FROMMER'S

COMPREHENSIVE
TRAVEL GUIDE

Santa Fe, Taos
&
Albuquerque
'95

by Lisa Legarde

MACMILLAN • USA

ABOUT THE AUTHOR

Lisa Legarde was born in New Orleans and graduated from Wellesley College with a B.A. in English. She has traveled extensively in Europe and North America and is author or co-author of 12 Frommer Guides.

MACMILLAN TRAVEL

A Prentice Hall Macmillan Company
15 Columbus Circle
New York, NY 10023

ISBN 0-02-860065-7
ISSN 0899-2789

Design by Michele Laseau
Maps by Geografix Inc. and Ortelius Design

Manufactured in the United States of America.

Contents

List of Maps

About this Frommer Guide

What Is a Frommer City Guide? It's a comprehensive, easy-to-use guide to the best travel values in all price ranges—from very expensive to budget. The one guidebook to take along on any trip.

What the Symbols Mean

⭐ **Frommer's Favorites**   Hotels, restaurants, attractions, and entertainments you should not miss

💲 **Super-Special Values**   Really exceptional values

In Hotel and Other Listings

The following symbols refer to the standard amenities available in all rooms:

A/C   air conditioning
TEL   telephone
TV   television
MINIBAR   refrigerator stocked with beverages and snacks

The following abbreviations are used for credit cards:

AE   American Express
CB   Carte Blanche
DC   Diners Club
DISC   Discover
ER   enRoute
EU   Eurocard
JCB   Japanese Credit Bureau
MC   MasterCard
V   Visa

Trip Planning with this Guide
USE THE FOLLOWING FEATURES:

Calendar of Events   To plan for or avoid

Suggested Itineraries   For seeing the cities

Easy-to-Read Maps   Walking tours, city sights, hotel and restaurant locations

Fast Facts   All the essentials at a glance: currency, embassies, emergencies, taxes, tipping, and more

ANOTHER SPECIAL FROMMER FEATURE

Cool for Kids   Hotels, restaurants, and attractions

Invitation to the Reader

In researching this book, I have come across many wonderful establishments, the best of which I have included here. I am sure that many of you will also come across appealing hotels, inns, restaurants, guesthouses, shops, and attractions. Please don't keep them to yourself. Share your experiences, especially if you want to comment on places that have been included in this edition that have changed for the worse. You can address your letters to:

Lisa Legarde
Frommer's Santa Fe, Taos & Albuquerque '95
c/o Macmillan Travel
15 Columbus Circle
New York, NY 10023

A Disclaimer

Readers are advised that prices fluctuate in the course of time, and travel information changes under the impact of the varied and volatile factors that affect the travel industry. Neither the author nor the publisher can be held responsible for the experiences of readers while traveling. Readers are invited to write to the publisher with ideas, comments, and suggestions for future editions.

Safety Advisory

Whenever you're traveling in an unfamiliar city or country, stay alert. Be aware of your immediate surroundings. Wear a moneybelt and keep a close eye on your possessions. Be particularly careful with cameras, purses, and wallets, all favorite targets of thieves and pickpockets.

1

Introducing Northern New Mexico

Sᴀɴᴛᴀ Fᴇ ɪꜱ ᴛʜᴇ ᴄᴇɴᴛᴇʀ ᴏꜰ ᴛʜᴇ ꜰᴀꜱᴛ-ɢʀᴏᴡɪɴɢ ɴᴏʀᴛʜᴇʀɴ Nᴇᴡ
Mexico tourist region, an area that also includes Taos, a one-time
frontier town now famed worldwide as an art colony and
downhill-skiing center; Albuquerque, a booming high-tech metropolis of half a million people; the 19 surviving settlements and numerous ruins of the centuries-old Native American Pueblo culture; and
a spectacular outdoors appealing to wilderness lovers of all ages and
fitness levels with its outstanding skiing, backpacking, fishing, hunting, rafting, and other pursuits.

Santa Fe is in some ways typical of many New Mexican cities and
towns—still, there's no other place like it. The longest continually
occupied capital city in the United States, founded by Spanish
colonists a full decade before the Pilgrims set foot on Plymouth Rock,
it is caught in a time warp between the 17th and 21st centuries,
between traditional Native American and Hispanic cultures and a
current-day onslaught of tourism.

Here in the purified air of New Mexico's state capital, 7,000 feet
up in the pastel foothills of the Sangre de Cristo Mountains, Native
Americans sell traditional crafts to eager shoppers beneath the portico
of the 380-year-old Palace of the Governors. As a visitor, you're just
as likely to share a park bench with a turquoise-adorned San Ildefonso
tribe member or a Stetson-hatted Hispanic rancher as with a tourist
from Dallas or Atlanta or New York, in town to patronize posh art
galleries or to take in the famed Santa Fe Opera. It's no accident that
locals call their town "The City Different."

A carefully considered plan to preserve and perpetuate
pre-20th-century architecture has made downtown Santa Fe look like
an adobe enclave. Much of the rest of this city of 60,000 has followed
suit. For miles in all directions, flat-topped earth-colored homes,
many of them valued in the millions of dollars, speckle the hills amid
sparse piñon and mesquite forests. Most of the construction is actually
stuccoed concrete. A standing joke in Santa Fe art circles is that the
city sanctions the use of 42 shades of brown.

1   Geography, History & the People

Geography

Forget any preconceptions about the New Mexico "desert." It can
be hot in the summer, certainly; but it's cold in the winter and on
spring and fall nights. Santa Fe is at 7,000 feet in elevation; Taos, at
6,950. Albuquerque is in the "lowlands" at 5,300 feet.

The most notable physical features of northern New Mexico are
the Sangre de Cristo (Blood of Christ) Mountains and the Rio Grande
(Big River). The Sangre de Cristos, with their summit at 13,161-foot
Wheeler Peak just north of Taos, are the southern extremity of the
Rockies. The Rio Grande flows through a deep north-south cut
dividing the mountains from the mesa country to the west.
Albuquerque is on the Rio Grande; both Santa Fe and Taos are within
25 miles east on tributary streams.

New Mexico is classified as having a "semiarid subtropical" climate. That means there's lots of sun; precipitation is light and relative humidity is low. But because of the elevation differences, temperatures at Santa Fe and Taos are often 10° F cooler than those at Albuquerque.

History

The Pueblo tribes of the upper Rio Grande valley are believed to be descendants of the Anasazi, who lived from the 9th to the 13th century in the Four Corners region, where the states of New Mexico, Arizona, Colorado, and Utah now meet. The Anasazi built spectacular structures; an idea of their scale and intricacy is hinted at by ruins at Chaco Canyon and Mesa Verde. It isn't known for certain why they abandoned their homes (some archeologists suggest drought; others, social unrest), but by the time the first Spanish arrived in the 1500s they were long gone, and the Pueblo culture was well established throughout northern and western New Mexico.

A distinguishing and unifying mark of the otherwise diverse Anasazi and Pueblo cultures was architectural style. Both built condominium-style communities of stone and mud adobe bricks, three and four stories high. Focused around central plazas, villages incorporated circular spiritual chambers called *kivas*. These people were primitive farmers who used the waters of the Rio Grande and its tributaries to irrigate fields of corn, beans, and squash and created elaborate works of pottery.

THE SPANISH OCCUPATION The Spanish ventured into the upper Rio Grande after their conquest of Mexico's Aztecs in 1519–21. In 1540 Francisco Vásquez de Coronado led an expedition in search of the fabled Seven Cities of Cibola, coincidentally introducing horses and sheep to the region. Neither Coronado nor a succession of wealth-thirsty conquistadors could locate the legendary cities of gold, so the Spanish turned their attention to exploiting the Native Americans.

Franciscan priests attempted to turn the Pueblo people into model Hispanic peasants. Their churches became the focal points of every pueblo, with Catholic schools an essential adjunct. By 1625 there were an estimated 50 churches in the valley. (Two of the pueblo missions, at Isleta and Acoma, are still in use today.) But the Pueblos weren't enthused about doing "God's work"—building new adobe missions, tilling fields for the Spanish, and weaving garments for export to Mexico—so soldiers came north to back the padres in extracting labor. For all practical purposes, the Pueblos were forced into slavery.

Santa Fe was founded in 1610 as the seat of Spanish government in the upper Rio Grande. Gov. Don Pedro de Peralta named the settlement La Villa Real de la Santa Fe de San Francisco de Asis ("The Royal City of the Holy Faith of St. Francis of Assisi"). His capitol, the Palace of the Governors, has been in continuous use as a public building ever since by Spanish, Mexicans, Americans, briefly by

Confederate troops, and for 12 years (1680–92) by the Pueblos. (Today it's the flagship of the state museum system.)

The Pueblo occupation signaled the culmination of decades of resentment against the Spanish colonials. Rebellions in the 1630s at Taos and Jemez left village priests dead, and were savagely repressed. In 1680 a unified Pueblo rebellion, orchestrated from Taos, succeeded in driving all Spanish from the upper Rio Grande. Forced to retreat to Mexico, the colonists could not reconquer Santa Fe until 12 years later. Bloody battles continued for the next several years, but by the beginning of the 18th century Nuevo Mexico was firmly in Spanish hands.

It remained so until Mexican independence in 1821. The most notable event in the intervening years was the departure in the mid-1700s of the Franciscans, exasperated by their failure to wipe out all vestiges of traditional Pueblo religion—eight generations of Pueblos had clung tenaciously to their way of life through the Spanish occupation. But by that time the number of Pueblo villages had shrunk by half.

ARRIVAL OF THE ANGLOS The first Anglos to linger in the upper Rio Grande valley were mountain men: itinerant hunters, trappers, and traders. Trailblazers of the United States' westward expansion, they began entering New Mexico in the first decade of the 19th century. Many married into Pueblo or Hispanic families. Perhaps the best known was Kit Carson, a sometime federal agent, sometime Native American scout, whose legend is inextricably interwoven with that of early Taos. The home in which he settled and lived for 40 years, until his death in 1868, is now a museum.

Wagon trains and eastern merchants followed Carson and the other pathfinders. Santa Fe, Taos, and Albuquerque, already major trading and commercial centers at the end of the Chihuahua Trail (the Camino Real from Veracruz, Mexico, 1,000 miles south), likewise became the western terminuses of the new Santa Fe Trail (from Independence, Missouri, 800 miles east).

Even though independent Mexico granted the Pueblo people full citizenship and abandoned the restrictive trade laws of their former Spanish rulers, the 25 years of direct rule from Mexico City were not peaceful in the upper Rio Grande. Instead they were marked by continual rebellions against severe taxation, especially in Taos. Neither did things quiet down immediately when the United States assumed control during the Mexican War. Soon after Gen. Stephen Kearney occupied Santa Fe (in a bloodless takeover) on orders of Pres. James Polk in 1846, a revolt in Taos in 1847 resulted in the slaying of the new governor of New Mexico, Charles Bent. In 1848 the Treaty of Guadalupe Hidalgo officially transferred to the United States title to New Mexico, along with Texas, Arizona, and California.

Aside from Kit Carson, perhaps the two most notable personalities of 19th-century New Mexico were priests. Father José Martinez (1793–1867) was one of the first native-born priests to serve his people. Ordained in Durango, Mexico, he took over the Taos parish and rocked the Catholic boat by abolishing the enforced church tithe because it was a hardship on poor parishioners, publishing the first newspaper in the territory (in 1835), and fighting large land takeovers by Anglos after the United States annexed the territory.

On all these issues he ran at loggerheads with Bishop Jean-Baptiste Lamy (1814–88), a Frenchman appointed in 1851 to direct the first independent New Mexican diocese. Lamy, on whose life Willa Cather's novel *Death Comes for the Archbishop* was based, served the diocese for 37 years. He didn't take kindly to Martinez's independent streak and, after repeated conflicts, excommunicated the maverick priest in 1857. But Martinez kept preaching. He formed a breakaway church and continued as northern New Mexico's spiritual leader until his death.

Nevertheless, Lamy did much for New Mexico, especially in the areas of education and architecture. Santa Fe's Romanesque Cathedral of St. Francis and the nearby Gothic-style Loretto Chapel, for instance, were constructed under his aegis. But he never willingly accepted other viewpoints. Martinez, on the other hand, embraced the folk tradition, including the craft of *santero* (religious icon) carving and a tolerance of the Penitentes, a flagellant sect that flourished after the departure of the Franciscans in the mid-18th century.

With the advent of the Atchison, Topeka & Santa Fe Railway in 1879, New Mexico began to boom. Albuquerque in particular blossomed in the wake of a series of major gold strikes in the Madrid Valley, close to ancient Native American turquoise mines. By the time the gold lodes began to shrink in the 1890s, cattle and sheep ranching had become well entrenched. The territory's growth culminated in statehood in 1912.

Territorial Gov. Lew Wallace, who served from 1878 to 1881, helped inspire the interest in arts that today is symbolic of life in northern New Mexico. Wallace penned the great biblical novel *Ben Hur* while occupying the Palace of the Governors. In the 1890s the Taos art colony was launched by Ernest Blumenschein, Bert Phillips, and Joseph Sharp; it boomed in the decade following World War I when Mabel Dodge Luhan, D. H. Lawrence, Georgia O'Keeffe, Willa Cather, and many others visited or established residence in the area.

During World War II the federal government purchased an isolated boys' camp west of Santa Fe and turned it into the Los Alamos National Laboratory, where the Manhattan Project and other top-secret atomic experiments were developed and perfected. Today Albuquerque is among the nation's leaders in defense contracts and high technology.

The People

The most thoroughly tricultural of the contiguous 48 states, New Mexico is an overlay of Native Americans, Hispanics, and Anglos (non-Hispanic Caucasians). The groups live and work side by side, yet each preserves its distinct communities and cultural nuances. Interaction with Pueblo artists displaying their jewelry and crafts at the plazas of Santa Fe and Taos, and the mouth-watering aroma of corn tortillas and hot chiles wafting through the air of Hispanic communities, are unforgettable memories of northern New Mexico.

2 Art, Architecture, Religion & Myth

ART   Since prehistoric times New Mexico has been a cradle of artistic genius for its native peoples. Prehistoric Anasazi pottery is unique in its design and color. Today's Pueblo people are noted not only for their pottery—each pueblo being distinctive in its touches from the next—but also for their weaving.

Hispanic art was by nature either religious or rustic—or both. Cut off for centuries from most of the rest of the world, Hispanic artisans handcrafted their own ornate furnishings while their paintings (*retablos*) and carved icons (*santos*) underscored their devotion to the Roman Catholic faith. Their traditional decorative tinwork and furniture are popular today, along with weaving and silversmithing.

Taos took its place in the world of art with the founding of the Taos Society of Artists in 1915. The society members—Kenneth Adams, Oscar Beringhaus, Ernest Blumenschein, Irving Couse, Herbert Dunton, Victor Higgins, E. Martin Hennings, Bert Phillips, Joseph Sharp, and Walter Ufer—chose Taos because of the remarkable play of light on its landscape. Though disbanded in 1927, the society was so successful in widely marketing the work of Taos's geographically isolated masters that it established a solid foundation for the prolific art community of today. Works by society members are proudly displayed in museums and private collections throughout northern New Mexico and beyond, including the Metropolitan Museum of Art in New York.

Santa Fe grew as an art community on the heels of Taos. By 1921, Los Cinco Pintores, a group of five avant-garde painters—Jozef Bakos, Fremont Ellis, Walter Mruk, Willard Nash, and Will Shuster—were establishing names of their own.

Perhaps the best-known artist who worked extensively and lived most of her later years in the area was Georgia O'Keeffe (1887–1986). Her first visit to New Mexico in 1929 inspired her extraordinary paintings of the area's desert landscape and bleached animal skulls. The house she lived in in Abiquiu (42 miles northwest of Santa Fe on U.S. 84) is still a private home.

The number of full-time professional artists in Santa Fe and Taos today easily exceeds 1,000, and thousands more dabble in the arts. Studios and galleries are spread throughout the region. Santa Fe, despite its relatively small size, is the third-largest art market in the United States.

Santa Fe is home to the Institute of American Indian Arts and the School of Indian Art, where many of today's leading Native American artists studied, including Apache sculptor Allan Houser. The best-known Native American painter today is R. C. Gorman, an Arizona Navajo who has made his home in Taos for over two decades. Now in his late 50s, Gorman is internationally acclaimed for his bright, somewhat surrealistic depictions of Navajo women.

ARCHITECTURE   Traditional New Mexican homes are built of adobe—sun-dried clay bricks mixed with grasses for strength, mortared with simple mud, and then covered with additional protective layers of mud. Their roofs are supported by a network of *vigas,* long beams whose ends protrude through the outer facades, and *latillas,* smaller stripped branches layered between the vigas. Other architectural elements may include a *portal,* or ground-floor porch, usually shading a brick floor set into the ground; *corbels,* carved wooden supports for the vertical posts and the vigas; and a plastered adobe-brick *banco* fireplace set into an outside wall. Adobe homes are distinguished by their flat roofs and soft, rounded contours.

Santa Fe, Taos, and Albuquerque once were towns of one- and two-story adobes. When the United States took over the New Mexico territory from Mexico in 1846 and trade began flowing by stagecoach and (later) by train from the eastern states, new tools and materials such as red bricks and large logs began to change the face of the city. The old adobes took on brick facades and roof decoration in what became known as the Territorial style.

In Santa Fe and Taos the flat roofs were retained, so that the cities never lost their unique low profiles. Santa Fe has a serenity found in no other American city and in only a few of the smaller towns of the Southwest, such as Taos.

Few true adobe homes remain in modern Santa Fe. The majority are imitation adobe made of stuccoed concrete. But the imitations are effective. Strict building codes have been enforced by the city's Historic Design Review Board since 1957, requiring that all new structures within the circumference of the Paseo de Peralta conform to one of two revival styles: Pueblo, reflecting the mud-daubed adobe look of the Pueblos and early Spanish colonists, or Territorial. Much of the rest of the city has conformed to the example set by downtown. In 1988 citywide standards were established to assure good taste in architecture in new developments and to restrict the use of neon, large signs, and the like.

RELIGION & MYTH   Religion has always been at the heart of the life of the Pueblo people, who view the cosmos as a single whole within which all living creatures are mutually dependent. Thus every relationship, whether with another person, an animal, or even a plant, carries spiritual meaning. A hunter will pray before killing a deer, for instance, to ask the creature to give itself to the tribe. The slain deer is then treated as a guest of honor before the hunter ritually sends its soul back to its comrades to be reborn. Even the harvesting of a plant requires prayer, thanks, and ritual.

The Pueblos believe that their ancestors originally lived underground, the source of life (and the place from which plants spring). Encouraged by burrowing animals, they entered the world of humans—the "fifth" world—through a hole, a *sipapu,* by clinging to a web woven for them by Spider Woman.

They honor Mother Earth and Father Sun. In this dry land, the sun can mean life and death. The tribes watch the skies closely, tracking solstices and planetary movements, to determine the optimum timing for crop-planting cycles.

Dances are ritual occasions. Usually held in conjunction with the feast days of Catholic saints (including Christmas Eve for Jesus), the ceremonies demonstrate how the Pueblos absorbed certain aspects of Christianity from the Spanish without surrendering their traditional beliefs. In a personal universe such as ours, they feel, spiritual beings actively participate in the material world—and the more, the merrier.

There are medicine dances, fertility rites, and prayers for rain and for good harvests. The spring and summer corn, or *tablita,* dances are among the most impressive. Ceremonies begin with an early-morning mass and a procession to the plaza with an image of the saint being honored. The rest of the day is devoted to song, dance, and feasting, with performers masked and clad as deer, buffalo, eagles, or other creatures.

Visitors are normally welcome to attend Pueblo dances but should respect the tribe's requests that they not be photographed or tape recorded. It was a lack of this simple respect that caused Zunis to ban outsiders from attending their famous Shalako ceremony.

Outside of the pueblos, the most visible places of worship are those of the Roman Catholics. Santa Fe's Cathedral of St. Francis is the state's best-known church, but a close second is El Santuario de Chimayo, an hour north of the state capital. Constructed in 1816, it has long been a site of pilgrimage for Catholics who attribute miraculous powers of healing to the earth in the chapel's anteroom. Hispanic Catholics believe strongly in miracles.

3 Food & Drink

Santa Feans take their eating seriously. In fact, they've coined a name for their unique blend of Hispanic and Pueblo recipes: northern New Mexico cuisine.

This isn't the same as Mexican cooking or even those American distortions sometimes called "Tex-Mex" or "Cal-Mex." It's a consequence of southwestern history: As the Native Americans taught the Spanish conquerors about their corn—how to roast it and how to make corn pudding, stewed corn, cornbread, cornmeal, and *posole* (hominy)—the Spanish introduced their beloved chiles, adding spice to the cuisine and ultimately developing such famous strains of chile as Chimayo, Pojoaque, and Española Improved.

The basic ingredients of northern New Mexico cooking are three locally grown vegetables: chiles, beans, and corn. Of these, perhaps most crucial is the **chile,** brilliant red or green, with various levels of spicy bite. The green chiles are hotter if the seeds are left in; red chiles are green chiles at their ripest stage. Strung together like a garland (a *ristra*) to dry in the sun, they make the base for the red sauce known everywhere in the Southwest as *salsa.* Both red and green salsas are served in most restaurants; the red is usually the hotter of the two, but it's wise to ask before tasting.

The **beans**—spotted or painted pinto beans with a nutty taste—are simmered with garlic, onion, cumin, and red chile powder to be served as a side dish. Then mashed and refried in oil, they become *frijoles refritos*.

Corn supplies the vital dough called *masa* for tortillas. New Mexican corn comes in six colors, of which the yellow, white, and blue are the most common.

Even if you think you know Mexican cooking, the dishes you love may not be served here quite as you've had them before. Here's a sampling of some of the regional dishes that might be hard to find outside the Southwest:

biscochito   A cookie with anise.

carne adovada   Tender pork marinated in red chile sauce, herbs, and spices, then baked.

chiles rellenos   Stuffed with cheese, deep-fried, then covered with green chile sauce.

chorizo burrito   (also called a breakfast burrito) Mexican sausage, scrambled eggs, potatoes, and scallions wrapped in a flour tortilla with red or green chile sauce and melted Jack cheese.

empanada   A fried pie with nuts and currants.

enchiladas   Tortillas filled with peppers or other foods.

fajitas   Strips of beef or chicken sautéed with onions, green peppers, and other vegetables and served on a sizzling platter.

green chile stew   Locally grown chiles cooked in a stew with chunks of meat, beans, and potatoes.

nuevos rancheres   Fried eggs on corn tortillas, topped with cheese and red or green chiles, served with pinto beans.

pan dulce   A Native American sweet bread.

pasale   A corn soup or stew (called hominy in other parts of the South), sometimes with pork and chiles.

sopaipillas   A lightly fried puff pastry served with honey as a dessert or stuffed with meat and vegetables as a side dish. Sopaipillas with honey are also often served with your meal—the honey has a cooling effect on your palate after you've eaten a spicy dish.

tacos   More often served in soft rolled tortillas than in the crispy shells.

tamales   Made from cornmeal mush, wrapped in husks and steamed.

vegetables and nuts   Unusual local ingredients, such as piñon nuts, jicama, and prickly pear cactus, will often be a part of your meals.

---

4 Recommended Books

Many well-known writers have made their homes in northern New Mexico in the 20th century. In the 1920s, the most noted were D. H. Lawrence and Willa Cather, both short-term Taos residents.

Lawrence, the romantic and controversial English novelist, was here for parts of 1922–25 and reflected on that period in *Mornings in Mexico* and *Etruscan Places*. Lawrence's Taos period is described in *Lorenzo in Taos,* written by his patron, Mabel Dodge Luhan. Cather, a Pulitzer Prize winner famous for her depictions of the pioneer spirit, penned *Death Comes for the Archbishop,* a fictionalization of the career of 19th-century Santa Fe Bishop Jean-Baptiste Lamy, as a result of her stay.

Many contemporary authors live in and write about New Mexico. John Nichols of Taos, whose *Milagro Beanfield War* was turned into a popular movie in 1987, writes with insight about the problems of poor Hispanic farming communities. Tony Hillerman of Albuquerque is renowned for two decades of weaving mysteries around Navajo tribal police in such books as *Listening Woman* and *A Thief of Time*. Hispanic novelist Rudolfo Anaya's *Bless Me, Ultima,* and Pueblo writer Leslie Marmon Silko's *Ceremony* capture the lifestyles of their respective peoples. Of desert environment and politics, no one wrote better than the late Edward Abbey; *Fire on the Mountain,* set in New Mexico, was one of his most powerful works.

Other Suggested Reading

GENERAL

Dozier, Edward P. *The Pueblo Indians of North America.* New York: Holt, Rinehart & Winston, 1970.

Hillerman, Tony, ed. *The Spell of New Mexico.* Albuquerque: University of New Mexico Press, 1976.

Horgan, Paul. *Great River: The Rio Grande in North American History.* New York: Holt, Rinehart & Winston, 1960.

Jenkins, Myra Ellen, and Albert H. Schroeder. *A Brief History of New Mexico.* Albuquerque: University of New Mexico Press, 1974.

Morrill, Claire. *A Taos Mosaic: Portrait of a New Mexico Village.* Albuquerque: University of New Mexico Press, 1973.

Nichols, John, and William Davis. *If Mountains Die: A New Mexico Memoir.* New York: Alfred A. Knopf, 1979.

Simmons, Marc. *New Mexico: An Interpretive History.* Albuquerque: University of New Mexico Press, 1988.

Williamson, Ray A. *Living the Sky: The Cosmos of the American Indian.* Norman: University of Oklahoma Press, 1987.

THE ARTS

Aspen Center for the Visual Arts. *Enduring Visions: 1,000 Years of Southwestern Indian Art.* New York: Publishing Center for Cultural Resources, 1969.

Boyd, E. *Popular Arts of Spanish New Mexico.* Santa Fe: Museum of New Mexico Press, 1974.

Bunting, Bainbridge. *Of Earth and Timbers Made.* Albuquerque: University of New Mexico Press, 1974.

Dickey, Roland F. *New Mexico Village Arts.* Albuquerque: University of New Mexico Press, 1990.

O'Keeffe, Georgia. *O'Keeffe*. New York: Viking Press, 1976.

School of American Research. *Representative Art and Artists of New Mexico*. Santa Fe: Museum of New Mexico Press, 1976.

TRAVEL

Casey, Robert L. *Journey to the High Southwest: A Traveler's Guide*. Seattle: Pacific Search Press, 1985.

Chilton, Lance and Katherine, et al. *New Mexico: A New Guide to the Colorful State*. Albuquerque: University of New Mexico Press, 1984.

2

Planning a Trip to Santa Fe, Taos & Albuquerque

AS WITH ANY TRIP, A LITTLE PREPARATION IS ESSENTIAL BEFORE YOU START. This chapter will provide you with a variety of planning tools, including information on when to go and how to get there.

1   Information & When to Go

Information

Numerous agencies can assist with your trip planning. The state body responsible for tourism is the **New Mexico Economic Development and Tourism Department,** whose Tourism and Travel Division is housed at 491 Old Santa Fe Trail, Santa Fe, NM 87503 (☎ toll free **800/545-2040**). Santa Fe, Taos, and Albuquerque each has its own organization that provides information for visitors (see the "Orientation" sections in Chapters 4, 12, and 18, respectively).

When to Go

CLIMATE   The high desert climate of this part of the world is generally dry but not always warm. Santa Fe and Taos, at 7,000 feet in elevation, have midsummer highs in the 80s, with lows in the 50s. Spring and fall highs run in the 60s, with lows in the 30s. Typical midwinter day temperatures are in the low 40s, and overnight lows are in the teens. Temperatures in Albuquerque, at 5,000 feet, often run about 10°F warmer.

Average annual precipitation ranges from 8 inches at Albuquerque to 12 inches at Taos and 14 at Santa Fe, most of it coming in July and August as afternoon thunderstorms. Snowfall is common from November through March and sometimes as late as May, though it seldom lasts long. Santa Fe averages 32 inches total annual snowfall. At the high-mountain ski resorts, as much as 300 inches (25 feet) may fall in a season—and stay.

Average Temperatures (°F) and Annual Rainfall

	Jan	Apr	July	Oct	Rainfall
	High–Low	High–Low	High–Low	High–Low	(Inches)
Albuquerque	47–28	70–41	91–66	72–45	8.9
Santa Fe	40–18	59–35	80–57	62–38	14.0
Taos	40–10	62–30	87–50	64–32	12.1

Northern New Mexico Calendar of Events

January

- **New Year's Day.** Parades, traditional dances, and masses at several pueblos, including Picuris, San Ildefonso, and Taos. January 1.

February

- **Candlemas Day,** Picuris Pueblo. Traditional dances. February 2.

⭐ **Winter Fiesta**

Santa Fe's annual retreat from the midwinter doldrums appeals to skiers and nonskiers alike. Highlights include the Great Santa Fe Chili Cookoff; ski races, both serious and frivolous; snow-sculpture contests; snowshoe races; and hot-air balloon rides.

Where: Santa Fe Ski Area. **When:** The last weekend in February. **How:** Most events are free. Call **505/982-4429** for information.

April

- **Easter,** Nambe, Picuris, and San Ildefonso Pueblos. Celebrations include masses, parades, and corn and other dances.
- **Gathering of Nations Powwow,** University Arena, Albuquerque. Dance competitions, arts-and-crafts exhibitions. Mid- to late April.

May

⭐ **Taos Spring Arts Celebration**

Contemporary visual, performing, and literary arts are highlighted over two weeks of gallery openings, studio tours, performances by visiting theatrical and dance troupes, live musical events, traditional ethnic entertainment, an Indian Market, a film festival, fashion shows, literary readings, and more.

Where: Venues throughout Taos and Taos County. **When:** May 1–15. **How:** Tickets are available from the Taos County Chamber of Commerce, P.O. Box 1691, Taos, NM 87571 (☎ **505/758-3873,** or toll free **800/732-TAOS**).

⭐ **Santa Fe Spring Festival of the Arts**

This citywide celebration includes exhibits, demonstrations, lectures, tours, open studios, music, dance, theater, and poster and book signings.

Where: Throughout Santa Fe. **When:** 11 days, concluding with the Memorial Day holiday. **How:** Most events are free. For information, contact the Santa Fe Festival of the Arts, 1524 Paseo de Peralta, Santa Fe, NM 87501 (☎ **505/988-3924**).

- **Santa Fe Powwow.** Native dances, singing, games, crafts, and food. Call **505/983-5220** for location. Memorial Day weekend.

June

- **Rodeo de Taos,** County Fairgrounds, Taos. See "Sports and Recreation" in Chapter 15 for details. The fourth weekend in June.

★ New Mexico Arts and Crafts Fair

The second-largest event of its type in the United States presents more than 200 artisans demonstrating and selling their crafts, plus nonstop entertainment.
Where: State Fairgrounds, Albuquerque. **When:** The last weekend in June (on Friday and Saturday from 10am to 10pm and on Sunday from 10am to 6pm). **How:** Admission varies. For information, call **505/884-9043.**

July

- **High Country Arts and Crafts Festival,** Picuris Pueblo. Traditional dances and other events. Proceeds go to the restoration of the San Lorenzo Mission. The first weekend in July.

★ Rodeo de Santa Fe

This four-day event starts with a western parade on Thursday morning and ends with a rodeo dance; in between, more than 20,000 people attend four performances of rodeo. Attracting 300 to 350 cowboys from all over the Southwest competing for a $35,000 purse, the events include Brahma bull and bronco riding, calf roping, steer wrestling, barrel racing, trick riding, clown and animal acts, and a local version of bullfighting in which neither the bull nor the matador is hurt.
Where: Rodeo grounds, 4801 Rodeo Rd., off Cerrillos Road, $5^1/2$ miles south of the Plaza. **When:** The first weekend following the Fourth of July (starting at 8pm Thursday through Saturday and at 2:30pm on Sunday). **How:** For tickets and information, call **505/471-4300.**

- **Taos Pueblo Powwow.** Intertribal competition in traditional and contemporary dances. The second weekend in July.
- **Eight Northern Pueblos Artist and Craftsman Show,** San Ildefonso Pueblo. More than 600 Native American artists exhibit their work. Traditional dances and food booths. The third weekend in July.

★ Fiesta de Santiago y Santa Ana

The fiesta begins with a Friday-night mass at Our Lady of Guadalupe Church, where the fiesta queen is crowned. During the weekend there are parades, crafts and food booths, and live entertainment.
Where: Taos Plaza. **When:** A three-day weekend in late July. **How:** Most events are free. For information, contact

the Taos Fiesta Council, P.O. Box 3300, Taos, NM 87571
(☎ toll free **800/732-TAOS**).

★ The Spanish Markets

More than 300 Hispanic artists from New Mexico and
southern Colorado exhibit and sell their work in this
lively community event. Artists are featured in special
demonstrations, while an entertaining mix of traditional
Hispanic music, dance, foods, and pageantry create the
ambience of a village celebration. Artwork for sale includes
painted and carved saints, textiles, tinwork, furniture, straw
appliqué, and metalwork.
Where: Santa Fe Plaza, Santa Fe. **When:** The last full
weekend in July. **How:** Markets are free. For information,
contact the Spanish Colonial Arts Society, P.O. Box 1611,
Santa Fe, NM 87504 (☎ **505/983-4038**).

August

★ The Indian Market

This is the largest all–Native American market in the
country. About 800 artisans display their baskets and
blankets, jewelry, pottery, wood carvings, rugs, sand
paintings, and sculptures at rows of booths. Sales are brisk.
Costumed tribal dancing and crafts demonstrations are
scheduled in the afternoon.
Where: Santa Fe Plaza and the surrounding streets.
When: The third weekend in August. **How:** The market
is free and hotels are booked months in advance. For
information, contact the Southwestern Association on
Indian Affairs, P.O. Box 1964, Santa Fe, NM 87501
(☎ **505/983-5220**).

★ Feria Artesana

Four centuries of Hispanic heritage are celebrated with
music, dancing, food, and an outdoor folk mass, plus juried
competitions of more than 250 artisans from all over the
state.
Where: Albuquerque Convention Center and Civic
Plaza. **When:** The last weekend in August. **How:**
Admission varies. For information, call **505/848-1334**
or **505/766-7660.**

September

• **Santa Fe Banjo and Fiddle Contest,** rodeo ground,
Santa Fe. Big-name folk musicians perform. On the
Sunday before Labor Day.

★ La Fiesta de Santa Fe

An exuberant combination of spirit, history, and general
merrymaking, La Fiesta is the oldest community
celebration in the United States. The first Fiesta was

celebrated in 1712, 20 years after the peaceful resettlement of New Mexico by Spanish conquistadors in 1692, following the Pueblo revolt of 1670. *La Conquistadora,* a carved Madonna credited with the victory, is the focus of the celebration, which includes masses, a parade for children and their pets, a historical/hysterical parade, mariachi concerts, dances, food, and arts, as well as local entertainment on the Plaza. Zozobra, "Old Man Gloom," a 40-foot-tall effigy of wood, canvas, and paper, is burned at dusk on Friday to revitalize the community.
Where: Santa Fe. **When:** The first Friday after Labor Day. **How:** For information, contact the Santa Fe Fiesta Council, P.O. Box 4516, Santa Fe, NM 87502-4516 (☎ **505/988-7575**).

★ New Mexico State Fair

One of America's top 10 fairs, it features parimutuel horse racing, a nationally acclaimed rodeo, entertainment by top country artists, Native American and Spanish villages, and the requisite midway and livestock shows.
Where: State Fairgrounds, Albuquerque. **When:** 17 days in September. **How:** Advance tickets can be ordered. Call **505/265-1791** for information.

★ Taos Fall Arts Festival

Highlights include arts-and-crafts exhibitions and competitions, studio tours, gallery openings, lectures, films, concerts, dances, and stage plays. Simultaneous events include the Old Taos Trade Fair, the Wool Festival, and San Geronimo Day at Taos Pueblo.
Where: Throughout Taos and Taos County. **When:** 17 days, from the last week in September through the first week in October. **How:** Events schedules and tickets (where required) can be obtained from the Taos County Chamber of Commerce, P.O. Drawer 1, Taos, NM 87571 (☎ **505/758-3873,** or toll free **800/732-TAOS**).

- **Old Taos Trade Fair,** Martinez Hacienda, Lower Ranchitos Road, Taos. This two-day affair reenacts Spanish colonial life of the mid-1820s with Hispanic and Native American music, weaving and crafts demonstrations, traditional foods, dancing, and "visits" by mountain men. The last full weekend in September.
- **Wool Festival,** Kit Carson Memorial State Park, Taos. Shearing and handcrafting demonstrations, spinning and fleecing competitions, exhibitions of wool-producing animals, sales booths, an auction, a fashion show, music, and entertainment are all part of the fun. The last weekend in September.

- **San Geronimo Feast Day,** Taos Pueblo. A mass and procession; traditional corn, buffalo, and Comanche dances; an arts-and-crafts fair; footraces; and pole climbs by clowns. The last weekend in September.

October

- **Santa Fe Fall Festival of the Arts,** Sweeney Convention Center. New Mexican painters, sculptors, ceramicists, weavers, and woodworkers are featured in this annual exhibition. 11 days concluding with the Columbus Day holiday.

★ **Kodak Albuquerque International Balloon Fiesta®**

The world's largest balloon rally brings together 600 colorful aerialists in races and contests. Mass ascensions leave at 7am on Saturday and Sunday. Various special events are staged all week long.

Where: Balloon Fiesta Park on Albuquerque's northern city limits, and elsewhere in Albuquerque. **When:** The first through the second weekend in October. **How:** For information, call **505/344-3501.**

- **Taos Mountain Balloon Rally** and **Taste of Taos.** The Albuquerque fiesta's "little brother" offers mass dawn ascensions, tethered balloon rides for the public, and a Saturday parade of balloon baskets (in pickup trucks) from Kit Carson Park around the Plaza. Taste of Taos includes food and product fairs, chili cookoffs, and creation of the "world's biggest burrito." The last full weekend in October.

November

- **Southwest Arts and Crafts Festival,** State Fairgrounds, Albuquerque. Nearly 200 artisans in mixed media from throughout the United States attend this invitational juried competition with an emphasis on southwestern art. A three-day weekend in mid-November.

December

★ **Yuletide in Taos**

This pre-Christmas event emphasizes New Mexican traditions, culture, and arts with carols, festive classical music, Hispanic and Native American songs and dances, historic walking tours, art exhibitions, dance performances, candlelight dinners, and more.

Where: Throughout Taos. **When:** December 1–15. **How:** Events are staged by the Taos County Chamber of Commerce, P.O. Drawer 1, Taos, NM 87571 (☎ toll free **800/732-TAOS**).

- **Pueblo dances,** at the Nambe, Picuris, San Ildefonso, San Juan, Santa Clara, Taos, and Tesuque Pueblos. Traditional dances. Christmas week.

- **Sundown Torchlight Procession of the Virgin,** San Ildefonso, Santa Clara, Taos, and Tesuque Pueblos. Vespers and Matachines dance. December 24.
- **Winter Spanish Market,** La Fonda Hotel, Santa Fe. See the Spanish Markets in July (above) for more information. The last full weekend in December.

2 Health & Insurance

HEALTH   One thing that sets New Mexico aside from most other states is its altitude. Santa Fe and Taos are about 7,000 feet above sea level, Albuquerque more than 5,000. The reduced oxygen and humidity can bring on some unique problems, not the least of which is acute **mountain sickness.** Characterized in its early stages by headaches, shortness of breath, appetite loss and/or nausea, tingling in the fingers or toes, lethargy, and insomnia, it ordinarily can be treated with aspirin and by getting plenty of rest, avoiding large meals, and drinking lots of nonalcoholic fluids (especially water). If it persists or worsens, you must descend to a lower altitude. Sunburn and hypothermia are other dangers of higher elevations and should not be lightly regarded.

INSURANCE   Before setting out on your trip, check your medical insurance policy to be sure it covers you away from home. If it doesn't, it's wise to purchase a relatively inexpensive traveler's policy, widely available at banks, travel agencies, and automobile clubs. In addition to medical assistance, including hospitalization and surgery, it should include the cost of an accident, death, or repatriation; loss or theft of baggage; costs of trip cancellation; and guaranteed bail in the event of an arrest or other legal difficulties.

3 What to Pack

Don't forget to pack a sweater and a rainproof jacket. Even in summer, it can get cold at night at 7,000 feet of elevation. You'll want shorts and a swimsuit (for hotel pools) in the summer and several layers of warm clothing, including gloves and a hat, in winter. Unless you plan to dine in one of the handful of very elegant restaurants in the state, you probably won't need a jacket and tie or a formal dress. No matter what your plans, a good pair of walking shoes (not just tennis shoes) are essential.

A few other easily forgotten items that could prove priceless during your stay: (1) a travel alarm clock, so as not to be at the mercy of your hotel for wakeup calls; (2) a Swiss Army knife, which has a multitude of uses, from bottle opener to screwdriver; (3) a magnifying glass to read the small print on maps; and (4) a small first-aid kit (containing an antibiotic ointment, bandages, aspirin, soap, a thermometer, motion-sickness pills, and required medications) to avoid dependence on others in minor emergencies.

Of course, don't forget your camera!

4 Tips for the Disabled, Seniors, Students & Families

FOR THE DISABLED   Throughout the state of New Mexico steps have been taken to provide access for the disabled. On my latest trip I found that several bed-and-breakfast inns had made one or more of their rooms completely wheelchair accessible, and in Taos there is a completely wheelchair-accessible trail in the state park. However, there is no state agency that provides information to persons with disabilities who wish to travel throughout New Mexico. In Albuquerque there is a car-rental company that caters to the disabled (see "Getting There," below), and information on handicapped accessibility is also available through the Albuquerque Convention and Visitors Bureau (see Chapter 18 for address and phone number). When traveling to Santa Fe and Taos, you should call the Chamber of Commerce in advance of your visit and they will be able to give you the information you need.

FOR SENIORS   Travelers over the age of 65—in many cases 60, sometimes even 55—may qualify for discounts not available to the younger adult traveler. Some hotels offer rates 10% to 20% lower than the published rate; inquire at the time you make reservations. Many attractions give seniors discounts of up to half the regular adult admission price. Get in the habit of asking for your discount.

If you're retired and are not already a member of the American Association of Retired Persons (AARP), consider joining. The AARP card is valuable throughout North America in your search for travel bargains.

FOR STUDENTS   Always carry your student identification. Tourist attractions, transportation systems, and other services may provide discounts with appropriate proof. Never be afraid to ask. A high-school or college ID card or International Student Card will suffice.

Student-oriented activities abound on and around college campuses, especially the University of New Mexico in Albuquerque. In Santa Fe, there are two small four-year colleges: the College of Santa Fe and St. John's College.

FOR FAMILIES   Children often get discounts that adults, even seniors, never dream of. For instance, many hotels allow children to stay free with their parents in the same room. The upper age limit of what defines a "child" may vary from 12 to 18.

Youngsters are almost always entitled to discounts on public transportation and admission to attractions. Though every entrance requirement is different, you'll often find that admission for kids 5 and under is free and for elementary-school–age children it's half price; and older students (through high school) may also get significant discounts.

5 Getting There

BY PLANE The gateway to Santa Fe, Taos, and other northern New Mexico communities is the **Albuquerque International Airport** (☎ **505/842-4366** for the administrative offices; call the individual airlines for flight information), recently expanded and renovated.

Airlines serving Albuquerque are **American** (☎ toll free **800/ 433-7300**), **America West** (☎ toll free **800/247-5692**), **Continental** (☎ toll free **800/525-0280**), **Delta** (☎ toll free **800/221-1212**), **Southwest** (☎ toll free **800/435-9792**), **TWA** (☎ toll free **800/221-2000**), **United** (☎ toll free **800/241-6522**), and the regional carrier, **Mesa** (☎ toll free **800/637-2247**).

The regional carrier, Mesa Airlines, serves Albuquerque, Santa Fe, Taos, and other smaller cities year-round and in winter flies from Albuquerque into such ski resorts as Angel Fire, Red River, and Rio Costilla.

BY TRAIN The National Railroad Passenger Corporation **Amtrak** (☎**505/842-9650,** or toll free **800/USA-RAIL**) passes through northern New Mexico twice daily. The *Southwest Chief,* which runs between Chicago and Los Angeles, stops once eastbound and once westbound in Gallup, Grants, Albuquerque, Lamy (for Santa Fe), Las Vegas, and Raton.

You can get a copy of Amtrak's National Timetable from any Amtrak station, from travel agents, or by writing Amtrak, 400 N. Capitol St. NW, Washington, DC 20001.

BY BUS Because Santa Fe is only about 58 miles northeast of Albuquerque via I-40, most visitors travel by bus directly from the Albuquerque airport. **Shuttlejack** buses (☎ **505/243-3244** in Albuquerque, **505/982-4311** in Santa Fe), make the 70-minute run between the airport and Santa Fe hotels 7 to 10 times daily each way, from 5am to 10:15pm (cost is $20, payable to the driver). Two

---

Frommer's Smart Traveler: Airfares

Value-Conscious Travelers Should Take Advantage of the Following:

1. Shop all the airlines that fly to Albuquerque.

2. Always ask for the lowest fare, not just a discount fare.

3. Keep calling the airline to check fares. Availability of inexpensive seats changes daily, and as the departure date draws nearer, more seats are sold at lower prices.

4. Ask about senior-citizen discounts (usually 10%).

other bus services shuttle between Albuquerque and Taos (via Santa Fe) for $25 one-way, $45 round-trip: **Pride of Taos Tours/Shuttles** (☎ 505/758-8340) twice daily and **Faust's Transportation** (☎ 505/758-3410) once daily.

The public bus depot in Albuquerque (☎ 505/243-4435) is located on Second Street at Silver Avenue. **Greyhound/Trailways** and **Texas, New Mexico & Oklahoma** (TNMO) run regular service between Albuquerque, Santa Fe, and Taos (four times daily between Albuquerque and Santa Fe, twice daily between Santa Fe and Taos). Fares run about $12 to Santa Fe, $24 to Taos. But bus stations in Santa Fe (858 St. Michael's Dr.; ☎ 505/471-0008) and Taos (at the Chevron bypass station at the corner of U.S. 64 and N.M. 68; ☎ 505/758-1144) are several miles south of the city centers. Additional taxi or shuttle service is needed to get to most accommodations, and most travelers find it more convenient to pay a few extra dollars for an airport-to-hotel shuttle.

BY CAR   The most convenient way to get around the Santa Fe region is by private car. **Auto and RV rentals** are widely available for those who arrive without their own transportation, either at the Albuquerque airport or at locations around each city.

I have received good rates and service on separate trips from **Avis** at the Albuquerque airport (☎ 505/842-4080, 505/982-4361 in Santa Fe, or toll free **800/331-1212**); **Thrifty,** 2039 Yale Blvd. SE, Albuquerque (☎ 505/842-8733, or toll free **800/367-2277**); **Hertz,** Albuquerque International Airport (☎ 505/842-4255, or toll free **800/654-3131**); **Dollar,** Albuquerque International Airport (☎ 505/842-4244, or toll free **800/369-4226**); **Budget,** Albuquerque International Airport (☎ 505/769-5900); **Alamo,** 2601 Yale SE (☎ 505/842-4057, or toll free **800/327-9633**); and **Payless,** 2200 Renard Place SE (☎ 505/247-9255).

Drivers who need wheelchair-accessible transportation should call **Wheelchair Gateways of New Mexico,** 1015 Tramway Lane NE (☎ 505/247-2626, or toll free **800/408-2626**); it rents vans by the day, week, or month.

If you're **arriving by car** from elsewhere in North America, Albuquerque is the crossroads of two major interstate highways. **I-40** runs from Wilmington, North Carolina (1,870 miles east), to Barstow, California (580 miles west). **I-25** extends from Buffalo, Wyoming (850 miles north), to El Paso, Texas (265 miles south). I-25 skims past Santa Fe's southern city limits. To reach Taos, you'll have to leave I-25 at Santa Fe and travel north 74 miles via **U.S. 84/285** and **N.M. 68,** or exit I-25 9 miles south of Raton, near the Colorado border, and proceed 100 miles west on **U.S. 64.**

The following table shows the approximate mileages to Santa Fe from various cities around the United States.

Distances to Santa Fe (in miles)

From	Distance	From	Distance
Atlanta	1,417	Minneapolis	1,199
Boston	2,190	New Orleans	1,181
Chicago	1,293	New York	1,971
Cleveland	1,558	Oklahoma City	533
Dallas	663	Phoenix	595
Denver	391	St. Louis	993
Detroit	1,514	Salt Lake City	634
Houston	900	San Francisco	1,149
Los Angeles	860	Seattle	1,477
Miami	2,011	Washington, D.C.	1,825

PACKAGE TOURS Tours within the state of New Mexico are offered by the following inbound operators:

Destination Southwest, 121 Tijeras NE, Suite 1100, Albuquerque, NM 87102 (☎ **505/766-9068,** or toll free **800/999-3109**).

Gray Line Tours, 800 Rio Grande NW, Suite 2, Albuquerque, NM 87104 (☎ **505/242-3880,** or toll free **800/256-8991**).

Jack Allen Tours, P.O. Box 11940, Albuquerque, NM 87192 (☎ **505/266-9688**).

Rojo Tours & Services, 228 Old Santa Fe Trail, Santa Fe, NM 87501 (☎ **505/983-8333**).

Sun Tours, 4300 San Mateo Blvd. NE, Suite B-155, Albuquerque, NM 87110 (☎ **505/889-8888**).

Travel New Mexico, Inc., 3317 Valencia NE, Albuquerque, NM 87110 (☎ **505/883-9178,** or toll free **800/333-7159**).

Zia Tours / A to Z Travelink, 6020 Indian School Rd., Albuquerque, NM 87110 (☎ **505/883-5865,** or toll free **800/366-0282**).

3

For Foreign Visitors

Aᴌᴛʜᴏᴜɢʜ Aᴍᴇʀɪᴄᴀɴ ꜰᴀᴅꜱ ᴀɴᴅ ꜰᴀꜱʜɪᴏɴꜱ ʜᴀᴠᴇ ꜱᴘʀᴇᴀᴅ ᴀᴄʀᴏꜱꜱ Eᴜʀᴏᴘᴇ and other parts of the world so much that the United States may seem like familiar territory before your arrival, there are still many peculiarities and uniquely American situations that any foreign visitor will encounter.

In this chapter I will point out to you many of the perhaps unexpected differences from what you are used to at home, and explain some of the more confusing aspects of daily life in the United States.

1 Preparing for Your Trip

Entry Requirements

DOCUMENT REQUIREMENTS   Canadian citizens may enter the United States without passports or visas; they need only proof of residence.

British subjects and citizens of New Zealand, Japan, and most western European countries traveling on valid passports may not need a visa for holiday or business travel to the United States for less than 90 days, providing that they hold a round-trip or return ticket and that they enter the United States on an airline or cruise line participating in the visa waiver program. (Note that citizens of these visa-exempt countries who first enter the United States may then visit Mexico, Canada, Bermuda, and/or the Caribbean islands and then reenter the United States by any mode of transportation, without needing a visa. Further information is available from any U.S. embassy or consulate.)

Citizens of countries other than those stipulated above, including citizens of Australia, must have two documents: (1) a valid passport with an expiration date at least six months later than the scheduled end of their visit to the United States; and (2) a tourist visa, available without charge from the nearest U.S. consulate.

To obtain a visa, the traveler must submit a completed application form (either in person or by mail) with a $1^1/_2$-inch-square photo and must demonstrate binding ties to a residence abroad. Usually you can obtain a visa at once or within 24 hours, but it may take longer during the summer rush from June to August. If you cannot go in person, contact the nearest U.S. embassy or consulate for directions on applying by mail. Your travel agent or airline office may also be able to provide you with visa applications and instructions. The U.S. embassy or consulate that issues your visa will determine whether you will be issued a multiple- or single-entry visa and any restrictions regarding the length of your stay.

MEDICAL REQUIREMENTS   No inoculations are needed to enter the United States unless you're coming from, or have stopped over in, areas known to be suffering from epidemics, particularly cholera or yellow fever.

If you have a disease requiring treatment with medications containing narcotics or drugs requiring a syringe, carry a valid signed prescription to allay any suspicions that you are smuggling drugs.

CUSTOMS REQUIREMENTS   Every adult visitor may bring in free of duty: one liter of wine or hard liquor; 200 cigarettes or 100 cigars (but no cigars from Cuba) or three pounds of smoking tobacco; and $100 worth of gifts. These exemptions are offered to travelers who spend at least 72 hours in the United States and who have not claimed them within the preceding six months. It's altogether forbidden to bring into the country foodstuffs (particularly cheese, fruit, cooked meats, and canned goods) and plants (vegetables, seeds, tropical plants, and so on). Foreign tourists may bring in or take out up to $10,000 in U.S. or foreign currency with no formalities; larger sums must be declared to Customs on entering or leaving the country.

Insurance

There is no national health-care system in the United States. Because the cost of medical care is extremely high, I strongly advise every traveler to secure health insurance coverage before setting out.

You may want to take out a comprehensive travel policy that covers (for a relatively low premium) sickness or injury costs (medical, surgical, and hospital); loss or theft of your baggage; trip-cancellation costs; guarantee of bail in case you are arrested; costs of accidents, repatriation, or death. Such packages (for example, "Europe Assistance" in Europe) are sold by automobile clubs at attractive rates, as well as by insurance companies and travel agencies.

Money

CURRENCY & EXCHANGE   The U.S. monetary system has a decimal base: one American dollar ($1) = 100 cents (100¢).

Dollar bills commonly come in $1 ("a buck"), $5, $10, $20, $50, and $100 denominations (the last two are not welcome when paying for small purchases and are not accepted in taxis or at subway ticket booths). There are also $2 bills (seldom encountered).

There are six denominations of coins: 1¢ (one cent or "a penny"), 5¢ (five cents or "a nickel"), 10¢ (ten cents or "a dime"), 25¢ (twenty-five cents or "a quarter"), 50¢ (fifty cents or "a half dollar"), and the rare $1 piece.

Note: The "foreign-exchange bureaus" so common in Europe are rare even at airports in the United States and nonexistent outside major cities. Try to avoid having to change foreign money, or traveler's checks denominated other than in U.S. dollars, at a small-town bank or even a branch bank in a big city. In fact, leave any currency other than U.S. dollars at home—it may prove more nuisance to you than it's worth.

TRAVELER'S CHECKS   Traveler's checks denominated in U.S. dollars are readily accepted at most hotels, motels, restaurants, and large stores. But the best place to change traveler's checks is at a bank. Do not bring traveler's checks denominated in other currencies.

CREDIT & CHARGE CARDS   The method of payment most widely used is credit and charge cards: Visa (Barclaycard in Britain),

MasterCard (EuroCard in Europe, Access in Britain, Chargex in Canada), American Express, Diners Club, Discover, and Carte Blanche. You can save yourself trouble by using "plastic money" rather than cash or traveler's checks in most hotels, motels, restaurants, and retail stores (a growing number of food and liquor stores now accept credit/charge cards). You must have a credit or charge card to rent a car. It can also be used as proof of identity (often carrying more weight than a passport) or as a "cash card," enabling you to draw money from banks and automated-teller machines (ATMs) that accept it.

Safety

GENERAL   While tourist areas are generally safe, crime is on the increase everywhere, and U.S. urban areas tend to be less safe than those in Europe or Japan. Visitors should always stay alert. This is particularly true of large U.S. cities. It is wise to ask the city or area's tourist office if you are in doubt about which neighborhoods are safe. Avoid deserted areas, especially at night. Don't go into any city park at night unless there is an event that attracts crowds. Generally speaking, you can feel safe in areas where there are many people and many open establishments.

Avoid carrying valuables with you on the street, and don't display expensive cameras or electronic equipment. Hold on to your pocketbook and place your billfold in an inside pocket. In restaurants, theaters, and other public places, keep your possessions in sight.

Remember also that hotels are open to the public, and in a large hotel, security may not be able to screen everyone entering. Always lock your room door; don't assume that once inside your hotel you are automatically safe and need no longer be aware of your surroundings.

DRIVING   Safety while driving is particularly important. Question your rental agency about personal safety, or ask for a brochure of traveler safety tips when you pick up your car. Obtain written directions, or a map with the route marked in red, from the agency showing how to get to your destination. And, if possible, arrive and depart during daylight hours.

Recently more and more crime has involved cars and drivers. If you drive off a highway into a doubtful neighborhood, leave the area as quickly as possible. If you have an accident, even on the highway, stay in your car with the doors locked until you assess the situation or until the police arrive. If you are bumped from behind on the street or are involved in a minor accident with no injuries and the situation appears to be suspicious, motion to the other driver to follow you. *Never* get out of your car in such situations. You can also keep a prepared sign in your car which reads PLEASE FOLLOW THIS VEHICLE TO REPORT THE ACCIDENT. Show the sign to the other driver and go directly to the nearest police precinct, well-lighted service station, or all-night store.

If you see someone on the road who indicates a need for help, do not stop. Take note of the location, drive on to a well-lighted area, and telephone the police by dialing **911.**

Park in well-lighted, well-traveled areas if possible. Always keep your car doors locked, whether the car is attended or unattended. Look around you before you get out of your car, and never leave any packages or valuables in sight. If someone attempts to rob you or steal your car, do *not* try to resist the thief/carjacker—report the incident to the police department immediately.

Also, make sure that you have enough gasoline in your tank to reach your intended destination, so that you're not forced to look for a service station in an unfamiliar and possibly unsafe neighborhood—especially at night.

You may wish to contact the local tourist information bureau in your destination before you arrive, as they may be able to provide you with a safety brochure. (See "Sources of Information," in Chapter 1, and the "Orientation" sections in Chapters 4, 12, and 18 for specific tourist organization names and addresses.)

Special Services

The **Santa Fe Council on International Relations,** P.O. Box 1223, Santa Fe, NM 87504 (☎ **505/982-4931**), assists foreign visitors by providing community information. An office in Room 281 of La Fonda Hotel on the Plaza is open Monday through Friday from 9am to noon.

2 Getting To & Around the U.S.

GETTING TO THE U.S. Travelers from overseas can take advantage of the **APEX (advance-purchase excursion) fares** offered by all the major international carriers. Aside from these, attractive values are offered by Icelandair on flights from Luxembourg to New York and by Virgin Atlantic Airways from London to New York/Newark and Los Angeles. To reach northern New Mexico from Europe, you'll probably stop at one of these airports anyway, to catch a connecting flight.

British travelers should check out **British Airways** (☎ **081/897-4000** in the U.K., or toll free **800/247-9297** in the U.S.), which offers direct flights from London to New York and to Los Angeles, as does **Virgin Atlantic Airways** (☎ **02/937-47747** in the U.K., or toll free **800/862-8621** in the U.S.). Canadian readers might book flights on **Air Canada** (☎ toll free **800/776-3000**), which offers service from Toronto, Montréal, and Calgary to New York and Los Angeles. In addition, many other international carriers also serve the New York and Los Angeles airports, including **Japan Airlines** (☎ toll free **800/525-3663** in the U.S.) and **SAS** (☎ toll free **800/221-2350** in the U.S.).

The visitor arriving by air, no matter what the port of entry, should cultivate patience and resignation before setting foot on U.S. soil. Getting through Immigration control may take as long as two hours on some days, especially summer weekends. Add the time it takes to clear Customs and you'll see that you should make very generous allowance for delay in planning connections between international and domestic flights—an average of two to three hours at least.

In contrast, for the traveler arriving by car or by rail from Canada, the border-crossing formalities have been streamlined practically to the vanishing point. And for the traveler by air from Canada, Bermuda, and some places in the Caribbean, you can sometimes go through Customs and Immigration at the point of departure, which is much quicker and less painful.

For further information about travel to and arriving in Santa Fe, Taos, and Albuquerque, see the "Orientation" sections in Chapters 4, 12, and 18, respectively.

GETTING AROUND THE U.S. • By Plane   Some large American airlines (for example, American Airlines, Delta, Northwest, TWA, and United) offer travelers on their transatlantic or transpacific flights special discount tickets under the name **Visit USA,** allowing travel between any U.S. destinations at minimum rates. They are not on sale in the United States—they must be purchased before you leave your foreign point of departure. This system is the best, easiest, and fastest way to see the United States at low cost. You should obtain information well in advance from your travel agent or the office of the airline concerned, since the conditions attached to these discount tickets can be changed without advance notice.

• **By Train**   Long-distance trains in the United States are operated by Amtrak, the national rail passenger corporation. International visitors can buy a **USA Railpass,** good for 15 or 30 days of unlimited travel on Amtrak. The pass is available through many foreign travel agents. Prices in 1994 for a 15-day pass were $208 off-peak, $308 peak; a 30-day pass cost $309 off-peak, $389 peak. (With a foreign passport, you can also buy passes at some Amtrak offices in the United States, including locations in Boston, Chicago, Los Angeles, Miami, New York, San Francisco, and Washington, D.C.) Reservations are generally required and should be made for each part of your trip as early as possible.

However, visitors should be aware of the limitations of long-distance rail travel in the United States. With a few notable exceptions (for instance, the Northeast Corridor line between Boston and Washington, D.C.), service is rarely up to European standards: Delays are common, routes are limited and often infrequently served, and fares are rarely significantly lower than discount airfares. Thus cross-country train travel should be approached with caution.

• **By Bus**   The cheapest way to travel the United States is by bus. Greyhound, the sole nationwide bus line, offers an **Ameripass** for unlimited travel for 7 days (for $250), 15 days (for $350), and 30 days (for $450). Bus travel in the United States can be both slow and uncomfortable, so this option is not for everyone.

• **By Car**   Travel by car gives visitors the freedom to make—and alter—their itineraries to suit their own needs and interests. And it offers the possibility of visiting some of the off-the-beaten-path locations, places that cannot be reached easily by public transportation. For information on renting cars in the United States, see "Automobile Organizations" and "Automobile Rentals" in "Fast Facts: For the Foreign Traveler," later in this chapter; "By Car" in "Getting There," in Chapter 2; and "By Car" in "Getting Around," in Chapters 4, 12, and 18.

Fast Facts: For the Foreign Traveler

Accommodations   Some of the major hotels listed in this book maintain overseas reservation networks and can be booked either directly or through travel agents. Some hotels are also included in tour operators' package tours. Since tour companies buy rooms in bulk, they can often offer them at a discount. Discuss this option with your travel agent and compare tour prices with those in this guide.

Automobile Organizations   Auto clubs will supply maps, suggested routes, guidebooks, accident and bail-bond insurance, and emergency road service. The major auto club in the United States, with 955 offices nationwide, is the American Automobile Association (AAA). Members of some foreign auto clubs have reciprocal arrangements with the AAA and enjoy its services at no charge. If you belong to an auto club in your home country, inquire about AAA reciprocity before you leave. You may be able to join the AAA even if you're not a member of a reciprocal club; to inquire, call the AAA (☎ toll free **800/336-4357**). The AAA can provide you with an International Driving Permit, validating your foreign license.

In addition, some automobile-rental agencies now provide many of these same services. Inquire about their availability when you rent your car.

Automobile Rentals   To rent a car you will need a major credit or charge card and a valid driver's license. In addition, you usually need to be at least 25 (some companies do rent to younger people but add a daily surcharge). Be sure to return your car with the same amount of gas you started out with; rental companies charge excessive prices for gasoline. See "By Car" in "Getting Around," in Chapters 4, 12, and 18, for the phone numbers of car-rental companies in Santa Fe, Taos, and Albuquerque, respectively.

Business Hours   **Banks** are generally open Monday through Friday from 9am to 3 or 4pm, although there's 24-hour access to the automated teller machines (ATMs) at most banks and other outlets. Generally, **offices** are open Monday through Friday from 9am to 5pm. **Stores** are open six days a week, with many open on Sunday too; department stores usually stay open until 9pm at least one night a week.

Climate   See "When to Go," in Chapter 2.

Currency   See "Money" in "Preparing for Your Trip," earlier in this chapter.

Currency Exchange   You'll find currency-exchange services in major airports with international service. Elsewhere, they may be quite difficult to come by. In the United States, a very reliable choice is Thomas Cook Currency Services, Inc., which has been in business since 1841 and offers a wide range of services. It sells commission-free foreign and U.S. traveler's checks, drafts, and wire transfers; it also does check collections (including Eurochecks). The rates are competitive and the service excellent. Thomas Cook maintains several offices in New York City, including a major one at 630 Fifth Ave. (☎ **212/757-6915**); at the JFK airport International Arrivals Terminal (☎ **718/656-8444**); and at LaGuardia Airport in the Delta terminal (☎ **718/533-0784**). In Los Angeles there's an office in the Hilton Hotel Center, 900 Wilshire Blvd. (☎ **213/624-4221**).

For northern New Mexcio banks that handle foreign-currency exchange, see "Fast Facts: Santa Fe," in Chapter 4, and "Fast Facts: Taos," in Chapter 12.

Drinking Laws   You must be 21 to purchase alcoholic beverages in New Mexico and most other states in the country. No alcohol can be served after 2am Monday through Saturday night; on Sunday liquor can be sold only between noon and midnight. No alcohol can be sold on election days.

Electricity   The United States uses 110–120 volts A.C., 60 cycles, compared to 220–240 volts A.C., 50 cycles, as in most of Europe. In addition to a 100-volt transformer, small appliances of non-American manufacture, such as hairdryers and shavers, will require a plug adapter, with two flat, parallel pins.

Embassies and Consulates   All embassies are located in the national capital, Washington, D.C.; some consulates are located in major U.S. cities, and most countries maintain a mission to the United Nations in New York City. The embassies and consulates of the major English-speaking countries—Australia, Canada, the Republic of Ireland, New Zealand, and the United Kingdom— are listed below. If you are from another country, you can get the telephone number of your embassy by calling "Information" in Washington, D.C. (☎ **202/555-1212**).

The embassy of **Australia** is at 1601 Massachusetts Ave. NW, Washington, DC 20036 (☎ **202/797-3000**). There is an Australian consulate at 611 N. Larchmont Blvd., Los Angeles, CA 90004 (☎ **213/469-4300**). Other Australian consulates are in Chicago, Honolulu, Houston, New York, and San Francisco.

The embassy of **Canada** is at 501 Pennsylvania Ave. NW, Washington, DC 20001 (☎ **202/682-1740**). There's a Canadian consulate in Los Angeles at 300 S. Grand Ave., 10th Floor, Los Angeles, CA 90071 (☎ **213/346-2700**). Other Canadian consulates are in Atlanta, Buffalo (N.Y.), Chicago, Cleveland, Dallas,

Detroit, Miami, Minneapolis, New York, San Francisco, and Seattle.

The embassy of the **Republic of Ireland** is at 2234 Massachusetts Ave. NW, Washington, DC 20008 (☎ 202/462-3939). The nearest Irish consulate is at 655 Montgomery St., Suite 930, San Francisco, CA 94111 (☎ 415/392-4214). Other Irish consulates are in Boston, Chicago, and New York.

The embassy of **New Zealand** is at 37 Observatory Circle NW, Washington, DC 20008 (☎ 202/328-4848). The only New Zealand consulate in the United States is at 12400 Wilshire Blvd., 11th Floor, Los Angeles, CA 90025 (☎ 310/477-8241).

The embassy of the **United Kingdom** is at 3100 Massachusetts Ave. NW, Washington, DC 20008 (☎ 202/462-1340). There's a British consulate in Los Angeles at 11766 Wilshire Blvd., Suite 400, Los Angeles, CA 90025 (☎ 310/477-3322). Other British consulates are in Atlanta, Chicago, Houston, Miami, and New York.

Emergencies   Call **911** to report a fire, call the police, or get an ambulance. This is a toll-free call (no coins are required at a public telephone).

If you encounter traveler's problems, check the local telephone directory to find an office of the **Traveler's Aid Society,** a nationwide, nonprofit, social-service organization geared to helping travelers in difficult straits. Their services might include reuniting families separated while traveling, providing food and/or shelter to people stranded without cash, or even emotional counseling. If you're in trouble, seek them out.

Gasoline (Petrol)   One U.S. gallon equal 3.8 liters or .85 Imperial gallons. There are usually several grades (and price levels) of gasoline available at most gas stations, and their names change from company to company. The unleaded ones with the highest octane rating are the most expensive (most rental cars take the least expensive "regular" unleaded gas); leaded gas is the least expensive, but only older cars can use this anymore, so check if you're not sure. And often the price is lower if you pay in cash instead of by credit or charge card. Also, many gas stations now offer lower-priced self-service gas pumps—in fact, some gas stations, particularly at night, are all self-service.

Holidays   On the following legal national holidays, banks, government offices, post offices, and many stores, restaurants, and museums are closed: January 1 (New Year's Day), the third Monday in January (Martin Luther King Day), the third Monday in February (Presidents Day, Washington's Birthday), the last Monday in May (Memorial Day), July 4 (Independence Day), the first Monday in September (Labor Day), the second Monday in October (Columbus Day), November 11 (Veterans Day/Armistice Day), the last Thursday in November (Thanksgiving Day), and December 25 (Christmas). Also, the Tuesday following the first

Monday in November is Election Day, and is a legal holiday in presidential-election years (next in 1996).

Information   See "Information and When to Go," in Chapter 2; and "Tourist Information" in "Orientation," in Chapters 4, 12, and 18, for Santa Fe, Taos, and Albuquerque, respectively.

Languages   Only major hotels may have multilingual employees, although Spanish-speaking staff members may be available. Other than that, in most places in northern New Mexico you'll have to rely on English.

Legal Aid   The foreign tourist, unless positively identified as a member of the Mafia or of a drug ring, will probably never become involved with the American legal system. If you are stopped for a minor infraction (for example, of the highway code, such as speeding), never attempt to pay the fine directly to a police officer; you may wind up arrested on the much more serious charge of attempted bribery. Pay fines by mail or directly into the hands of the clerk of the court. If you're accused of a more serious offense, it's wise to say and do nothing before consulting a lawyer. Under U.S. law, an arrested person is allowed one telephone call to a party of his or her choice. Call your embassy or consulate.

Mail   If you want your mail to follow you on your vacation and you aren't sure of your address, your mail can be sent to you, in your name, **c/o General Delivery** (Poste Restante) at the main post office of the city or region where you expect to be. (For Santa Fe, Taos, and Albuquerque, see the "Fast Facts" sections in Chapters 4, 12, and 18, respectively, for addresses and telephone numbers.) The addressee must pick it up in person and must produce proof of identity (driver's license, credit or charge card, passport, etc.).

Domestic **postage rates** are 19¢ for a postcard and 29¢ for a letter. Check with any local post office for current international postage rates to your home country.

Generally found at intersections, **mailboxes** are blue with a red-and-white stripe and carry the designation U.S. MAIL. If your mail is addressed to a U.S. destination, don't forget to add the five-digit **postal code,** or ZIP (Zone Improvement Plan) Code, after the two-letter abbreviation of the state to which the mail is addressed (CA for California, NM for New Mexico, NY for New York, and so on).

Medical Emergencies   To call an ambulance, dial **911** from any phone. No coins are needed. For a list of hospitals and other emergency information in northern New Mexico, see the "Fast Facts" sections in Chapters 4, 12, and 18.

Newspapers and Magazines   National newspapers include the *New York Times, USA Today,* and the *Wall Street Journal.* National news weeklies include *Newsweek, Time,* and *U.S. News & World Report.* In large cities most newsstands offer a small selection of the most popular foreign periodicals and newspapers, such as *The*

Economist, Le Monde, and *Der Spiegel.* For information on local publications, see the "Fast Facts" sections in Chapters 4, 12, and 18.

Radio and Television   Audiovisual media, with four coast-to-coast networks—ABC, CBS, NBC, and Fox—joined in recent years by the Public Broadcasting System (PBS) and the cable network CNN, play a major part in American life. In big cities, televiewers have a choice of about a dozen channels (including the UHF channels), most of them transmitting 24 hours a day, without counting the pay-TV channels showing recent movies or sports events. All options are usually indicated on your hotel TV set. You'll also find a wide choice of local radio stations, both AM and FM, each broadcasting particular kinds of talk shows and/or music— classical, country, jazz, pop, gospel—punctuated by news broadcasts and frequent commercials.

Safety   See "Safety" in "Preparing for Your Trip," earlier in this chapter.

Taxes   In the United States there is no VAT (value-added tax) or other indirect tax at a national level. Every state, and each county and city in it, has the right to levy its own local tax on purchases (including hotel and restaurant checks, airline tickets, and so on) and services. Taxes are already included in the price of certain services, such as public transportation, cab fares, telephone calls, and gasoline. The amount of sales tax varies from about 4% to 12%, depending on the state and city, so when you're making major purchases, such as photographic equipment, clothing, or stereo components, it can be a significant part of the cost.

New Mexico levies a 6.875% state tax on gross receipts, including hotel bills and shop purchases (food is exempted). And each city or county levies an additional lodging tax of 2.75% to 5.25% to support the local tax base. Since this could add 9% to 11.50% to your hotel bills, travelers on a budget should keep this tax in mind when making accommodations choices.

Telephone, Telegraph, Telex, and Fax   The telephone system in the United States is run by private corporations, so rates, especially for long-distance service and operator-assisted calls, can vary widely—even on calls made from public telephones. Local calls in the United States usually cost 25¢ (they're 25¢ throughout New Mexico).

Generally, hotel surcharges on long-distance and local calls are astronomical. You're usually better off by calling collect, using a telephone charge card, or using a **public pay telephone,** which you'll find clearly marked in most public buildings and private establishments as well as on the street. Outside metropolitan areas, public telephones are more difficult to find. Stores and gas stations are your best bet.

Most **long-distance and international calls** can be dialed directly from any phone (stock up on quarters if you're calling from a pay phone or use a telephone charge card). For calls to Canada and other parts of the United States, dial 1 followed by the area code and the seven-digit number. For international calls, dial 011 followed by the country code (Australia, 61; Republic of Ireland, 353; New Zealand, 64; United Kingdom, 44), then the city code (for example, 71 or 81 for London, 21 for Birmingham) and the telephone number of the person you wish to call.

Note that all calls to area code 800 are toll free. However, calls to numbers in area codes 700 and 900 (chat lines, bulletin boards, "dating" services, etc.) can be very expensive—usually a charge of 95¢ to $3 or more per minute, and they sometimes have minimum charges that can run as high as $15 or more.

For **reversed-charge or collect calls**, and for **person-to-person calls**, dial 0 (zero, *not* the letter "O") followed by the area code and number you want; an operator will then come on the line, and you should specify that you are calling collect, or person-to-person, or both. If your operator-assisted call is international, ask for the overseas operator.

For local **directory assistance** ("information"), dial **411**; for long-distance information, dial **1**, then the appropriate area code and **555-1212.**

Like the telephone system, **telegraph** and **telex** services are provided by private corporations like ITT, MCI, and above all, Western Union, the most important. You can bring your telegram in to the nearest Western Union office (there are hundreds across the country) or dictate it over the phone (a toll-free call, **800/325-6000**). You can also telegraph money (using a major credit or charge card), or have it telegraphed to you, very quickly over the Western Union system. (Note, however, that this service can be very expensive—the service charge can run as high as 15% to 25% of the amount sent.)

Most hotels have **fax** machines available for guest use (be sure to ask about the charge to use it), and many hotel rooms are even wired for guests' fax machines. You'll probably also see signs for public faxes in the windows of local shops.

Telephone Directory   There are two kinds of telephone directories available to you. The general directory is the so-called *White Pages,* in which private and business subscribers are listed in alphabetical order. The inside front cover lists the emergency number for police, fire, and ambulance, and other vital numbers (like the poison-control center, crime-victims hotline, and so on). The first few pages are devoted to community-service numbers, including a guide to long-distance and international calling, complete with country codes and area codes.

The second directory, printed on yellow paper (hence its name, *Yellow Pages*), lists all local services, businesses, and industries by type of activity, with an index at the back. The listings cover not only such obvious items as automobile repairs by make of car or drugstores (pharmacies), often by geographical location, but also restaurants by type of cuisine and geographical location, bookstores by special subject and/or language, places of worship by religious denomination, and other information that the tourist might otherwise not readily find. The *Yellow Pages* also often include city plans or detailed area maps, often showing ZIP Codes and public transportation routes.

Time   The United States is divided into six **time zones:** From east to west, eastern standard time (EST), central standard time (CST), mountain standard time (MST), Pacific standard time (PST), Alaska standard time (AST), and Hawaii standard time (HST). Always keep the changing time zones in mind if you are traveling (or even telephoning) long distances in the United States. For example, noon in New York City (EST) is 11am in Chicago (CST), 10am in Santa Fe (MST), 9am in Los Angeles (PST), 8am in Anchorage (AST), and 7am in Honolulu (HST).

New Mexico is on mountain standard time (MST), seven hours behind Greenwich mean time. **Daylight saving time** is in effect from the last Sunday in April through the last Saturday in October (actually, the change is made at 2am on Sunday), except in Arizona, Hawaii, part of Indiana, and Puerto Rico. Daylight saving time moves the clock one hour ahead of standard time. (Americans use the adage "Spring ahead, fall back" to remember which way to change their clocks and watches.)

Tipping   This is part of the American way of life, on the principle that you must expect to pay for any service you get (many service personnel receive little direct salary and must depend on tips for their income). Here are some rules of thumb:

In **hotels,** tip bellhops $1 per piece and tip the chamber staff $1 per day. Tip the doorman or concierge only if he or she has provided you with some specific service (for example, calling a cab for you or obtaining difficult-to-get theater tickets).

In **restaurants, bars, and nightclubs,** tip the service staff 15% of the check, tip bartenders 10% to 15%, tip checkroom attendants $1 per garment, and tip valet-parking attendants $1 per vehicle. Tip the doorman only if he has provided you with some specific service (such as calling a cab for you). Tipping is not expected in cafeterias and fast-food restaurants.

Tip **cab drivers** 15% of the fare.

As for **other service personnel,** tip redcaps at airports or railroad stations $1 per piece and tip hairdressers and barbers 15% to 20%.

Tipping ushers in cinemas, movies, and theaters and gas-station attendants is not expected.

Toilets   Foreign visitors often complain that public toilets (euphemistically referred to as "restrooms") are hard to find in most U.S. cities. True, there are none on the streets, but the visitor can usually find one in a bar, restaurant, hotel, museum, department store, or service station—and it will probably be clean (although the last-mentioned sometimes leaves much to be desired). Note, however, a growing practice in some restaurants and bars of displaying a notice like RESTROOMS ARE FOR THE USE OF PATRONS ONLY. You can ignore this sign or, better yet, avoid arguments by paying for a cup of coffee or a soft drink, which will qualify you as a patron. The cleanliness of toilets at railroad stations and bus depots may be more open to question, and some public places are equipped with pay toilets, which require you to insert one or more coins into a slot on the door before it will open. In restrooms with attendants, leaving at least a 25¢ tip is customary.

The American System of Measurements

Length

1 inch (in.)			=	2.54cm			
1 foot (ft.)	=	12 in.	=	30.48cm	=	.305m	
1 yard (yd.)	=	3 ft.			=	.915m	
1 mile	=	5,280 ft.					= 1.609km

To convert miles to kilometers, multiply the number of miles by 1.61. Also use to convert speeds from miles per hour (m.p.h.) to kilometers per hour (kmph).
To convert kilometers to miles, multiply the number of kilometers by .62. Also use to convert speeds from kmph to m.p.h.

Capacity

1 fluid ounce (fl. oz.)			=	.03 liters	
1 pint (pt.)	=	16 fl. oz.	=	.47 liters	
1 quart	=	2 pints	=	.94 liters	
1 gallon (gal.) =		4 quarts	=	3.79 liters	= .83 Imperial gal.

To convert U.S. gallons to liters, multiply the number of gallons by 3.79.
To convert liters to U.S. gallons, multiply the number of liters by .26.
To convert U.S. gallons to Imperial gallons, multiply the number of U.S. gallons by .83.
To convert Imperial gallons to U.S. gallons, multiply the number of Imperial gallons by 1.2.

Weight

1 ounce (oz.)			=	28.35g			
1 pound (lb.) =		16 oz.	=	453.6g	=	.45kg	
1 ton	=	2,000 lb.			=	907kg	= .91metric ton

To convert pounds to kilograms, multiply the number of pounds by .45.
To convert kilograms to pounds, multiply the number of kilograms by 2.2.

Area

1 acre		=	.41ha		
1 square mile	=	640 acres	=	259ha	=	2.6km²

To convert acres to hectares, multiply the number of acres by .41.
To convert hectares to acres, multiply the number of hectares by 2.47.

To convert square miles to square kilometers, multiply the number of square miles by 2.6.

To convert square kilometers to square miles, multiply the number of square kilometers by .39.

Temperature

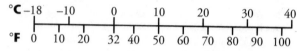

To convert degrees Fahrenheit to degrees Celsius, subtract 32 from °F, multiply by 5, then divide by 9 (example: 85°F – 32 × 5 ÷ 9 = 29.4°C).

To convert degrees Celsius to degrees Fahrenheit, multiply °C by 9, divide by 5, and add 32 (example: 20°C × 9 ÷ 5 + 32 = 68°F).

4

Getting to Know Santa Fe

Part of the charm of Santa Fe is that it's so easy to get around. Like most cities of Hispanic origin, it was built around a parklike central plaza, with its centuries-old adobe buildings and churches lining the narrow streets. Many of them now house shops, restaurants, art galleries, and museums.

Santa Fe is situated high and dry at the foot of the rugged Sangre de Cristo range. Santa Fe Baldy rises to more than 12,600 feet a mere 12 miles northeast of the Plaza. The city's downtown straddles the Santa Fe River, a tiny tributary of the Rio Grande that's little more than a trickle for much of the year.

North is the Española valley (a beautiful view of which is afforded from the Santa Fe Opera grounds) and beyond that, the village of Taos, about 66 miles distant. South are ancient Native American turquoise mines in the Cerrillos Hills; southwest is metropolitan Albuquerque, some 58 miles away. To the west, across the Caja del Rio Plateau, is the Rio Grande, and beyond that, the 11,000-foot Jemez Mountains and Valle Grande, an ancient and massive volcanic caldera. Pueblos dot the entire Rio Grande valley an hour's drive in any direction.

1 Orientation

Arriving

BY AIR The **Santa Fe Municipal Airport** (☎ 505/473-7243), just outside the southwestern city limits on Airport Road off Cerrillos Road, has three paved runways, primarily used by private planes. Commercial service is offered by **Mesa Airlines** (☎ 505/473-4118, or toll free **800/MESA-AIR**), which shuttles up to seven times a day between Albuquerque and Santa Fe and offers direct flights to Taos and Denver. The nine-passenger Cessna Caravans have a 25-minute flying time from Albuquerque International Airport, with interline connections with all major carriers. Charter services include **Capital Aviation** (☎ 505/471-2525) and **Santa Fe Aviation** (☎ 505/471-6533).

Getting to and from the Airport: Typically, air travelers to Santa Fe arrive in Albuquerque and either rent a car there or take one of a number of bus services. See "Getting There," in Chapter 2, for details.

BY TRAIN & BUS For detailed information about train and bus service to Santa Fe, see "Getting There," in Chapter 2.

BY CAR **I-25** skims past Santa Fe's southern city limits, connecting it north and south with points from Billings, Montana, to El Paso, Texas. **I-40,** the state's major east-west thoroughfare that bisects Albuquerque, affords coast-to-coast access to "The City Different." (From the west, motorists leave I-40 in Albuquerque and take I-25 north; from the east, travelers exit I-40 at Clines Corners, an hour's drive east of Albuquerque, and continue 52 miles to Santa Fe via

U.S. 285.) For travelers coming from the northwest, the most direct route is via Durango, Colorado, on U.S. 160, entering Santa Fe on U.S. 84.

For information on **car rentals** in Albuquerque, see "Getting There," in Chapter 2; and for agencies in Santa Fe, see "Getting Around," later in this chapter.

Tourist Information

The **Santa Fe Convention and Visitors Bureau** is located at 201 W. Marcy St., in Sweeney Center at the corner of Grant Street downtown (P.O. Box 909), Santa Fe, NM 87504-0909 (☎ **505/984-6760,** or toll free **800/777-CITY**). The Santa Fe County Chamber of Commerce is at 510 N. Guadalupe St. (☎ **505/988-3279**).

City Layout

The limits of downtown Santa Fe are demarcated on three sides by the horseshoe-shaped **Paseo de Peralta** and on the west by **St. Francis Drive,** otherwise known as U.S. 84/285. **Alameda Street** follows the north shore of the Santa Fe River through downtown, with the State Capitol and other federal buildings on the south side of the stream and most buildings of historic and tourist interest on the north, east of Guadalupe Street.

The **Plaza** is Santa Fe's universally accepted point of orientation. Its four diagonal walkways meet at a central fountain, around which a strange and wonderful assortment of people, of all ages, nationalities, and lifestyles, can be found at nearly any hour of the day or night.

If you stand in the center of the Plaza looking north, you're gazing directly at the Palace of the Governors. In front of you is Palace Avenue; behind you, San Francisco Street. To your left is Lincoln Avenue and to your right **Washington Avenue,** which divides downtown avenues into "East" and "West." St. Francis Cathedral is the massive Romanesque structure a block east, down San Francisco Street. Alameda Street is two full blocks behind you.

Streaking diagonally to the southwest from the downtown area, beginning opposite the state office buildings on Galisteo Avenue, is **Cerrillos Road.** Once the main north-south highway connecting New Mexico's state capital with its largest city, it is now a six-mile-long motel and fast-food "strip." St. Francis Drive, which crosses Cerrillos Road three blocks south of Guadalupe Street, is a far less tawdry byway, linking Santa Fe with I-25 four miles southeast of downtown. The **Old Pecos Trail,** on the east side of the city, also joins downtown and the freeway. **St. Michael's Drive** interconnects the three arterials.

MAPS   Free city and state maps are easily obtained at tourist information offices. An excellent state highway map is published by the New Mexico Department of Tourism, 491 Old Santa Fe Trail, Santa Fe, NM 87504 (☎ toll free **800/545-2040**). There's also a Santa Fe Visitors Center in the same building. More specific county and city maps are available from the State Highway and Transportation Department, 1120 Cerrillos Rd., Santa Fe, NM 87501 (☎ 505/827-5250). Members of the American Automobile Association, 1644 St. Michael's Dr. (☎ 471-6620), can get maps at no cost from the AAA office. Other good regional maps can be purchased at area bookstores. Gousha publishes a laminated "FastMap" of Santa Fe and Taos that has proved indispensable during my travels.

2 Getting Around

BY BUS In 1993, Santa Fe opened **Santa Fe Trails** (☎ 984-6730), its first public bus system. There are six routes, and visitors can pick up a map from the Convention and Visitors Bureau. Buses operate Monday through Friday from 6:30am to 7:30pm and on Saturday from 7am to 7pm. There is no service on Sunday or holidays. Call for current schedule and fare information.

BY TAXI It's best to telephone for a cab, for they are difficult to flag from the street. Taxis have no meters, but fares are set for given distances. Expect to pay an average of about $2.50 per mile. **Capital City Cab** (☎ 982-9990) is the main company in Santa Fe.

BY CAR Cars can be rented from any of the following firms in Santa Fe: **Adopt-a-Car,** 3574 Cerrillos Rd. (☎ 505/473-3189); **Agency Rent-A-Car,** 3347 Cerrillos Rd. (☎ 505/473-2983); **Avis,** Garrett's Desert Inn, 311 Old Santa Fe Trail (☎ 505/982-4361); **Budget,** 1946 Cerrillos Rd. (☎ 505/984-8028); **Capitol Ford,** 4490 Cerrillos Rd. (☎ 505/473-3673); **Enterprise,** 1911 Fifth St. (☎ 505/473-3600); **Hertz,** 100 Sandoval St. (☎ 505/982-1844); and **Snappy Car Rental,** 3012 Cielo Court (☎ 505/473-2277).

If Santa Fe is merely your base for an extended self-driving exploration of New Mexico, be sure to give the vehicle a thorough road check before starting out. There are a lot of wide-open desert and wilderness spaces in New Mexico, and it wouldn't be fun to be stranded in the heat or cold with a vehicle that didn't run. Check your lights, windshield wipers, horn, tires, battery, drive belts, fluid levels, alignment, and other possible trouble spots.

Make sure your driver's license, vehicle registration, safety inspection sticker, and auto club membership (if you're a member) are valid. Check with your auto insurance company to make sure you're covered when out of state and/or when driving a rental car.

If you're having car trouble, **Payne Bros. Automotive,** 1121 Calle La Resolana (☎ 471-8958), is well established. Many other garages, including import specialists, are listed in the telephone directory. For **AAA Towing Service,** call 471-6620.

Street **parking** is difficult to find during the summer months. There's a parking lot near the federal courthouse, two blocks north of the Plaza; another one behind Santa Fe Village, a block south of the Plaza; and a third at Water and Sandoval Streets. If you stop by the Santa Fe Convention and Visitors Bureau, at the corner of Grant and Marcy Streets, you can pick up a wallet-size guide to Santa Fe parking areas. The map shows both street and lot parking.

Unless otherwise posted, the **speed limit** on freeways is 65 m.p.h.; on most other two-lane open roads it's 55 m.p.h. Minimum age for drivers is 16. Safety belts are required for drivers and all passengers age 5 and over; children under 5 must use approved child seats.

Native American reservations are considered sovereign nations and enforce their own laws. For instance, on the Navajo reservation (New Mexico's largest), it is prohibited to transport alcoholic beverages, to leave established roadways, or to go without a seatbelt. Motorcyclists must wear helmets. If you are caught breaking reservation laws you are subject to reservation punishment.

Gas is readily available at service stations throughout the state. Prices are lowest in Albuquerque and are 10% to 15% more in more isolated communities. All prices are subject to the same fluctuations as anywhere in the United States.

The State Highway and Transportation Department has a toll-free hotline (☎ toll free **800/432-4269**) providing up-to-the-hour information on **road closures and conditions.**

In case of an **accident or road emergency,** contact the New Mexico State Police. District offices include Albuquerque (☎ **841-9256**), Española (☎ **753-2277**), Farmington (☎ **325-7547**), Gallup (☎ **287-4141**), Las Vegas (☎ **425-6771**), Raton (☎ **445-5571**), Santa Fe (☎ **827-5213**), and Taos (☎ **758-8878**).

Words of Warning: New Mexico has the highest per capita rate of traffic deaths of any American state. Drive carefully!

BY BICYCLE/ON FOOT A bicycle is a perfect way to get around town. Check with **Palace Bike Rentals,** at 409 E. Palace Ave. (☎ **984-2151**), for rentals.

The best way of all is to meander through downtown Santa Fe on foot. Free walking-tour maps are available at the tourist information center in Sweeney Center, 201 W. Marcy St. (☎ **984-6760**).

Fast Facts: Santa Fe

Airport See "Orientation," earlier in this chapter.

American Express There is no representative in Santa Fe; the nearest is in Albuquerque (see "Fast Facts: Albuquerque," in Chapter 18, for information on its representative there and other services).

Area Code All of New Mexico is in area code **505.**

Babysitters Most hotels can arrange for sitters on request. Alternatively, call the Santa Fe Kid Connection, 1015 Valerie Circle (☎ **471-3100**).

Business Hours **Offices and stores** are generally open Monday through Friday from 9am to 5pm, with many stores also open Friday nights, Saturday, and Sunday in the summer season. Most

banks are open Monday through Thursday from 10am to 3pm and on Friday from 10am to 6pm; drive-up windows may be open later. Some may also open Saturday mornings. Most branches have cash machines available 24 hours. See also "Liquor Laws," below.

Car Rentals   See "Getting Around," earlier in this chapter.

Climate   Santa Fe is consistently 10°F cooler than the nearby desert but gets the same sunny skies, averaging more than 300 days of sunshine out of 365. Midsummer (July and August) days are dry and sunny (around 80°F), with brief afternoon thunderstorms common; evenings are typically in the upper 50s. Winters are mild and fair, with occasional and short-lived snow (average annual snowfall is 32 inches, although the ski basin gets an average of 225 inches). Average annual rainfall is 14 inches a year, most of it in summer; the relative humidity is 45%. (Also see "When to Go," in Chapter 2.) For current weather information, call **988-5151.**

Currency Exchange   Four banks in Santa Fe will exchange foreign currency. SunWest Bank, 1234 St. Michael's Dr. (☎ **471-1234**), offers same-day sales of 20 different currencies. First Interstate Bank, 150 Washington Ave. (☎ **982-3671**); First National Bank of Santa Fe, on the Plaza (☎ **984-7400**); and the Bank of Santa Fe, 241 Washington Ave. (☎ **984-0500**), will also buy currencies—but this usually takes two to three days.

Dentist   Most work in the medical office area several miles south of downtown. Among those near downtown, Dr. Leslie E. La Kind, 400 Botulph Lane (☎ **988-3500**), offers 24-hour emergency service. You might also call the Dental Referral Service (☎ **989-9158**) for help in finding a dentist.

Doctor   The Lovelace Alameda clinic, 901 W. Alameda St. (☎ **986-3600**), is in the Solano Center near St. Francis Drive. It's open daily from 8am to 8pm for urgent care, with no appointments required. For Physicians and Surgeons Referral and Information Services, call the American Board of Medical Specialties (☎ toll free **800/776-2378**).

Drugstores   The R&R Professional Pharmacy, at 1691 Galisteo St. (☎ **988-9797**), is open Monday through Friday from 9am to 6pm and on Saturday from 9am to 5pm. Emergency and delivery service can be arranged with the Medical Center Pharmacy, adjacent to St. Vincent Hospital on St. Michael's Drive (☎ **983-4359**).

Emergencies   For police, fire, or ambulance emergency, dial **911.**

Eyeglasses   The Quintana Optical Dispensary, 109 E. Marcy St. (☎ **988-4234**), offers one-hour prescription service Monday through Friday from 9am to 5pm and on Saturday from 9am to noon.

Hairdressers and Barbers   You can get your hair cut in the Inn at Loretto, La Fonda Hotel, or numerous other locations throughout the city. Santa Fe's Supercuts franchise is at 1936 Cerrillos Rd.

(☎ **988-7559**). Your best bet for finding a good hairstylist is to ask locals who they'd recommend.

Hospitals   St. Vincent Hospital, 455 St. Michael's Dr. (☎ **983-3361**), is a 268-bed regional health center. Patient services include urgent and emergency-room care and ambulatory surgery. Other health services include the AIDS Wellness Program (☎ **983-1822**) and Women's Health Services Family Care and Counseling Center (☎ **988-8869**). Lovelace Health Systems has two walk-in offices, one at 901 W. Alameda St. (☎ **986-3666**) and the other at 440 St. Michael's Dr. (☎ **986-8566**).

Hotlines   The following hotlines are available in Santa Fe: battered families (☎ **473-5200**), poison control (☎ toll free **800/432-6866**), psychiatric emergencies (☎ **983-3361**), sexual assault (☎ **473-7818**), teen suicide (☎ **989-5242**), and emergency lodging (☎ **986-0043** after 4pm daily).

Information   See "Tourist Information" in "Orientation," earlier in this chapter; and "Information and When to Go," in Chapter 2.

Language   English is the lingua franca, but Spanish is almost as frequently spoken. You'll also hear the various Native American languages: Navajo (the most widely spoken surviving dialect), Apache, Zuni, Tanoan, and Keresan.

Laundry and Dry Cleaning   Just outside the downtown perimeter is Shockey's Coinop Laundry, 755 Cerrillos Rd. (☎ **983-9881**), open daily from 6am to 10:30pm. You can drop off laundry ($5 a load) at Adobe Laundromat, 411 W. Water St. (☎ **982-9063**). Solano Center Laundromat and Dry Cleaners, 949¹/₂ W. Alameda St. (☎ **989-8905**), offers dropoff service, as well as dry-cleaning service, daily from 7am to 9:30pm.

Libraries   The Santa Fe Public Library is half a block from the Plaza at 145 Washington Ave. (☎ **984-6780**). There are branch libraries at Villa Linda Mall and at 1713 Llano St., just off St. Michael's Drive. The New Mexico State Library is at 325 Don Gaspar Ave. (☎ **827-3800**). Specialty libraries include the Archives of New Mexico, 404 Montezuma St., and the New Mexico History Library, 110 Washington Ave.

Liquor Laws   The legal drinking age is 21 throughout New Mexico. Bars may remain open until 2am Monday through Saturday and until midnight on Sunday. Wine, beer, and spirits are sold at licensed supermarkets and liquor stores. There are no package sales on Sunday and no sales of any alcohol on election days. Some restaurants are licensed to serve beer, wine, and hard liquor; some may sell beer and wine only; others are unlicensed. The distinctions are noted in restaurant descriptions in this book. A special allowance must be granted for liquor to be dispensed in proximity to any church. It is illegal to transport liquor through most reservations.

Lost Property   Contact the city police at **473-5000.**

Mail   The Main Post Office is at 120 S. Federal Place, Santa Fe, NM 87501 (☎ **988-6351**), two blocks north and a block west of the Plaza. The Coronado Station branch is at 541 W. Cordova Rd. (☎ **438-8452**). Both are open Monday through Friday from 8am to 4pm and on Saturday from 9am to noon. Most of the major hotels have stamp machines and mailboxes with twice-daily pickup. The ZIP Code for central Santa Fe is 87501.

Newspapers and Magazines   The *New Mexican,* a Gannett publication, is Santa Fe's daily newspaper. Offices are at 202 E. Marcy St. (☎ **983-3303**). The weekly *Santa Fe Reporter,* published on Wednesday, is often more willing to be controversial; its entertainment listings are excellent. Regional magazines published locally are *New Mexico Magazine* (monthly, statewide interest), *The Santa Fean Magazine* (monthly, local interest), *Santa Fe Lifestyle* (quarterly, local interest), and *Southwest Profile* (eight times a year, regional art).

Photographic Needs   Everything from film purchases to camera repairs to 24-hour processing can be handled by the Camera Shop, 109 E. San Francisco St. (☎ **983-6591**), or Camera & Darkroom, 216 Galisteo St. (☎ **983-2948**).

Police   In case of emergency, dial **911**. All other inquiries should be directed to the main Santa Fe Police Station, 2515 Camino Entrada (☎ **473-5000,** or **473-5080** after 5pm and weekends). The Santa Fe County Sheriff's Office is in the county courthouse, Grant Avenue and Johnson Street (☎ **984-5060**). The New Mexico State Police search-and-rescue line is **827-9300.**

Radio   Santa Fe's radio stations include KMIK-AM 810 (all-news CBS affiliate), KTRC-AM 1400 (nostalgia music and early radio dramas), KSFR-FM 90.7 (classical), KNYN-FM 95.5 (country), KBAC-FM 98.1 (adult contemporary), KLSK-FM 104.1 (adult alternative), KBOM-FM 106.7 (Spanish), and KVSF, 1260 AM (news and talk). Albuquerque stations are easily received in Santa Fe.

Religious Services   Roman Catholics are the highest-profile group in Santa Fe, with eight churches and the venerable St. Francis Cathedral. Visitors may attend services at the Franciscan cathedral, 131 Cathedral Place, one block east of the Plaza (☎ **982-5619**). Other denominations active in Santa Fe include Anglican, Assembly of God, Baptist, Charismatic, Christian and Missionary Alliance, Christian Science, Church of Christ, Church of God, Disciples of Christ, Episcopal, Foursquare Gospel, Friends, Jehovah's Witnesses, Lutheran, Methodist, Mormon, Nazarene, Seventh-day Adventist, and United Church of Christ. There is also a Jewish synagogue. The Galisteo News & Ticket Center, 201 Galisteo St. (☎ **984-1316**), is a good clearing house of information on metaphysical pursuits.

Restrooms   Most hotels, restaurants, bars, department stores, gasoline stations, museums, and other tourist attractions have toilets available for use. In a restaurant or bar, it's usually appropriate to order a cup of coffee or soft drink to qualify you as a customer.

Shoe Repairs   Most convenient to downtown Santa Fe is the Jacobs Shoe Repair Shop, 646 Old Santa Fe Trail (☎ **982-9774**).

Taxes   A city bed tax of 3.875% is added onto all lodging bills, over and above the state gross-receipts tax of 6.875%.

Telephone, Telegraph, and Fax   The area code for New Mexico is **505**. If you're calling from Santa Fe to anywhere else in the state you must use the 505 area code. Local calls are normally 25¢. Telegrams can be sent through Western Union, 519 Airport Rd. (☎ **438-3141**). Numerous agencies, including most hotels, will send and receive faxes, among them Kinko's Copies, 333 Montezuma Ave. (☎ **982-6311**).

Television   Two local independent television stations are KKTO-TV (Channel 2) and KCHF-TV (Channel 11), the latter offering Christian programming. The three Albuquerque network affiliates—KOB-TV (Channel 4, NBC), KOAT-TV (Channel 7, ABC) and KQRE-TV (Channel 13, CBS) all have offices at the State Capitol.

Time   New Mexico is on mountain standard time, one hour ahead of the West Coast and two hours behind the East Coast. When it's 10am in Santa Fe, it's noon in New York, 11am in Chicago, and 9am in San Francisco. Daylight saving time is in effect from late April to late October.

Useful Telephone Numbers   Information on road conditions in the Santa Fe area can be obtained from the state police (☎ **827-9300**). For time and temperature, call **473-2211.** For weather forecasts, call **988-5151.**

5

Santa Fe Accommodations

T HERE MAY NOT BE A "BAD" PLACE TO STAY IN SANTA FE. FROM DOWNTOWN
hotels to Cerrillos Road motels, from ranch-style resorts to quaint
B&Bs, the standard of accommodation is universally high.

When perusing the following listings, be aware of the highly
seasonal nature of the tourist industry in Santa Fe. Accommodations
are often booked solid through the summer months, and most
establishments raise their prices accordingly. Rates are usually
increased further for Indian Market, the third weekend of August.
It's essential to make reservations well in advance at these times.

But there's little agreement on the dates marking the beginning
and end of the tourist season; whereas one hotel may not raise its
rates until July 1 and may drop them again in mid-September, another may have higher rates from May to November. Some hotels
increase rates again over the Christmas holidays or recognize a shoulder season. It pays to shop around during these "in-between" seasons of May to June and September to October.

In any season, senior, group, corporate, and other special rates are
often available. If you have any questions about your eligibility for
these rates, be sure to ask.

A combined city-state tax of 10.75% is imposed on every hotel
bill in Santa Fe. And, unless otherwise indicated, all my recommended
accommodations come with private bath.

ACCOMMODATIONS CATEGORIES   In this chapter, hotels/
motels are listed first by geographical area (downtown, Northside,
or Southside) and then by price range, based on midsummer rates:
"Very Expensive," with high-season doubles averaging $150 or more
per night; "Expensive," with doubles in high season for $110 to $150;
"Moderate," with high-season doubles for $75 to $110; "Inexpensive," with doubles for $45 to $75 in high season; and "Budget,"
offering high-season double rooms for less than $45 per night.

Following my hotel/motel and bed-and-breakfast recommenda-
tions, you'll find suggestions for campgrounds and RV parks.

RESERVATIONS SERVICES   Although Santa Fe has more than
50 hotels, motels, bed-and-breakfast establishments, and other accommodations, rooms can still be hard to come by at the peak of the
tourist season. You can get year-round assistance from **Santa Fe Central Reservations,** 320 Artist Rd., no. 10 (☎ **505/983-8200,** or
toll free **800/776-7669;** fax 505/984-8682). The service will also
book transportation and activities. **Emergency Lodging Assistance**
especially helpful around Fiesta time in September—is available free
after 4pm daily (☎ **505/986-0043**).

1 Downtown

Everything within the horseshoe-shaped Paseo de Peralta, and east a
few blocks on either side of the Santa Fe River, is considered downtown Santa Fe. None of these accommodations is beyond walking
distance from the Plaza.

Very Expensive

Eldorado Hotel, 309 W. San Francisco St., Santa Fe, NM 87501.
☎ **505/988-4455,** or toll free **800/955-4455.** Fax 505/982-0713.
219 rms, 18 suites. A/C MINIBAR TV TEL

Rates: July–Aug and major holidays, $239 single or double; $349–$750 suite. Mar–June and Sept–Oct, $209 single or double; $319–$700 suite. Nov–Feb (excluding holidays), $169 single or double; $279–$500 suite. AE, DC, DISC, MC, V. **Parking:** Free, 24-hour valet.

A five-story pueblo-style structure built around a lovely courtyard two blocks west of the Plaza, the Eldorado boasts a southwestern interior with an art collection appraised at more than $500,000, including antique furniture, Native American pottery, carved animals, and other works mainly by Santa Fe artists.

The guest rooms continue the regional theme. Many of them have traditional kiva fireplaces, handmade furniture, and decks or terraces. The upper rooms in particular afford outstanding views of the surrounding mountains. Each room—tastefully appointed in southwestern colors—has one king-size bed or two double beds, easy chairs, a double closet, a remote-control TV in an armoire, and a minirefrigerator with an honor bar. Rooms on the fifth floor have the added luxury of butler service. Just down the street from the main hotel is Zona Rosa, which houses two-, three-, and four-bedroom suites.

Dining/Entertainment: The innovative and elegant Old House restaurant was built on the preserved foundation of an early 1800s Santa Fe house. Its viga-latilla ceiling, polished wood floor, and pottery and kachinas in niches give it a distinct regional touch, present also in its preparation of creative continental cuisine. Open for dinner Tuesday through Sunday from 6pm, its main courses are in the $14 to $21 range. The Old House Tavern is open Tuesday through Sunday from 6 to 11pm. More casual meals are served in the spacious Eldorado Court, open daily for breakfast from 7am to 11pm and lunch from 11:30am to 2pm. Dinner is served Monday through Saturday from 5:30pm to 9:30pm, and Sunday brunch is offered from 11:30am to 2pm. Dinner prices range from $6 to $16 for anything from cheese enchiladas to seared filet of salmon. The lobby lounge has low-key entertainment.

Services: Room service, concierge, butlers, laundry, twice-daily maid service, safe-deposit boxes.

Facilities: Rooms for nonsmokers and the disabled; pets are welcome; heated rooftop swimming pool and Jacuzzi, exercise room, his-and-hers saunas, professional masseuse, beauty salon, free membership in Santa Fe Spa, shopping arcade (with Southwest artifacts, jewelry, gifts, apparel, news, and a real estate showcase).

Hilton of Santa Fe, 100 Sandoval St. (P.O. Box 25104), Santa Fe, NM 87504-2387. ☎ **505/988-2811,** or toll free **800/336-3676** or **800/HILTONS.** Fax 505/986-6439. 158 rms, 6 suites. A/C MINI-BAR TV TEL

Rates (based on single or double occupancy): Jan 1–May 1, $100–$200; May 2–June 29, $130–$230; June 30–Sept 3, $150–$250; Sept 4–Oct 28, $130–$230; Oct 29–Dec 21, $100–$200; Dec 22–Dec 31, $150–$250. Suites $375–$500 year round. Additional person $20 extra. AE, CB, DC, DISC, MC, V. **Parking:** Free.

With its city-landmark belltower, the Hilton covers a full city block two blocks west of the Plaza, between Sandoval, San Francisco, Guadalupe, and Alameda Streets. It's built around a central pool and patio area. There's cozy lobby seating around a traditional fireplace, flanked on one side by a cactus, on the other by a folk-art sculpture of a howling coyote.

The units are clean and spacious, furnished with king-size, queen-size, or double beds. Each room has a deck or balcony, a couch or two easy chairs, a four-drawer credenza, and in-room movies. There are two sinks, one inside the bathroom, one outside at a dressing table; and every room has a coffee pot.

In June of 1994 the Hilton opened Casa Ortiz de Santa Fe, a small building located adjacent to the main hotel, that houses three exclusive guesthouses. The building was once the coach house (c. 1625) of Nicholas Ortiz III. Today the thick adobe walls hold two one-bedroom units and one two-bedroom suite. Each has a living room with a kiva fireplace, a fully stocked kitchenette, and a bathroom with a whirlpool tub. One of the one-bedroom units also has a fireplace in the bedroom.

Dining/Entertainment: Two restaurants occupy the premises of the early 18th-century Casa Ortiz, which has been incorporated into the hotel. In the Piñon Grill, with its intimate candlelight service from 5 to 11pm daily, you can't miss the ancient beams and pillars of the main house construction. Lunch is served from 11am to 5pm. All main courses are prepared on the wood-fired grill, including fresh wild game, chile-marinated lamb, and Rocky Mountain trout; dinner prices range from $14.95 to $19.95. The Chamisa Courtyard serves breakfast daily from 6:30 to 11am; featuring casual garden-style tables amid lush greenery under a large skylight, it's built on the home's enclosed patio. El Cañon wine and coffee bar specializes in fine wines by the glass and gourmet coffees. Open from 7am to midnight, El Cañon also serves house-baked breads and pastries as well as tapas (from 5pm).

Services: Room service, concierge, courtesy car, valet laundry.

Facilities: Rooms for nonsmokers and the disabled; outdoor swimming pool, Jacuzzi, gift shop, car-rental agency.

Homewood Suites, 400 Griffin St., Santa Fe, NM 87501.

☎ **505/988-3300,** or toll free **800/225-5466.** Fax 505/988-4700. 105 suites. A/C TV TEL

Rates (including continental breakfast): Jan–June 25 and Oct 31–Dec 15, $145–$165 one-bedroom suite; $255 two-bedroom suite. June 26–Oct 30 and Dec 16–31, $155–$175 one-bedroom suite; $310 two-bedroom suite. AE, DC, DISC, MC, V. **Parking:** Free.

Homewood Suites is Santa Fe's only downtown all-suite hotel. The apartment-style units are perfect for families or single travelers who prefer having the option of cooking for themselves while on vacation. Each suite has a living room, bedroom, kitchen, and bathroom with separate dressing area. Master Suites are just larger versions of Homewood Suites. There are also a few suites with two bedrooms and two baths. The kitchens are fully equipped and have microwaves, two-burner stoves, and full-size refrigerators with ice makers. All suites also have ironing boards and irons. Both living rooms and bedrooms have TVs, and the living room couches convert into full-size beds (perfect for the kids). Each suite has a recliner chair with an ottoman. Many of the suites have fireplaces and all have VCRs. Video rentals are available in the "Suite Shop" on the lobby level. Business travelers enjoy the convenience of the business center where use of computer, copier, and typewriter are free of charge. A complimentary continental breakfast is served in the Lodge daily, and there are free social functions Monday through Thursday evenings.

Services: Concierge, complimentary shopping service.

Facilities: Outdoor pool, outdoor hot tubs, exercise center (with bikes, weights, a step machine, and a rower), activity court, guest laundry, business center, "Suite Shop" (for sundries, food, and video rentals).

⭐ **Inn of the Anasazi,** 113 Washington Ave., Santa Fe, NM 87501. ☎ **505/988-3030,** or toll free **800/688-8100.** Fax 505/988-3277. 51 rms, 8 suites. A/C MINIBAR TV TEL

Rates: Nov–Apr, $180–$245 single or double; $305–$335 suite. May–Oct, $230–$260 single or double; $390–$415 suite. Holiday and festival rates may be higher. AE, CB, DC, DISC, MC, V. **Parking:** $10 per night.

Fancy
Right on
the Plaza

The Inn of the Anasazi, located near the Palace of the Governors, can definitely be described as a luxury hostelry. It's named in celebration of the "enduring and creative spirit" of the Native American people known as the Anasazi. It opened in 1991, a project of Robert Zimmer, a man well known for his exciting and innovative concepts in hotels. According to Zimmer, the Inn of the Anasazi is "committed to ecological and environmental awareness, the interconnectedness and diversity of all people, land, heritage, and sentient beings, and makes every effort to operate in a sound and conscious manner." Basically, the inn seeks to teach by example. Every piece of paper used in the inn is recycled; the fireplaces are gas- rather than wood-burning; the linens, soaps, and shampoos are all natural; and the food in the restaurant is chemical free and organic.

None of this is to say that the hotel skimps on amenities—there are TVs, VCRs, and stereos in all the rooms, as well as minibars, private safes, coffee makers, bathroom telephones, and walk-in closets. The place abounds in original artwork, and there's a living room with a fireplace, as well as a library where you can sit and relax before dinner.

Dining/Entertainment: The Inn of the Anasazi restaurant serves breakfast, lunch, and dinner every day, and it features Native

Downtown Santa Fe Accommodations

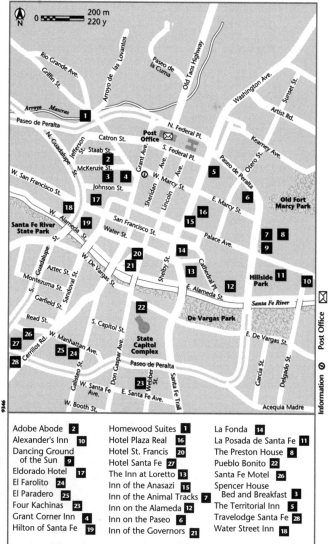

Adobe Abode **2**	Homewood Suites **1**	La Fonda **14**
Alexander's Inn **10**	Hotel Plaza Real **16**	La Posada de Santa Fe **11**
Dancing Ground of the Sun **9**	Hotel St. Francis **20**	The Preston House **8**
Eldorado Hotel **17**	Hotel Santa Fe **27**	Pueblo Bonito **22**
El Farolito **24**	The Inn at Loretto **13**	Santa Fe Motel **26**
El Paradero **25**	Inn of the Anasazi **15**	Spencer House Bed and Breakfast **3**
Four Kachinas **23**	Inn of the Animal Tracks **7**	The Territorial Inn **5**
Grant Corner Inn **4**	Inn on the Alameda **12**	Travelodge Santa Fe **28**
Hilton of Santa Fe **19**	Inn on the Paseo **6**	Water Street Inn **18**
	Inn of the Governors **21**	

American and northern New Mexican food. (See Chapter 6, "Santa Fe Dining," for a full description.)

Services: Room service, concierge, twice-daily maid service, complimentary newspaper, tours of galleries and museums, massage and aromatherapy treatments, stationary bicycles available for use in guest rooms; access to spas and fitness centers can easily be arranged.

★ **Inn on the Alameda,** 303 E. Alameda St., Santa Fe, NM 87501.
☎ **505/984-2121,** or toll free **800/289-2122.** Fax 505/986-8325.
66 rms, 8 suites. A/C TV TEL

Rates (including breakfast): Nov–Mar, $130–$170 single; $140–$180 double; $190–$235 suite. Apr–Oct, $155–$200 single; $170–$215 double; $245–$350 suite. Holiday and special-event rates may be higher. AE, CB, DC, MC, V. **Parking:** Free.

This might be just the ticket for visitors who prefer more intimacy than large hotels can offer. Just two blocks from the Plaza and one block from gallery-intense Canyon Road, opposite the Santa Fe River at the corner of Paseo de Peralta, the Inn on the Alameda preserves the spirit of old Santa Fe behind an exterior of adobe and adz-hewn wood pillars. You'll catch the flavor as soon as you enter the lobby, with its traditional viga-latilla ceiling construction. Just past the unobtrusive reception desk is a sitting room/library with handcrafted furnishings, soft pillows, and a rocking chair all placed around an inviting kiva fireplace.

The mood continues to the guest rooms, done in warm pastel shades of contemporary southwestern decor. Each room features a king-size bed or two queen-size beds, a desk with three-drawer credenza, an additional table and chairs, and cable TV with built-in AM/FM radio. Fresh-cut flower bouquets brighten each room, charming prints hang on the walls, and wood-slat blinds add warmth and privacy. Heating and air conditioning are individually controlled. Some rooms have outdoor patios or private balconies, refrigerators, and kiva fireplaces.

A new wing has recently been added to the inn. It includes 19 more rooms, a guest laundry, a fitness facility, and a massage room. Eight individually designed suites have such luxuries as enclosed courtyards and portals, and traditional, kiva fireplaces and TVs in both the living room and the bedroom, and minirefrigerators. Their furnishings are much the same as those of the rest of the hotel, and they're set away from the main building with their own parking areas. Be sure to ask about the inn's unique packages.

Dining/Entertainment: An elaborate complimentary "Breakfast of Enchantment" is served each morning in the outdoor courtyard, Agoyo Room, or in the privacy of your own room. A full-service bar is open nightly.

Services: Room service (7 to 11am), concierge, valet laundry, complimentary morning newspaper; child care can be arranged; pets are accepted and the hotel offers a pet program which features pet amenities and pet-walking map.

Facilities: Two open-air Jacuzzi spas, fitness facility, massage room, guest laundry, rooms for nonsmokers and the disabled.

Expensive

Hotel St. Francis, 210 Don Gaspar Ave., Santa Fe, NM 87501.
☎ **505/983-5700,** or toll free **800/529-5700.** Fax 505/989-7690.
83 rms, 2 suites. A/C TV TEL

Rates: May 4–Oct plus Thanksgiving, Christmas, and New Year's weeks. $110–$195 single or double; $225–$350 suite. Nov–Feb, $80–$145 single or double; $175–$275 suite. Mar–Apr, $85–$150 single or double; $190–$225 suite. Children under 12 stay free in parents' room. AE, DC, DISC, MC, V. **Parking:** Free.

Listed in the National Register of Historic Places, this was once the De Vargas Hotel, a 1924-vintage politicians' gathering place where more business may have been conducted in the 1930s and '40s than in the State Capitol. The DeVargas closed its doors in 1984, and following a $6-million makeover, reopened as the Hotel St. Francis in 1986. With its original tile floor, high-backed Edwardian chairs and sofas around glass tables, and big fireplace (with Cupid designs), it's also an ideal setting for afternoon teas.

All rooms have high ceilings and casement windows. Thirty of them are tiny "baby rooms" with barely enough room for a double bed, two chairs, and a table. But like all other rooms, these also have a refrigerator, a closet safe, and an individual thermostat. Most units have maroon carpeting, big brass or iron beds with paisley bedspreads and drapes, brass lamps, cushioned rattan chairs, antique cherrywood desks or tables, remote-control cable TVs in Santa Fe–style armoires, and full baths of Mexican marble.

Dining/Entertainment: On Water Street, the hotel's restaurant, is open daily for breakfast from 7 to 10:30am, lunch from 11:30am to 2pm, and dinner from 5:30 to 9:30pm. The DeVargas Bar, which incorporates the earlier hotel's copper-topped counter, offers sidewalk seating for people-watchers. Then there's the silver tea service, daily from 3 to 5:30pm in the lobby. Finger sandwiches, scones, and pastries are served with six varieties of tea from India, Sri Lanka, China, and France. Walk-ins are welcome.

Services: Room service, valet laundry.

Facilities: Rooms for nonsmokers and one for the disabled, guest membership at nearby health club.

Hotel Santa Fe, 1501 Paseo de Peralta (at Cerrillos Rd.), Santa Fe, NM 87501. ☎ **505/982-1200,** or toll free **800/825-9876.** Fax 505/984-2211. 131 rms, 91 suites. A/C MINIBAR TV TEL

Rates: May–Oct 15 plus Thanksgiving and Christmas, $139 single; $159 double; $139–$165 junior suite; $185–$210 deluxe suite. Oct 16–Apr, $95 single; $115 double; $125–$140 junior suite; $165–$185 deluxe suite. Additional person $20 extra; children 17 and under stay free in parents' room. AE, CB, DC, DISC, MC, V. **Parking:** Free.

This is the first-ever partnership in New Mexico between a Native American tribe—in this case, Picuris Pueblo—and private business located off reservation trust land. The three-story pueblo-style building, cruciform in shape and featuring Picuris tribal motifs throughout, is about half a mile south of the Plaza.

Most of the rooms have king-size beds, and all have Taos-style furnishings, remote-control TVs, and fully stocked minibars. Each suite has a separate living room and bedroom, with a TV and phone in each room, a safe-deposit box, and a microwave oven.

Dining/Entertainment: The hotel offers a continental breakfast menu and a deli on the lobby level. The Lobby Lounge serves complimentary hors d'oeuvres daily from 5 to 7pm.

Services: Valet laundry, 24-hour security, safe-deposit boxes, courtesy shuttle to the Plaza and Canyon Road.

Facilities: Rooms for nonsmokers and the disabled; massage room, guest laundry, Picuris Pueblo gift shop, pool; access to the Club International fitness center can be arranged.

Inn at Loretto, 211 Old Santa Fe Trail (P.O. Box 1417), Santa Fe, NM 87501. ☎ **505/988-5531,** or toll free **800/727-5531.** Fax 505/984-7988. 137 rms, 3 suites. A/C TV TEL

Rates: $95–$195 single; $125–$210 double; $300–$550 suite. Additional person $15 extra; children 12 and under, stay free in parents' room. AE, CB, DC, DISC, MC, V. **Parking:** Free.

This handsome, Pueblo Revival–style building stands on the site of the original Loretto Academy, a Catholic girls' school built in the late 19th century under the direction of Bishop Lamy. Although the building (which opened as a hotel in 1975) has been fully renovated and expanded, bits and pieces of the original academy remain, including the famous chapel of Our Lady of Light with its mysterious spiral staircase (see "More Attractions" in Chapter 7). Another unique element of the Inn at Loretto is the use of hand-painted Mimbres designs. There are about 1,000 of these colorful motifs, all different, throughout the building. Artist Ross Martinez re-created work found on pottery of the 11th- and 12th-century Mimbres people of southwestern New Mexico.

The hotel, a little over one block from the southeastern corner of the Plaza, is horseshoe-shaped, with room balconies or patios surrounding a landscaped outdoor courtyard with a pool. Half the guest rooms have a king-size bed; the remainder, a pair of double beds. Southwestern decor dominates with etched-tin shades on intricate pottery-style lamps, Mexican tiles inset in writing and bedside tables, and colorful patterned comforters. All rooms have either a sofa or an easy chair or an activity table with two chairs.

Dining/Entertainment: Bimi's, styled after the rambling haciendas of northern New Mexico, is open daily from 6:30am to 9pm, with extended summer hours. Breakfasts run $5.75 to $8.50; lunches cost $6.25 to $9. Dinners, including pastas and regional and continental specialties, range from $7.50 to $17. The warm, mezzanine-ringed hotel lounge has live entertainment nightly, and complimentary chips and salsa are available daily at 4pm.

Services: Room service, concierge, valet laundry.

Facilities: Rooms for nonsmokers and the disabled; outdoor swimming pool, shopping arcade (with a fine-art gallery, four boutiques, a gold designer, a bookstore, three gift shops, a sundries shop, and a hair salon); tennis and golf privileges nearby can be arranged.

⭐ **Inn of the Governors,** Alameda St. and Don Gaspar Ave., Santa Fe, NM 87501. ☎ **505/982-4333,** or toll free **800/234-4534.** Fax 505/989-9149. 100 rms. A/C TV TEL

Rates: July–Oct, $125–$150 standard double, $135–$175 superior double, $155–$185 deluxe double. Nov–June, $80–$120 standard double, $110–$140 superior double, $175–$215 deluxe double. Additional person $10 extra; children under 18 stay free in parents' room. AE, DC, MC, V. **Parking:** Free.

Considered one of the best examples of Territorial architecture in downtown Santa Fe, the inn has been an institution in the city since 1965. Located two blocks from the Plaza, it consists of three sections—56 standard rooms, 24 rooms in the Superior Wing, and 20 deluxe accommodations in the Governors Wing.

The guest rooms have white stuccoed walls and color schemes of coral and pale jade with bedspreads of tribal-feather motif, refrigerators, and remote-control TVs in Santa Fe–style armoires. The creatively decorated units have handcrafted Mexican furniture and headboards, folk art, wrought-iron lamps, hand-painted tin mirrors, and washed turquoise writing desks. The spacious Governors rooms include wood balconies, wall-size 19th-century pueblo photographs, and L-shaped seating to divide the sleeping and living areas. Many of the superior and deluxe rooms have fireplaces (wood provided daily) and minibars. Stereos are available in some rooms.

Dining/Entertainment: The Mañana Bar and Restaurant serves three meals daily (6:30am to 2:30pm and 5:30 to 10pm) in a casual atmosphere. Regional watercolors brighten the walls, and on warm days meals are served in an outdoor courtyard. Cuisine is southwestern, Italian, and contemporary American, with most dinner prices in the $6.50 to $14.95 range. Wood-fired pizzas are a treat, and the Milagro bread pudding in a warm whiskey sauce is a killer. The adjacent bar is rustic, with cowhide chairs at a copper-topped bar beneath a viga ceiling; a pianist performs six nights a week.

Services: Room service, concierge, valet laundry.

Facilities: Rooms for nonsmokers and the disabled; outdoor swimming pool with patio and outdoor kiva fireplace.

⭐ **La Fonda,** 100 E. San Francisco St. (P.O. Box 1209), Santa Fe, NM 87501. ☎ **505/982-5511,** or toll free **800/523-5002.** Fax 505/988-2952. 153 rms, 21 suites. A/C TV TEL

Rates: $150–$185 standard single or double; $165–$200 deluxe double; $225–$500 suite. Additional person $15 extra; children under 12 stay free in parents' room. AE, CB, DC, MC, V. **Parking:** $2 per day in three-story garage.

"The Inn at the End of the Trail" occupies a full block between the southeast corner of the Plaza, where a marker denotes the terminus of the Santa Fe Trail, and Bishop Lamy's St. Francis Cathedral. When the first Americans to pioneer the trail arrived in Santa Fe in 1821, they found an inn—a *fonda*—on this site. As trappers, traders, and merchants began flocking to Santa Fe, a saloon and casino were added. Among the inn's 19th-century patrons were Pres. Rutherford B. Hayes, Gen. Ulysses S. Grant, and Gen. William Tecumseh Sherman. The original inn was dying of old age in 1920 when it was razed and replaced by the current La Fonda. Its architecture is Pueblo

Revival, imitation adobe with wooden balconies and beam ends protruding over the tops of windows.

Every room is a bit different from the next. Each piece of hand-carved Spanish-style furniture is individually painted in a Hispanic folk motif, color-coordinated to other pieces in the room. Beds are king-size, queen-size, or double. Suites and deluxe rooms have minirefrigerators, tiled baths, and sophisticated artwork, including etched tin and stonework. Full suites have fireplaces, private balconies, antique furniture, Oriental carpets, and a large amount of closet and shelf space.

Dining/Entertainment: La Plazuela Restaurant, a tiled skylit garden patio, is open for three meals daily from 7am to 10pm. Furniture is solid-wood Spanish Colonial, and the waiters and waitresses are garbed accordingly. Cuisine is regional with contemporary flair, ranging at dinner from blue-corn enchiladas to shrimp scampi cilantro. The adjacent La Fiesta Lounge, open Monday through Saturday from 11am to 1am and on Sunday from noon to midnight, has nightly entertainment. Weather permitting, La Terraza, an outdoor patio on the third floor, offers lunches. The Bell Tower Bar, at the southwest corner of the hotel, is the highest point in downtown Santa Fe, a great place for a cocktail and a view of the city.

Services: Room service, concierge, tour desk, laundry.

Facilities: Rooms for nonsmokers and the disabled; outdoor swimming pool, two indoor Jacuzzis, cold plunge, massage room, ballroom, shopping arcade (with galleries, leather shop, boutique, French pastry shop, and newsstand with sundries).

★ **La Posada de Santa Fe**, 330 E. Palace Ave., Santa Fe, NM
87501. ☎ **505/986-0000**, or toll free **800/727-5276.**
$ Fax 505/982-6850. 119 rms, 40 suites. A/C TV TEL

Rates: May–Oct plus the Thanksgiving and Christmas seasons, $115–$295 single or double; $195–$347 suite. Nov–Apr (except holidays), $88–$215 single or double; $125–$285 suite. Various packages are available. AE, CB, DC, MC, V. **Parking:** Free.

This lovely hotel has 19 adobe-style buildings spread across six acres of thoughtfully landscaped grounds. It's constructed around the Staab House, a historic mansion built two blocks east of the Plaza in 1882 by Abraham Staab, a German immigrant, for his bride, Julia. Santa Fe's first brick building, it was equally well known for its richly carved walnut interior woodwork and the decorative scrolls and fluting on its doors and windows. Today, several rooms of the house have been fully restored in classical fashion as a Victorian lounge, with period furnishings and museum-quality 19th-century art. Julia Staab, who died in 1896, continues to haunt half a dozen upstairs sleeping rooms. Mischievous but good-natured, she is Santa Fe's best-known and most frequently witnessed ghost.

Each of the hotel's charming rooms is a little different from the next, with variations in size, shape, layout, and detail. Many objects d'art are one of a kind—a factor that inspires repeat visitors to request "their" room year after year. But the *casitas*, "little houses," share many common traits: outside entrances with carved wood portals, handcrafted furniture and wrought-iron garden chairs, wood floors with throw rugs, and painted tiles built into walls. Eighty-six rooms have fireplaces or wood stoves; piñon firewood is provided daily. Some larger units have wet bars or refrigerators, walk-in closets, and dressing tables. But finding your way around the hotel grounds may be confusing: Get a map from the desk. The room numbers are in no particular order.

Dining/Entertainment: The Staab House Restaurant, open for three meals daily from 7am to 2pm and 6 to 10pm, has been fully restored with ceiling vigas and pueblo weavings and tinwork on the walls. From spring to early fall, food is also served outside on a big patio. New Mexican cuisine is a house specialty, with breakfasts like eggs Robles (with chorizo sausage and cactus chile); lunch, including fresh fish in corn husks and a jicama-chicken salad; and dinner, featuring scallops Encinada, pork Mezcal, and prime rib. The lounge has frequent happy-hour entertainment (usually local musicians).

Services: Room service, concierge, valet laundry.

Facilities: Rooms for nonsmokers and the disabled; outdoor swimming pool, guest use of local health club, boutique, beauty salon.

Moderate

Hotel Plaza Real, 125 Washington Ave., Santa Fe, NM 87501.
☎ **505/988-4900,** or toll free **800/279-REAL.** 56 rms, 44 suites. A/C TV TEL

Rates (including breakfast): Nov–Apr, $130–$209 double. May–June, $139–$219 double. July–Oct, $159–$249 double. Year-round, $295–$475 suite. Additional person $15 extra; children under 12 stay free in parents' room. AE, DC, MC, V. **Parking:** $5 per day.

This three-story hotel opened in 1990 and is located half a block north of the Plaza. It's built in traditional Territorial style, complete with red-brick coping along the roof lines and windows trimmed in white. Native American designs and wood beams complement the Santa Fe–style furnishings in the rooms, most of which have fireplaces and outdoor patios. Rooms overlook a peaceful inner courtyard, away from the bustle of the Plaza. Complimentary breakfast with the daily paper is served in the Santa Clara Room and Patio or delivered to guest rooms. La Piazza is the hotel's sidewalk café where guests enjoy pastries, cappuccino, sandwiches, and cocktails. An intimate lounge also serves cocktails in the evening. Services include a concierge, a complimentary walking tour, a 24-hour desk, valet laundry, and rooms for the disabled.

Inexpensive

Santa Fe Motel, 510 Cerrillos Rd., Santa Fe, NM 87501.
☎ **505/982-1039,** or toll free **800/999-1039.** Fax 505/986-1275. 22 rms, 1 house. A/C TV TEL

Rates: May–Oct, $75–$85 single; $80–$90 double; $145 Thomas House, Nov–Apr, $65–$75 single; $70–$80 double; $150 Thomas House. AE, MC, V. **Parking:** Free.

One of the bonuses of staying at this adobe-style motel south of the Santa Fe River is that most rooms have kitchenettes, complete with two-burner stoves and minirefrigerators, as well as pans, dishes, and utensils. Southwestern motifs predominate in the rooms, spread across four turn-of-the-century buildings. Fresh-brewed coffee is served each morning in the office, where a bulletin board posts listings of Santa Fe activities. The nearby Thomas House, on West Manhattan Drive, is a fully equipped rental home with living and dining rooms and off-street parking. If you're planning to stay here, I'd recommend that you call ahead to see if the hotel has completed renovations that are scheduled as this book goes to press. Otherwise, expect, very outdated decor.

Santa Fe Plaza Travelodge, 646 Cerrillos Rd., Santa Fe, NM 87501. ☎ **505/982-3551,** or toll free **800/255-3050.** Fax 505/983-8624. 49 rms. A/C TV TEL

Rates: Nov–Apr, $60–$70 single or double. May–Oct, $72–$84 single or double. AE, CB, DC, DISC, MC, V. **Parking:** Free.

Practically next door to the Santa Fe Motel (above) is this inn with a heated swimming pool. Each room has a king-size bed or two queen-size beds with floral-patterned bedspreads and drapes, a two-drawer credenza, table and chairs, cable TV, and telephone (local calls 50¢). Some rooms also have small desks.

Frommer's Smart Traveler: Hotels

1. Always remember that at any time of year a hotel room is a perishable commodity: If it's not rented, the revenue is lost forever. Therefore, it is a fact that rates are linked to the hotel's occupancy level. If it's 90% occupied the price goes up; if it's 50% occupied the price goes down. Even at check-in, ask if the stated rate is the best they can give you, especially in the off-seasons.

2. Many hotels in the ski-resort areas offer package deals including ski rentals and lift tickets; some may even include instruction.

3. Ask if the 6.25% state tax and the city bed taxes—3.875% in Santa Fe, 3% in Taos, and 4.25% in Albuquerque—are included in the room rate quoted.

4. Find out if the hotel provides free transportation to and from the airport.

5. Ask about special rates that might be offered to groups you may be a member of (AAA or AARP, for instance) and when traveling with children, if they can stay in your room free.

[handwritten annotations: "we stayed here but out of town" / "but food was delicious"]

2 Northside

This area, within easy reach of the Plaza, includes accommodations that lie beyond the loop of the Paseo de Peralta on the north.

Very Expensive

★ **The Bishop's Lodge,** Bishop's Lodge Rd. (P.O. Box 2367), Santa Fe, NM 87504. ☎ **505/983-6377.** Fax 505/989-8739. 68 rms and 20 suites. A/C TV TEL

Rates: European Plan (meals not included), Mar 25–May 26 and Sept 6–Dec, $140 standard double, $215 deluxe double, $245 super-deluxe double; $170 standard suite, $285 deluxe suite. May 27–June, $160 standard double, $245 deluxe double, $275 super-deluxe double; $210 standard suite, $315 deluxe suite. July–Sept 5, $195 standard double, $295 deluxe double, $325 super-deluxe double; $245 standard suite, $355 deluxe suite. Modified American Plan (available May 27–Labor Day), $236–$271 standard double, $321–$371 deluxe double, $351–$401 super-deluxe double; $286–$321 standard suite, $391–$431 deluxe suite. Jan–Mar 24, $150 standard double, $225 deluxe double, $265 super deluxe double, $180 standard suite, $295 deluxe suite. No credit cards. **Parking:** Free.

More than a century ago, when Bishop Jean-Baptiste Lamy was the spiritual leader of northern New Mexico's Roman Catholic population, he often escaped clerical politics by hiking 3½ miles north over a ridge into the Little Tesuque Valley. There he built a retreat he named Villa Pintoresca (Picturesque Villa) for its lovely vistas, and a humble chapel (now on the National Register of Historic Places) with high-vaulted ceilings and a hand-built altar. Today Lamy's 1,000-acre getaway has become the Bishop's Lodge. Purchased in 1918 from the Pulitzer family (of publishing fame) by Denver mining executive James R. Thorpe, it has remained in that one family's hands for more than seven decades.

The guest rooms, spread through 10 buildings, all feature handcrafted cottonwood furniture and regional artwork. Guests receive a complimentary fruit basket upon arrival. Standard rooms

---

Frommer's Cool for Kids: Hotels

The Bishop's Lodge (see p. 61) A children's pony ring, riding lessons, tennis courts with instruction, a pool with lifeguard, stocked trout pond just for kids, a summer daytime program, horseback trail trips, and more make this a veritable day camp for all ages.

Rancho Encantado (see p. 62) Horseback riding on trails or in a pony ring, a pool, tennis courts, and a number of indoor and outdoor games will keep kids happily busy here.

El Rey Inn (see p. 67) Kids will enjoy the play area, table games, and pool; parents will appreciate the kitchenettes and laundry facilities.

have balconies and either king-size beds or two twin beds. Deluxe rooms have traditional kiva fireplaces, private decks or patios, and walk-in closets; some older units have flagstone floors and viga ceilings. Super-deluxe rooms have a combination bedroom/sitting room. Deluxe suites are extremely spacious, with living rooms, separate bedrooms, private patios and decks, and artwork of near-museum quality. All "deluxe" units have fireplaces, refrigerators, and in-room safes.

Dining/Entertainment: Three large adjoining rooms with wrought-iron chandeliers and wall-size Native American–theme oil paintings comprise the Bishop's Lodge dining room. Santa Feans flock here for its breakfast, $12 (7:30 to 10am); lunch, $7 to $12; Sunday brunch, $22 (noon to 2pm); and dinner (main courses $12 to $25), creative regional cuisine with continental flair, served from 6:30 to 9pm daily. Attire is casual at breakfast and lunch but more formal at dinner, when men are asked to wear a sport coat and women a dress or pants suit. There's a full vintage wine list, and El Charro Bar serves before- and after-dinner drinks.

Services: Room service, seasonal cookouts, valet laundry.

Facilities: Daily guided horseback rides, introductory riding lessons, children's pony ring; four surfaced tennis courts, pro shop and instruction; supervised skeet and trap shooting; outdoor pool with lifeguard, saunas, and whirlpool; aerobics classes; stocked trout pond for children; shuffleboard, croquet, Ping-Pong; summer daytime program with counselors for children.

Rancho Encantado, Rte. 4, Box 57C, Santa Fe, NM 87501. ☎ **505/982-3537.** Fax 505/983-8269. 88 rms, 41 suites. A/C TV TEL

Rates: Nov–Apr 1 (excluding Thanksgiving and Christmas), $115–$125 suites; $175 one-bedroom villa; $215 two-bedroom villa. Apr 2–Oct, $190–$210 suite; $315 one-bedroom villa; $375 two-bedroom villa. AE, DC, MC, V. **Parking:** Free.

Located eight miles north of Santa Fe in the foothills of the Sangre de Cristo Mountains, Rancho Encantado, with its sweeping panoramic views, claims to be "where the magic of New Mexico comes to life." Indeed, it does have a rather magical history, which began when the ranch was the subject of the 1956 bestselling novel *Guestward Ho*. The book was later adapted for a television series of the same name which was filmed on location at the ranch. Not long after the series end, the property was sold, deteriorated, and eventually abandoned. In the mid-1960s, Betty Egan, formerly a World War II captain in the Women's Army Corps, purchased the property despite her lack of experience in the hospitality business. A recently widowed housewife, Mrs. Egan was determined to begin a new and prosperous life with her family, and so in 1968 the 168-acre ranch became Rancho Encantado. Today the property is still owned by the Egan family.

Accommodations & Dining on Cerrillos Road

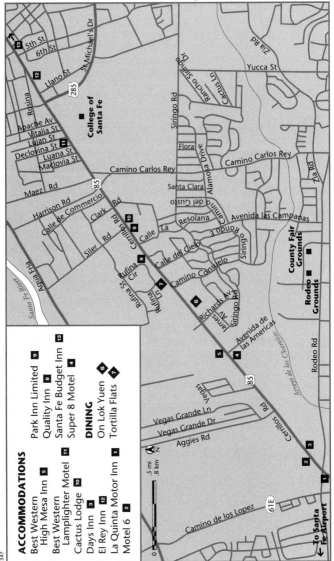

The handsome main lodge is done in traditional southwestern decor with hand-painted tiles, ceiling vigas, brick floors, antique furnishings, pueblo rugs, and Hispanic art objects hanging on stuccoed walls. The large fireplace in the living room/lounge is a focal point, especially on cold winter afternoons. In the main lodge and the immediate area there are seven standard rooms, five cottages with fireplaces, and 10 suites with living rooms, fireplaces, and refrigerators.

All rooms have coffee makers and are supplied with coffee for those who can't make it out the front door without their first cup. Across the street from the main building are two-bedroom/two-bath "villas." These split-level adobe units have fireplaces in the living room and master bedroom and each has a fully equipped kitchen. Whatever you choose, you're sure to find the accommodations here more than adequate—Princess Anne, Robert Redford, Jimmy Stewart, Whoopi Goldberg, and John Wayne certainly did.

Dining/Entertainment: Rancho Encantado's Cactus Rose Restaurant, with its exceptional western decor, ranks among the most beautiful in the Santa Fe area. The west wall of the dining room has picture windows that overlook the Jemez Mountains and offers diners a first-rate view of the spectacular New Mexico sunset. Full dinners ($16 to $23) include prime grilled steaks, seafood, free-range chicken, and pork, in addition to a fine selection of appetizers and desserts. Dinner is served from 6 to 9pm, and breakfast/lunch from 7:30am to 2pm. The Cantina, with its big-screen TV, is a popular gathering spot, and there is also a snack bar on the premises.

Facilities: Tennis courts, horseback riding, hiking trails, pool, hot tub, library.

Expensive

Picacho Plaza Hotel, 750 N. St. Francis Dr., Santa Fe, NM 87501. ☎ **505/982-5591,** or toll free **800/441-5591.** Fax 505/988-2821. 127 rms, 13 suites, 34 condominium units. A/C TV TEL

Rates: Jan 2–Feb and Nov 18–Dec 21, $78–$133 single; $88–$133 double. Mar–Apr, $88–$143 single; $98–$143 double. May–Nov 17 and Dec 22–Jan 1, $108–$178 single; $123–$178 double. AE, DC, MC, V. **Parking:** Free.

If you're in town for the Santa Fe Opera, you'll have a hard time finding an accommodation closer than the newly renovated Picacho Plaza. The amphitheater is only about three miles north up U.S. 84/285; the Picacho Plaza provides free dropoff and pickup. In fact, there's complimentary shuttle service anywhere within the city limits—including the Santa Fe Plaza, 1¼ miles southeast—from 6am to 10pm daily. Once you're in this landscaped garden-style hotel, though, you may find it hard to leave. Standard rooms, with soft southwestern decor, have either king-size beds or two double beds and subtle Southwest furnishings. Mini-suites are more spacious, with Santa Fe–style furnishings, TVs, and private balconies. In addition to all the above, each parlor suite has a Murphy bed and traditional kiva fireplace in the living room, a big dining area, a wet bar and refrigerator, and a jetted bathtub. Cielo Grande condo units have fully equipped kitchens, fireplaces, and private decks.

Dining/Entertainment: The Petroglyph Bar and Restaurant serves three meals a day from 6:30am to 10pm amid antique local crafts and reproductions of rock drawings. Dinner main courses ($9.95 to $21) are international cuisine with a bit of southwestern flair, like grilled chicken jalapeño, marinated in olive oil and fresh herbs and basted with orange jalepeño marmalade; or shrimp spaghetti with mussels, crushed red peppers, and "lots of garlic." A jazz combo plays Thursday through Saturday in the Petroglyph bar, and the nightclub features the Spanish quick-steps of New Mexico's best-known flamenco dancer and her Estampa Flamenco troupe.

Services: Room service, complimentary shuttle, valet laundry, complimentary *USA Today;* child care can be arranged.

Facilities: Rooms for nonsmokers and the disabled; outdoor swimming pool, hot tub, Santa Fe Spa (indoor pool, racquetball courts, weights, massage, steam rooms, aerobics, dance, yoga and karate classes), coin-op guest laundry, gift and sundries shop; use of adjacent Santa Fe Spa health club.

$ Santa Fe Accommodations/Fort Marcy Compound/ Las Palomas/527, 320 Artist Rd., Santa Fe, NM 87501. ☎ **505/98C-ONDO,** or toll free **800/745-9910.** Fax 505/984-8682. 140 units. A/C

Rates: Jan 6–Mar 1, Apr 1–May 15 and Nov 1–Dec 15 from $65 1-bedroom, $140 2-bedroom, $210 3-bedroom; Mar 1–Mar 31, May 15–June 30, and Sept 1–Oct 31 from $75 1-bedroom, $160 2-bedroom, $230 3-bedroom; July 1–Aug 31 and Dec 15–Jan 6 from $85 1-bedroom, $180 2-bedroom, $250 3-bedroom. Extra person $20. Children 18 and under stay free in parents' room.

These privately owned condominiums, nestled throughout Santa Fe on tastefully landscaped grounds, are an excellent choice. Each condo unit is a full apartment, most with a living and dining room, a full kitchen, one to three bedrooms, and 2 or 2$\frac{1}{2}$ baths. A typical unit has handcrafted wood-and-leather furnishings and is decorated with regional arts and crafts. In most living rooms are a sofa bed, an easy chair with ottoman, a coffee table, a fireplace, a cable TV with VCR, a stereo tape deck, and a private phone line with voice mail. The kitchen, in addition to a four-burner stove and refrigerator, has a microwave, coffeemaker, and toaster, and the cupboards are stocked with some staples, as well as dishes, pots and pans, glasses, and cutlery. Bedrooms have queen-size beds and private balconies. Daily linen exchange is available. Room rates listed above are for two in a one-bedroom unit, four in a two-bedroom unit, and six in a three-bedroom unit. Guests of Fort Marcy Compound have access to the swimming pool and hot tub at the Fort Marcy Sports Complex.

3 Southside

Santa Fe's major strip, Cerrillos Road, is U.S. 85, the main route to and from Albuquerque and the I-25 freeway. It's about 5$\frac{1}{4}$ miles from the Plaza to the Villa Linda Mall, which marks the southern extent of the city limits. Most motels are on this strip, although a couple of them are east, closer to St. Francis Drive (U.S. 84) or the Las Vegas Highway.

Expensive

$ **Residence Inn,** 1698 Galisteo St., Santa Fe, NM 87501.
☎ **505/988-7300,** or toll free **800/331-3131.** Fax 505/988-3243.
120 suites. A/C TV TEL

Rates (including continental breakfast): $120–$160 studio suite; $170–
$225 penthouse suite. Rates depend on season (high season is usually
mid-July to early Sept; low season, early Jan to early May.) Weekly rate
$5 less per night. AE, CB, DC, DISC, JCB, MC, V. **Parking:** Free.

This travelers' community, a division of Marriott, consists of 15 separate buildings on landscaped grounds. Three-quarters of the suites
are one-bedroom studios; the remainder are deluxe penthouse suites.
All are fully self-contained, with their own hot-water heaters.

Furnishings for each studio include a sofa sleeper or love seat and
chair beside the fireplace, two spacious closets, and a remote-control
TV. Each kitchen has a full refrigerator and range, a microwave oven,
a coffee maker, even a popcorn popper. A vanity with its own sink is
outside the bathroom. In addition, each penthouse suite has an open
sleeping loft, a queen-size Murphy bed in the living room, a full dining room table, and two baths.

Dining/Entertainment: Breakfasts are served weekdays from 6:30
to 10am and on Saturday and Sunday from 6:30 to 10:30am. Social
hour with complimentary hors d'oeuvres is Monday, Wednesday, and
Thursday from 5 to 6:30pm.

Services: Valet laundry, complimentary local newspaper delivered
to room in morning; child care can be arranged.

Facilities: Outdoor swimming pool, three hot tubs, jogging trail,
sports court, guest membership at nearby health club, coin-op guest
laundry, barbecue grills on patio.

Moderate

$ **Best Western High Mesa Inn,** 3347 Cerrillos Rd., Santa Fe,
NM 87501. ☎ **505/473-2800,** or toll free **800/777-3347.**
Fax 505/473-5128. 210 rms, 33 suites. A/C TV TEL

Rates (including buffet breakfast): High season, $99–$139 double;
$115–$300 suite. Low season, $69–$85 double; $89–$129 suite. Guests
over 55 get a 10% discount; children 12 and under stay free in parents'
room. AE, CB, DC, DISC, MC, V. **Parking:** Free.

Though about four miles south of the Plaza, the High Mesa wins
kudos as one of the city's better hostelries. In the user-friendly lobby
is a message board with information on current local events. The
rooms feature Southwest regional decor, each with a king-size or two
queen-size beds, plush carpeting, a wet bar and refrigerator, a desk/
dresser, and a satellite TV with in-room movies. Each suite has a
separate sitting room with a couch and TV, and each suite also comes
equipped with a microwave and coffee maker. Five luxury suites have
full kitchens and huge desks.

Dining/Entertainment: Kids' menus are available.

Services: Room service, courtesy car, valet laundry, child care on request; masseuse available by appointment; car-rental, ski-rental, and tour desk.

Facilities: Rooms for nonsmokers and the disabled; indoor pool, two 24-hour Jacuzzis, weight/exercise room, coin-op guest laundry, gift shop.

Days Inn, 3650 Cerrillos Rd., Santa Fe, NM 87501. ☎ **505/438-3822,** or toll free **800/325-2525.** Fax 505/438-3795. 96 rms, 20 suites. A/C TV TEL

Rates (including continental breakfast): Apr–Sept, $85–$95 single; $95–$105 double; $135–$155 suite. Oct–Mar, $60–$70 single; $65–$75 double; $85–$95 suite. Children 12 and under stay free in parents' room. AE, CB, DC, DISC, MC, V. **Parking:** Free.

A three-story pink palace, the Days Inn opened in 1990 as an impressive new motel on the south side of Santa Fe. It's a security-conscious hostelry, with all room entrances off interior corridors and private safes in each room. Typical rooms have soft southwestern decor, each with a queen-size bed or two double beds and a sofa or easy chair. Deluxe suites and 14 upgraded "king" rooms have wet bars and refrigerators. Some suites also boast Jacuzzi tubs and private balconies.

Services: 24-hour desk, coin-op guest laundry.

Facilities: Rooms for nonsmokers and the disabled; indoor swimming pool, hot tub.

Inexpensive

Best Western Lamplighter Motel, 2405 Cerrillos Rd., Santa Fe, NM 87505. ☎ **505/471-8000,** or toll free **800/767-5267.** 80 rms. A/C TV TEL

Rates: June to mid-Oct and Christmas season, $55–$65 single; $69–$85 double; $85–$95 kitchenette rooms. Mid-Oct to June, $39–$55 single; $45–$65 double; $65–$75 kitchenette rooms. AE, DC, DISC, MC, V. **Parking:** Free.

Trees and shrubbery surround a grassy inner courtyard, located adjacent to a large heated indoor pool and hot tub. The motel consists of a well-kept older building and two newer annexes. All rooms feature regional decor, cable color TVs, and in-room coffee makers. Andrea's Mexican Restaurant serves local cuisine and is open daily from 7am to 10pm, serving breakfast, lunch, and dinner. Patio dining is available in season.

El Rey Inn, 1862 Cerrillos Rd. (P.O. Box 130), Santa Fe, NM 87504. ☎ **505/982-1931,** or toll free **800/521-1349.** Fax 505/989-9249. 85 rms, 8 suites. A/C TV TEL

Rates (including continental breakfast): June–Sept and holidays, $56–$89 single or double; $91–$127 suite. The rest of the year, $56–$89 single or double; $87–$125 suite. AE, CB, DC, MC, V. **Parking:** Free.

"The King" is notable for its carefully tended, shaded grounds and thoughtfully maintained, recently renovated units. The white stucco buildings are adorned with bright trim around the doors and hand-painted Mexican tiles in the walls. No two rooms are alike. Most have viga ceilings and Santa Fe–style wood furnishings, a walk-in closet, and a handsome blue-and-white-tiled bathroom. Some have kitchenettes; others, refrigerators and/or fireplaces. Eight stylish poolside terrace units feature private patio areas. Facilities include a Territorial-style sitting room with a library and games tables, a swimming pool, a hot tub, a picnic area, a children's play area, and a guest laundry. The owners recently purchased the motel next door and at press time had begun renovations over there. In my opinion, the El Rey is Santa Fe's best inexpensively priced lodging choice.

La Quinta Motor Inn, 4298 Cerrillos Rd., Santa Fe, NM 87501. ☎ **505/471-1142,** or toll free **800/531-5900.** Fax 505/438-7219. 130 rms. A/C TV TEL

Rates (including continental breakfast): June to late Oct, $81 single; $89 double. Late Oct to May, $57 single; $68 double. Large discount for AAA members. AE, CB, DC, DISC, ER, JCB, MC, V. **Parking:** Free.

Right at Villa Linda Mall is this gracious motel. The rooms are appointed with light-wood decor, adobe-colored carpets, and specially commissioned prints on beige walls. Each room has a king-size bed or two extra-long double beds and standard motel furnishings. Eight rooms are designed for disabled travelers, and nearly 50% are designated for nonsmokers. The Kettle, a 24-hour coffee shop, is adjacent. La Quinta has a heated outdoor swimming pool, a 24-hour desk, valet laundry service, and complimentary coffee at all times in the lobby. Pets are accepted.

Park Inn Limited, 2900 Cerillos Rd., Santa Fe, NM 87501. ☎ **505/473-4281,** or toll free **800/279-0894.** 84 rms. A/C TV TEL **Rates:** Jan 3–Mar and Oct 10–Dec 16 (excluding holidays), $39–$45 single or double. Apr–May, $65–$75 single or double. June–Oct 9, Nov 23–27, and Dec 17–Jan 2, $75–$85 single or double. AE, CB, DC, DISC, MC, V. **Parking:** Free.

One of Santa Fe's older lodgings, dating to 1961, this former Holiday Inn, Rodeway Inn, and Del Camino Inn has been reincarnated under new owners. Painted pink and refurbished and reupholstered in a southwestern decor, it has a seasonal swimming pool, a spacious lobby, and a variety of rooms with a king-size bed or two double beds. Furnishings include desks and sofas. There's complimentary coffee and a small meeting room. Half a dozen economy rooms with queen-size beds are available year-round at budget rates.

Quality Inn, 3011 Cerrillos Rd., Santa Fe, NM 87505. ☎ **505/471-1211,** or toll free **800/228-5151.** 99 rms. A/C TV TEL **Rates:** Mar–July, $65–$75 single; $71–$81 double. Aug–Oct, $90 single or double. Nov–Feb, $50–$60 single; $56–$66 double. AE, CB, DC, DISC, ER, JCB, MC, V. **Parking:** Free.

An impressive outdoor pool is surrounded by balconies or patio decks extending from each guest room. Each unit has a southwestern decor, a queen-size bed or two double beds, reading lamps, a dresser with two deep drawers, a table and chairs, and an individual thermostat. Deluxe rooms with king-size beds have refrigerators and dressing tables. There are rooms for nonsmokers and a courtesy airport van. Pets are accepted and child care can be arranged. The Quality Inn coffee shop and dining room, open daily from 7am to 10pm, offers American and New Mexican fare, with full dinners from $8.50.

Santa Fe Budget Inn, 725 Cerrillos Rd., Santa Fe, NM 87501.
☎ **505/982-5952,** or toll free **800/288-7600.** Fax 505/984-8879. 160 rms. A/C TV TEL

Rates: July 4–Oct 25 and Dec 25–Jan 2, $75 single; $75–$86 double ($10–$20 higher for Indian Market). The rest of the year, $45 single; $50–$58 double. A Sun–Thurs "super-saver" rate may apply in the off-season. AAA and AARP members get $3 discounts. AE, CB, DC, MC, V. **Parking:** Free.

Santa Fe Opera and Fiesta posters add color to the predominantly brown rooms of this hostelry at the north end of Cerrillos Road. Its modest units each contain one queen-size or two double beds, striped bedspreads, reading lamps, and a desk with a built-in dresser. Each room has satellite TV. Rooms for nonsmokers and the disabled are available. There are an outdoor swimming pool and plenty of parking, plus a restaurant adjacent to the motel.

Budget

Cactus Lodge, 2864 Cerillos Rd., Santa Fe, NM 87501.
☎ **505/471-7699.** 25 rms, 4 suites. A/C TV TEL

Rates: Mar 15–Oct, $48–$68 double with one bed, $68–$75 double with two beds. Nov–Mar 14, $32–$48 double with one bed, $38–$58 double with two beds. Suites $75–$90. Additional person $4 extra. AE, DISC, MC, V. **Parking:** Free.

Typical of many small privately owned motels on the Cerrillos Road strip, this ma-and-pa operation includes four two-bedroom suites that can sleep up to seven people. Each room is furnished with one queen-size bed or two double beds, a desk or three-drawer dresser, a table and chairs, and cable TV. Pets are accepted with certain restrictions.

Motel 6, 3695 Cerrillos Rd., Santa Fe, NM 87501. ☎ **505/471-4140.** Fax 505/474-4370. 121 rms. A/C TV TEL

Rates: $36 single; $42 double. AE, CB, DC, DISC, MC, V. **Parking:** Free.

Vaguely Spanish-looking, with its red-tile roof and white stucco exterior, this Motel 6 offers adequate lodgings for the money. The rooms are appointed in deep tones of brown and green, with average furnishings. There are an outdoor swimming pool and an elaborate snack-vending room. Pets are permitted. A renovation is planned for 1995.

Super 8 Motel, 3358 Cerrillos Rd., Santa Fe, NM 87501.
☎ **505/471-8811,** or toll free **800/800-8000.** Fax 505/471-3239. 96 rms. A/C TV TEL

Rates: May–Sept, $39.90 single; $45.90 double. Oct–Apr, $36.90 single; $41.90 double. AE, CB, DC, DISC, MC, V. **Parking:** Free.

It's nothing flashy, but this boxlike hotel attracts a regular following as a known quantity: clean, comfortable rooms with standard furnishings, each including double beds, a working desk, a TV, and a phone with free local calls. Rooms for nonsmokers are available. The motel has a 24-hour desk and a coin-op guest laundry.

4 Bed-and-Breakfasts

If you favor a homey, intimate environment over the sometimes-impersonal ambience of a large hotel, one of Santa Fe's bed-and-breakfast inns may be for you. All those listed here are located in or close to downtown Santa Fe and offer comfortable accommodations at moderate to inexpensive prices.

★ **Adobe Abode,** 202 Chapelle, Santa Fe, NM 87501. ☎ **505/983-3133.** 5 rms. TEL

Rates (including breakfast): $90–$135 single; $95–$140 double. DISC, MC, V. **Parking:** Free.

Without a doubt, Adobe Abode is one of Santa Fe's most luxurious and eclectic bed-and-breakfasts. The living room has a fireplace and is filled with everything from Mexican folk art and pottery to Buddhas and ethnic masks. The open kitchen features bar stools with cowhide seats, as well as Balinese puppets. The creativity of proprietress Pat Harbor shines through in each of the guest rooms as well. The Bloomsbury Room, in the main house, is named for the English literary and artistic circle of the early part of this century. Laura Ashley created some Bloomsbury-inspired fabrics, which can be seen hanging from the queen-size four-poster bed in the Bloomsbury Room. Another unique feature in this room is the bathroom tiles that were handcrafted for the Adobe Abode by a local artist. The English Garden Room features Ralph Lauren floral fabrics, an antique marble-topped desk, and a French armoire. Casita de Corazon is known for its custom-designed aspen-pole twin beds, and is the perfect room for friends who are traveling together. Amenities in the casita include a coffee maker, minirefrigerator, skylights, and cable TV, and the bathroom even has a towel warmer. The artwork in Casita de Corazon is captivating. The Cactus Room features a variety of fabrics that were hand-loomed in Oaxaca, Mexico, and colorful, hand-painted furnishings. The bathroom in this room also features locally handmade tiles as well as an oversize shower. Finally, the Bronco Room is just filled with cowboy paraphernalia—hats, Pendleton blankets, pioneer chests, and my favorite, an entire shelf lined with children's cowboy boots. Two rooms have fireplaces and several have private patios. All rooms feature fine bed linens, writing desks, and terrycloth robes. Complimentary sherry, fruit, and Santa Fe cookies are served daily in the living room. Every morning a healthy breakfast of fresh-squeezed orange juice, fresh fruit, homemade muffins, scones or pastries, and a hot dish is served in the kitchen. You'll have no complaints if you stay at Adobe Abode.

Alexander's Inn, 529 East Palace Ave., Santa Fe, NM 87501.
☎ **505/986-1431.** 6 rms (3 with bath), 1 cottage. A/C

Rates (including continental breakfast): $80–$120 double. MC, V.
Parking: Free.

Located not too far from the center of downtown Santa Fe in a quiet residential area, Alexander's Inn is unlike most of the places in Santa Fe because it isn't done in southwestern decor. Instead, the eight-year-old inn is done in a Victorian/New England style with stenciling on the walls, pastel Dhurri rugs, muted colors like apricot and lilac, and white iron or four-poster queen-size beds. You might begin to think you're in a country inn in Vermont. One of the rooms has a private deck. There's also a new cottage complete with a kitchen, a living room with a kiva fireplace, and a porch. All guests can enjoy privileges at the El Gancho Tennis Club. Mountain bikes are available for guest use. A continental breakfast of homemade baked goods is served every morning, and afternoon tea and cookies are available to guests.

⭐ **Dancing Ground of the Sun,** 711 Paseo de Peralta, Santa Fe, NM 87501. ☎ **505/986-9797,** or toll free **800/645-5673.** 5 casitas. TV TEL

Rates (including breakfast): Nov–Apr, $115–$145 casita for two. May–Oct, $130–$160 casita for two. MC, V. **Parking:** Free.

Sometimes it amazes me that bed-and-breakfast owners are able to come up with new and creative theme ideas for their inns, and the day I saw Dancing Ground of the Sun was one of those times. The owners of this bed-and-breakfast put a great deal of thought and energy into decorating their units—and it shows. Each of the five casitas has been outfitted with handcrafted Santa Fe–style furnishings made by local artisans, and the decor of each room centers around a mythological Native American figure, the likenesses of which have been hand-painted on the walls of each unit. Corn Dancer represents the anticipation of an abundant harvest and is the motif for the studio casita which has a queen-size bed. The Kokopelli Casita is a one-bedroom unit with a dining room, living room, and king-size bed; Kokopelli is a flute player who is thought to bring good fortune and abundance to the Native American people. The Rainbow Dancer represents power, beauty, and strength through the colors of the rainbow. In the Buffalo Dancer Casita beautiful Native American drums are used as end tables and are meant to remind visitors of the rhythm of life. The one-bedroom Clown (or Koshari) Dancer Casita is delightfully representational of the "spirit of the classic Native American prankster." Four of the casitas have fireplaces, and all have fully equipped kitchens; the Buffalo and Rainbow casitas have washers and dryers. Each morning a breakfast of healthful, fresh-baked goods is delivered (along with the paper) to your front door in a basket for you to enjoy at your leisure. Smoking and pets are not permitted.

El Farolito, 514 Galisteo St., Santa Fe, NM 87501. ☎ **505/988-1631.**
7 casitas. TV TEL

Rates (including continental breakfast): $110–$125 casita for two. MC,
V. **Parking:** Free.

El Farolito is just a five-minute walk from downtown Santa Fe, but
it's far enough away from the center of town that guests will be able
to enjoy some peace and quiet after a long day of shopping and
sightseeing. All seven of the casitas here have kiva fireplaces, and all
are decorated in true Santa Fe style. The floors in each unit are either brick or tile and are covered with Mexican rugs, walls are adobe
colored, and bedspreads are southwestern in style. Some rooms have
semiprivate patios, some have wet bars, and one of the larger rooms
has a kitchenette. A continental breakfast of fruit, pastry, cereals, and
coffee and tea is served each morning in the breakfast room (which
also has a fireplace).

El Paradero, 220 W. Manhattan Ave., Santa Fe, NM 87501.
☎ **505/988-1177.** 14 rms (8 with bath), 2 suites. A/C TEL

Rates (including breakfast): Apr–June, $50–$90 single; $60–$100
double; $120 suite. July–Oct, $55–$95 single; $65–$110 double; $135
suite. Nov–Mar, $45–$85 single; $55–$95 double; $115 suite. No credit
cards. **Parking:** Free.

Located a few blocks south of the Santa Fe River, El Paradero (The
Stopping Place) began as a circa-1810 Spanish adobe farmhouse;
doubled in size in 1878, when Territorial-style details were added;
and incorporated Victorian touches, clear in the styling of its doors
and windows, in 1912. Nine ground-level rooms surround a central
courtyard; they have clean white decor, hardwood floors, folk art and
hand-woven textiles on the walls. Three more luxurious upstairs
rooms have tile floors and baths and private balconies. Three rooms
have fireplaces. Eight rooms have private baths; four others share.
All rooms have telephones; there are no TVs. Two suites in a separate brick Victorian building have living rooms with fireplaces,
kitchen nooks, bedrooms with queen-size beds, full baths, TVs, and
phones.

The downstairs of the main building, with its impressive viga-latilla
ceiling, includes a parlor; a living room with a piano and fireplace;
and the dining room, where a full gourmet breakfast is served daily
from 8 to 9:30am and afternoon tea at 5pm. Also, if you'd like to
take a trip up the mountain and have a picnic, they'll prepare a lunch
for you.

Four Kachinas Inn, 512 Webber St., Santa Fe, NM 87501.
☎ **505/982-2550,** or toll free **800/397-2564.** 4 rms. TV TEL

Rates (including breakfast): $88–$113 double. MC, V. **Parking:** Free.

Located on a quiet, residential street, but still well within walking
distance of downtown Santa Fe, the Four Kachinas Inn is a wonderful little bed-and-breakfast. The rooms are decorated with southwestern artwork, including beautiful antique Navajo rugs, kachinas, and
handmade furniture (in fact, some of the furniture was made from

the wood salvaged from the old barn that once stood on the property here). As you might have guessed, each of the rooms is named for a Hopi kachina: The Koyemsi Room is named for the "fun-loving, mudhead clown kachina"; the Poko Room, for the dog kachina that "represents the spirits of domestic animals"; the Hon Room, for the "powerful healing bear kachina"; and the Tawa Room, for the sun god kachina. Three of the rooms are on the ground floor. The upstairs room has a beautiful view of the Sangre de Cristo Mountains. In a separate building, which is constructed of adobe bricks that were made on the property, is a guest lounge where guests gather at any time during the day to enjoy complimentary beverages and snacks. The snacks, whatever they are, will be a treat—one of the owners won "Best Baker of Santa Fe" at the county fair a couple of years ago. Also in the guest lounge are pieces of art for sale and a library of art and travel books. An extended continental breakfast of juice, coffee or tea, pastries, yogurt, and fresh fruit is brought to guests' rooms each morning. One of the rooms here is completely handicapped-accessible.

★ **Grant Corner Inn,** 122 Grant Ave., Santa Fe, NM 87501. ☎ 505/983-6678 for reservations, **505/984-9001** for guest rooms. 12 rms (10 with bath). A/C TV TEL   *Sun · Brunch*
Rates (including breakfast): $85–$95 single or double without bath; $100–$140 single or double with bath. MC, V.

This early 20th-century manor at the corner of Grant Avenue and Johnson Street is just three blocks west of the Plaza. Each room is furnished with antiques, from brass or four-poster beds to armoires and quilts, and all provide monogrammed terrycloth robes. Most rooms also have ceiling fans and small refrigerators, and 10 have baths. But each room also has its own character. No. 3, for instance, has a hand-painted German wardrobe closet dating from 1772 and a wash basin with brass fittings in the shape of a fish, no. 8 has an exclusive outdoor deck that catches the morning sun, and no. 11 has an antique collection of dolls and stuffed animals. The inn's office doubles as a library and gift shop and has hot coffee and tea at all hours. Children 6 and under are not accepted.

Breakfast is served each morning in front of the living-room fireplace or on the front veranda in summer. The meals are so good, an enthusiastic public pays $10.50 a head ($7 for young children) to brunch here on Saturday from 8 to 11am and on Sunday from 8am to 1pm. (It's included in the room price for Grant Corner Inn guests, of course.)

Inn of the Animal Tracks, 707 Paseo de Peralta, Santa Fe, NM 87501. ☎ **505/988-1546.** 5 rms.
Rates (including breakfast): $90–$130 single or double. AE, MC, V.
Parking: Free.

The Inn of the Animal Tracks is a great little place. All the rooms, including the common spaces, are named under the signs of different animals, which are the patron spirits of the rooms. There are five in all: the Sign of the Rabbit, the Soaring Eagle, the Gentle Deer, the Playful Otter, and the Loyal Wolf. Each room, with a platform bed and private bath, reflects the presence of the patron animal. The Sign of the Rabbit room, for instance, is just overflowing with rabbits—stuffed rabbits, rabbit paintings, and rabbit books. There are handmade furnishings, and the rooms are all pleasant and bright. The Sign of the Soaring Eagle is the only one with a fireplace.

The Sign of the Bear room has a wonderful living room with a fireplace and a big overstuffed sofa. There's a small library from which you can borrow a book. Breakfast, served in the Sign of the Buffalo room or on a shaded landscaped patio, includes fresh bread, juice, fruit, and a different main course daily. Afternoon refreshments are also served. The inn does not permit smoking. Appropriately, there are several house pets.

Inn on the Paseo, 630 Paseo de Peralta, Santa Fe, NM 87501. ☎ **505/984-8200,** or toll free **800/457-9045.** Fax 505/989-3979. 19 rms, 2 suites.

Rates (including breakfast): $99–$190 double. AE, DC, MC, V. **Parking:** Free.

Located just a few blocks from the Plaza, the Inn on the Paseo is a good choice for travelers who want to be able to walk to the shops, galleries, and restaurants but would rather not stay in one of the larger hotels. When you enter the inn you'll be welcomed by the warmth of the large fireplace in the foyer. Southwestern furnishings dot the spacious public areas and the work of local artists adorns the walls. The guest rooms are large, meticulously clean, and very comfortable. Many of the rooms have fireplaces, and the focal point of each room is an original, handmade patchwork quilt. The owner is a third-generation quilter and she made all the quilts you'll see hanging throughout the inn. A breakfast buffet is served out on the sun deck in warmer weather, indoors by the fire on cooler days. It consists of muffins, breads, granola, fresh fruit, and coffee and tea. Complimentary refreshments are served every afternoon.

The Preston House, 106 Faithway St., Santa Fe, NM 87501. ☎ **505/982-3465.** 15 rms (13 with bath), 2 cottages, 1 adobe house. A/C TV TEL

Rates (including continental breakfast): High season, $70–$80 double without bath, $100–$145 double with bath; $140 cottage or adobe house. Low season, $48–$58 double without bath, $78–$98 double with bath; $115 cottage or adobe house. Additional person $15 extra. MC, V. **Parking:** Free.

This is a different sort of building for "The City Different"—a century-old Queen Anne home. That style of architecture is rarely seen in New Mexico, especially painted sky blue with white trim. The house's owner, noted silk-screen artist and muralist Signe Bergman, adores its original stained glass.

Located five blocks east of the Plaza, off Palace Avenue near La Posada hotel, the Preston House has several types of rooms. Six in the main house have period antiques and exquisitely feminine decor, with floral wallpaper and lace drapes. Many have brass beds covered with quilts; some have decks, several have fireplaces, and only two must share a bath. All rooms have phones. Seven more rooms with bath are in an adobe building catty-corner from the house. Two private cottages in the rear of the Preston House, and an adobe home across the street, have more deluxe facilities. All rooms are stocked with sherry and terrycloth robes. A continental buffet breakfast is served daily, as is afternoon tea with homemade cookies, cakes, and pies. Children 10 and under not accepted.

Pueblo Bonito, 138 W. Manhattan St., Santa Fe, NM 87501. ☎ 505/984-8001. 18 rms, 6 suites. TV TEL

Rates (including continental breakfast): June–Oct and holidays, $75–$90 single; $85–$100 double; $135 suite. Nov–May, $55–$70 single; $65–$80 double; $125 suite. MC, V. **Parking:** Free.

Private courtyards and narrow flagstone paths lend a look of elegance to this former circuit judge's 19th-century adobe hacienda and stables, located a few blocks south of the Santa Fe River. Adobe archways lead to hybrid rose gardens shaded by prolific apricot and pear trees; guests are invited to help themselves to the fruit.

Each of the guest rooms is named for a Pueblo tribe of the surrounding countryside. Every one—decorated with Native American rugs on wood or brick floors—has a queen-size bed, fireplace, cable TV, and radio/alarm clock. Bathrooms are small but attractively tiled. Six rooms are suites, each with an elaborate and fully stocked kitchen, a living/dining room with fireside seating, and a bedroom. A couple of other rooms have refrigerators and wet bars. The remainder are standard units with locally made willow headboards and couches, dining alcoves, and old Spanish-style lace curtains. Continental breakfast is served daily from 8 to 10am in the dining room or on the sun deck; or if you prefer, there's room service. Afternoon tea is served every day from 4 to 6pm. There's also a coin-op laundry.

★ **Spencer House Bed & Breakfast Inn,** 222 McKenzie St., Santa Fe, NM 87501. ☎ 505/988-3024, or toll free 800/647-0530 (7am to 7pm). 3 rms.

Rates (including breakfast): $85–$95 double. MC, V. **Parking:** Free.

The Spencer House is unique among Santa Fe bed-and-breakfasts. Instead of southwestern-style furnishings you'll find beautiful antiques from England, Ireland, and colonial America. One guest room features an antique brass bed, another a pencil-post bed, and all rooms are done in Ralph Lauren fabrics and linens (in fact, the Spencer House was recently featured in Ralph Lauren ads). Each of the beds is also outfitted with a fluffy down comforter. All bathrooms are completely new, modern, and very spacious. Owners Keith and Michael keep the inn spotlessly clean and take great pride in the Spencer House. From the old Bissell carpet sweeper and drop-front desk in the reading nook to antique trunks in the bedrooms, no detail has been overlooked. In summer a full breakfast—coffee, tea, yogurt, cereal, fresh fruit, and a different main course daily is served on the outdoor patio. In winter guests dine indoors by the wood-burning stove. A full afternoon tea is served in the breakfast room. Keith and Michael, who live next door, recently received an award from the Santa Fe Historical Board for the restoration of the Spencer House. They plan to have two more rooms by the summer of 1995.

The Territorial Inn, 215 Washington Ave., Santa Fe, NM 87501.
☎ **505/989-7737.** Fax 505/986-1411, attn: Lela. 10 rms (8 with bath). TV TEL

Rates (including continental breakfast): $80–$90 single or double without bath; $130–$150 single or double with bath. Indian Market, Thanksgiving, and Christmas, rates are higher. Additional person $15 extra. MC, V. **Parking:** Free.

This two-story Territorial-style building, built a block and a half from the Plaza in the 1890s, is the last of the private homes on Washington Avenue. Constructed of stone and adobe with a pitched roof, it features a curving tiled stairway.

All but two of its rooms, most of them furnished with Early American antiques, have private baths; the remaining pair share. Rooms have ceiling fans and sitting areas, and two have fireplaces. The back garden, shaded by large cottonwoods, boasts a patio where breakfast is served in warm weather, as well as a rose garden and a gazebo-enclosed hot tub.

Water Street Inn, 427 Water St., Santa Fe, NM 87501.
☎ **505/984-1193.** 6 rms. A/C TV TEL

Rates (including continental breakfast): $110–$145 single or double. MC, V. **Parking:** Free.

An award-winning adobe restoration on the west side of the Hilton hotel four blocks from the Plaza, this friendly inn features beautiful Mexican-tile baths, some kiva fireplaces or wood stoves, and antique furnishings. Each room is packed with southwestern art and books. Wine, fruit, chips, and salsa are offered in the living room or on the upstairs portal in the afternoon.

All rooms have king-size or queen-size beds. Room 3 features a queen-size hideaway sofa to accommodate families. (Yes, children are welcomed, as are pets, with prior approval.) Room 4 has special regional touches in its decor and boasts a chaise longue, a fur rug, built-in seating, and a corner fireplace.

5 RV Parks & Campgrounds

RV Parks

At least four private camping areas, mainly for recreational vehicles, are located within a few minutes' drive of downtown Santa Fe. Typical rates are $20 for full RV hookups, $15 for tents. Be sure to book ahead at busy times.

Los Campos RV Park, 3574 Cerrillos Rd., Santa Fe, NM 87501.
☎ **505/473-1949.**

The resort has 95 spaces with full hookups, picnic tables, showers, restrooms, a laundry, and a grocery store. It's just five miles south of the Plaza.

Rancheros de Santa Fe Camping Park, Exit 290 off I-25 (Rte. 3, Box 94, Santa Fe, NM 87505). ☎ **505/466-3482.**

Tents, motor homes, and trailers requiring full hookups are welcome here. The park's 130 sites are set in 22 acres of piñon and juniper forest. Facilities include tables, grills and fireplaces, hot showers, restrooms, a laundry, a grocery store, a swimming pool, a playground, a games room, free nightly movies, public telephones, and propane. It's located about six miles southeast of Santa Fe.

Santa Fe KOA, Exit 290 or 294 off I-25 (Rte. 3, Box 95A, Santa Fe, NM 87501). ☎ **505/982-1419.**

This campground offers full hookups, pull-through sites, tent sites, picnic tables, showers, restrooms, a laundry, a store, a "Santa Fe–style" gift shop, a playground, a recreation room, propane, and a dumping station. It's located about 11 miles northeast of Santa Fe.

Tesuque Pueblo RV Campground, U.S. 84/285 (Rte. 5, Box 360H, Santa Fe, NM 87501). ☎ **505/455-2661,** or toll free **800/ TRY-RV-PARK.**

This campground has 63 full hookups, pull-through sites, tent sites, showers, restrooms, a laundry, a seasonal swimming pool and hot tub, and a store selling Native American jewelry and fishing gear. It's approximately 10 miles north of Santa Fe.

Campgrounds

There are three forest sites along N.M. 475 toward the Santa Fe Ski Basin. All are open from May to October. Overnight rates start at about $6, depending on site choice.

Hyde Memorial State Park, N.M. 475 (P.O. Box 1147, Santa Fe, NM 87503). ☎ **505/983-7175.**

The park is about eight miles from the city. Its campground has shelters, water, tables, fireplaces, and pit toilets. Maps of Santa Fe with firewood supply locations indicated are supplied. There are also a small ice-skating pond and nature trails.

Santa Fe National Forest, N.M. 475 (P.O. Box 1689, Santa Fe, NM 87504). ☎ **505/988-6940.**

Black Canyon campground, with 44 sites, is just past the state park; it has clean water and sites for trailers up to 32 feet long. Big Tesuque campground, with 10 units, is about 12 miles from town; it has fishing but no drinking water. Both campgrounds have pit toilets.

6

Santa Fe Dining

1. Swiss Palace Bakery

2. Chili Shop

3. Downtown Subscription—
   Coffee shop

THERE ARE LITERALLY HUNDREDS OF RESTAURANTS IN SANTA FE, FROM LUXURY establishments with strict dress codes right down to corner hamburger stands. This is a sophisticated city, and a great variety of cuisines flourish here. Some chefs create recipes incorporating traditional southwestern foods with nonindigenous ingredients; their restaurants are referred to in listings as "creative southwestern." Others stick with steak and seafood. Many offer continental, European, or Asian menu options.

Especially during peak tourist seasons, dinner reservations may be essential. Reservations are always recommended at better restaurants. There's no tax on restaurant meals in New Mexico, but it's appropriate to tip 15% to 20% on top of your tab for service.

The categories below define "Very Expensive" restaurant as one in which most dinner main courses are priced above $25; "Expensive" restaurants are those where most main courses cost between $18 and $25; "Moderate," $12 to $18; "Inexpensive," $7 to $12; and "Budget," less than $7.

1 Downtown

This includes eateries within the circle defined by the Paseo de Peralta and St. Francis Drive, as well as those on Canyon Road.

Very Expensive

The Compound, 653 Canyon Rd. ☎ **982-4353.**
   Cuisine: CONTINENTAL. **Reservations:** Required.
   Prices: Main courses $17.50–$28. AE
   Open: Dinner only, Tues–Sat 6pm–until the last diners leave.

The Compound, designed by noted architect Alexander Girard, is set on beautifully landscaped grounds amid tall firs and pines on the south bank of the Santa Fe River. It's reached by a long driveway off Canyon Road, at the rear of an exclusive housing compound. The interior decor is simple but refined, yielding to the natural setting. Service is attentive and elegant: A coat and tie are de rigueur for a gentleman, and young children are not admitted.

There's typically a wide choice of seafood, chicken, and meat dishes. A favorite house special is roast rack of lamb with mint sauce. A different special is offered nightly. Main courses are served with rice, potatoes, a vegetable, and fresh-baked rolls. Seafood and vegetables are delivered daily; bread and pastries are baked on the premises. There is, of course, an extensive wine list.

Expensive

Coyote Cafe, 132 W. Water St. ☎ **983-1615.**
   Cuisine: CREATIVE SOUTHWESTERN. **Reservations:** Required.
   Prices: Appetizers $2.25–$5.95; main courses $6.50–$12.50; fixed-price dinner $39. MC, V.
   Open: Lunch Sat–Sun 11:30am–2pm; dinner daily 5:30–10pm.

This is still the number-one "trendy" place to dine in Santa Fe. Owner Mark Miller has talked extensively about his restaurant and cuisine on national television, with the result that he is universally identified with "Santa Fe cuisine." Tourists throng here: In summer, in fact, reservations are recommended days in advance. The café overlooks Water Street from tall windows on the second floor of a downtown building. Beneath the skylight, set in a cathedral ceiling, is a veritable zoo of animal sculptures in modern folk-art forms. Smoking is not allowed here.

The cuisine, prepared on a pecan-wood grill in an open kitchen, is southwestern with a modern twist. The menu changes seasonally, but diners might start with wild-boar bacon and fresh corn tamale with glazed granny apples and corn-cumin coulis or griddled buttermilk-and-wild-rice corn cakes with chipotle shrimp and salsa fresca. Main courses might include pecan-grilled pork tenderloin or grilled tolenas farm sonoma quail with spicy bourbon-apple stuffing and la caretta cider glaze. You can get drinks from the full bar or wines by the glass.

The Coyote Café has two adjunct establishments. The Rooftop Cantina (open April through October) serves light Mexican fare and cocktails. It's open daily from 11am to 10pm and main-course prices range from $5 to $16. On the ground floor is the Coyote Café General Store, a retail gourmet southwestern food market, featuring the Coyote Café's own food line (called Coyote Cocina), as well as hot sauces and salsas from all over the world.

Geronimo, 724 Canyon Rd. ☎ **982-1500.**

Cuisine: CREATIVE NEW MEXICAN. **Reservations:** Recommended.
Prices: Appetizers $6.50–$8.50; main courses $16.50–$21.50. AE, MC, V.
Open: Lunch Tues–Sun 11:30am–2:30pm; dinner daily 6–10:30pm.

When Geronimo opened in 1991, no one was sure that it would make it because so many other restaurants at this location had failed miserably. But Geronimo has done more than just survive—it has flourished. Located in an old adobe structure known as the Borrego House, the restaurant has been restored but, with its numerous small dining rooms, it still retains the comfortable feel of an old Santa Fe home. On my recent visit, the menu appetizer offerings included barbecued shrimp quesadilla with Bermuda onion, goat cheese, crème fraîche, and yellow-tomato salsa or crispy relleno stuffed with chicken mole and served with a lime crème faîche and an ancho chile purée. Favorite main courses were the white-cornmeal–dusted, pan-seared, free-range chicken served with a fresh peach-ginger salsa, baby spinach, and roasted new potatoes; lime-grilled halibut with smoky red posole and a blackened-tomato/roasted-yellow-pepper vinaigrette; and mesquite-grilled Black Angus ribeye steak with a roasted-pepper/grilled-summer-vegetable salsa and white Cheddar/green-chile-layered potatoes. The menu changes seasonally, and there is a well-selected wine list.

Inn of the Anasazi Restaurant, 113 Washington St.
☎ **988-3236.**
Cuisine: NORTHERN NEW MEXICAN/NATIVE AMERICAN. **Reservations:** Recommended.
Prices: Appetizers $6.50–$8 at lunch, $6.50–$9.50 at dinner; main courses $8.50–$11.75 at lunch, $17.50–$29 at dinner; breakfast $4–$9. AE, D, DC, DISC, MC, V.
Open: Breakfast Mon–Fri 7–10:30am, Sat–Sun 7–11am; lunch daily 11:30am–2:30pm; dinner Mon–Fri 5:30–10pm, Sat–Sun 5:30–11pm.

In keeping with the theory behind the Inn of the Anasazi (see Chapter 5), everything offered in this restaurant is all-natural. The meats are chemical free and the fruits and vegetables are organic whenever possible. They even serve water only on request "in the interest of conservation." The setting is comfortable, with an exposed-beam ceiling, exposed adobe walls, and traditional Southwest decor—very elegant surroundings.

For breakfast you can have anything from fruit to a breakfast burrito with ranchero sauce and chile potatoes or a soft-scrambled-egg quesadilla with yellow tomatoes, apple-smoked bacon, and fresh avocados. At lunch, you might try the Anasazi flatbread with fire-roasted sweet peppers and tomato-olive salsa to start, followed by achiote charred rare tuna with Wasabi aioli and snow pea slaw, or the mesquite-grilled buffalo burger on white Cheddar jalapeño brioche with seasoned fries and yellow ketchup. For dinner, try tortilla soup with barbecued pork pot stickers, then perhaps follow with pecan-grilled range chicken with garlic and sage and corn pudding. Or maybe you'd rather have dried guava-and-citrus–seared halibut with apricot essence and green rice.

There are daily specials, as well as a nice list of wines by the glass and special wines of the day.

La Casa Sena, 125 E. Palace Ave. ☎ **988-9232.**
Cuisine: CREATIVE SOUTHWESTERN. **Reservations:** Recommended.
Prices: Appetizers $2.75–$8 at lunch, $5–$7 at dinner; main courses $7.75–$11 at lunch, $18–$23 at dinner. La Cantina, tapas $3.25–$11; main courses $10–$18.50. AE, CB, DC, DISC, MC, V.
Open: Lunch Mon–Sat 11:30am–3pm; dinner daily 5:30–10pm; brunch (in main dining room only) Sun 11am–3pm.

Opposite St. Francis Cathedral, two restaurants look into a spacious garden patio. The elegant main dining room occupies the Territorial-style adobe house built in 1867 by Civil War hero Maj. José Sena for his wife and 23 children. Today it's a veritable art gallery with museum-quality landscapes on the walls and Taos-style handcrafted furniture. In the adjacent La Cantina, waiters and waitresses sing arias and tunes from Broadway shows as they carry platters from kitchen to table.

The cuisine in the main dining room might be described as northern New Mexican with a continental flair. Lunches include chicken enchiladas on blue-corn tortillas and baby coho salmon with a cilantro-lime pesto. In the evenings, diners might start with caldo de frijole negro (purée of black beans with amontillado sherry), then move to piñon free-range chicken breast with mulato chile-lignonberry sauce or wild-boar scaloppine.

The more moderately priced Cantina menu offers the likes of fire-roasted chicken salad and carne adovada burrito (prime pork roasted with red-chile sauce, served with Hatch green chiles and cheeses). Both restaurants have exquisite desserts and fine wines by the glass.

The Pink Adobe, 406 Old Santa Fe Trail. ☎ **983-7712.**

Cuisine: CONTINENTAL/SOUTHWESTERN. **Reservations:** Recommended.

Prices: Appetizers $5.75–$7.50; main courses $6.50–$9.50 at lunch, $10.75–$22.25 at dinner. AE, CB, DC, DISC, MC, V.

Open: Lunch Mon–Fri 11:30am–2:30pm; dinner daily 5:30–10pm.

San Pasqual, patron saint of the kitchen, keeps a close eye on this popular restaurant in the center of the 17th-century Barrio de Analco and across the street from the San Miguel mission. A Santa Fe institution since 1946, it occupies an adobe home believed to be at least 350 years old. Guests enter through a narrow side door into a series of quaint, informal dining rooms with tile or hardwood floors. Stuccoed walls display original modern art or Priscilla Hoback pottery on built-in shelves.

At the dinner hour the Pink Adobe offers the likes of escargots and shrimp rémoulade as appetizers. Main courses include shrimp Créole, poulet Marengo, tournedos bordelaise, lamb curry, and porc Napoleone. The steak Dunnigan is a house specialty. Lunch has more New Mexican and Cajun dishes, including a house enchilada topped with an egg, turkey-seafood gumbo, and gypsy stew (chicken, green chiles, tomatoes, and onions in sherry broth).

Smoking is allowed only in the Dragon Room, the lounge across the alleyway from the restaurant. Under the same ownership, the charming Dragon Room (which is much more popular with locals than is the Pink Adobe's main dining room) has a separate menu from its parent establishment with traditional Mexican food. The full bar is open daily from 11:30am to 2am, until midnight on Sunday, and there's live entertainment Sunday through Thursday.

★ **Santacafe,** 231 Washington Ave. ☎ **984-1788.**

Cuisine: NEW AMERICAN. **Reservations:** Recommended.

Prices: Appetizers $5–$10; main courses $8–$12 at lunch, $18–$24 at dinner. MC, V.

Open: Lunch Mon–Sat 11:30am–2pm; dinner daily 6–10pm (5:30–10:30pm in summer).

A casually formal restaurant in the 18th-century Padre Gallegos House, 2^1/$_2$ blocks north of the Plaza, Santacafe has service and presentation that are impeccable. Noted for its minimalist decor, art-free soft white adobe interior, and "Zen-inspired" courtyard, Santacafe has been a favorite of tourists and locals alike since 1983. Each room has a fireplace, and there's an outside courtyard for summer diners.

Downtown Santa Fe Dining

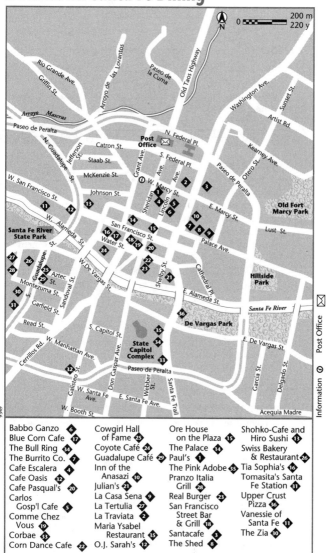

Babbo Ganzo 6	Cowgirl Hall	Ore House	Shohko-Cafe and
Blue Corn Cafe 17	of Fame 25	on the Plaza 15	Hiro Sushi 13
The Bull Ring 34	Coyote Café 24	The Palace 14	Swiss Bakery
The Burrito Co. 7	Guadalupe Café 29	Paul's 1	& Restaurant 26
Cafe Escalera 4	Inn of the	The Pink Adobe 35	Tia Sophia's 16
Cafe Oasis 32	Anasazi 10	Pranzo Italia	Tomasita's Santa
Cafe Pasqual's 20	Julian's 21	Grill 28	Fe Station 31
Carlos	La Casa Sena 9	Real Burger 23	Upper Crust
Gosp'l Cafe 5	La Tertulia 27	San Francisco	Pizza 36
Comme Chez	La Traviata 2	Street Bar	Vanessie of
Vous 19	Maria Ysabel	& Grill 18	Santa Fe 11
Corbae 33	Restaurant 35	Santacafe 3	The Zia 30
Corn Dance Cafe 22	O.J. Sarah's 12	The Shed 8	

Its unique modern American cooking also features southwestern and
Asian influences. Menus change seasonally. Recent menu offerings
included Dungeness crabcakes with cucumber-and-carrot salad and
house-smoked chicken spring rolls with a three-chile dipping sauce
as appetizers. Main courses included red-chile ravioli filled with goat
and feta cheeses, fresh oregano, sun-dried tomato, and a basil/
green-chile sauce or Atlantic salmon with roasted new potatoes. All

breads and desserts are homemade, and the full bar offers wines by the glass.

Moderate

Babbo Ganzo Trattoria, 130 Lincoln Ave. ☎ **986-3835.**

Cuisine: ITALIAN. **Reservations:** Recommended.
Prices: Appetizers $4.75–$10.95; main courses $6.25–$15.75. MC, V.
Open: Lunch Mon–Sat 11:30am–2:30pm; dinner Mon–Sat 5:30–10:30pm.

Located atop the only escalator in Santa Fe, the Babbo Ganzo is a great little Italian place that serves lunch and dinner. As you walk into the restaurant, you'll see on your right a wall of pasta for sale and on your left a large bar. There's a wonderful mural, as well as a fireplace and a wine rack.

For lunch you can start with bruschetta (grilled bread topped with garlic, tomato, and basil) and then follow with an allo zenzero pizza with red chiles, tomato, and mozzarella cheese. At dinner, start with insalata e funghi fritti, shiitake and oyster mushrooms sautéed in balsamic vinegar and served over a bed of lettuce. Move on to pappardelle sui cinghiale (homemade pasta with wild boar in a light tomato sauce), or if you feel like having fish, the Babbo Ganzo offers a variety plus a fresh fish of the day. This is one of the more authentic Italian restaurants in the area.

The Bull Ring, 414 Old Santa Fe Trail. ☎ **983-3328.**

Cuisine: STEAKS/SEAFOOD. **Reservations:** Recommended.
Prices: Appetizers $3.95–$6; main courses $10.95–$25. AE, DISC, MC, V.
Open: Lunch Mon–Fri 11:30am–2:30pm; dinner daily 5:30–9:30pm.
Closed: Sun in winter.

Legislators and lobbyists from the adjacent State Capitol make a habit of dining and drinking at the Bull Ring. Impressive impressionistic paintings adorn the walls of this old adobe hacienda, now a series of small dining rooms. Steaks are the dinner specialty. Much ballyhooed is the Bull Ring steak, a 12-ounce charcoal-broiled New York cut with sautéed mushrooms or onions, red or green chiles, or au poivre sauce. Seafood dishes include grilled shrimp skewer served on a bed of rice with garlic-herb butter. Enchiladas Nuevo Mexico (blue-corn tortillas with red or green chile, cheese, beef, or chicken) highlights the small regional portion of the menu. Midday diners can also select half-pound hamburgers or other sandwiches.

Cafe Escalera, 130 Lincoln Ave. ☎ **989-8188.**

Cuisine: CREATIVE CONTINENTAL/SOUTHWESTERN. **Reservations:** Recommended.
Prices: Appetizers $2–$6.50; main courses $8.75–$22.50. AE, DISC, MC, V.
Open: Mon–Sat 8:30am–10pm, Sun 5–9pm.

When Cafe Escalera opened a few years ago, the quality of the food wasn't too consistent; however, it has now become one of Santa Fe's most popular restaurants. The spacious, open, warehouselike space is bright, airy, and filled with energy. The decor is understated in a modern way—the focus here is on the food. At lunch I like to start my meal with an order of Mediterranean olives and perhaps roasted almonds. If you're in the mood for something more substantial to start, try the roasted peppers and goat cheese or the vegetarian black-bean chili. On my last visit to Cafe Escalera for lunch I enjoyed the grilled-tuna salad with arugula, new potatoes, green beans, beets, and aioli. Dinner appetizers are usually the same as at lunch, but the main courses differ greatly. The risotto timbale with summer squash, spinach, and basil pesto is a good choice, and so is the grilled king salmon with a tomato-basil vinaigrette. Those with a heartier appetite will enjoy the roast New York strip steak with saffron-garlic mashed potatoes and summer chantarelles. For dessert I had the Grand Marnier ice, which was delicious. There's also always something for chocoholics. Breakfast is served in the bar Monday through Saturday.

$ Cafe Pasqual's, 121 Don Gaspar Ave. ☎ 983-9340.
Cuisine: NEW MEXICAN. **Reservations:** Recommended for dinner.
Prices: Appetizers $4.95–$8.95; main courses $13.75–$18.75; breakfast $4.25–$7.50; lunch $6.25–$8.95. MC, V.
Open: Breakfast Mon–Sat 7am–3pm; lunch Mon–Sat 11am–3pm; dinner Mon–Thurs 6–10pm, Fri–Sat 6–10:30pm; brunch Sun 8am–2pm.

This intimate establishment, located across from the Hotel St. Francis, has a common table where solo journeyers can get acquainted and an innovative menu that appeals to budget watchers at breakfast and lunch. Omelets, pancakes, and huevos motuleños (two eggs over easy on blue-corn tortillas and black beans topped with sautéed bananas, feta cheese, salsa, and green chiles) are among the breakfast options. Soups, salads, burgers, and Mexican dishes are popular at lunch, and there's a delectable grilled-salmon burrito with herbed goat cheese and cucumber salsa. The frequently changing dinner menu offers grilled meats and seafoods, plus vegetarian specials. Oaxacan mango, warm Brie with whole roasted garlic, and cornmeal pizzetta with alderwood-smoked salmon, herbed goat cheese, and roasted jalapeño salsa are typical appetizers. Main courses might include blue-cornmeal-crusted soft-shell crabs, charcoal-grilled marinated quail, or pan-roasted chimayo-chile-rubbed salmon filet. Pasqual's also boasts homemade desserts, imported beers, and wine by the bottle or glass.

Celebrations, 613 Canyon Rd. ☎ 989-8904.
Cuisine: NEW AMERICAN. **Reservations:** Recommended.
Prices: Appetizers $5–$7.50; main courses $12.50–$18.75; breakfast $2.50–$6.25; lunch $4–$6.95. AE, MC, V.
Open: Summer, breakfast/lunch daily 7:30am–2:30pm; dinner Tues–Sun 5–9pm. Winter, breakfast/lunch daily 7:30am–2:30pm; dinner Wed–Sat 5–9pm.

Housed in a former art gallery with beautiful stained-glass windows and a kiva fireplace, Celebrations boasts "the ambience of a bistro and the simple charm of another era." In summer, guests can dine on a brick patio facing Canyon Road.

Three meals are served daily, starting with breakfast—an omelet with black beans or French toast with orange syrup, for example. Lunch offers soup, salad, and pasta specials, Swiss raclette, sandwiches like the oyster poor boy, and ploughman's lunch. Casseroles, pot pies, and hearty soups are always on in winter. The dinner menu changes with chef's whim. Diners might start with fried bocconcini with fresh tomato-and-basil sauce, then progress to a main course like red snapper with avocados and lemon sauce, shrimp brochettes with Chimayo-chile-and-pineapple salsa, or grilled ribeye with rosemary potatoes. All desserts are homemade. A choice of beers and California wines by the bottle or glass is available.

$ El Farol, 808 Canyon Rd. ☎ **988-9912.**
Cuisine: SPANISH. **Reservations:** Recommended.
Prices: Main courses $9.95–$22.95. DC, DISC, MC, V.
Open: Daily 11am–10pm.

This is the place to head for local ambience and old-time flavor. The Canyon Road artists' quarter's original neighborhood bar, El Farol means "The Lantern." Its low ceilings and dark-brown walls have now also become the home of one of Santa Fe's largest and most unusual selections of tapas (bar snacks and appetizers). There are 35 varieties offered, including such delicacies as pulpo a la Gallega (octopus with Spanish paprika sauce), grilled cactus with ramesco sauce, conejo y vino (rabbit with tomatoes, olives, and wine), and Moroccan eggplant. Guests who proceed to the main courses often opt for the Cornish game hen—butterflied, cooked with rosemary, and served with ginger sauce. Jazz, folk, and ethnic musicians play every night beginning at 9:30pm. In summer, an outdoor patio, seating 50, is open to diners.

★ **Julian's,** 221 Shelby St. ☎ **988-2355.**
Cuisine: ITALIAN. **Reservations:** Recommended.
Prices: Appetizers $5–$8; main courses $12–$19. AE, CB, DC, DISC, MC, V.
Open: Dinner only, daily 6pm until the last diners leave.

Devotees of Julian's in Telluride, Colorado, may be pleased to discover that their favorite northern Italian restaurant resurfaced in Santa Fe in 1989. Elizabeth (Lou) and Wayne Gustafson have moved to an unpretentious setting just off Alameda Street. Meals are served in an atmosphere of simple elegance, around a central kiva fireplace, to the strains of light jazz music. Meals are principally Tuscan, though other regional dishes find their way onto the menu. Diners can start with prosciutto di Parma con fichi (fresh figs with Italian ham), carne al Albese (thinly sliced raw beef served with olive oil, oregano, capers, and parmesan), or melanzana griglia con peperoni (grilled eggplant with roasted peppers and balsamic vinegar); then move on to the generous main courses—for instance, fresh fish, pollo agro dolci (chicken sautéed with shallots, raisins, and capers in a sweet brown sauce) or veal piccata alla limone. All main courses include bread and

Josie's - lunch
The Pontchatrain - n.o. style

a side of pasta. You can order a salad à la carte. There are a full bar and an extensive list of Italian and Californian wines priced from $14 to $55.

⭐ **La Tertulia,** 416 Agua Fria St. ☎ 988-2769.
$ **Cuisine:** NEW MEXICAN. **Reservations:** Recommended.
Prices: Lunch $4.95–$7.25; dinner $7.25–$17.95. AE, MC, V.
Open: Lunch Tues–Sun 11:30am–2pm; dinner Tues–Sun 5–9pm.

Housed in a former 18th-century convent, La Tertulia's thick adobe walls separate six dining rooms, among them the old chapel and a restored *sala* (living room) containing a valuable Spanish Colonial art collection. There's also an outside garden patio for summer dining. Dim lighting and viga-beamed ceilings, shuttered windows and wrought-iron chandeliers, lace tablecloths and hand-carved santos in wall niches lend a feeling of historic authenticity. *La tertulia* means "the gathering place." A highlight of the menu is Spanish paella (for two or more), an olio of seafood, chicken, chorizo sausage, vegetables, and rice, served with black-bean/jalapeño soup and sopaipillas. Gourmet regional dishes include filet y rellenos, carne adovada, pollo adovo, and camarones con pimientos y tomates (shrimp with peppers and tomatoes). If you feel like dessert, try the chocolate piñon-nut truffle torte or natillas (custard). The bar features homemade sangría.

La Traviata, 95 W. Marcy St. ☎ 984-1091.
Cuisine: SOUTHERN ITALIAN. **Reservations:** Recommended.
Prices: Appetizers $3.75–$7.75; main courses $8.25–$19.50. MC, V.
Open: Continental breakfast Mon–Fri 8:30–11:30am; lunch Mon–Fri 11:30am–2:30pm; dinner daily 6–10pm.

This simple Italian bistro, just a block off the Plaza, hits its stride during the annual July-August opera season. Photos of opera singers and classical composers share wall space with prints of Italian scenes amid the refined strains of classical music. The menu focuses on antipasti, pastas, and a handful of seasonal specials. Grilled eggplant, smoked salmon, and roast pepper dishes are popular starters. Favored homemade pastas include linguine con gamberi (with shrimp in a tomato-saffron sauce) and tagliatelle arrabbiata (with mushrooms in a spicy tomato-basil sauce). Featured main dishes are fresh fish and shellfish and veal dishes—like the costolette di vitello alla saltimbocca, a grilled veal chop with prosciutto, Fontina cheese, and sage. La Traviata also offers delectable desserts, espresso coffees, and a wine list full of Italian imports.

Ore House on the Plaza, 50 Lincoln Ave. ☎ 983-8687.
Cuisine: STEAKS/SEAFOOD. **Reservations:** Recommended.
Prices: Appetizers $3.50–$9.75; main courses $12.95–$20. AE, MC, V.
Open: Lunch daily 10:30am–2:30pm; dinner daily 5:30–10pm.

The Ore House's second-story balcony, at the southwest corner of the Plaza, is an ideal spot from which to watch the passing parade while enjoying lunch or cocktails. The decor is southwestern, with plants and lanterns hanging amid white walls and booths. The menu is heavy on fresh seafood and steaks. Daily fresh fish specials include salmon and swordfish (poached, blackened, teriyaki, or lemon), rainbow trout, lobster, and shellfish. Steak Ore House (wrapped in bacon and topped with crabmeat and béarnaise sauce) and chicken Ore House (a grilled breast stuffed with ham, Swiss cheese, green chiles, and béarnaise) are local favorites. The Ore House also caters to non–meat-eaters with vegetable platters.

The bar, with solo music Wednesday through Saturday night, is proud of its 66 "custom margaritas." It has a selection of domestic and imported beers and an excellent wine list. An appetizer menu is served from 2:30 to 5pm daily, and the bar stays open until midnight or later (only until midnight on Sunday).

The Palace, 142 W. Palace Ave. ☎ 982-9891.

Cuisine: NORTHERN ITALIAN/CONTINENTAL. **Reservations:** Recommended.
Prices: Appetizers $5.95–$8.50; main courses $9.50–$18.95; lunch $5.25–$10.50. AE, MC, V.
Open: Lunch Mon–Sat 11:30am–5pm; dinner Mon–Sat 5:45–10pm.

When the Burro Alley site of Doña Tules' 19th-century gambling hall was excavated in 1959, an unusual artifact was discovered: a brass door-knocker, shaped half like a horseshoe, half like a saloon girl's stockinged leg. That knocker today is the logo of the Palace, which maintains the Victorian flavor but none of the ill repute of its predecessor.

Brothers Lino, Pietro, and Bruno Pertusini have carried a long family tradition into the restaurant business: Their father was chef at the Villa d'Este on Lake Como, Italy. The Pertusinis' menu is northern Italian with a few French and continental dishes. Lunches include Caesar salad and roasted "7 Aromas" chicken salad, bruschetta caprini, ruby trout, housemade pasta, and breads. Dinners include crab-stuffed shrimp, scaloppine fontina, New Mexican lamb, steaks, gnocchi, and a variety of vegetarian dishes. There are fresh pastas daily; the wine list is long and well considered.

There is outdoor dining, and the bar is open Monday through Saturday from 11:30am to 2am, with a nightly piano bar.

Paul's, 72 W. Marcy St. ☎ 982-8738.

Cuisine: INTERNATIONAL. **Reservations:** Recommended for dinner.
Prices: Main courses $12.95–$17.95; lunch $5.50–$6.95. DISC, MC, V.
Open: Lunch Mon–Sat 11:30am–2pm; dinner daily 5:30–9:30pm.

Once just a home-style deli, then a little gourmet restaurant called Santa Fe Gourmet, Paul's (opened in 1990) is a great place for lunch or dinner. The lunch menu has a few main courses, like sausage and lentils or fettuccine; hot or cold sandwiches; and a short vegetarian menu. At dinner, the lights are dimmed and the bright Santa Fe interior (with folk art on the walls and colorfully painted screens that divide the restaurant into smaller, more intimate areas) becomes a great place for a romantic dinner. The menu might include a black-bean crêpe filled with curried vegetables to start, and as a main course, stuffed pumpkin bread with pine nuts, corn, green chiles, red-chile sauce, queso blanco, and caramelized apples. Paul's won the Taste of Santa Fe for best main course in 1992 and best dessert in 1994. A wine list is available, and there is no smoking anywhere in the restaurant.

★ **Pranzo Italia Grill,** 540 Montezuma St., Sanbusco Center. ☎ 984-2645. *Wonderful, nice grown up atmosphere*

Cuisine: NORTHERN ITALIAN. **Reservations:** Recommended.
Prices: Appetizers $4.25–$6.95; main courses $4.50–$7.95 at lunch, $6.95–$17.95 at dinner. AE, DC, DISC, MC, V.
Open: Lunch daily 11:30am–3pm; dinner Sun–Thurs 5–10pm, Fri–Sat 5–11pm. *but kid friendly*

Housed in a renovated warehouse, this sister to Albuquerque's redoubtable Scalo restaurant caters to local Santa Feans with a contemporary atmosphere of modern abstract art and food prepared on an open grill. Homemade soups, salads, creative pizzas, and fresh pastas mark the low end of the menu. Bianchi e nere al capesante (black-and-white linguine with bay scallops in a light seafood sauce) and pizza pollo affumicato (with smoked chicken, pesto, and roasted peppers) are consistent favorites. Steaks, chicken, veal, and fresh seafood grills—heavy on the garlic—dominate the dinner menu. The bar boasts the Southwest's largest collection of grappas, as well as a wide selection of wines and champagnes by the glass. The restaurant's deli, Portare Via, offers Santa Fe's largest selection of Italian deli meats and cheeses.

Shohko-Cafe and Hiro Sushi, 321 Johnson St. ☎ 983-7288 or 983-7364.

Cuisine: JAPANESE. **Reservations:** Recommended.
Prices: Lunch $5.25–$11; dinner $7.25–$15. AE, MC, V.
Open: Lunch Mon–Fri 11:30am–2pm; dinner Mon–Sat 5:30–9:30pm.

Opened in the late 1970s as Santa Fe's first Japanese restaurant, Shohko is located at the corner of Guadalupe Street next to the Eldorado Hotel. Its 36-foot sushi bar serves up 30 fresh varieties of raw seafood including sushi and sashimi. Here is where to indulge in teriyaki dishes, sukiyaki, yakitori (skewered chicken), and yakisoba (fried noodles), and a uniquely southwestern Japanese treat: green-chile tempura. There are also some Chinese plates and vegetarian dishes on the menu. Wine, imported beers, and hot saké are available.

$ **Vanessie of Santa Fe,** 434 W. San Francisco St. ☎ 982-9966.
Cuisine: STEAKS/SEAFOOD. **Reservations:** Not accepted.
Prices: Dinner $9.95–$15.95. AE, DC, MC, V.
Open: Dinner only, daily 5:30–10:30pm.

Vanessie is as much a piano bar as it is a restaurant. The talented Doug Montgomery and Taylor Kundolf hold forth at the keyboard, caressing the ivories with a repertoire that ranges from Bach to Gershwin to Barry Manilow. A five-item menu, served at large, round wooden tables beneath hanging plants, never varies: roast chicken, fresh fish, New York sirloin, filet mignon, and rack of lamb. Portions are large and are served with baked potatoes or onion loaf, fresh vegetables or Saratoga chips for $2.95 extra per sidedish. The cheesecake served for dessert is large enough to feed three. There's a short wine list.

Inexpensive

Cowgirl Hall of Fame, 319 S. Guadalupe St. ☎ 982-2565.
> **Cuisine:** REGIONAL AMERICAN/BARBECUE. **Reservations:** Recommended.
> **Prices:** Appetizers $4.25–$4.95; main courses $3.95–$12.95. AE, DISC, MC, V.
> **Open:** Daily 11am–11pm.

Mention the Cowgirl Hall of Fame to any Santa Fean and you'll hear one word: "fun." Everything at this restaurant has been done with a playful spirit—from the cowgirl paraphernalia that decorates the walls to the menu which features items like "chicken wing dings" (eight chicken wings in a "dandy" citrus-Tabasco marinade served with a special dressing). The chuckwagon chili is another house favorite, and so is the honey-fried chicken. The bunkhouse smoked brisket with potato salad, barbecue beans, and cole slaw is excellent, as is the cracker fried catfish with jalapeño-tartar sauce. There's even a special "kid's corral" which has horseshoes, a play area, and pin-the-tail-on-the-cow to keep children entertained during dinner. The dessert specialty of the house is the original ice cream baked potato (ice cream molded into a potato shape, rolled in spices, and topped with green pecans and whipped cream). Happy hour is from 4 to 6pm, and the bar stays open until 2am.

$ Guadalupe Cafe, 313 Guadalupe St. ☎ 982-9762.
> **Cuisine:** NEW MEXICAN.
> **Prices:** Appetizers $1.95–$5.25; main courses $6.95–$12.95; breakfast $4.50–$8.75; lunch $5.25–$10. MC, V.
> **Open:** Breakfast/lunch Tues–Fri 7am–2pm; dinner Tues–Sat 5:30–10pm; brunch Sat–Sun 11am–2pm.

Santa Feans line up at all hours to dine in this casually elegant café. Breakfasts include chorizo burritos and huevos rancheros; on the lunch menu are Mexican chicken salad and blue-corn enchiladas.

Frommer's Smart Traveler: Restaurants

1. Have lunch instead of dinner at expensive restaurants you really want to try. The food is often the same, but the prices are noticeably lower.

2. Make a picnic for lunch in good weather and head for the parks and plazas in town or to one of the beautiful scenic spots mentioned in this book.

3. Watch the booze—it can add greatly to the price of any meal.

4. If you're traveling with kids, ask if restaurants have a children's menu.

Dinner includes everything from breast of chicken relleno to chile-cheese chimichangas. Daily specials feature fresh fish, crêpes, and pastas; don't miss the famous chocolate-amaretto adobe pie for dessert. Beer and wine are served.

⭐ **San Francisco Street Bar and Grill,** 114 W. San Francisco St. ☎ 982-2044.

Small nice

$ **Cuisine:** AMERICAN. **Reservations:** Not accepted.
Prices: Lunch $4.50–$6.50; dinner $4.50–$12.95. DISC, MC, V.
Open: Daily 11am–11pm.

This easy-going eatery offers casual dining amid simple decor in three seating areas: the main restaurant, an indoor courtyard beneath the three-story Plaza Mercado atrium, and an outdoor patio with its own summer grill. It's perhaps best known for its hamburgers, yet it offers a variety of daily specials. The lunch menu consists mainly of soups, sandwiches, and salads; dinners include fresh deep-fried catfish, grilled pork tenderloin medallions, and New York strip steak. There are also nightly pasta specials. The full bar service includes draft beers and daily wine specials.

$ **Tomasita's Santa Fe Station,** 500 S. Guadalupe St. ☎ 983-5721.

Cheap good busy

Cuisine: NEW MEXICAN. **Reservations:** Not accepted.
Prices: Appetizers $1.95–$4.95; main courses $4.25–$9.25 at lunch, $4.75–$9.75 at dinner. MC, V.
Open: Mon–Sat 11am–10pm.

This may be the restaurant most consistently recommended by local Santa Feans. Why? Some point to the atmosphere; others cite the food and prices. Hanging plants and wood decor accent this spacious brick building, adjacent to the old Santa Fe railroad station. Traditional New Mexican main dishes like chiles rellenos and enchiladas (house specialties), as well as stuffed sopaipillas, chalupas, and tacos. Vegetarian dishes, as well as burgers and steaks and daily specials, are offered; and there's full bar service.

Upper Crust Pizza, 329 Old Santa Fe Trail. ☎ 983-4140.

Cuisine: PIZZA. **Reservations:** Not accepted.
Prices: $3.95–$12.95. No credit cards.
Open: Winter, Mon–Sat 11am–10pm, Sun noon–10pm. Summer, Mon–Sat 11am–11pm, Sun noon–11pm.

Santa Fe's best pizzas may be served here, in an adobe house with its front patio adjacent to the old San Miguel mission. Meals-in-a-dish include the likes of the Grecian gourmet pizza (feta and olives) and the whole-wheat vegetarian pizza (topped with sesame seeds). You can choose between indoor seating or 30-minute free delivery to downtown hotels. Beer and wine are served, as well as salads, calzones, and stromboli.

The Zia Diner, 326 S. Guadalupe St. ☎ 988-7008.

Cuisine: INTERNATIONAL/AMERICAN. **Reservations:** Accepted only for parties of six or more.

Prices: Appetizers $2.25–$4.75; main courses $3.50–$7.50 at lunch, $5.95–$11.25 at dinner. AE, MC, V.
Open: Daily 11:30am–10pm.

In a renovated 1880 coal warehouse, this art deco diner boasts a stainless-steel soda fountain, a shaded patio, and pueblo motifs throughout. The varied menu features homemade soups, salads, fish and chips, meatloaf, and, of course, enchiladas are served anytime. Specials range from East Indian curry to spanakopita, Thai-style trout to three-cheese calzone. There are fine wines, gourmet desserts, and an espresso bar.

Budget

The Burrito Co., 111 Washington Ave. ☎ 982-4453.
Cuisine: NEW MEXICAN.
Prices: $1.90–$4.75. MC, V.
Open: Mon–Sat 7:30am–11pm.

This is probably downtown Santa Fe's best fast-food establishment. You can people-watch as you dine on the outdoor patio or enjoy the garden-style poster gallery indoors. Order and pick up at the counter. Breakfast burritos are popular in the morning; after 11am you can get traditional Mexican meals with lots of chiles.

$ Carlos' Gosp'l Cafe, 125 Lincoln Ave. ☎ 983-1841.
Cuisine: DELI.
Prices: $2.65–$6.90. No credit cards.
Open: Mon–Sat 11am–4pm.

You may sing the praises of the "Say Amen" desserts at this café in the inner courtyard of the First Interstate Bank Building. First, though, try the tortilla or hangover (potato-corn) soups or the deli sandwiches. Carlos's has outdoor tables, but many diners prefer to sit indoors, reading newspapers or sharing conversation at the large common table. Gospel and soul music play continually; paintings of churches and performers cover the walls.

La Choza, 905 Alarid St. ☎ 982-0909.
Cuisine: NEW MEXICAN. **Reservations:** Not accepted.
Prices: Lunch $4.50–$5.50; dinner $5.50–$6.50. MC, V.
Open: Mon–Thurs 11am–8pm, Fri–Sat 11am–9pm.

The sister restaurant of the Shed (see below) is located near Cerrillos Road's intersection with St. Francis Drive. A casual eatery with round tables beneath a viga ceiling, it's especially popular on cold days when diners gather around the wood-burning stove and fireplace. The menu offers traditional enchiladas, tacos, and burritos on blue-corn tortillas, as well as green-chile stew, chili con carne, and carne adovada. Vegetarians and children have their own menus. Beer and wine are served.

O. J. Sarah's, 106 N. Guadalupe St. ☎ 984-1675.
Cuisine: CREATIVE AMERICAN. **Reservations:** Not accepted.
Prices: Breakfast $3–$6; lunch $3.50–$7.75. No credit cards.
Open: Daily 7am–2pm.

Named for a since-departed owner who had a penchant for orange juice and other wholesome foods, this café offers such unusual breakfasts as cottage-cheese pancakes topped with hot raspberry sauce and three-egg omelets filled with spinach, avocado, cheese, and mushrooms. For lunch, consider a spinach-artichoke salad, a guacamole burrito, or a sour-cream chicken enchilada—or play it safe with sandwiches on home-baked bread and a fruit smoothie.

Real Burger, 227 Don Gaspar Ave. ☎ **988-3717.**

> **Cuisine:** AMERICAN/NEW MEXICAN.
> **Prices:** $2.25–$5.75. No credit cards.
> **Open:** Mon–Sat 7am–5pm.

Downtown Santa Fe's preferred hamburger stand is across the street from the St. Francis Hotel. Don't come for atmosphere—come for burgers with "the works," chili dogs, fajitas, or the enchilada plate. In the morning, you can get steak and eggs or a breakfast burrito.

$ The Shed, 113 1/2 E. Palace Ave. ☎ **982-9030.** *GOOD FOR*

> **Cuisine:** NEW MEXICAN. **Reservations:** Not accepted. *LUNCH*
> **Prices:** Main dishes $3.50–$6.75. No credit cards. *DOWN TOWN*
> **Open:** Mon–Sat 11am–2:30pm.

Queues often form outside the Shed, half a block east of the Palace of the Governors. A luncheon institution since 1954, it occupies several rooms and the patio of a rambling hacienda built in 1692. Festive folk art adorns the doorways and walls. The food is basic but delicious, a compliment to traditional Hispanic Pueblo cooking. Blue-corn enchiladas, tacos, and burritos, all served on blue-corn tortillas with pinto beans and posoles, are standard courses. The green-chile soup is a local favorite. There are dessert specials, and beer and wine are available.

Tia Sophia's, 210 W. San Francisco St. ☎ **983-9880.**

> **Cuisine:** NEW MEXICAN.
> **Prices:** Breakfast $1.35–$5.75; lunch $3.95–$7.25. MC, V.
> **Open:** Mon–Sat 7am–2pm.

Diners in this friendly downtown restaurant sit at big wooden booths. Daily breakfast specials include eggs with blue-corn enchiladas (Tuesday) and burritos with chorizo, potatoes, chile, and cheese (Saturday); a popular lunch is the Atrisco plate: green-chile stew, a cheese enchilada, beans, posole, and a sopaipilla.

2 Northside

Expensive

El Nido, N.M. 22, Tesuque. ☎ **988-4340.**

> **Cuisine:** STEAK/SEAFOOD. **Reservations:** Recommended.
> **Prices:** Appetizers $2.95–$8.95; main courses $9.95–$25.95. MC, V.
> **Open:** Lunch Tues–Sat 11:30am–2pm; dinner Tues–Sun 5:30–10pm.

Life has never been dull at El Nido ("The Nest"). Located five miles north of the Plaza, this 1920s adobe home was a dance hall and later

Ma Nelson's brothel, before the restaurant opened in 1939. It has been drawing throngs of Santa Feans ever since for its food and atmosphere, lively bar, and occasional flamenco dance performances. Scandinavian wood tables and chairs sit beneath viga ceilings, surrounded by kiva fireplaces and stuccoed walls covered with local artwork.

The appetizer list features ceviche, steamed mussels, and half-shell or deep-fried oysters when available. Main courses include a variety of steaks, aged and prime rib, stuffed chicken breast, king crab, shrimp, scallops, and a variety of broiled fresh fish specials. Desserts are highlighted by profiteroles, a puff pastry filled with vanilla ice cream and covered with chocolate sauce.

3 Southside

Santa Fe's motel strip and other streets south of the Paseo de Peralta have their share of good, reasonably priced restaurants.

Moderate

Corn Dance Cafe, 409 W. Water St. ☎ **986-1662.**
Cuisine: CREATIVE NATIVE AMERICAN. **Reservations:** Recommended.
Prices: Appetizers $4.50–$8.50; main courses $13.50–$23.50. AE, DC, DISC, MC, V.
Open: Lunch daily 11am–3pm; dinner daily 5:30–10pm.

The recently opened Corn Dance Cafe is unique to the Santa Fe restaurant scene because it focuses on Native American, rather than New Mexican, cuisine and aims to "promote healthy well-being and ecological respect for Mother Earth." Start with the Potawatomi Little Big Pie (Native American flatbread topped with savory chicken, grilled mushrooms, and corn chili) or the "Kick Ass Buffalo Chili" in a jalapeño bread bowl. The alderwood-smoked chinook salmon on red-corn cakes is very tasty. My favorite main dish here is the fire-roasted Colorado golden trout with blue-corn wild-rice johnnycakes. Other interesting dishes include grilled pueblo rabbit with Roma tomatoes, cilantro, and hazelnuts; and sassafras

Frommer's Cool for Kids: Restaurants

Cowgirl Hall of Fame (see p. 90) All kids love the Kid's Corrale where, among other things, they can play a game of horseshoes.

Upper Crust Pizza (see p. 91) Not only do many say they have the best pizza in town, but they'll deliver to tired tots and their families at downtown hotels.

Bobcat Bite (see p. 98) The name and the ranch-style atmosphere will appeal to families set on great steaks and huge hamburgers with low price tags.

wood-smoked bobwhite quails with grilled red banana, papaya, and achiote cream. At press time the restaurant was still awaiting a beer and wine license, so call ahead to see if you'll need to bring your own. The restaurant is smoke-free.

Hunan Restaurant, 2440 Cerrillos Rd., College Plaza South.
☎ **471-6688.**
Cuisine: NORTHERN & CENTRAL CHINESE. **Reservations:** Recommended.
Prices: Lunch buffet $6.55; dinner $6.95–$25.95. AE, MC, V.
Open: Mon–Thurs 11am–9:30pm, Fri 10am–11pm. Sat–Sun 11:30am–9:30pm.

A pair of stone lions guard the ostentatious dragon-gate entrance to this Asian delight. The red-and-white decor, with a large aquarium and antique Oriental furniture, is reminiscent of a Chinese palace. The hot, spicy Hunan- and Peking-style recipes prepared by chef/owner Alex Lee are equally fascinating. Family dinners of Hunan shredded pork, sha-cha beef, and spiced chicken and shrimp include eggroll, wonton soup, fried rice, tea, and fortune cookies. Or you can order à la carte, including whole fish with hot bean sauce or Peking duck. There's a 10-dish luncheon buffet (with children's prices), and food take-out.

⭐ **Old Mexico Grill,** 2434 Cerrillos Rd., College Plaza South.
☎ **473-0338.**
Cuisine: MEXICAN. **Reservations:** Recommended for large parties.
Prices: Appetizers $2.95–$6.75; main courses $8.75–$16.95. DISC, MC, V.
Open: Lunch Mon–Fri 11:30am–3pm; dinner daily 5–9:30pm (hours extended in summer).

Here's something unique in Santa Fe: a restaurant that specializes not in northern New Mexico food, but in authentic Mexico City and regional Mexican cuisine. Servers are attentive; the centerpiece is an exhibition cooking area with an open mesquite grill and French rôtisserie where a tempting array of fajitas, tacos al carbon, and other specialties are prepared. Popular dishes include turkey mole poblano, costillas de puerro en barbacou de Oaxaca (hickory-smoked baby back ribs baked in a chipotle and mulato chile, honey, mustard barbecue sauce), shrimp in orange-lime/tequila sauce, and paella mexicana. There's a good choice of soups and salads at lunch, and a selection of homemade desserts. A full bar serves Mexican beers and margaritas, and there's a guitarist during the week.

⭐ **Steaksmith at El Gancho,** Old Las Vegas Hwy. ☎ **988-3333.**
Cuisine: STEAKS/SEAFOOD. **Reservations:** Recommended.
Prices: Appetizers $3.50–$5.75; main courses $8.95–$28.95. AE, MC, V.
Open: Dinner only, Mon–Sat 5:30–10pm, Sun 5–9pm.

Santa Fe's most highly regarded steakhouse is a 15-minute drive up the Old Pecos Trail toward Las Vegas. Guests enjoy attentive service in a pioneer atmosphere of brick walls and viga ceilings. New York sirloin, filet mignon, and other complete steak dinners are served, along with barbecued ribs and such nightly fresh seafood specials as oysters, trout, and salmon. A creative appetizer menu ranges from ceviche Acapulco to grilled pasilla peppers and beef chupadero. There are also a choice of salads, homemade desserts and bread, and a full bar and lounge that even caters to cappuccino lovers.

Szechwan Chinese Cuisine, 1965 Cerrillos Rd. ☎ **983-1558.**
Cuisine: NORTHERN CHINESE. **Reservations:** Recommended.
Prices: Lunch $4.50–$5.25; dinner $5.25–$20. MC, V.
Open: Daily 11am–9:30pm.

Spicy northern Chinese cuisine pleases the southwestern palate, a favorite here being the Peking duck, made to order with 24 hours' notice, served with traditional pancakes and plum sauce. Also excellent is the seafood platter of shrimp, scallops, crab, fish, and vegetables stir-fried in a wine sauce. Other specialties are Lake Tung Ting shrimp, sesame beef, and General Chung's chicken. Wine and Tsingtao beer from China are served.

Toushie's, 4220 Airport Rd. ☎ **473-4159.**
Cuisine: MEXICAN/AMERICAN. **Reservations:** Recommended on weekends.
Prices: Appetizers $4.25–$6.50; main courses $5.25–$8.50 at lunch, $6.95–$18.50 at dinner. AE, CB, DC, MC, V.
Open: Mon–Fri 11am–9:30pm, Sat–Sun 4–11:30pm.

Located just one block from the Villa Linda Mall, this is an oft-overlooked surprise on the south side of town. Its spacious, semicircular seating area is an ideal place to listen to the mellow dance music on Saturday nights and an intimate area in which to enjoy a relaxing meal at other times. Appetizers include escargots and sautéed mushrooms. A wide choice of main dishes features a 16-ounce T-bone steak, prime rib and baked shrimp, and coquille of sea scallops and shrimp. Regional dishes highlight the lunch menu, from menudo (Spanish-style tripe stew) to a combination plate of taco, tamale, and rolled enchilada. Children's plates are also served. A favored dessert is Toushie's Delight, a flaming sopaipilla.

Inexpensive

Blue Corn Cafe, 133 W. Water. ☎ **984-1800.**
Cuisine: NEW MEXICAN. **Reservations:** Not accepted.
Prices: Main courses $4.95–$8.25. AE, DC, DISC, MC, V.
Open: Daily 11am–11pm.

This lively, attractively decorated southwestern-style restaurant opened in 1992 and is just what downtown Santa Fe needed—great food at low prices. While you peruse the menu your waiter will bring freshly made tortilla chips to your table. While you're reading, keep in mind that the Blue Corn Cafe is known for its chiles rellenos and its burritos. The mercado burrito (a homemade flour tortilla filled with potatoes, bacon, and red or green chile and served with refried beans and blue-corn posole) is a good choice. So is the carne adovada

Greater Santa Fe Dining

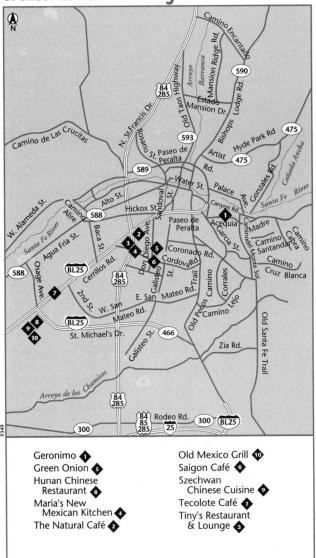

Geronimo **1**
Green Onion **5**
Hunan Chinese
  Restaurant **8**
Maria's New
  Mexican Kitchen **4**
The Natural Café **2**

Old Mexico Grill **10**
Saigon Café **6**
Szechwan
  Chinese Cuisine **9**
Tecolote Café **7**
Tiny's Restaurant
  & Lounge **3**

(marinated pork in red chile). For the more adventurous, the tortilla burger (a beef patty covered with cheeses and red or green chile, wrapped in a flour tortilla and served with chile fries) is a good bet. And those who can't decide, the combination plates will satisfy. For dessert, try the Mexican brownies, the flan, or the fried ice cream. Prices are the same at dinner as they are at lunch.

$ Bobcat Bite, Old Las Vegas Hwy. ☎ 983-5319.

Cuisine: STEAKS/BURGERS. **Reservations:** Not accepted.
Prices: $3.50–$11.95. No credit cards.
Open: Wed–Sat 11am–7:50pm.

This local classic, about five miles southeast of Santa Fe, is famed for its high-quality steaks—like the 13-ounce ribeye—and huge hamburgers, including a remarkable green-chile cheeseburger. The ranch-style atmosphere appeals to families.

Café Oasis, 526 Galisteo St. ☎ 983-9599.

Cuisine: INTERNATIONAL/NATURAL. **Reservations:** Not accepted.
Prices: Breakfast $3.75–$7.75; lunch $2.50–$7.75; dinner $6.75–$10.75. No credit cards.
Open: Sun–Thurs 9am–11:30pm, Fri–Sat 9am–1am.

Located on the corner of Paseo de Peralta and Galisteo Street, the Cafe Oasis advertises itself as "funky and elegant" in atmosphere—the kind of place "for those who want something different." It certainly lives up to its reputation, but I might call it one of the last hippie holdouts of the Southwest. Within the walls of Cafe Oasis are four rooms, each one unique in its experience. There's a "Mystical Room of blue violet," a "Smoking Room of green," a "Social Room of marigold," and a "Romantic Room." There's no fluorescent lighting here; instead there's an eclectic mix of floor and table lamps. Tables and chairs that look like great garage-sale finds come in all different shapes and sizes—there's even a couch or two. The breakfast menu is served all day and includes specialties like blue-corn huevos rancheros with red or green chile, sour cream, black beans, and rice; and Amalia's fruit-sweetened, wheat-free blue-corn silver-dollar pancakes; a stack of three large buckwheat pancakes; or cinnamon-raisin challah-bread French toast. At lunch you can begin your meal with the hummus appetizer with feta, olives, cucumbers, tomatoes, and pita, or cold sesame noodles with tahini sauce and crudités. Sandwiches come with a "side o' homies" and might include blue-corn catfish on a baguette with tartar sauce, an Oasis lamb burger with a choice of one filling or cheese, or a Cajun blackened-chicken sandwich on a honey-wheat bun with barbecue sauce. The dinner menu features full courses like blue-corn catfish with potato pancakes or yaki soba noodles simmered in ginger-soy broth topped with seasonal vegetables and fresh fish yakitori. There are daily specials available.

Corbae, 422 Old Santa Fe Trail. ☎ 983-2422.

Cuisine: ECLECTIC. **Reservations:** Recommended.
Prices: Breakfast/lunch $4.50–$9.50; dinner $6.50–$19. MC, V.
Open: Daily 7:45am–the last diners leave.

Corbae, formerly Patis Corbae, offers "seasonal eclectic" cuisine in a comfortable atmosphere. In cooler months diners are treated to the warmth of the fireplace, and in the summer the dining room extends to the outdoor patio. Lunch is served all day and includes a green-chile stew (with potatoes, pork, and mushrooms) ribboned with sour cream. As a main course, the ruby trout with corn fritters, with fresh pico de gallo salsa and pure maple syrup on the side, is an excellent choice, as is the vegetarian club (a sandwich of avocado, tomato, onions, and greens with a chipotle mayonnaise). At dinner you might like to start with the sopa de lima (shredded open-range chicken, avocado, tomato, and Mexican herbs in a savory chicken broth with a squeeze of lime) or the gazpacho. Main courses run the gamut from beef tenderloin (sautéed tenderloin medallions with shiitake mushrooms, sherry, and garlic) to citrus-marinated chicken (roasted half breast of free-range chicken served with chayote squash, zucchini, fresh corn, and couscous) and pan-roasted salmon (served with lemon, avocado, and roasted vegetables). Coffees are organically grown, and there is a large selection of freshly baked breads and desserts. The wine list is short but well selected.

$ Maria's New Mexican Kitchen, 555 W. Cordova Rd. near St. Francis Dr. ☎ 983-7929.

Cuisine: NEW MEXICAN. **Reservations:** Accepted.
Prices: Main courses $5.25–$8.95 at lunch. $5.75–$15.95 dinner. MC, V.
Open: Mon–Fri 11am–10pm, Sat–Sun noon–10pm.

Built in 1949 by Maria Lopez and her politician husband, Gilbert, the restaurant is a prime example of what charm can come from scavenging: Its bricks came from the old New Mexico State Penitentiary and most of its furniture was once used in La Fonda Hotel. The five wall frescoes in the cantina were painted by master muralist Alfred Morang (1901–58) in barter for food. Maria's boasts an open tortilla grill, where cooks can be seen making flour tortillas by hand. Generous portions are on every plate, from the award-winning beef, chicken, and vegetarian fajitas to blue-corn enchiladas, chiles rellenos, green-chile and posole stews, and huge steaks. If you're a margarita fan, this is the place to taste a variety of them—Maria's features over 40 "real margaritas," ranging in price from $3.75 to $20. Children's plates are available. Strolling mariachi troubadours perform nightly. The restaurant offers patio dining in the summer, and two fireplaces warm the dining room in winter.

The Natural Cafe, 1494 Cerrillos Rd. ☎ 983-1411.

Cuisine: CREATIVE INTERNATIONAL. **Reservations:** Recommended.
Prices: Main courses $5–$8 at lunch, $8.50–$15, at dinner. MC, V.
Open: Lunch Tues–Fri 11:30am–2:30pm; dinner Tues–Sun 5–9:30pm.

An international menu of tasty and healthy dishes is served in an artsy garden atmosphere by a competent cosmopolitan staff. Seven national cuisines—Mexican (black-bean enchiladas), Chinese (Szechuan chicken), Indian (East Indian tempeh curry), Japanese (par-broiled trout), Lebanese (hummus with pita bread), Italian (pasta of the day), and American—are represented on the menu. There are a few seafood and chicken daily specials. A children's menu is available. Homemade desserts are sweetened with maple syrup, raw sugar, or honey. Wine and beer are served.

On Lok Yuen, 3242 Cerrillos Rd. ☎ **473-4133.**
> **Cuisine:** CHINESE/AMERICAN. **Reservations:** Not accepted for Fri evenings.
> **Prices:** Lunch $2.95–$4.95; dinner $4.95–$7.95. MC, V.
> **Open:** Mon–Thurs 11am–2:30pm and 4:30–9pm, Fri–Sat 11am–9pm.

Behind the adobe walls you'll find typical Chinese-American fare—longtime favorites like beef and chicken chow mein, chop suey, egg foo yung, sweet-and-sour pork, and shrimp fried rice. Luncheon specials include soup, wonton, rice, and fortune cookie. There's a choice of several dinner combinations.

Tiny's Restaurant & Lounge, in the Penn Road Shopping Center, 1015 Penn Rd. ☎ **983-9817** or **983-1100.**
> **Cuisine:** STEAKS/NEW MEXICAN. **Reservations:** Recommended.
> **Prices:** Lunch $5–$8; dinner $6.25–$14. AE, CB, DC, MC, V.
> **Open:** Lunch Mon–Fri 11:30am–2pm; dinner Mon–Sat 6–10pm. (Bar, Mon–Sat 10pm–2am.)

A longtime favorite of Santa Feans, Tiny's first opened in 1948. It has added an elegant indoor/outdoor patio and garden room with full food and cocktail service. Steaks and shrimp complement a menu that features fajitas and northern New Mexico main courses, such as chicken and guacamole tacos. Try the house specialty, baked chicken flautas. A very popular lounge has live entertainment weekends from 9pm.

Budget

Green Onion, 1851 St. Michael's Dr. ☎ **983-5198.**
> **Cuisine:** NEW MEXICAN.
> **Prices:** Lunch $1.75–$5.25; dinner $4.50–$9. AE, MC, V.
> **Open:** Daily 11am–10pm.

The Onion offers up some of the hottest chilis and one of the liveliest local bars in Santa Fe. Roast-beef burritos and chicken enchiladas highlight an established menu that also features a selection of sandwiches and a wide variety of daily specials.

Saigon Cafe, 501 W. Cordova Rd. ☎ **988-4951.**
> **Cuisine:** VIETNAMESE/CHINESE.
> **Prices:** Lunch $3.25–$4.75; dinner $4.50–$8.95. AE, MC, V.
> **Open:** Lunch Mon–Sat 11am–2:30pm; dinner Mon–Sat 5–8:30pm.

Daily lunch buffets and low-priced dinner main courses, such as cashew chicken and eggrolls, are the fare here. The Saigon prepares orders to go and has beer and wine for those who prefer to dine in.

$ Tecolote Cafe, 1203 Cerrillos Rd. ☎ **988-1362.**
> **Cuisine:** NEW MEXICAN/AMERICAN.
> **Prices:** Main dishes $2.95–$8.95. AE, CB, DC, DISC, MC, V.
> **Open:** Tues–Sun 7am–2pm.

This is a breakfast-lovers' favorite. The decor is simple, but the food is elaborate: eggs any style, omelets, huevos rancheros, all served with fresh-baked muffins or biscuits and maple syrup. Give the atole piñon hotcakes (made with blue-corn meal) a try. Luncheon specials include carne adovada burritos and green-chile stew, served with beer or wine.

Tortilla Flats, 3139 Cerrillos Rd. ☎ **471-8685.**

> **Cuisine:** NEW MEXICAN.
> **Prices:** Breakfast $1.75–$6.25; lunch $1.25–$6.50; dinner $4.75–$9.75. DISC, MC, V.
> **Open:** Daily 7am–10pm.

This casual restaurant prides itself on its all-natural ingredients and vegetarian menu selections. It offers the likes of homemade blueberry pancakes, fajitas and eggs with a side of black beans, and blue-corn enchiladas, quesadillas, chiles rellenos, tacos, and chimichangas. Santa Fe Trail steak (eight ounces of prime ribeye smothered with red or green chiles and topped with grilled onions) and green-chile pork chops (smothered with green chiles and topped with grilled tomatoes and onions) are house specialties. Beer and wine are served, and there are a children's menu and take-out service.

4 Out of Town

A couple of very popular area restaurants take a little extra effort to get to . . . but they're worth it.

Expensive

The Evergreen, Hyde Park Rd., eight miles east of Santa Fe.
> ☎ **984-8190.**
> **Cuisine:** CONTEMPORARY CONTINENTAL. **Reservations:** Recommended.
> **Prices:** Appetizers $6.50–$8.95; main courses $14.95–$23.50. AE, CB, DC, MC, V.
> **Open:** Lunch seasonal (call for hours); dinner Fri–Sun 6–9pm; brunch Sun 11am–2:30pm.

If the views en route to the Santa Fe Ski Basin don't take your breath away, the elevation might—you're 8,400 feet up in the Sangre de Cristo range. The restaurant is nestled in a grove of spruce and pine at the entrance to Hyde Memorial State Park. Diners can enjoy an intimate candlelit atmosphere beside the fireplace or, in summer, bask in twilight on a flagstone patio.

The menu, designed by award-winning chef Jonathan Coady, features apple-wood-smoked lamb, pheasant breast, free-range beef tenderloin, black- and white-bean sausages, fresh fish, and many daily specials.

Moderate

⭐ **The Legal Tender,** Lamy. ☎ **982-8425.**
> **Cuisine:** STEAKS/SEAFOOD. **Reservations:** Recommended.
> **Prices:** Appetizers $3.95–$5.95: main courses lunch. $12.50–$22.95. DISC, MC, V.
> **Open:** Lunch daily noon–3pm; dinner Sun–Thurs 5–8:30pm, Fri–Sat 5–9pm.

About 17 miles from the Plaza, but just across the road from the old Atchison, Topeka & Santa Fe Railway station in Lamy, the Legal Tender is spectacularly faithful to the Wild West theme of the late 19th century. Built as a general store in 1881, it has gone through a lot of changes—but the Victorian decor remains. The hand-carved cherrywood bar is the same one its first owner imported from Germany. Two murals on the balcony, depicting the coming of the iron horse to the West, were commissioned for the 1916 Pan-Pacific Exposition in San Francisco. The tin ceiling of the Americana Room was from the original Hilton Hotel in San Francisco, and its drapes and chandeliers came from the presidential suite of Chicago's Sherman Hotel. Of course, the building is on the National Register of Historic Places.

The food is equally worthy of recognition. Beef, chops, and seafood highlight the menu. For lunch, diners can consider a Tender's beef sandwich, red snapper Veracruz, or Bombay chicken salad. Dinner main courses include ribeye steak, teriyaki beef kebab, quail, mountain rainbow trout, shrimp Fiji, and top sirloin and shrimp. The bar is fully licensed. During lunch on Tuesday, Thursday, and Saturday a ragtime pianist entertains, and on Friday and Saturday nights, as well as at Sunday lunch, there's country music.

To reach the Legal Tender, take I-25 North (actually southeast) toward Las Vegas, get off at Exit 290, and follow U.S. 285 south until you see the signs for the Lamy turnoff.

7

What to See & Do in Santa Fe

Best Gallery is Fenn's
Paseo de Peralto
(sculpture garden
Indian artifacts)

---

6 Palace of the Govr.
① St. Francis Cathedral
③ Museum of Fine Arts
④ Loretto Chapel
⑤ Folk Art Museum —
Canyon Rd.
(GIFTS?)

Sᴀɴᴛᴀ Fᴇ ɪs ᴏɴᴇ ᴏꜰ ᴛʜᴇ ᴏʟᴅᴇsᴛ ᴄɪᴛɪᴇs ɪɴ ᴛʜᴇ Uɴɪᴛᴇᴅ Sᴛᴀᴛᴇs ᴀɴᴅ ʜᴀs long been a center for both the creative and the performing arts, so it's not surprising that its major sights have to do with history and the arts. The Museum of New Mexico system, the art galleries and studios, the historic churches, and the Native American and Hispanic communities all warrant visits. It would be easy to spend a full week sightseeing in the city without ever heading out to any nearby attractions.

Suggested Itineraries

If You Have Two Days

For an overview, start your first day at the Palace of the Governors and, as you leave, visit the Native Americans selling their crafts and jewelry beneath the portal facing the Plaza. After lunch, take a self-guided walking tour of old Santa Fe, starting at the Plaza.

On Day 2, spend the morning at the Museum of Fine Arts and the afternoon browsing galleries, perhaps on Canyon Road.

If You Have Three Days

On your first two days, follow the outline above.

On the third day, visit the cluster of museums on Camino Lejo—the Museum of International Folk Art, the Museum of Indian Arts and Crafts, and the Wheelwright Museum of the American Indian. Then wander through the historic Barrio de Analco and spend the rest of the afternoon shopping.

If You Have Four Days or More

For the first three days, follow the outline above.

Devote your fourth day to exploring the pueblos, including San Juan Pueblo, headquarters of the Eight Northern Indian Pueblos Council, and Santa Clara Pueblo, with its Puye Cliff Dwellings.

On Day 5, go out along the High Road to Taos, with a stop at El Santuario de Chimayo, returning down the Rio Grande valley.

If you have more time, take a trip to Los Alamos, birthplace of the atomic bomb and home of the Bradbury Science Museum, and Bandelier National Monument.

1 The Top Attractions

Palace of the Governors, North Plaza. ☎ 827-6483.
Built in 1610 as the original capitol of New Mexico, the Palace has been in continuous public use longer than any other structure in the United States. Designated the Museum of New Mexico in 1909, it has become the state history museum, with an adjoining library and photo archives. Some cutaways of doors and windows show off early architecture.

A series of exhibits chronicle four centuries of New Mexico's Hispanic and American history, from the 16th-century Spanish explorations through the frontier era to modern times. Among Hispanic artifacts, there are early maps and rare hide paintings—historic chronicles on elk and buffalo hides—from the early 1700s. There's even an entire mid-19th-century chapel, with a simple, bright-colored altarpiece made in 1830 for a Taos church by folk artist José Rafael Aragón.

Governor's offices of the Mexican and 19th-century U.S. eras have been restored and preserved. Displays of artifacts from early New Mexican life include a stagecoach, an early working printing press, and a collection of *mestizajes,* portraits of early Spanish colonists detailing typical costumes of the time. Also on display are pieces from the silver service used aboard the battleship U.S.S. *New Mexico* from 1918 to 1939 and a tiny New Mexico state flag, three by four inches, that was smuggled to the moon on one of the Apollo missions.

Reminders of the Native American heritage are scant in this museum, most having been moved to the Museum of Indian Arts and Culture. Among those remaining are some ancient pottery from the Puye Plateau culture and a series of artifacts and photographs depicting a museum-sponsored study of Mayan sites in Mexico's Yucatán.

There are two shops that visitors should not miss. One is the bookstore, with one of the finest selections of art, history, and anthropology books in the Southwest. The other is the print shop and bindery, in which limited-edition works are produced on hand-operated presses.

One of the most lasting impressions Santa Fe visitors bring home is not of the museum itself, but of the Native American artisans sitting shoulder-to-shoulder beneath the long covered portal facing the Plaza. Here on the shaded sidewalk, several dozen colorfully dressed members of local Pueblo tribes, plus an occasional Navajo, Apache, or Hopi, spread their handcrafts: mainly jewelry and pottery, but also woven carpets, beadwork, and paintings. The museum's Portal Program restricts selling space to Native Americans only.

The Palace is the flagship of the Museum of New Mexico system, with head offices at 113 Lincoln Ave. (☎ 982-6366, or 827-6463 for recorded information). The system comprises five state monuments and four Santa Fe museums—the Palace of the Governors, the Museum of Fine Arts, the Museum of International Folk Art, and the Museum of Indian Arts and Culture.

Admission: $3.50 adults, free for children under 16. Two-day passes good at all four branches of the Museum of New Mexico cost $6 for those 16 and older.

Open: Jan–Feb, Tues–Sun 10am–5pm; Mar–Dec, daily 10am–5pm. **Closed:** Mon in Feb, and New Year's, Thanksgiving, and Christmas Days.

⭐ **Museum of Fine Arts,** Palace and Lincoln Ave. ☎ 827-4455. Located catty-corner from the Plaza and immediately opposite the Palace of the Governors, this was the first Pueblo Revival–style building constructed in Santa Fe, in 1917. As such, it was a major stimulus in Santa Fe's development as an art colony earlier in this century.

The museum's permanent collection of more than 8,000 works emphasizes regional art and includes landscapes and portraits by all the Taos masters and more recent works by such contemporary artists as R. C. Gorman, Amado Pena, Jr., and Georgia O'Keeffe.

The museum also has a collection of photographic works by masters such as Ansel Adams, Edward Weston, and Elliot Porter. Modern artists, many of them far from the mainstream of traditional southwestern art, are featured in temporary exhibits throughout the year. Two sculpture gardens present a range of three-dimensional art from the traditional to the abstract.

Beautiful St. Francis Auditorium, patterned after the interiors of traditional Hispanic mission churches, adjoins the art museum (see Chapter 10). A museum shop sells books on southwestern art, prints, and postcards of the collection.

Admission: $4 adults, free for children under 17. Three-day passes are available.

Open: Jan–Feb, Tues–Sun 10am–5pm; Mar–Dec, daily 10am–5pm, **Closed:** Easter Sunday and Thanksgiving, Christmas, and New Year's Days.

★ **St. Francis Cathedral,** Cathedral Place at San Francisco St. ☎ 982-5619.

Santa Fe's grandest religious structure is just a block east of the Plaza. An architectural anomaly in Santa Fe, it was built between 1869 and 1886 by Archbishop Jean-Baptiste Lamy to resemble the great cathedrals of Europe. French architects designed the Romanesque building—named after Santa Fe's patron saint—and Italian masons assisted with its construction.

The small adobe Our Lady of the Rosary chapel on the northeast side of the cathedral reflects a Spanish look. Built in 1807, it's the only parcel remaining from Our Lady of the Assumption Church, founded along with Santa Fe in 1610. The new cathedral was built over and around the old church.

A wooden icon set in a niche in the wall of the north chapel, *La Conquistadora,* "Our Lady of the Conquest," is the oldest representation of the Madonna in the United States. Rescued from the old church during the 1680 Pueblo Rebellion, it was carried back by Don Diego de Vargas on his peaceful reconquest 12 years later, thus the name. Today *La Conquistadora* plays an important part in the annual Feast of Corpus Christi in June and July.

In 1986 a $600,000 renovation project relocated an early 18th-century wooden statue of St. Francis of Assisi to the center of the altar screen. Around the cathedral's exterior are front doors featuring 16 carved panels of historic note and a plaque memorializing the 38 Franciscan friars who were martyred in New Mexico's early years. There's also a large bronze statue of Bishop Lamy himself; his grave is under the main altar of the cathedral.

Admission: Donations appreciated.

Open: Daily. Visitors may attend mass Mon–Sat at 6am, 7am, and 5:15pm, Sun at 6, 8, and 10am, noon, and 7pm.

2 More Attractions

Museums

Catholic Museum, 223 Cathedral Place. ☎ **983-3811.**

Housed in a complex of buildings that date from 1832, the Catholic Museum is one of New Mexico's newest museums, where visitors have the opportunity to learn about the development and significance of Catholicism in New Mexico. Opened in 1994 by the Archdiocese of Santa Fe, the museum houses a collection of religious relics that include a book printed by Padre Antonio José Martinez of Taos, the Lamy chalice that was given to Archbishop Lamy by Pope Pius IX in 1845, as well as the document that formally reestablished royal possession of the Villa and Capital of Santa Fe and that was signed by Diego de Vargas in 1692. There are also photographs on display that document events pertaining to the 11 archbishops of Santa Fe. The museum shop is stocked with books on New Mexico's religious history.

Admission: $1.50 adults, $1 students and seniors, free for children.

Open: Mon–Fri 8:30am–4:30pm, Sat hours vary (call ahead).

⭐ **El Rancho de las Golondrinas,** 334 Los Pinos Rd. ☎ **471-2261.**

This 200-acre ranch, about 15 miles south of the Santa Fe Plaza via I-25 (take Exit 276), was once the last stopping place on the 1,000-mile El Camino Real from Mexico City to Santa Fe. Today it's a living 18th- and 19th-century Spanish village, comprising a hacienda, a village store, a schoolhouse, and several chapels and kitchens. There's also a working molasses mill, wheelwright and blacksmith shops, shearing and weaving rooms, a threshing ground, a winery and vineyard, and four water mills, as well as dozens of farm animals. A walk around the entire property is $1^3/4$ miles in length.

Highlights of the year for Las Golondrinas ("The Swallows") are the Spring Festival (the first weekend of June) and the Harvest Festival (the first weekend of October). On these festival Sundays the museum opens with a procession and mass dedicated to San Ysidro, patron saint of farmers. Other festivals and theme weekends are held throughout the year. Authentically costumed volunteers demonstrate shearing, spinning, weaving, embroidery, wood carving, grain milling, blacksmithing, tinsmithing, soapmaking, and other activities. There's an exciting atmosphere of Spanish folk dancing, music, theater, and traditional food.

Admission: $3.50 adults, $2.50 seniors and teens, $1.50 children 5–12. Free for children under 5. Festival weekends, $5 adults, $3 seniors and teens, $2 children 5–12.

Open: June–Sept, Wed–Sun 10am–4pm; Apr–May and Oct, guided by advance arrangement. **Closed:** Nov–Mar.

Indian Art Research Center, School of American Research, 660 Garcia St., off Canyon Rd. ☎ **982-3584.**

With 10,000 objects, the center holds one of the world's best collections of Southwest Indian art. Admission, however, is highly restricted. The School of American Research, of which it is a division, was established in 1907 as a center for advanced studies in anthropology and related fields. It sponsors scholarship, academic research, publications, and educational programs.

Admission: Free for Native Americans; $15 per person for others, by appointment only.

Open: Tours given by appointment, Fri at 2pm.

Institute of American Indian Arts Museum, 108 Cathedral Place. ☎ **988-6211.**

The Institute of American Indian Arts (IAIA) is the nation's only congressionally chartered institute of higher education devoted solely to the study and practice of the artistic and cultural traditions of all American Indian and Alaska native peoples. Many of the best Native American artists of the last three decades have passed through the IAIA. Their works can often be seen as part of the many exhibitions offered at the museum throughout the year. The museum's National Collection of Contemporary Indian Art comprises painting, sculpture, ceramics, textiles, jewelry, beadwork, basketry, and graphic arts. The institute's museum is the official repository of the most comprehensive collection of contemporary Native American art in the world and has loaned items from its collection to museums all over the world. The museum presents the artistic achievements of IAIA alumni, current students, and other nationally recognized Native American and Alaskan artists.

Admission: (two-day pass); $4 adults, $2 seniors and students, free for children 16 and under.

Open: Jan–Feb, Tues–Sat 10am–5pm, Sun noon–5pm. Mar–Dec, Mon–Sat 10am–5pm, Sun noon–5pm.

⭐ **Museum of Indian Arts and Culture,** 710 Camino Lejo. ☎ **827-6344.**

Next door to the folk-art museum, this museum opened in 1987 as the showcase for the adjoining Laboratory of Anthropology. Interpretive displays detail tribal history and contemporary life-styles of New Mexico's Pueblo, Navajo, and Apache cultures. More than 50,000 pieces of basketry, pottery, clothing, carpets, and jewelry—much of it quite ancient—are on continual rotating display.

There are frequent demonstrations of traditional skills by tribal artisans and regular programs in a 70-seat multimedia theater. Native American educators run a year-round workshop that encourages visitors to try such activities as weaving and corn grinding. There also are regular performances of Native American music and dancing by tribal groups. Concession booths purvey Native American foods during summer months.

Downtown Santa Fe Attractions

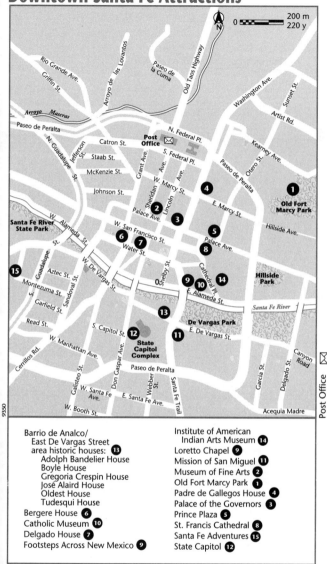

0   200 m
    220 y

Rio Grande Ave.
Griffin St.
Arroyo de las Lovantos
Paseo de la Cuma
Old Taos Highway
Washington Ave.
Sunset St.
Arroyo Mascras
Paseo de Peralta
Artist Rd.
Kearney Ave.
Catron St.
N. Federal Pl.
Post Office
S. Federal Pl.
Otero St.
Paseo de Peralta
Staab St.
Jefferson St.
N. Guadalupe St.
McKenzie St.
Grant Ave.
Sheridan Ave.
Johnson St.
W. Marcy St.
Lincoln Ave.
E. Marcy St.
4
1
Old Fort Marcy Park
2
Palace Ave.
3
Hillside Ave.
Santa Fe River State Park
W. Alameda St.
W. San Francisco St.
6
7
Palace Ave.
5
Aztec St.
Water St.
8
Montezuma St.
Guadalupe St.
W. De Vargas St.
Sandoval St.
Shelby St.
Cathedral Pl.
9
10
14
Hillside Park
Garfield St.
15
E. Alameda St.
Read St.
13
Santa Fe River
S. Capitol St.
12
De Vargas Park
11
State Capitol Complex
E. De Vargas St.
Cerrillos Rd.
W. Manhattan Ave.
Don Gaspar Ave.
Paseo de Peralta
Canyon Road
Galisteo St.
Webber St.
Garcia St.
Delgado St.
W. Santa Fe Ave.
E. Santa Fe Ave.
Santa Fe Trail
Post Office
W. Booth St.
Acequia Madre
9350

Barrio de Analco/
East De Vargas Street
area historic houses: **13**
  Adolph Bandelier House
  Boyle House
  Gregoria Crespin House
  José Alaird House
  Oldest House
  Tudesqui House
Bergere House **6**
Catholic Museum **10**
Delgado House **7**
Footsteps Across New Mexico **9**

Institute of American
Indian Arts Museum **14**
Loretto Chapel **9**
Mission of San Miguel **11**
Museum of Fine Arts **2**
Old Fort Marcy Park **1**
Padre de Gallegos House **4**
Palace of the Governors **3**
Prince Plaza **5**
St. Francis Cathedral **8**
Santa Fe Adventures **15**
State Capitol **12**

The laboratory is a point of interest in itself, an exquisite example of Pueblo Revival architecture by well-known Santa Fe architect John Gaw Meem. Since the museum opened, the lab has expanded its research and library facilities into its former display wing. It was founded in 1931 by John D. Rockefeller, Jr.

Admission: $4 adults, children under 17 free.

Open: Mar–Dec, daily 10am–5pm; Jan–Feb, Tues–Sun 10am–5pm. **Closed:** Mon in Jan and Feb, Easter Sunday, Thanksgiving, Christmas, and New Year's Day.

⭐ **Museum of International Folk Art,** 706 Camino Lejo. ☎ **827-6350.**

Excellent for Kids

This branch of the Museum of New Mexico may not seem quite as typically southwestern as other Santa Fe museums, but it's the largest of its kind in the world. With a collection of around 130,000 objects from more than 100 countries, it is my personal favorite of the city museums.

It was founded in 1953 by Chicago collector Florence Dibell Bartlett, who said: "If peoples of different countries could have the opportunity to study each others' cultures, it would be one avenue for a closer understanding between men." That's the basis on which the museum operates today.

The special collections include Spanish Colonial silver, traditional and contemporary New Mexican religious art, Mexican tribal costumes, Mexican majolica ceramics, Brazilian folk art, European glass, African sculptures, East Indian textiles, and the marvelous Morris Miniature Circus. Particularly delightful are numerous dioramas—all done with colorful miniatures—of people around the world at work and play in typical town, village, and home settings. Recent acquisitions include American weathervanes and quilts, Palestinian costume jewelry and amulets, and Bhutanese and Indonesian textiles. Children love to look at the hundreds of toys on display. About half the pieces comprise the 1982 contribution of Alexander and Susan Girard. A new wing was built to hold the vast assemblage of dolls, animals, and dioramas of entire towns.

In 1989 the museum opened a new Hispanic Heritage Wing. Folk-art demonstrations, performances, and workshops are often presented here. The 80,000-square-foot museum also has a lecture room, a research library, and a gift shop where a variety of folk art is available for purchase.

Admission: $4 adults, Free for children under 17.

Open: Jan–Feb, Tues–Sun 10am–5pm; Mar–Dec, daily 10am–5pm. **Closed:** New Year's, Thanksgiving, and Christmas Days. **Directions:** The museum is located about two miles south of the Plaza, in the Sangre de Cristo foothills: Drive southeast on Old Santa Fe Trail, which becomes Old Pecos Trail, and look for signs pointing left onto Camino Lejo.

Wheelwright Museum of the American Indian, 704 Camino Lejo. ☎ **982-4636.**

Though not member of the state museum system, the Wheelwright is often lumped in with a trip to the folk-art and Native American arts museums by virtue of its proximity—it's next door. Once known as the Museum of Navajo Ceremonial Art, it was founded in 1937 by Boston scholar Mary Cabot Wheelwright in collaboration with a Navajo medicine man, Hastiin Klah, to preserve and document Navajo ritual beliefs and practices. Klah took the designs of sand paintings used in healing ceremonies and adapted them into the woven pictographs that are a major part of the museum's treasure.

In 1976 the museum's focus was changed to include the living arts of all Native American cultures. Built of adobe in the shape of a Navajo hogan, with its doorway facing east (toward the rising sun) and its ceiling made in the interlocking "whirling log" style, it offers rotating single-subject shows of silverwork, jewelry, tapestry, pottery, basketry, and paintings. There's a permanent collection, of course, plus an outdoor sculpture garden with works by Allan Houser and other noted artisans.

In the basement is the Case Trading Post, an arts-and-crafts shop built to resemble the sort of turn-of-the-century trading post that was found on Navajo reservations. Storyteller Joe Hayes gathers listeners outside a tepee at dusk on certain days in July and August.

Admission: Free; donations appreciated.

Open: Mon–Sat 10am–5pm, Sun 1–5pm. **Closed:** New Year's, Thanksgiving, and Christmas Days.

Churches

Cristo Rey Church, Upper Canyon Rd. at Camino Cabra.
☎ 983-8528.

This Catholic church, a huge adobe structure, was built in 1940 to commemorate the 400th anniversary of Coronado's exploration of the Southwest. Parishioners did most of the construction work, even making adobe bricks from the earth where the church stands. Architect John Gaw Meem designed the building, in missionary style, as a place to keep some magnificent stone reredos (altar screens) created by the Spanish during the colonial era and recovered and restored in the 20th century.

Admission: Free.

Open: Most days; call for hours.

★ **Loretto Chapel,** at the Inn at Loretto, 211 Old Santa Fe Trail, at Water St. ☎ 984-7971.

Though no longer consecrated for worship, the Loretto Chapel is an important site in Santa Fe. Patterned after the famous Sainte-Chapelle church in Paris, it was constructed in 1873—by the same French architects and Italian masons who were building Archbishop Lamy's cathedral—as a chapel for the Sisters of Loretto, who had established a school for young ladies in Santa Fe in 1852.

The chapel is especially notable for its remarkable spiral staircase: It makes two complete 360° turns with no central or other visible support! (A railing was added later.) Legend has it that the building was nearly finished in 1878 when workers realized the stairs to the choir loft wouldn't fit. Hoping for a solution more attractive than a ladder, the sisters made a novena to St. Joseph—and were rewarded when a mysterious carpenter appeared astride a donkey and offered to build a staircase. Armed with only a saw, a hammer, and a T-square, the master constructed this work of genius by soaking slats of wood in tubs of water to curve them and holding them together with

Attractions, Accommodations & Dining in
Greater Santa Fe

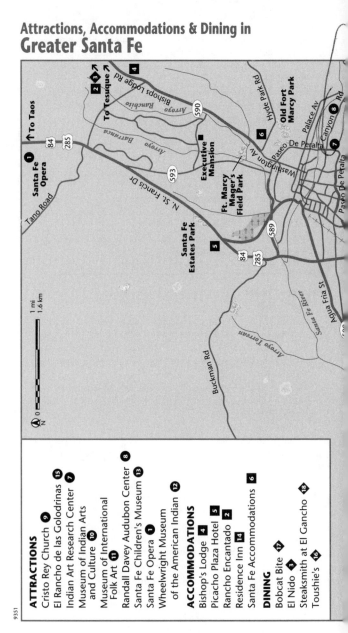

9351

wooden pegs. Then he disappeared without waiting to collect his fee.
Today the chapel is maintained by the Inn at Loretto Hotel.

Admission: $1 adults, free for children 6 and under.

Open: Daily 9am–4:30pm. Entry is through the Inn at Loretto.

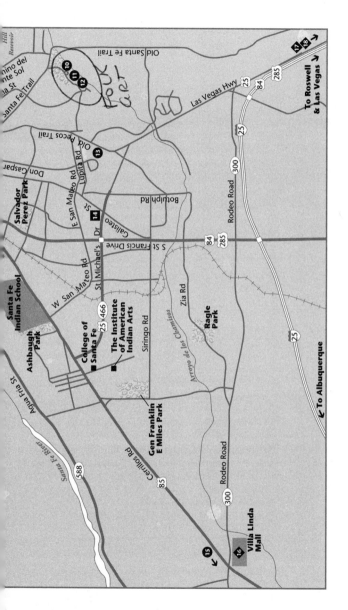

Mission of San Miguel, Old Santa Fe Trail at East De Vargas St.
☎ 983-3974.

This is one of the oldest churches in America, having been erected
within a couple of years of the 1610 founding of Santa Fe. Tlaxcala

tribe members, servants of early Spanish soldiers and missionaries, may have used fragments of a 12th-century pueblo on this site in its construction. Severely damaged in the 1680 Pueblo Revolt, it was almost completely rebuilt in 1710 and has been altered numerous times since.

Because of its design, with high windows and thick walls, the structure was occasionally used as a temporary fortress during times of attack by raiding tribes. One painting in the sanctuary has holes that, according to legend, were made by arrows.

The mission and a nearby house—today a gift shop billed as "The Oldest House," though there's no way of knowing for sure—were bought by the Christian Brothers from Archbishop Lamy for $3,000 in 1881, and the order still operates both structures. Among the treasures in the mission are the San José Bell, reputedly cast in Spain in 1356 and brought to Santa Fe via Mexico several centuries later; and a series of buffalo hides and deerskins decorated with Bible stories for Native American converts.

Admission: Free; donations appreciated.

Open: Mon–Sat 11:30am–4pm, Sun 1–4:30pm. Summer hours start earlier. Mass is said daily at 5pm.

Santuario de Nuestra Señora de Guadalupe, 100 Guadalupe St. ☎ 988-2027.

Built between 1795 and 1800 at the end of El Camino Real by Franciscan missionaries, this is believed to be the oldest shrine in the United States honoring the Virgin of Guadalupe, patroness of Mexico. Better known as Santuario de Guadalupe, the sanctuary's adobe walls are almost three feet thick, and the deep-red plaster wall behind the altar was dyed with oxblood in traditional fashion when the church was restored earlier this century.

On one wall is a famous oil painting, *Our Lady of Guadalupe,* created in 1783 by renowned Mexican artist José de Alzibar. Painted expressly for the church, it was brought from Mexico City by mule caravan.

Today administered as a museum by the nonprofit Guadalupe Historic Foundation, the sanctuary is frequently used for chamber music concerts, flamenco dance programs, dramas, lectures, and religious art shows.

Admission: Free; donations appreciated.

Open: Mon–Sat 9am–4pm, Sun noon–4pm.

Parks and Refuges

Old Fort Marcy Park, Artist Rd.

Marking the 1846 site of the first U.S. military reservation in the Southwest, this park overlooks the northeast corner of downtown. Only a few mounds remain from the fort, but the Cross of the Martyrs, at the top of a winding brick walkway from Paseo de Peralta near Otero Street, is a popular spot for bird's-eye photographs. The cross was erected in 1920 by the Knights of Columbus and the Historical Society of New Mexico to commemorate Franciscans killed in the Pueblo Revolt of 1680. It has since played a role in numerous religious processions.

Randall Davey Audubon Center, Upper Canyon Rd.
☎ 983-4609.

Named for the late Santa Fe artist who willed his home to the National Audubon Society, this wildlife refuge occupies 135 acres at the mouth of Santa Fe Canyon. More than 100 species of birds and 120 types of plants live here, and a variety of mammals have been spotted—including black bears, mule deer, mountain lions, bobcats, raccoons, and coyotes. Trails winding through more than 100 acres of the nature sanctuary are open to day hikers.

Admission: $1 donation requested.

Open: Daily 9am–5pm. House tours, sporadically during the summer; call for hours.

Santa Fe River State Park, Alameda St.

This is a lovely spot for an early-morning jog, a midday walk beneath the trees, or perhaps a sack lunch at a picnic table. The green strip follows the midtown stream for about four miles as it meanders along the Alameda from St. Francis Drive upstream beyond Camino Cabra, near its source.

Other Attractions

Footsteps Across New Mexico, at the Inn at Loretto, 211 Old Santa Fe Trail. ☎ 982-9297.

This multimedia presentation is an impressive introduction to the state. Slides, music, and a sculptured three-dimensional map combine to tell the New Mexico story from pre-Hispanic Pueblo culture to the landing of the space shuttle at White Sands. There's a fine bookstore here for browsing before or after the show.

Admission: $3.50 adults, $2.50 children 6–16, free for children 5 and under.

Open: Shows every half hour, Mon–Sat 9:30am–5pm, Sun 9:30am–4pm.

State Capitol, Paseo de Peralta and Old Santa Fe Trail. ☎ 827-4011.

Some are surprised to learn that this is the only round capitol building in America. It's also the newest. Built in 1966 in the shape of a Pueblo zia emblem, it symbolizes the Circle of Life: four winds, four seasons, four directions, and four sacred obligations. Surrounding the capitol is a lush 6 1/2-acre garden boasting more than 100 varieties of plants—roses, plums, almonds, nectarines, Russian olive trees, and sequoias among them. Benches are placed around the grounds for the enjoyment of visitors.

COOKING & ART CLASSES

If you have the time and you're looking for something to do that's a little off the beaten tourist path, take a cooking or art class.

You can master the flavors of Santa Fe with an entertaining three-hour demonstration cooking class at the ★ **Santa Fe School of Cooking**, on the upper level of the Plaza Mercado, 116 W. San Francisco St. (☎ 983-4511; fax 505/983-7540). The class discusses the flavors and history of traditional New Mexican and contemporary southwestern cuisines. Cooking-light classes are offered for those who prefer to learn how to cook with less fat. Prices start at $25 and include a meal; call for a class schedule.

The adjoining market offers a variety of regional foods and cookbooks, with gift baskets available.

If southwestern art has you hooked, you can take some drawing and painting classes led by Santa Fe artist Jane Shoenfield. Students work outdoors with subjects that include adobe architecture and the Santa Fe landscape. All experience levels are welcome. Contact Joan at **Sketching Santa Fe,** P.O. Box 5912, Santa Fe, NM 87501 (☎ **505/986-1108**).

WINE TASTINGS

If you enjoy tasting regional wines, consider visiting the wineries within easy driving distance of Santa Fe: **Balagna Winery/San Ysidro Vineyards,** 223 Rio Bravo Dr., in Los Alamos (☎ **505/672-3678**), north on U.S. 84/285 and then west on N.M. 501; **Santa Fe Vineyards,** about 20 miles north of Santa Fe on U.S. 84/285 (☎ **505/753-8100**); **Madison Vineyards & Winery,** in Ribera (☎ **505/421-8020**), about 45 miles east on I-25 North; and the **Black Mesa Winery,** 1502 N.M. 68, in Velarde (☎ toll free **800/852-MESA**), north on U.S. 84/285 to N.M. 68.

Be sure to call in advance to find out when the wineries are open for tastings and to get specific directions.

3 Cool for Kids

Don't miss taking the kids to the **Museum of International Folk Art,** where they'll love the international dioramas and the toys, or to **El Rancho de las Golondrinas,** a living Spanish Colonial village. (Both are discussed earlier in this chapter.)

Santa Fe Children's Museum, 1050 Old Pecos Trail.
☎ **989-8359.**

Designed for whole families to share, this museum offers interactive exhibits and hands-on activities in the arts, humanities, science, and technology. Special theater performances for the younger set are regularly scheduled.

Admission: $2.50 adults, $1.50 children under 12.
Open: Thurs–Sat 10am–5pm, Sun noon–5pm.

4 Organized Tours

Bus and Car Tours

Chamisa Touring Service, 2076 Calle Ensenada. ☎ **438-9656,** or toll free **800/631-TOURS.**

Chamisa's Nicholas and Sandra Cobb offer customized tours in your private car or a rental vehicle. They will plan specific tours based on your interests and at the pace you desire.

Gray Line Tours, 1330 Hickox St. ☎ **983-9491.**

The trolleylike Roadrunner departs several times daily in summer (less often than in winter) from the Plaza, beginning at 9am, for 2 ¹/₂-hour city tours. Buy tickets as you board. Daily tours to Taos, Chimayo, and Bandelier National Monument are also offered.

Rocky Mountain Tours, 1323 Paseo de Peralta. ☎ **984-1684.**

With this tour service, you can arrange a custom tour with a private guide (in your car or a four-wheel-drive vehicle) to Chaco Canyon (usually requires an overnight stay), the "Four Corners" region (usually requires two nights on the road), and other areas. River-rafting trips, hot-air-balloon flights, airplane sightseeing rides over Santa Fe, and horseback riding trips are also offered.

Walking Tours

Afoot in Santa Fe, at the Inn at Loretto, 211 Old Santa Fe Trail. ☎ **983-3701.**

Personalized 2¹/₂-hour tours begin twice daily from the Inn at Loretto.

Ghost Tours of Santa Fe, 142 Lincoln Ave. ☎ **983-0111.**

This tour visits 14 haunted places around the city, including the Staab Mansion for dinner. Walks are held nightly June through August, on weekends in April, May, September, and October. Winter tours for groups are available by appointment.

Historical Walking Tours of Santa Fe, 418 Cerrillos Rd. ☎ **984-8235.**

Three basic tours are offered several times daily, from morning to early evening.

Santa Fe Walks, at La Fonda Hotel, 100 E. San Francisco St. ☎ **983-6565,** or toll free **800/338-6877.**

Tours of 2¹/₂ hours leave twice daily in summer.

Miscellaneous Tours

Pathways Customized Tours, 161-F Calle Ojo Feliz. ☎ **982-5382.**

Don Dietz offers several planned tours, including a downtown Santa Fe walking tour, a full city tour, a trip to the cliff dwellings and native pueblos, a "Taos adventure," and a trip to Georgia O'Keeffe country; he will try to accommodate any special requests you might have. The tours mentioned above run anywhere from 1¹/₂ to 9 hours, depending on the one you choose. Don has extensive knowledge of the area's culture, history, geology, and flora and fauna, and will make the most of your precious vacation time.

Rain Parrish, 535 Cordova Rd., Suite 250. ☎ **984-8236.**

A Navajo anthropologist, artist, and freelance curator offers custom guide services focusing on cultural anthropology, Native American arts, and the history of the Native Americans of the Southwest. Ms. Parrish includes visits to local pueblo villages.

118

Recursos de Santa Fe, 826 Camino de Monte Rey. ☎ **982-9301.**

This organization is a full-service destination management company with an emphasis on custom-designed itineraries to meet the interests of any group. They'll design a custom itinerary that focuses on the archeology, art, literature, spirituality, architecture, environment, food, or history of the Southwest.

Rojo Tours & Services, Inc., 228 Old Santa Fe Trail, Suite 201. ☎ **983-8333.**

Customized private tours are arranged to pueblos, cliff dwellings, and ruins, as well as adventure travel like river rafting and horseback riding.

Santa Fe Detours, at La Fonda Hotel, 100 E. San Francisco St. ☎ **983-6565,** or toll free **800/DETOURS.**

Santa Fe's most extensive tour-booking agency panders to almost all travelers' tastes, from bus and rail tours to river rafting to backpacking and cross-country skiing.

Southwest Safaris, P.O. Box 945, Santa Fe, NM 87504. ☎ **988-4246** or toll free **800/842-4246.**

One day air/land excursions are offered from Santa Fe to Monument Valley, Grand Canyon, Canyon de Chelly, Mesa Verde, and Arches/Canyonlands.

Studio Entrada, 132 Romero. ☎ **983-8786.**

Small groups are offered personalized tours to studios of leading painters, sculptors, craftspersons, and furniture makers.

---

5 Sports & Recreation

Spectator Sports

HORSE RACING The ponies run at **The Downs at Santa Fe** (☎ **471-3311**), about 11 miles south of Santa Fe off U.S. 85, near La Cienega, from Memorial Day through September. Post time for 10-race cards is 3:30pm on Wednesday and Friday; for 12-race cards, 1:30pm on Saturday and Sunday, plus Memorial Day, the Fourth of July, and Labor Day. Admission starts at $1 and climbs depending on seating. A closed-circuit TV system shows instant replays of each race's final-stretch run and transmits out-of-state races for legal betting.

RODEO The **Rodeo de Santa Fe,** 2801 Rodeo Rd. (☎ **471-4300**), is held annually the weekend following the Fourth of July. (See "Northern New Mexico Calendar of Events," in Chapter 2, for details.)

Recreation

BALLOONING Rocky Mountain Tours, at 1323 Paseo de Peralta (☎ **984-1684,** or toll free **800/231-7238**), offers hot-air-balloon flights daily on a custom basis. Summer flights take place at dawn only, but winter flights are offered at dawn or late afternoon.

BICYCLING   Palace Bike Rentals, 409 E. Palace Ave. (☎ **984-2151**), rents mountain bikes and caters to tourists. Half-day, full-day, and weekly rentals can be arranged. Accessories, repairs, maps, and trail information are also supplied.

FISHING   Rainbow trout are the favorite fish for most high-lakes anglers: The season runs April through December. Check with the **New Mexico Game and Fish Department** (☎ 505/827-7911 for information, **827-7880** for licenses). **High Desert Angler,** 435 S. Guadalupe St. (☎ **988-7688**), specializes in fly-fishing gear.

GOLF   There are two public courses in the Santa Fe area: the 18-hole **Santa Fe Country Club,** on Airport Road (☎ **471-0601**); and the oft-praised, 18-hole **Cochiti Lake Golf Course,** 5200 Cochiti Hwy., Cochiti Lake, about 35 miles southwest of Santa Fe via I-25 and N.M. 16 and 22.

HIKING/BACKPACKING   It's hard to decide which of the 900 miles of nearby national forest trails to challenge. Three wilderness areas are especially attractive: **Pecos Wilderness,** with 223,000 acres east of Santa Fe; Dome Wilderness, 5,200 acres of rugged canyonland adjacent to Bandelier National Monument; and **San Pedro Parks Wilderness,** 41,000 acres west of Los Alamos. Information on these and other wilderness areas is available from the **Santa Fe National Forest,** 1220 St. Francis Dr. (P.O. Box 1689), Santa Fe, NM 87504 (☎ **505/988-6940**). If you're looking for company on your trek, contact the Santa Fe group of the **Sierra Club** (☎ **505/983-2703**) or **Tracks,** P.O. Box 173, Santa Fe, NM 87504 (☎ **505/982-2586**).

HORSEBACK RIDING   Trips ranging in length from a few hours to overnight can be arranged by **Galarosa Stable,** on Hwy. 41 in Galisteo (☎ **983-6565,** or toll free **800/338-6877**). Rides are also major activities at two local guest ranches: **The Bishop's Lodge** and **Rancho Encantado** (see "Santa Fe Accommodations," Chapter 5).

HUNTING   Mule deer and elk are taken by hunters in the Pecos Wilderness and Jemez Mountains, as well as occasional black bear and bighorn sheep. Wild turkey and grouse are frequently bagged in the uplands, geese and ducks at lower elevations. Check with the **New Mexico Game and Fish Department** (☎ **505/827-7911** for information, **827-7880** for licenses).

RIVER RAFTING   Although Taos is the real rafting center of New Mexico, several companies serve Santa Fe during the April to October white-water season. They include the **Southwest Wilderness Adventures,** P.O. Box 9380, Santa Fe, NM 87501 (☎ **505/ 983-7262** or toll free **800/869-7238**); **New Wave Rafting,** 107 Washington Ave. (☎ **505/984-1444**); and the **Santa Fe Rafting Co.,** 80 E. San Francisco St. (☎ **505/988-4914**).

RUNNING   Despite its elevation, Santa Fe is popular with runners and hosts numerous competitions, including the annual Old Santa Fe Trail Run on Labor Day. Fun runs begin from the Plaza on Wednesday at 6pm year-round (5:30pm in winter).

SKIING   There's something for all ability levels at the **Santa Fe Ski Area,** about 16 miles northeast of Santa Fe via Hyde Park (Ski Basin) Road. Built on the upper reaches of 12,000-foot Tesuque Peak, the area has an average annual snowfall of 225 inches and a vertical drop of 1,650 feet. Seven lifts, including a 5,000-foot triple chair and a new quad chair, serve 39 runs and 590 acres of terrain, with a total capacity of 7,300 an hour. Base facilities, at 10,350 feet, center around La Casa Mall, with a cafeteria, lounge, ski shop, and boutique. Another restaurant, Totemoff's, has a midmountain patio.

The ski area is open daily from 9am to 4pm; the season often runs from Thanksgiving to Easter, depending on snow conditions. Rates for all lifts are $35 for adults, $22 for children and seniors, free for kids under 46 inches (in their ski boots). For more information, contact the Santa Fe Ski Area, 1210 Luisa St., Suite 10, Santa Fe, NM 87505 (☎ **505/982-4429**). For 24-hour taped reports on snow conditions, call **983-9155.** The New Mexico Snophone (☎ **984-0606**) gives statewide reports.

Cross-country skiers find seemingly endless miles of snow to track in the **Santa Fe National Forest** (☎ **988-6940**). A favorite place to start is at the Black Canyon campground, about nine miles from downtown en route to the Santa Fe Ski Area. In the same area are the Borrego Trail (high intermediate) and the Norski Trail, seven miles up from Black Canyon. Basic Nordic lessons and backcountry tours are offered by Bill Neuwirth's Tracks, P.O. Box 173, Santa Fe, NM 87504 (☎ **505/982-2586**).

SPAS   A common stop for skiers coming down the mountain road from the Santa Fe Ski Area is **Ten Thousand Waves,** a Japanese-style health spa about three miles northeast of Santa Fe on Hyde Park Road (☎ **505/988-1047** or **982-9304**). This serene retreat, nestled in a grove of piñon, offers hot tubs, saunas, and cold plunges, plus a variety of massage and other bodywork techniques.

Bathing suits are optional in the 10-foot communal hot tub, where you can stay as long as you want for $12. Nine private hot tubs cost $15 to $20 an hour, with discounts for seniors and children. You can also get therapeutic massage, hot-oil massage, in-water watsu massage, herbal wraps, and salt glows. The spa is open on Sunday, Monday, Wednesday, and Thursday from 10am to 10pm; on Tuesday from 4:30 to 10pm; and on Friday and Saturday from 10am to 11:30pm. Reservations are recommended, especially on weekends.

SWIMMING   The City of Santa Fe operates four indoor pools and one outdoor pool. Nearest downtown is the **Fort Marcy Complex** (☎ **984-6725**) on Camino Santiago off Bishop's Lodge Road. Admission is $1.75 for adults, $1.25 for students, and 75¢ for children 8 to 13.

TENNIS   Santa Fe has 27 public tennis courts and four major private facilities. The City Recreation Department (☎ **984-6862**) can locate all indoor, outdoor, and lighted public courts.

8

Strolling Around Santa Fe

Sᴀɴᴛᴀ Fᴇ ʟᴇɴᴅs ɪᴛsᴇʟꜰ ᴛᴏ ᴡᴀʟᴋɪɴɢ. Tʜᴇ ᴄɪᴛʏ's ʜɪsᴛᴏʀɪᴄ ᴅᴏᴡɴᴛᴏᴡɴ core extends only a few blocks in any direction from the Plaza, and the ancient Barrio de Analco and the Canyon Road artists' colony are a mere stone's throw away.

Walking Tour 1
The Plaza Area

[handwritten: Georgia O'Keefe Museum near here]

Start   The Plaza.
Finish   Loretto Chapel.
Time   One to five hours, depending on how long you spend in the museums and churches.
Best Times   Any morning after breakfast, before the afternoon heat but after the native traders have spread their wares.

[handwritten: all of this is interesting]

1. **The Plaza** has been the heart and soul of Santa Fe since it was established with the city in 1610. Originally designed as a meeting place, it has been the location of innumerable festivals and other historical, cultural, and social events, and for many years it was a dusty hive of activity as the staging ground and terminus of the Santa Fe Trail. Today those who sit around its central fountain are afforded the best people-watching in New Mexico.

    Facing the Plaza on its north side is the:

2. **Palace of the Governors,** continually operated as a public building since it was built in 1610 as the capitol of Nuevo Mexico. Today it's the flagship of the New Mexico State Museum system (see "The Top Attractions," in Chapter 7). Native American artisans spread their crafts for sale beneath its portico daily.

    Immediately opposite the Palace, at Lincoln and Palace Avenues, is the:

3. **Museum of Fine Arts,** with its renowned St. Francis Auditorium (see "The Top Attractions" in Chapter 7, and "The Performing Arts," in Chapter 10). The works of Georgia O'Keeffe and other famed Taos and Santa Fe artists of the 20th century are a highlight of a visit here. The building is a fine model of Pueblo Revival–style architecture.

    Virtually across the street is the:

4. **Delgado House,** 124 W. Palace Ave., an 1890 Victorian mansion that now belongs to the Historic Santa Fe Foundation.

    If you continue west on Palace past numerous small shops and restaurants, you'll see a narrow lane—Burro Alley—cutting south toward San Francisco Street. Turn right on Grant Street to the:

5. **Tully House,** 136 Grant Ave., built in 1851 in Territorial style. This is the headquarters of the Historic Santa Fe Foundation. (A publication of the foundation, *Old Santa*

Walking Tour–The Plaza Area

Fe Today, gives detailed descriptions, with a map and
photos, of 50 sites within walking distance of the Plaza.)
  Across the street is the:

6. **Bergere House,** 135 Grant Ave., built around 1870. It
hosted U.S. Pres. Ulysses S. Grant and his wife, Julia,
during an 1880 visit to Santa Fe.

Proceed north on Grant, turning right on Marcy. On the north side of this corner is the Sweeney Convention Center, host of major exhibitions and home of the Santa Fe Convention and Visitors Bureau.

Three blocks farther east, through a residential, office, and restaurant district, turn left on Washington Avenue. A short distance on your right, note the:

7. Padre de Gallegos House, 227-237 Washington Ave., built in 1857 in the Territorial style. It now houses the Santacafé restaurant (see Chapter 6). Padre de Gallegos was a priest who, in the eyes of newly arrived Archbishop Jean-Baptiste Lamy, kept too high a social profile and was defrocked in 1852. Gallegos later represented the territory in Congress and eventually became the federal superintendent of Native American affairs.

Reverse course and turn south again on Washington Avenue, passing en route the public library and some handsomely renovated accommodations—the Territorial Inn and the Plaza Real. On your right is the entrance to the Palace of the Governors' archives. As you approach the Plaza, turn left (east) on Palace Avenue. A short distance on your left is:

8. Prince Plaza, 113 E. Palace Ave., a former governor's home. This Territorial-style structure, which now quarters the Shed restaurant, had huge wooden gates to keep out tribal attacks.

Next door is:

9. Sena Plaza, 125 E. Palace Ave. This city landmark offers a quiet respite from the busy streets with its parklike patio. La Casa Sena restaurant is the primary occupant of what was once the 31-room Sena family adobe hacienda, built in 1831. The Territorial legislature met in the upper rooms of the hacienda in the 1890s (see Chapter 6).

Turn right (south) on Cathedral Place to enter the doors of:

10. St. Francis Cathedral, built in Romanesque style between 1869 and 1886 by Archbishop Lamy. Santa Fe's grandest religious edifice, it contains a famous 17th-century wooden Madonna known as *La Conquistadora* (see "The Top Attractions," in Chapter 7).

After leaving the cathedral, walk around the back side of the illustrious La Fonda Hotel—south on Cathedral Place and west on Water Street—to the intersection of the Old Santa Fe Trail. Here, in the northwest corner of the Best Western Inn at Loretto, you'll find the:

11. Loretto Chapel, more properly known as the Chapel of Our Lady of Light. Lamy was also behind the construction of this chapel, built for the Sisters of Loretto. It is remarkable for its spiral staircase that has no central or other visible support (see "More Attractions," in Chapter 7).

Walking Tour 2
Barrio de Analco/Canyon Road

Start   Don Gaspar Avenue and East De Vargas Street.
Finish   Any one of the quaint restaurants on Canyon Road.
Time   One to three hours, depending on how long you dawdle in the art galleries.
Best Time   Anytime.

The Barrio de Analco, now East De Vargas Street, is beyond question one of the oldest continuously inhabited avenues in the United States. Spanish colonists and their Mexican–Native American servants built homes here in the early 1600s, when Santa Fe was founded, and some of them survive to this day.

Most of the houses you'll see as you walk east on De Vargas are private residences, not open for inspection inside. But they are well worth the exterior look for the feeling of Santa Fe life of bygone days that they import. Most have interpretive historical plaques on their outer walls. The first you'll see is:

1.   **Tudesqui House,** 129 E. De Vargas St., dating from the early 19th century, now recognizable for the wisteria growing over its adobe walls.

Across the street is the:

2.   **Gregoria Crespin House,** 132 E. De Vargas St., whose records date back at least to 1747 (when it was sold for 50 pesos). Originally of pueblo design, it later had Territorial embellishments added in the trim of bricks along its roofline.

Just down the road is the:

3.   **Santa Fe Community Theatre,** 142 E. De Vargas St., home of the oldest existing thespian group in New Mexico. Actors still perform in this original adobe theater (see "The Performing Arts," in Chapter 10).

In the next block, just east of the Old Santa Fe Trail, is the:

4.   **Mission of San Miguel,** built about 1612 and certainly one of the oldest churches in America (see "More Attractions," in Chapter 7). Today it's maintained and operated by the Christian Brothers.

Across De Vargas Street is the so-called:

5.   **Oldest House in the U.S.A.** Whether it is or not is anybody's guess, but it's among the last of the poured-mud adobe houses and may have been built by Pueblo people. It's sad that modern graffiti has defiled some interior walls. Entrance is through a gift shop.

Walking Tour–Barrio de Analco/Canyon Road

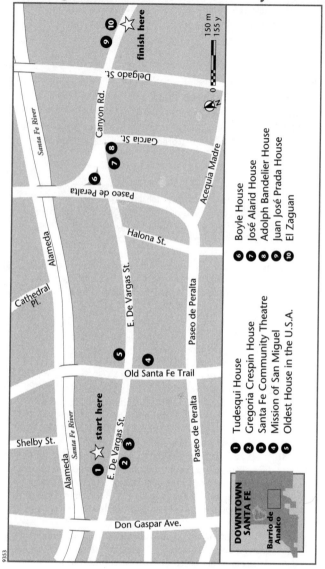

★ finish here

10 El Zaguan
9 Juan José Prada House
8 Adolph Bandelier House
7 José Alarid House
6 Boyle House

1 Tudesqui House
2 Gregoria Crespin House
3 Santa Fe Community Theatre
4 Mission of San Miguel
5 Oldest House in the U.S.A.

Delgado St.
Canyon Rd.
Garcia St.
Acequia Madre
Santa Fe River
Paseo de Peralta
Halona St.
Alameda
Cathedral Pl.
E. De Vargas St.
Old Santa Fe Trail
Paseo de Peralta
Paseo de Peralta
★ start here
E. De Vargas St.
Shelby St.
Alameda   Santa Fe River
Don Gaspar Ave.

150 m
155 y
0

N

DOWNTOWN
SANTA FE

Barrio de
Analco

9353

There are more homes at the east end of De Vargas, before its junction with Canyon Road. Among them is the:

6. Boyle House, 327 E. De Vargas St., built in the mid-18th century as a hacienda.

Nearby is the:

7. **José Alarid House,** 338 E. De Vargas St., built in the 1830s and now an art gallery.

A few houses down the road is the:

8. **Adolph Bandelier House,** 352 E. De Vargas St., home of the famous archeologist who unearthed the prehistoric ruins at Bandelier National Monument.

De Vargas intersects narrow, winding Canyon Road after crossing the Paseo de Peralta. Extending about two miles from the Paseo to Camino Cabra, this quaint road today is lined with art galleries, shops, and restaurants. But it was once a Native American trail down which Pueblo tribes came to launch their 1680 insurrection against the Spanish colonists. Historic buildings include the:

9. **Juan José Prada House,** 519 Canyon Rd., which dates from about 1760.

Farther up the road is:

10. **El Zaguan,** a hacienda at 545 Canyon Rd.

9

Santa Fe Shopping

1. Canyon Rd. Stores
2. Square Stores

* art - furniture

For traditional Native American crafts to Hispanic folk art to abstract contemporary works, Santa Fe is the place to shop. Galleries speckle the downtown area, and Canyon Road is well known as an artists' thoroughfare. Of course, the greatest concentration of Native American crafts is displayed beneath the portal of the Palace of the Governors. And any serious arts aficionado will try to attend one or more of the city's great arts festivals—the Spring Festival of the Arts in May, the Spanish Market in July, the Indian Market in August, and the Fall Festival of the Arts in October.

1   The Shopping Scene

Few visitors to Santa Fe leave the city without having bought at least one item—and often several—from the Native American artisans at the Palace of the Governors. In considering purchases, keep the following pointers in mind:

Silver jewelry should have a harmony of design, clean lines, and neatness in soldering. Navajo jewelry typically features large stones, with designs shaped around the stone. Zuni jewelry usually has patterns of small or inlaid stones. Hopi jewelry rarely uses stones, instead displaying a motif incised into the top layer of silver and darkened.

Turquoise of a deeper color is usually higher quality, so long as it hasn't been color treated. Heishi bead necklaces usually use stabilized turquoise.

Pottery is traditionally hand-coiled and of natural clay, not thrown on a potter's wheel using commercial clay. It is hand-polished with a stone, hand-painted, and fired in an outdoor oven rather than an electric kiln. Look for an even shape; clean, accurate painting; a high polish (if it is a polished piece); and an artist's signature.

Navajo rugs are appraised according to tightness and evenness of weave, symmetry of design, and whether natural (preferred) or commercial dyes have been used.

Kachina dolls are more highly valued according to the detail of their carving: fingers, toes, muscles, rib cages, feathers, etc. Elaborate costumes are also desirable. Oil staining is preferred to the use of bright acrylic paints.

Sand paintings should display clean narrow lines, even colors, balance, an intricacy of design, and smooth craftsmanship.

Local museums, particularly the Wheelwright Museum and the Institute of American Indian Art, can give a good orientation to contemporary craftsmanship.

Contemporary artists are mainly painters, sculptors, ceramicists, and fiber artists, including weavers. Peruse one of the outstanding **catalogs** that introduce local galleries—*The Collector's Guide to Santa Fe & Taos* by Wingspread Incorporated (P.O. Box 13566, Albuquerque, NM 87192), *Santa Fe & Taos Arts* by The Book of Santa Fe (535 Cordova Rd., Suite 241, Santa Fe, NM 87501), or *The Santa Fe Catalogue* by Modell Associates (P.O. Box 1007, Aspen, CO

81612). They're widely distributed at shops or can be ordered directly from the publishers.

An outstanding introduction to Santa Fe art and artists is the personalized studio tours offered by ✪ **Studio Entrada,** P.O. Box 4934, Santa Fe, NM 87502 (☎ **983-8786**). For $100 for two people, director Linda Morton takes small groups into private studios to meet the artists and learn about their work. Each itinerary lasts about 2¹/₂ hours, and includes two or three studio gallery visits.

Business hours vary quite a bit between establishments, but nearly everyone is open *at least* Monday through Friday from 10am to 5pm, with mall stores open until 9pm. Most shops are open similar hours on Saturday; and many are also open on Sunday afternoon during the summer. Winter hours are often more limited.

2 Shopping A to Z

Antiques

Scarlett's Antique Shop & Gallery, 225 Canyon Rd. ☎ **983-7092.**
Early American antiques, fine crystal, vintage jewelry, H. Koller Native American portraits, and Vi Andrews leather.

William R. Talbot Fine Art, 129 W. San Francisco St. ☎ **982-1559.**
Antique maps, natural-history paintings and prints.

Susan Tarman Antiques & Fine Art, 923 Paseo de Peralta. ☎ **983-2336.**
Seventeenth- to 19th-century American, Oriental, and European furniture, porcelain, silver, and paintings.

Art

Blue Door Art & Antiques, 300 Garcia. ☎ **983-9635.**
Specializes in decorative arts, furniture, and antiques as well as painting and sculpture by contemporary artists.

Bobby's Plaza Gallery, 233 Canyon Rd. ☎ **989-7193.**
Beautiful kachinas, Native American, New Mexican, and Mexican artworks. Represents artists E. J. Predika, Leroy Metzgar, Marsha Howe, Ann Marie Eastburn, Cruz Flores, Napoleon Montoya, O. T. Bonnet, and Lloyd Pinay. Also featured are antiques and garden sculpture.

Glenn Green Galleries, 50 E. San Francisco St. ☎ **988-4168.**
Exclusive representatives for Allan Houser, bronze and stone sculptures. Paintings, prints, and photographs, and jewelry by other important artists.

Horwitch Lewallen Gallery, 129 W. Palace Ave. ☎ **988-8997.**
Contemporary art gallery exhibiting works done on canvas and paper; sculpture in stone, bronze, and glass; ceramics; southwestern folk art; and jewelry by Native American and contemporary southwestern jewelers.

Chuck Jones Showroom–Animation Gallery, 135 W. Palace Ave., Suite 203. ☎ **983-5999.**

A comprehensive representation of animation artwork from Warner Bros. director Chuck Jones. Original production cels, lithographs, sculpture, drawings, and limited editions.

Alan Kessler, 836 Canyon Rd. ☎ **986-0123.**

Fine-quality antique Native American art of the Plains, Southwest, Woodlands, and Northwest Coast peoples. Also featured are beadwork, historic kachinas, and Southwest pottery.

Adieb Khadoure Fine Art, 610 Canyon Rd. ☎ **820-2666.**

This is a working artist's studio with contemporary artist Hal Larsen and Santa Fe artist Phyllis Kapp. Works are shown in the gallery daily from 10am to 6pm, and Adieb Khadoure also features beautiful rugs from around the world.

★ **Nedra Matteucci's Fenn Galleries,** 1075 Paseo de Peralta. ☎ **982-4631.**

Excellent gallery

Early Taos and Santa Fe painters; classic American impressionism, historical western, modernism, as well as contemporary southwestern landscapes and sculpture, including monumental pieces displayed in the sculpture garden.

Leonor & Ernesto Mayans Galleries, 601 Canyon Rd. ☎ **983-8068.**

Twentieth-century American and Latin American paintings, photography, prints, and sculpture.

Linda McAdoo Gallery, 503 Canyon Rd. ☎ **983-7182.**

Nationally known artists are represented here, with an emphasis on impressionistic and realistic works.

★ **Owings-Dewey Fine Art,** 74 E. San Francisco St. ☎ **982-6244.**

Nineteenth- and 20th-century American art, including works by Georgia O'Keeffe, Charles Russell, Robert Henri, and Andrew Dasburg.

★ **Gerald Peters Gallery,** 439 Camino del Monte Sol. ☎ **988-8961.**

Taos School and other classical artists; modern oils and watercolors.

Photography: Platinum Plus, Inc., 943 Canyon Rd. ☎ **982-8920.**

The world's first gallery to specialize in platinum prints. Works by such 19th- and 20th-century masters as Emerson, Evans, Curtis, Strand, Weston, Bravo, Horst, and Mapplethorpe. This is a wonderful gallery!

Rettig y Martinez Gallery, 901 W. San Mateo Rd. ☎ **983-4640.**

Contemporary American and Mexican art; monumental works of sculpture in outdoor sculpture gardens. Represents Garo Antreasian, Enrique Bostelmann, Carol Brown, Bob Haosous, Russell Hamilton, Susan Contreras, and Sebastian. Also works by Cuevas, Felguerez, Rojo, and Toledo.

Rio Grande Gallery, 80 E. San Francisco St. ☎ **983-2458.**
Exclusive representation of R. C. Gorman lithographs, bronzes, and originals.

Santa Fe East, 200 Old Santa Fe Trail. ☎ **988-3103.**
Across from the Loretto Chapel, this gallery has some great museum-quality artwork, including sculpture, pottery, paintings, and one-of-a-kind pieces of jewelry.

★ **Shidoni Foundry and Gallery,** Bishop's Lodge Rd., Tesuque. ☎ **988-8001.**
Sculpture garden, with bronze castings; foundry tour available.

Sigel & Sigel Fine Art, 403 Canyon Rd. ☎ **983-3348.**
Specializes in limited-edition prints by Georgia O'Keeffe and Eyvind Earle, as well as lithographs of O'Keeffe drawings from 1915. Represents contemporary artists like Warhol, Haring, Peter Max, Thomas McKnight, Erté, and Jennifer Markes. There's always an exhibit of local artists as well.

Summerfield Gallery, 1512 Paseo de Peralta. ☎ **820-1427.**
Contemporary art including paintings, sculpture, and an outdoor art garden.

Wadle Galleries, Ltd., 128 W. Palace Ave. ☎ **983-9219.**
Fine southwestern art, including paintings, bronzes, pottery, folk art, and traditional as well as contemporary jewelry.

Wilson Woodrow Fine Arts, 319 Road St. ☎ **983-2444.**
High-profile Taos and Santa Fe artists, plus modern impressionist and realist works.

Books

Caxton Books & Maps, 216 W. San Francisco St. ☎ **982-6911.**
A major downtown bookstore, its collection includes a wide choice of regional works, art books, music, and maps.

★ **Footsteps Across New Mexico,** at the Inn at Loretto, 211 Old Santa Fe Trail. ☎ **982-9297.**
The bookstore here specializes only in works about New Mexico and the Southwest. Visitors can also learn a bit about New Mexico history in the historical theater.

Horizons, 328 S. Guadalupe St. ☎ **983-1554.**
Children's books, travel, natural sciences, outdoor guides, and maps.

Margolis & Moss, 129 W. San Francisco St. ☎ **982-1028.**
Rare books, maps, photographs, and prints.

Parker Books of the West, 142 W. Palace Ave. ☎ **988-1076.**
New and out-of-print works on western history and fiction.

Nicholas Potter, Bookseller, 203 E. Palace Ave. ☎ **983-5434.**
Used and rare hardcover books.

Santa Fe Bookseller, 203 W. San Francisco St. ☎ **983-5278.**
New and out-of-print art books.

Crafts

⭐ **Joshua Baer & Company,** 116 E. Palace Ave. ☎ **988-8944.**
Nineteenth-century Navajo blankets, pottery, jewelry, and tribal art.

Cristof's, 106 W. San Francisco St. ☎ **988-9881.**
Fine contemporary Navajo weavings and jewelry.

Davis Mather Folk Art Gallery, 141 Lincoln Ave. ☎ **983-1660.**
New Mexican animal wood carvings, as well as folk and Hispanic arts.

Gallery 10, 225 Canyon Rd. ☎ **983-9707.**
Museum-quality pottery, weavings, basketry, and contemporary painting.

Kania-Ferrin Gallery, 662 Canyon Rd. ☎ **982-8767.**
Fine Native American baskets, pottery, jewelry, textiles, beadwork, santos, retablos, and Oceanic art and artifacts.

⭐ **Nambe Mills, Inc.,** 924 Paseo de Peralta, at Canyon Rd.
☎ **988-5528.**
An exquisite alloy is sand-cast and handcrafted to create cooking, serving, and decorating pieces. Also at Plaza Mercado, 112 W. San Francisco St. (☎ **988-3574**), and 216 Paseo del Pueblo Norte (Yucca Plaza), Taos (☎ **758-8221**).

Prairie Edge, in El Centro Mall, 102 E. Water St. ☎ **984-1336.**
Plains tribal art, artifacts, and jewelry.

Streets of Taos, 200 Canyon Rd. ☎ **983-8268.**
Navajo rugs, Pueblo jewelry, pottery, and baskets.

Fashions

Origins, 135 W. San Francisco St. ☎ **988-2323.**
Wearable art, folk art, work of local designers, as well as imports and jewelry.

Santa Fe Fiesta Fashions, 651 Cerrillos Rd. ☎ **983-1632.**
Designer and manufacturer of traditional southwestern wear for the entire family since 1969 by Lindee. Also local handcrafted Native American accessories.

Santa Fe Pendleton, 53 Old Santa Fe Trail. ☎ **983-5855.**
Native American trade blankets and men's and women's apparel.

Three Sisters, at the Inn at Loretto, 211 Old Santa Fe Trail.
☎ **988-5045.**
Casual southwestern clothing and fiesta ribbon shirts.

Furniture

Southwest Spanish Craftsmen, 328 S. Guadalupe St.
☎ **982-1767.**
Spanish Colonial and Spanish provincial furniture, doors, and home accessories.

Taos Furniture, 232 Galisteo St. ☎ **988-1229.**

Classic southwestern furnishings handcrafted in solid Ponderosa pine, both contemporary and traditional pieces.

Gifts and Souvenirs

El Nicho, 227 Don Gaspar Ave. ☎ **984-2830.**

Handcrafted folk art, including kachinas, jewelry, tiles, and drums.

Wharton's Crafted Gifts, in the De Vargas Center Mall, N. Guadalupe St. and Paseo de Peralta. ☎ **983-3066.**

Native crafts including kachinas, sand paintings, and jewelry; also art supplies and glass blowing.

Jewelry

Mineral & Fossil Gallery of Santa Fe, 127 W. San Francisco St. ☎ **984-1682.**

Fossils, meteorites, and lapidary items.

James Reid Ltd., 114 E. Palace Ave. ☎ **988-1147.**

Gold and silver jewelry and buckle sets, antique American and Native American art, contemporary furniture and paintings, and folk sculpture.

Malls and Shopping Centers

De Vargas Center Mall, N. Guadalupe St. and Paseo de Peralta. ☎ **982-2655.**

Over 55 merchants and restaurants are in this mall just northwest of downtown. Open Monday through Thursday from 10am to 7pm, on Friday from 10am to 9pm, on Saturday from 10am to 6pm, and on Sunday from noon to 5pm.

Sanbusco Market Center, 500 Montezuma St. ☎ **983-9136.**

Unique shops and restaurants occupy this remodeled warehouse near the old Santa Fe Railroad Yard. There's a farmers market in the south parking lot. Open from 7am to noon on Tuesday and Saturday in summer.

Villa Linda Mall, 4250 Cerrillos Rd. at Rodeo Rd. ☎ **473-4253.**

Santa Fe's largest mall, including department stores, is near the southwestern/city limits, not far from the I-25 on-ramp. Open Monday through Friday from 10am to 9pm, on Saturday from 10am to 6pm, and on Sunday from noon to 5pm.

Markets

Santa Fe Traders Market, 1241 Siler Rd. ☎ **438-0011.**

This huge indoor flea market, offering new and antique goods, is open Friday through Sunday from 10:30am to 5:30pm.

Wines

The Winery, 500 Montezuma St. ☎ **982-WINE.**

Perhaps the most extensive wine shop in New Mexico, it carries gourmet foods and beers and gift baskets, and it publishes a monthly newsletter.

10

Santa Fe Nights

Santa Fe is a city committed to the arts. Its night scene is dominated by high-brow cultural events, with the club and music scene running a distant second.

Full information on all major cultural events can be obtained from the **Santa Fe Convention and Visitors Bureau** (☎ **505/984-6760**, or toll free **800/777-CITY**) or from the City of **Santa Fe Arts Commission** (☎ **505/984-6707**). Current listings can be found in Friday's "Pasatiempo" edition of *The New Mexican,* Santa Fe's daily newspaper, and in the *Santa Fe Reporter,* published weekly on Wednesday.

The **Galisteo News & Ticket Center,** 201 Galisteo St. (☎ **984-1316**), is the primary outlet for tickets to the opera and other major entertainment events. **Nicholas Potter, Bookseller,** 203 E. Palace Ave. (☎ **983-5434**), also has tickets to select events. You can order by phone from **TicketMaster** (☎ **842-5387** for information, **884-0999** to order). Discount tickets may be available on the nights of performances; the opera, for example, makes standing-room tickets available at a greatly reduced rate just one hour ahead of time.

A variety of free concerts, lectures, and other events are presented in the summer, cosponsored by the City of Santa Fe and the chamber of commerce under the name **Santa Fe Summerscene.** From mid-June through August, on Tuesday and Thursday at noon and 6pm, they are held on the Plaza or in Fort Marcy Park, and run the gamut from light opera to blues, jazz, Cajun, and bluegrass to hot salsa and New Mexican folk music. Call **983-7317** for more information.

The **Santa Fe Summer Concert Series,** at Paolo Soleri Outdoor Amphitheatre on the Santa Fe Indian School campus on Cerrillos Road, has brought such name performers as Frank Zappa, Kenny Loggins, and B. B. King to the city. More than two dozen concerts and special events are scheduled each summer.

Note: Many companies listed here perform at locations other than their headquarters, so check the site of the performance you plan to attend.

---

1 The Performing Arts

No fewer than 24 performing-arts groups flourish in Santa Fe. Many of these groups perform year-round, but others are active only seasonally. The internationally acclaimed Santa Fe Opera, for instance, has a two-month summer season: July and August.

Major Performing-Arts Companies

OPERA & CLASSICAL MUSIC

★ **Santa Fe Opera,** P.O. Box 2408, Santa Fe, NM 87504. ☎ **986-5955,** or **986-5900** for tickets.

Even if your visit isn't timed to coincide with the opera season, you shouldn't miss seeing its open-air amphitheater. Located on a wooded hilltop seven miles north of the city off U.S. 84/285, the sweeping curves of this serene structure seem perfectly attuned to the contour of the surrounding terrain. At night, the lights of Los Alamos can be seen in the distance under clear skies.

Many rank the Santa Fe Opera second only to the Metropolitan Opera of New York as the finest company in the United States today. Established in 1957 by John Crosby, still the opera's artistic director, it consistently attracts famed conductors, directors, and singers, the list of whom has included Igor Stravinsky. At the height of the season the company is 500 strong, including the skilled craftspeople and designers who work on the sets.

The opera is noted for its performances of great classics, little-known works by classical European composers, and American premières of 20th-century works.

The nine-week, 40-performance opera season runs from the first week in July through the last week in August. All performances begin at 9pm.

Tours: First Mon in July to last Fri in Aug, Mon–Sat at 1pm; $8 adults, free for children 15 and under.

Admission: Tickets, $19, $34, $50, $60, $71, $96 Mon–Thurs; $25, $40, $56, $66, $77, $102 Fri–Sat; wheelchair seating, $14 Mon–Thurs, $20 Fri–Sat; standing room (sold on day of performance beginning at 10am), $6 Mon–Thurs, $8 Fri–Sat, $15 Opening Night Gala.

Orchestral and Chamber Music

Ensemble of Santa Fe, P.O. Box 8427, Santa Fe, NM 87504. ☎ 984-2501.

The Ensemble is a professional chamber-music group composed of leading musicians from the western United States and guests of national and international acclaim. The Ensemble performs monthly public concerts from October through May in the historic Loretto Chapel and the Santuario de Guadalupe. Christmas and Holy Week concerts sell out in advance.

Admission: Tickets, $12–$20.

Orchestra of New Mexico, 111 Guadalupe St. (P.O. Box 2091), Santa Fe, NM 87504. ☎ 988-4640.

Founded in 1974, this chamber orchestra is best known for its holiday production of Handel's *Messiah* and its January-February Bach

---

The Major Concert and Performance Halls

Center for Contemporary Arts, 291 E. Barcelona Rd. (☎ 982-1338).

St. Francis Auditorium at the Museum of Fine Arts, Lincoln and Palace Avenues (☎ 827-4455).

Sweeney Convention Center, Marcy and Grant Streets (☎ 984-6760)

or Mozart festivals. In all, it offers 15 mostly classical (some pops, one baroque) concerts a year, between mid-September and early May.

All regular concert performances are at the Lensic Theatre, 211 W. San Francisco St. This early 20th-century Spanish Colonial–style theater, otherwise an 850-seat United Artists cinema, has a state-of-the-art acoustical sound shell installed in 1989. Noon lectures are given five times a season each at the St. Francis Auditorium and in Los Alamos.

Admission: Tickets, $6–$27 (five seating categories); students pay half price. Ask about the Sunday family-saver package.

★ **Santa Fe Symphony Orchestra and Chorus,** P.O. Box 9692, Santa Fe, NM 87504. ☎ **983-3530.**

This 60-piece professional symphony orchestra has grown rapidly in stature since its founding in 1984. Matinee and evening performances of classical and popular works are presented in a subscription series at Sweeney Center from August to May. There's a preconcert lecture before each performance. During the spring there are music festivals and in the fall there are free concerts in the park (call for details).

Admission: Tickets, $12–$30 (six seating categories).

Serenata of Santa Fe, P.O. Box 5771, Santa Fe, NM 87502. ☎ **989-9258.**

This professional chamber-music group specializes in bringing the lesser-known works of the masters to the concert stage. Four or five concerts are presented from September to May at the Santuario de Guadalupe, 100 Guadalupe St. Call the number above or the Santuario (☎ **988-2027**) for dates and details.

Tickets: $10 general admission, $15 reserved seats.

Choral Groups

Desert Chorale, 219 Shelby St. (P.O. Box 2813), Santa Fe, NM 87501. ☎ **988-7505,** or toll free **800/244-4011.**

This 24- to 30-member vocal ensemble, New Mexico's only professional choral group, recruits members from all over the country. It's nationally recognized for its eclectic blend of both Renaissance melodies and modern avant-garde compositions. During the summer months the chorale performs both Classic concerts at the historic Santuario de Guadalupe and the St. Francis Auditorium, as well as smaller cameo concerts in more intimate settings throughout Santa Fe and Albuquerque. The chorale also performs a popular series of Christmas concerts during the month of December. Most concerts begin at 8pm (3 or 6pm on Sunday).

Admission: Tickets, $18–$32 adults; half price for students.

Sangre de Cristo Chorale, P.O. Box 4462, Santa Fe, NM 87502. ☎ **662-9717.**

This 34-member ensemble has a repertoire ranging from classical, baroque, and Renaissance works to more recent folk music and spirituals. Much of it is presented a cappella. The group gives fall and spring concerts at the Santuario de Guadalupe or St. Francis

Auditorium, and its Christmas dinner concerts at St. John's College (1160 Camino Cruz Blanca) are avidly attended.

Admission: Tickets, $8–$30.

Santa Fe Women's Ensemble, 424 Kathryn Place, Santa Fe, NM 87501. ☎ **984-4075.**

This choral group of 12 semiprofessional singers, sponsored by the Santa Fe Concert Association (see below), offers classical works sung a cappella as well as with a variety of instrumental accompaniment during the spring and fall season. Both the "A Christmas Offering" concerts (in mid-December) and the annual "Spring Offering" concerts are held in the Loretto Chapel. Tickets are sold by Nicholas Potter, Bookseller (see "Books" in "Shopping A to Z," in Chapter 9), through mail order, and at the door.

Admission: Tickets, $12 general admission, $15 reserved seats.

Music Festivals and Concert Series

Santa Fe Chamber Music Festival, 640 Paseo de Peralta (P.O. Box 853), Santa Fe, NM 87504. ☎ **983-2075,** or **982-1890** for the box office, or toll free **800/962-7286.**

The festival brings an extraordinary group of international artists to Santa Fe every summer. Its six-week season of some 50 concerts runs from the second week of July through the third week of August and has been held in the beautiful St. Francis Auditorium since its founding in 1973. Each festival season features chamber-music masterpieces, new music by a composer-in-residence, jazz, free youth concerts, preconcert lectures, and open rehearsals. Festival concerts are recorded for broadcast in a 13-week nationally syndicated radio series.

Performances are Monday through Friday at 8pm and on Saturday and Sunday at 6pm. Open rehearsals, youth concerts, and preconcert lectures are free to the public.

Admission: Tickets, $20–$32.

Santa Fe Concert Association, P.O. Box 4626, Santa Fe, NM 87502. ☎ **984-8759.**

Founded in 1938, the oldest musical organization in northern New Mexico has a September to May season that includes approximately 20 annual events. Among them are a distinguished artists series featuring renowned instrumental and vocal soloists and chamber ensembles, a free youth concert series, a special Christmas Eve concert, and sponsored performances by local artists. All performances are at the St. Francis Auditorium; tickets are sold by Nicholas Potter, Bookseller (see "Books" in "Shopping A to Z," in Chapter 9).

Admission: Tickets, $15–$65.

THEATER COMPANIES

Greer Garson Theater Center, College of Santa Fe, St. Michael's Dr. ☎ **473-6511** or **473-6439.**

The college's Performing Arts Department produces four plays annually, with five presentations of each, between October and May.

Usually they include a comedy, a drama, a musical, and a classic.

Admission: Tickets, $5–$11 adults, $4–$10 students and seniors.

Santa Fe Actors' Theatre, 430 W. Manhattan St. ☎ 982-8309.

This company, new in 1987, offers a year-round schedule, with six to eight productions a year of works ranging from ancient Greek to late 20th century, as well as occasional dance performances and poetry readings. It's lodged in a 99-seat, modular performance space in a renovated Guadalupe district warehouse. At press time, the theater still had plans to move to the Center for Contemporary Arts, so be sure to check the address before heading out.

Admission: Tickets, $10–$12 adults, $7–$9 students and seniors.

⭐ **Santa Fe Community Theatre,** 142 E. De Vargas St. (P.O. Box 2084), Santa Fe, NM 87504. ☎ 988-4262.

Founded in the 1920s, this is the oldest existing theater group in New Mexico. Still performing in a historic adobe theater in the Barrio de Analco, it attracts thousands for its dramas, avant-garde theater, and musical comedy. Its popular one-act melodramas call on the public to boo the sneering villain and swoon for the damsel in distress.

Admission: Tickets, $10 adults, $8 students and seniors; for previews they often ask that you "pay what you like."

DANCE COMPANIES

⭐ **Maria Benitez Spanish Dance Company,** Institute for Spanish Arts, P.O. Box 8418, Santa Fe, NM 87501. ☎ 983-8477.

The Benitez Company's "Estampa Flamenca" summer series is performed from mid-June to mid-September. True flamenco is one of the most thrilling of all dance forms, displaying the inner spirit and verve of the gypsies of Spanish Andalusia.

Admission: Tickets, $15–$20 (subject to change).

Major Concert Halls and All-Purpose Auditoriums ——

Center for Contemporary Arts, 291 E. Barcelona Rd. ☎ 982-1338.

The Center for Contemporary Arts (CCA) presents the work of internationally, nationally, and regionally known contemporary artists in art exhibitions, dance, new music concerts, poetry readings, performance-art events, theater, and video screenings. The CCA Cinématique screens films from around the world nightly, with special series occurring regularly. A permanent outdoor James Turrell Skyspace is located on the CCA grounds. The CCA Warehouse/Teen Project is a unique program designed to encourage creativity, individuality, and free expression by giving teens a safe, free place to create programs and events, including workshops, art exhibitions, a radio show and publication, theater ensemble, café (with open mike opportunities), and concerts featuring local teen bands. CCA's galleries are open Monday through Friday from 10am to 4pm and on Saturday from noon to 4pm.

Admission: Tickets, films $6; prices for other performance events vary.

Paolo Soleri Amphitheatre, at the Santa Fe Indian School, 1501 Cerrillos St. ☎ **989-6310.**

This outdoor arena is the locale of many warm-weather events. More than two dozen concerts are presented here each summer, including the Santa Fe Summer Concert Series. In recent years the series has attracted such big-name acts as Joan Armatrading, the Grateful Dead, B. B. King, Kenny Loggins, Anne Murray, Suzanne Vega, Frank Zappa, and the Reggae Sunsplash. For information on who may be performing while you're there, contact Big River Productions, P.O. Box 8036, Albuquerque, NM 87198 (☎ **505/256-1777**).

Admission: Ticket prices vary according to performer.

★ **St. Francis Auditorium,** in the Museum of Fine Arts, Lincoln and Palace Ave. ☎ **827-4455.**

This beautiful music hall, patterned after the interiors of traditional Hispanic mission churches, is noted for its acoustics. It hosts a wide variety of musical events, including the Santa Fe Chamber Music Festival in July and August. The Santa Fe Symphony Festival Series, the Santa Fe Concert Association, the Santa Fe Women's Ensemble, and various other programs are also held here.

Admission: Tickets, $5–$25, depending on the event; see above for specific performing-arts companies.

Sweeney Convention Center, Marcy and Grant Sts. ☎ **984-6760.**

Santa Fe's largest indoor arena hosts a wide variety of trade expositions and other events during the year. It's also the home of the Santa Fe Symphony Orchestra and the New Mexico Symphony Orchestra's annual Santa Fe Series.

Admission: Tickets, $10–$30, depending on seating and performances.

---

2 The Club & Music Scene

Country, Jazz, and Folk ───────────

★ **El Farol,** 808 Canyon Rd. ☎ **983-9912.**

The original neighborhood bar of the Canyon Road artists' quarter (its name means "the lantern") is the place to head for local ambience. Its low ceilings and dark-brown walls are the home of Santa Fe's largest and most unusual selection of tapas (bar snacks and appetizers), from pulpo a la Gallega (octopus with Spanish paprika sauce) to grilled cactus with ramesco sauce. Jazz, folk, and ethnic musicians, some of national note, perform most nights.

Admission: $2–$6.

Fiesta Lounge, in La Fonda Hotel, 110 E. San Francisco St. ☎ **982-5511.**

This lively lobby bar offers cocktails and live entertainment nightly.
Admission: Free.

Rodeo Nites, 2911 Cerrillos Rd. ☎ 473-4138.

There's live country dance music nightly at this popular club.
Admission: Free Mon–Thurs, $3 Fri–Sat, $2 Sun.

Rock and Disco

The Bull Ring, 414 Old Santa Fe Trail. ☎ 983-3328.

This steakhouse near the State Capitol is also a lively bar with dance
music Wednesday through Sunday after 9pm. Bands, normally
booked for a week at a time, may play rock or tunes from the 1960s
and 1970s.
Admission: Free Wed and Sun, $4 Thurs–Sat.

Chelsea Street Pub, in the Villa Linda Mall, Rodeo and Cerrillos
Rds. ☎ 473-5105.

Burgers and beer are served here during the lunch and dinner hours,
but when the shopping mall closes at 9pm the pub really starts hopping. Top bands from throughout the Southwest play dance music
Monday through Saturday until 2am, on Sunday until 7pm.
Admission: Free.

Chez What, 213 W. Alameda St. ☎ 982-0099.

The nightly live music here runs the gamut from rock to alternative
pop, to reggae, to jazz and blues. There is a jazz dinner every Saturday from 7 to 9pm, and on other nights you might catch an act like
Michael Hedges (Windham Hill acoustic guitar) or Meat Puppets,
an alternative rock group. There's a huge dance floor.
Admission: Mon–Thurs, $2–$3; Fri–Sun, $5–$6. Major acts $10
or more.

Edge, 135 W. Palace Ave. ☎ 986-1720.

Located on the third floor of the Palace Court, Edge is popular with
a cross-section of the Santa Fe population (including the gay crowd).
The nightclub features live entertainment during most of the week
and dance music on Friday and Saturday nights. There is an adjoining restaurant with a short but satisfying menu. Open: Monday to
Saturday from 6pm to 2am, Sunday from 6pm to midnight.
Admission: Cover varies according to performer.

Luna, 519 Cerrillos Rd. ☎ 989-4888.

Originally built as a movie theater, Luna is a 9,000-square-foot dance
club that hosts a range of nationally recognized rock bands throughout the week and features DJ music on Friday and Saturday nights.
There's no food available, but the bar is enormous. Open: Monday
to Saturday 7pm to 2am, Sun 7pm to midnight.
Admission: Cover varies according to performer.

3   The Bar Scene

Evangelo's, 200 W. San Francisco St. ☎ 982-9014.

There's no food offered at Evangelo's, but the tropical decor and
mahogany bar are unique to Santa Fe. There are over 250 varieties

of imported beer available, and pool tables are an added attraction. Evangelo's is extremely popular with the local crowd. Open: Daily from noon until 1 or 2am.

Admission: Free.

Vanessie of Santa Fe, 434 W. San Francisco St. ☎ 982-9966.

This is unquestionably Santa Fe's most popular piano bar. The talented Doug Montgomery and Taylor Kundolf have a loyal local following. Their repertoire ranges from Bach to Billy Joel, Gershwin to Barry Manilow. They play Monday through Saturday from 4:30pm to 2am and on Sunday from 4:30pm to midnight.

Admission: Free.

11

Excursions from Santa Fe

Bandolier Monument –
   Canyon people   ✳

Drive to Tesuque / Shidoni
   (sculpture garden)

On Rd. to Opera –
   out door mkt –
      great finds

NATIVE AMERICAN PUEBLOS AND RUINS, TWO NATIONAL MONUMENTS, LOS Alamos—the A-bomb capital of the United States—and the scenic and culturally fascinating High Road to Taos are all within an easy day trip of Santa Fe.

1 Pueblos

The "Eight Northern Pueblos" are quickly reached from Santa Fe. Nambe, Pojoaque, San Ildefonso, San Juan, Santa Clara, and Tesuque are all within about 30 miles. Picuris (San Lorenzo) is on the High Road to Taos (see Section 3, below), and Taos Pueblo, of course, is just outside the northern New Mexican town of Taos.

The southern six pueblos described below can easily be seen in a single day's round-trip from Santa Fe. Plan to focus most of your attention on San Juan and Santa Clara, including the former's arts cooperative and the latter's Puye Cliff Dwellings.

Certain **rules of etiquette** apply in visits to pueblos. These are personal dwellings and must be respected as such. Don't climb on the buildings or peek into doors or windows. Don't enter sacred grounds, such as cemeteries and kivas. If you attend a dance or ceremony, remain silent during it and refrain from applause when it's over. Many pueblos prohibit photography or sketches; others require you to pay a fee for a permit. Again, any rules that apply to visiting a pueblo must be followed. If you don't respect the privacy of the Native Americans who live at the pueblo you'll be asked to leave.

Tesuque Pueblo, U.S. 84/285 (Rte. 11, Box 1. Santa Fe, NM 87501). ☎ 983-2667.

Tesuque (Teh-*soo*-keh) Pueblo is located about eight miles north of Santa Fe northbound on U.S. 84/285. The most visible signs that you are approaching the pueblo are the unusual Camel Rock and a large roadside bingo operation. Despite this concession to the late 20th century, the 400 pueblo dwellers are faithful to traditional religion, ritual, and ceremony. Excavations confirm that there was a pueblo here as long ago as A.D. 1250; a mission church and adobe houses surround the plaza.

Some Tesuque women are skilled potters; Ignacia Duran's black-and-white and red micaceous pottery and Teresa Tapia's miniatures and pots with animal figures are particularly notable. The **San Diego Feast Day,** featuring buffalo, deer, flag, or Comanche dances, is November 12.

Tesuque Pueblo Bingo (☎ **984-8414**) is open every night from 6:30 to 11pm. There is a snack bar on the premises.

Admission: Free. Still cameras $10, movie cameras $50, sketching $100.

Open: Daily 9am–5pm.

Pojoaque Pueblo, U.S. 84/285 (Rte. 11, Box 71, Santa Fe, NM 87501). ☎ 455-2278.

About seven miles farther north on U.S. 84/285, at the junction of N.M. 503, is Pojoaque (Po-*hwa*-keh). Though small (pop. 200) and without a definable village, Pojoaque is important as a center for traveler services. Indigenous pottery, embroidery, silverwork, and beadwork are available for sale at the Pojoaque Pueblo Tourist Center.

A modern community center is located near the site of the old pueblo and church. **Our Lady of Guadalupe Day,** the annual feast day celebrated on December 12, features a bow-and-arrow or buffalo dance.

Admission: Free. Contact the Governor's Office for information about sketching and camera fees.

Open: Daily, daylight hours.

Nambe Pueblo, Rte. 1, Box 117, Santa Fe, NM 87501. ☎ **455-2036,** or **455-2304** for the Ranger Station.

Drive east about three miles from Pojoaque on N.M. 503, then turn right at the Bureau of Reclamation sign for Nambe Falls. Approximately two miles farther is Nambe, a 700-year-old Tewa-speaking pueblo (pop. 450) with a solar-powered tribal headquarters, at the foot of the Sangre de Cristo range. A few of the original pueblo buildings still exist, including a large round kiva, used today in ceremonies. Pueblo artisans make woven belts, beadwork, and brown micaceous pottery.

Nambe Falls make a stunning three-tier drop through a cleft in a rock face about four miles beyond the pueblo, tumbling into Nambe Reservoir. A recreational site at the reservoir offers fishing, boating, hiking, camping, and picnicking. The **Waterfall Dances** on July 4 and the **San Francisco Feast Day** on October 4, which has an elk dance ceremony, are observed at the sacred falls.

Admission: Pueblo free; still cameras $5, movie cameras $10, sketching $10. Recreational site, fishing, $5 per day adults, $3 per day children; camping, $7 first night, $4 additional nights.

Open: Pueblo, daily 8am–5pm. Recreational site, Apr–May and Sept–Oct, daily 7am–7pm; June–Aug, daily 6am–9pm.

San Ildefonso Pueblo, off N.M. 502 (Rte. 5, Box 315A, Santa Fe, NM 87501). ☎ **455-3549** or **455-2273.**

If you turn left on N.M. 502 at Pojoaque, it's about six miles to the turnoff to this pueblo, nationally famous for the matte-finish black-on-black pottery developed by tribeswoman Maria Martinez in the 1920s. The pottery-making process is explained at the **San Ildefonso Pueblo Museum,** where exhibits of pueblo history, arts, and crafts are presented Monday through Friday. Tours of the pueblo (pop. 650) may be offered from the visitor center upon arrangement.

San Ildefonso Feast Day, January 22–23, is a good time to observe the social and religious traditions of the pueblo, when buffalo, deer, and Comanche dances are presented. There may be dances scheduled for **Easter,** the **Harvest Festival** in early September, and **Christmas.**

The pueblo has a 4$^1/_2$-acre **fishing lake** open April through October. Picnicking is encouraged; camping is not.

Admission: $1 noncommercial vehicle, $10 commercial vehicle, plus 50¢ per passenger. Still cameras $5, movie cameras and sketching $15. Fishing, $5 adults, $3 children 6–12, free for children under 6.

Open: Summer, Mon–Fri 8am–5pm, Sat–Sun 9am–6pm; winter, Mon–Fri 8am–4:30pm. **Closed:** Major holidays and tribal events.

⭐ **San Juan Pueblo,** P.O. Box 1099, San Juan Pueblo, NM 87566. ☎ 852-4400.

The largest (pop. 1,950) and northernmost of the Tewa- (not Tiwa-) speaking pueblos and the headquarters of the Eight Northern Indian Pueblos Council, San Juan is located on the east side of the Rio Grande—opposite the 1598 site of San Gabriel, the first Spanish settlement west of the Mississippi River and the first capital of New Spain. Continuing north on U.S. 84/285, the pueblo is reached via N.M. 74, a mile off N.M. 68, about four miles north of Española.

Past and present cohabit here. The San Juan tribe, though Roman Catholics, still practice traditional religious rituals; thus two rectangular kivas flank the church in the main plaza, and *caciques* (pueblo priests) share influence with civil authorities. The annual **San Juan Fiesta** is June 23–24, with buffalo and Comanche dances. Other annual ceremonies include a **turtle dance** on December 26.

The **Eight Northern Indian Pueblos Council** (☎ 852-4265) is a sort of chamber of commerce and social-service agency.

A crafts store, **O'ke Oweenge Arts and Crafts Cooperative** (☎ 852-2372), focuses on local wares: This is a fine place to seek out San Juan's distinctive red pottery, a lustrous ceramic incised with traditional geometric symbols. Also exhibited and sold are seed, turquoise, and silver jewelry; wood and stone carvings; indigenous clothing and weavings; embroidery; and paintings. Artisans often work in the center for visitors to watch. The co-op is open Monday through Saturday from 9am to 4:30pm; closed San Juan Feast Day. **Sunrise Crafts,** another crafts store, is located to the right of the co-op. There you'll find one-of-a-kind handcrafted pipes, beadwork, and burned and painted gourds.

Right on the main road through the pueblo is the **Tewa Indian Restaurant,** serving traditional pueblo chile stews, breads, blue-corn dishes, posole, teas, and desserts. It's open Monday through Friday from 9am to 2:30pm; closed holidays and feast days.

Fishing and picnicking are encouraged at the **San Juan Tribal Lakes,** open year-round.

Like most of the other pueblos, San Juan also offers bingo. In summer, doors are open Wednesday through Sunday at 5:30pm; in winter, on Sunday afternoon at noon.

Admission: Free. Photography or sketching may be allowed with prior permission from the Governor's Office. Fishing, $8 adults, $5 children and seniors.

Open: Daily, daylight hours.

Santa Clara Pueblo, P.O. Box 580, Española, NM 87532. ☎ 753-7326.

Just across the Rio Grande from Española on N.M. 5, Santa Clara has a population of about 1,600, making it one of the larger pueblos. Driving and walking tours are offered Monday through Friday, with a week's notice, and include visit's to the pueblo's historic church and artists' studios. Visitors are welcome to enter studios so marked and watch the artists making baskets and a highly polished red-and-black pottery.

There are corn and harvest dances on **Santa Clara Feast Day** (August 12); other special days include buffalo and deer dances in early February and children's dances (December 28).

The Puye Cliff Dwellings (see below) are on the Santa Clara reservation.

Admission: Free. Still cameras $5, movie cameras $15, sketching $15.

Open: Daily, daylight hours. Visitor's center open daily 9am–4:30pm.

★ **Puye Cliff Dwellings,** Santa Clara Pueblo. ☎ 753-7326.

The Santa Clara people migrated to their home on the Rio Grande in the 13th century from a former home high on the Pajarito Plateau to the west. The ruins of that past life have been preserved in this site, an 11-mile climb west of the pueblo. Thought to have been occupied from about 1250 to 1577, this site at the mouth of the Santa Clara Canyon is a national landmark.

High on a nearly featureless plateau, the volcanic tuff rises in a soft tan facade 200 feet high. Here the Anasazi found niches to build their houses. Visitors can descend via staircases and ladders from the 7,000-foot mesa top into the 740-room pueblo ruin, which includes a ceremonial chamber and community house. Petroglyphs are evident in many of the rocky cliff walls.

About six miles farther west is the **Santa Clara Canyon Recreational Area,** a sylvan summer setting for camping, open year-round for picnicking, hiking, and fishing in ponds and Santa Clara Creek.

Admission: $5 adults, $4 children and seniors. Guided tours additional $1 charge with advance notice of one week.

Open: Summer, daily 8am–8pm; winter, daily 9am–4:30pm.

2 Los Alamos

Pueblo tribes lived in this rugged area for well over 1,000 years, and an exclusive boys' school operated atop the 7,300-foot plateau from 1928 to 1943. Then the Los Alamos National Laboratory was founded in secrecy as Project Y of the Manhattan Engineer District, the hush-hush wartime program that developed the world's first nuclear weapons.

Project director J. Robert Oppenheimer, later succeeded by Norris E. Bradbury, worked with a team of 30 to 100 scientists in research, development, and production of the weapons. Today 3,000 scientists and another 4,800 support staff work at the **Los Alamos National Laboratory,** making it the largest employer in northern New Mexico. Still operated by the University of California for the federal Department of Energy, its 32 technical areas occupy 43 square miles of mesa-top land.

The laboratory is known today as one of the world's foremost scientific institutions. It's still geared heavily to the defense industry—the Trident and Minuteman strategic warheads were created here, for example—but it has many other research programs, including studies in nuclear fusion and fission, energy conservation, nuclear safety, the environment, and nuclear wastes. Its international resources include a genetic-sequence data bank, with wide implications for medicine and agriculture, and an Institute for Geophysics and Planetary Physics.

Orientation/Useful Information

Los Alamos is located about 33 miles west of Santa Fe and about 66 miles southwest of Taos. From Santa Fe, take U.S. 84/285 north approximately 16 miles to the Pojoaque junction, then turn west on N.M. 502. Driving time is only about 50 minutes.

Los Alamos is a city of 12,000 spread on the craggy, fingerlike mesas of the Pajarito Plateau, between the Jemez Mountains and Rio Grande valley. As it enters the Los Alamos area from Santa Fe, N.M. 502 separates into Trinity Drive (westbound) and Central Avenue (eastbound) through the downtown area where accommodations, restaurants, and other services are located. Both intersect Diamond Drive at their western ends; it's only a short distance south on this road to the Bradbury Science Museum, the city's star attraction.

The **Los Alamos Chamber of Commerce,** Fuller Lodge, 2132 Central Ave. (P.O. Box 460), Los Alamos, NM 87544 (☎ 505/662-8105), has a visitor center open Monday through Friday from 8am to 5pm.

Events

Los Alamos's events schedule includes a **Sports Skiesta** in late March or early April; **art-and-crafts fairs** in May, August, October, and November; the **Tour de Los Alamos bicycle race** and **Atomic City golf tourney** in July; a **county fair, rodeo,** and **arts festival** in August; and a **triathlon** in August/September.

What to See and Do

Aside from the sights described below, Los Alamos offers the **Pajarito Mountain ski area,** Camp May Road (P.O. Box 155), Los Alamos, NM 87544 (☎ 662-SNOW), with four chair lifts; and **Los Alamos Municipal Golf Course,** Diamond Drive (☎ 662-8139) at the edges of town; and the **Larry R. Walkup Aquatic Center,** 2760 Canyon Rd. (☎ 662-8170), the highest-altitude indoor Olympic-size swimming pool in the United States. There's even an **outdoor ice-skating rink.**

Excursions from Santa Fe

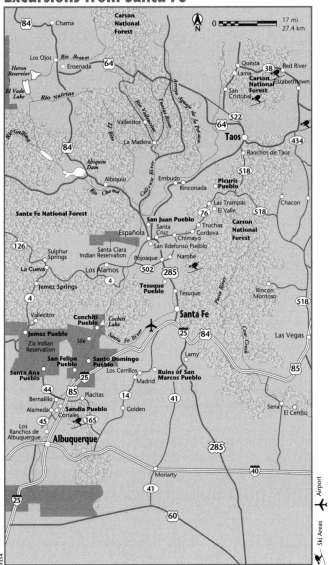

IN LOS ALAMOS

⭐ **Bradbury Science Museum,** at the Los Alamos National
Laboratory, 15th St. and Central Ave. ☎ **667-4444.**

This outstanding museum is the lab's public showcase. It focuses on
atomic research in a wide variety of scientific and historical displays,
including more than 35 hands-on exhibits. Visitors can peruse

photographs and documents highlighting the earliest days of Project Y, including a 1939 letter from Albert Einstein to Pres. Franklin D. Roosevelt suggesting research into uranium as a new and important source of energy. There are exhibits on weapons research, including an overview of the nation's nuclear arsenal; achievements in alternative-energy research, from solar and geothermal to laser and magnetic-fusion energy; biomedical research and development; computer technology; and basic research into the nature of nuclei, atoms, and molecules. Visitors may explore the museum, experiment with lasers, use computers, and view laboratory research in energy, defense, environment, and health. Self-guided exhibits have interesting hands-on features and video monitors. Educational and historical films are shown continuously.

Admission: Free.

Open: Tues–Fri 9am–5pm, Sat–Mon 1–5pm. **Closed:** Major holidays.

Fuller Lodge Art Center, 2132 Central Ave. ☎ 662-9331.

Works of northern New Mexico artists and traveling exhibitions of regional and national importance are displayed here. Four annual arts-and-crafts fares are also held here—in May, August, October, and November.

Admission: Free.

Open: Mon–Sat 10am–4pm, Sun 1–4pm.

Los Alamos Historical Museum, 2132 Central Ave.
☎ 662-4493.

The massive log building that once housed the dining and recreation hall for the Los Alamos Ranch School for boys is now a National Historic Landmark known as the Fuller Lodge. Its current occupants include the museum office and research archives, the Fuller Lodge Art Center (see below), and the Los Alamos County Chamber of Commerce, which doubles as a visitor information center. The museum, located in the small log-and-stone building to the north of Fuller Lodge, recounts area history, from prehistoric cliff dwellers to the present, with a variety of exhibits ranging from Native American artifacts to school memorabilia and wartime displays. The museum sponsors guest speakers and operates a bookstore.

Admission: Free.

Open: Summer, Mon–Sat 9:30am–4:30pm, Sun 11am–5pm, winter, Mon–Sat 10am–4pm, Sun 1–4pm.

NEARBY

⭐ **Bandelier National Monument**, N. M. 4 (HCR 1, Box 1, Suite 15, Los Alamos, NM 87544). ☎ 672-3861.

Less than 15 miles south of Los Alamos along N.M. 4, this is the National Park Service Area containing cliff dwellings that is nearest to Santa Fe. It combines the extensive ruins of an ancient cliff-dwelling Anasazi pueblo culture with 46 square miles of canyon-and-mesa wilderness.

Most visitors, after an orientation stop in the visitor center and museum to learn about the culture that existed here between A.D. 1100 and 1550, follow a trail along Frijoles Creek to the principal ruins. The pueblo site, including an underground kiva, has been stabilized. The biggest thrill for most folks, though, is climbing hardy Ponderosa pine ladders to visit an alcove 140 feet above the canyon floor that was once home to prehistoric people. Tours are self-guided or led by a National Park Service ranger.

On summer nights rangers offer campfire talks about the history, culture, and geology of the area. On some evenings in summer, the guided night walks reveal a different, spooky aspect of the ruins and cave houses, outlined in the two-dimensional chiaroscuro of the thin cold light from the starry sky. During the day, nature programs may be offered for adults and children. The small museum at the visitor center shows artifacts found in the area.

Elsewhere in the monument area, 70 miles of maintained trails lead to more tribal ruins, waterfalls, and wildlife habitats. The separate **Tsankawi** section, reached by an ancient two-mile trail close to White Rock, contains a large unexcavated ruin on a high mesa overlooking the Rio Grande valley.

Areas are set aside for picnicking and camping. Admission is $5 per vehicle. The national monument is named after Swiss-American archeologist Adolph Bandelier, who explored here in the 1880s.

Admission: $5 per vehicle.

Open: Daily, daylight hours. **Closed:** New Year's and Christmas Days.

Valle Grande, N.M. 4.

Most people are surprised to learn that the largest volcanic caldera in the world is here in northern New Mexico. Past Bandelier National Monument on N.M. 4, beginning about 15 miles from Los Alamos, is Valle Grande, a vast meadow 16 miles in diameter and 76 square miles in area, all that remains of a massive volcano that erupted nearly a million years ago. When the mountain spewed ashes and dust as far as Kansas and Nebraska, its underground magma chambers collapsed, forming this great valley. Lava domes that pushed up after the collapse obstruct a full view across the expanse. Valle Grande is now privately owned land.

White Rock, N.M. 4.

The town of White Rock, about 10 miles south of Los Alamos on N.M. 4, offers spectacular panoramas of the Rio Grande valley toward Santa Fe. Many folks enjoy picnicking at the White Rock Overlook.

3 Along the High Road to Taos

Unless you're in a hurry to get from Santa Fe to Taos, the "high road"—also called the Mountain Road or the King's Road—is by far the most fascinating route. It runs through tiny ridgetop villages where Hispanic lifestyles and traditions continue much as they were a century ago.

Chimayo

About 28 miles north of Santa Fe on N.M. 84/285 is the historic weaving center of Chimayo. It's approximately 16 miles past the Pojoaque junction, at the junction of N.M. 520 and N.M. 76 via N.M. 503. In this small village families like the Ortegas maintain a tradition of crafting hand-woven textiles begun by their ancestors seven generations ago, in the early 1800s. Both **Ortega's Weaving Shop** and **Galeria Ortega** are fine places to take a close look at this ancient craft.

Today, however, many more people come to Chimayo to visit ★ **El Santuario de Nuestro Señor de Esquipulas** (the Shrine of Our Lord of Esquipulas), better known simply as "El Santuario de Chimayo." Attributed with miraculous powers of healing, this church has been the destination of countless thousands of pilgrims since its construction in 1814–16. Some 30,000 people may participate in the annual Good Friday pilgrimage, many of them walking from as far away as Albuquerque.

Although only the earth in the anteroom beside the altar has healing powers ascribed to it, the entire shrine has a special serene feeling that's hard to ignore. It's quite moving to peruse the testimonies of rapid recoveries from illness or injury on the walls of the anteroom, and equally poignant to read the as-yet-unanswered entreaties made on behalf of loved ones.

A National Historic Landmark, the church contains five beautiful reredos, or panels of sacred paintings, one behind the main altar and two on each side of the nave. Each year during the fourth weekend in July, the 9th-century military exploits of the Spanish saint Santiago are celebrated in a weekend fiesta, including the historic play *Los Moros y Cristianos* (Moors and Christians).

Lovely **Santa Cruz Lake** has a dual purpose: The artificial lake provides water for Chimayo valley farms, but also offers a recreation site for trout fishing and camping at the edge of the Pecos Wilderness. To reach it, turn south four miles on N.M. 503, about two miles east of Chimayo.

WHERE TO DINE

★ **Restaurante Rancho de Chimayo,** N.M. 76. ☎ 351-4444.

Cuisine: NEW MEXICAN. **Reservations:** Recommended.
Prices: Lunch $6–$10; dinner $10–$15. MC, V.
Open: Tues–Sun noon–9pm.

Many travelers schedule their drives to have lunch at this well-known restaurant. The adobe home, built by Hermenegildo Jaramillo in the 1880s, has been in the food business for nearly three decades. Native New Mexican cuisine, prepared from generations-old Jaramillo family recipes, is served on terraced patios and in cozy dining rooms beneath hand-stripped vigas.

Cordova

Just as Chimayo is famous for its weaving, the village of Cordova, about seven miles east on N.M. 76, is noted for its wood carvers. Small shops and studios along the highway display santos (carved saints) and various decorative items carved from aspen and cedar.

Truchas

Anyone who saw Robert Redford's 1988 movie *The Milagro Beanfield War* has seen Truchas. A former Spanish Colonial outpost built at 8,000 feet atop a mesa four miles east of Cordova, it was chosen as the site for filming in part because traditional Hispanic culture is still very much in evidence. Subsistence *acequia* farming has a high profile here. The scenery is spectacular: 13,101-foot Truchas Peak dominates one side of the mesa and the broad Rio Grande valley dominates the other.

About six miles east of Truchas on N.M. 76 is the small town of **Las Trampas,** most notable for its **San José Church,** called by some the most beautiful of all churches built during the Spanish Colonial period.

Picuris (San Lorenzo) Pueblo

Near the regional education center of **Peñasco,** about 24 miles from Chimayo near the junction of N.M. 75 and N.M. 76, is the Picuris (San Lorenzo) Pueblo (☎ 587-2519). The 270 citizens of this 15,000-acre mountain pueblo, native Tiwa speakers, consider themselves a sovereign nation: Their forebears never made a treaty with any foreign country, the United States included. Thus they observe a traditional form of tribal council government. Their annual **feast day** at San Lorenzo church is August 10.

Still, the people are modern enough to have fully computerized their public showcase operations, Picuris Tribal Enterprises. Besides the Hotel Santa Fe they run in the state capital, ventures include the **Picuris Pueblo Museum,** where weaving, beadwork, and distinctive reddish-brown clay cooking pottery are exhibited Monday through Friday from 8am to 4:30pm. Guided tours through the old village ruins begin from the museum; camera fees start at $5. There's also an information center, crafts shop, grocery, and other shops, and a café serves Pueblo and American food at lunchtime. Permits ($4 for adults and children) are available to fish or camp at Pu-Na and Tu-Tah Lakes, regularly stocked with trout.

About a mile east of Peñasco on N.M. 75 is **Vadito,** which early this century was the center for the conservative Catholic brotherhood, the Penitentes.

Dixon and Embudo

Taos is about 24 miles north of Peñasco via N.M. 518. But day-trippers from Santa Fe can loop back to the capital by taking N.M. 75 west from Picuris Pueblo. **Dixon,** approximately 12 miles west of Picuris, and its twin village of **Embudo,** a mile farther on

N.M. 68 at the Rio Grande, are the homes of many artists and craftspeople who exhibit their works during an annual **autumn show** sponsored by the Dixon Arts Association. If you're in need of refreshments, you can follow signs to **La Chiripada Winery** (☎ 579-4437), whose product is surprisingly good. Local pottery is also sold in the tasting room. The winery is open Monday through Saturday from 10am to 5pm.

Near Dixon is the **Harding Mine,** a University of New Mexico property where visitors can gather mineral specimens without going underground. If you haven't signed a liability release at the Albuquerque campus, ask at Labeo's Store in Dixon. They'll direct you to the home of a local resident who can get you started on your fossil hunt almost immediately.

Two more small villages lie in the Rio Grande valley at six-mile intervals south of Embudo on N.M. 68. **Velarde** is a fruit-growing center; in season, the road here is lined with stands selling fresh fruit or crimson chile ristras and wreaths of native plants. **Alcalde** is the location of Los Luceros, an early 17th-century home that is to be refurbished as an arts and history center. The unique Dance of the Matachines, a Moorish-influenced production brought from Spain by the conquistadors, is performed here on holidays and feast days.

Española

The commercial center of Española (pop. 7,000) no longer has the railroad that was responsible for its establishment in the 1880s, but it does have perhaps New Mexico's greatest concentration of "low riders." Their owners give much loving attention to these late-model customized cars, so called because their suspension leaves them sitting exceedingly close to the ground. You can't miss seeing them cruise the main streets of town, especially on weekend evenings.

Significant sights in Española include the **Bond House Museum,** a Victorian-era adobe home displaying exhibits of local history and art; and the **Santa Cruz Church,** built in 1733 and renovated in 1979, which houses many fine examples of Spanish Colonial religious art. Major events include the July **Fiesta de Oñate,** commemorating the valley's founding in 1596; the **Tri-Cultural Art Festival** in October on the Northern New Mexico Community College campus; and the week-long **Summer Solstice** celebration, staged in June by the nearby, 200-strong Ram Das Puri ashram of the Sikhs (☎ 753-9438).

Full information on Española and vicinity can be obtained from the **Española Valley Chamber of Commerce,** 417 Big Rock Center, Española, NM 87532 (☎ 505/753-2831).

4 Pecos National Monument

About 15 miles east of Santa Fe, I-25 meanders through **Glorieta Pass,** site of an important Civil War skirmish. In March 1862, volunteers from Colorado and New Mexico, along with Fort Union regulars, defeated a Confederate force marching on Santa Fe, thereby turning the tide of Southern encroachment in the West.

Take N.M. 50 east to **Pecos,** a distance of about seven miles. This quaint town, well off the beaten track since the interstate was constructed, is the site of a noted Benedictine monastery. North of here about 26 miles on N.M. 63 is the village of **Cowles,** gateway to the natural wonderland of the Pecos Wilderness. There are many camping, picnicking, and fishing locales en route.

Pecos National Monument (☎ **757-6414**), about two miles south of the town of Pecos off N.M. 63, contains the ruins of a 14th-century pueblo and 17th-century mission. The **Pecos Pueblo** was well known to Coronado in 1540: "It is feared through the land," he wrote. With a population of about 2,000, the Native Americans farmed in irrigated fields and hunted wild game. Their pueblo had 660 rooms and many kivas. By 1620 Franciscan monks had established a church and convent. Military and natural disasters took their toll on the pueblo, and in 1838 the 20 surviving Pecos tribe members abandoned their ancestral home and took up residence with relatives at the Jemez Pueblo.

The **E. E. Fogelson Visitor Center** tells the history of the Pecos people in a well-done, chronologically organized exhibit, complete with dioramas of pre-Hispanic lifestyles. A 1¼-mile loop trail departs from the center and leads through Pecos Pueblo and the **Mission de Nuestra Señora de Los Angeles de Porciuncula,** as the church was formally known. This excavated structure—170 feet long and 90 feet wide at the transept—was once the most magnificent church north of Mexico City.

Pecos National Monument is open Memorial Day to Labor Day, daily from 8am to 6pm; the rest of the year, daily from 8am to 5pm; closed New Year's and Christmas Days. The $1 admission charge goes to further preservation efforts.

12

Getting to Know Taos

Sɪᴛᴜᴀᴛᴇᴅ ᴡʜᴇʀᴇ ᴛʜᴇ ᴡᴇsᴛᴇʀɴ ꜰʟᴀɴᴋ ᴏꜰ ᴛʜᴇ Sᴀɴɢʀᴇ ᴅᴇ Cʀɪsᴛᴏ ʀᴀɴɢᴇ meets the semi-arid high desert of the upper Rio Grande Valley, Taos combines nature and culture, history and progress. There's much less commercialization here than in the state capital.

Located just 40 miles south of the Colorado border, about 70 miles north of Santa Fe, and approximately 130 miles from Albuquerque, Taos is best known for its thriving art colony, its historic Native American pueblo, and its nearby ski area, one of the most highly regarded in the Rockies. It also has several fine museums (with a new one on the way as this book goes to press) and a wide choice of accommodations and restaurants for visitors.

About 4,500 people consider themselves Taoseños (permanent residents of Taos) today. They carry on a legacy of habitation that may have begun as long as 5,000 years ago; prehistoric ruins more than a millennium old exist throughout the Taos valley.

The Spanish first visited in 1540 and colonized the area in 1598, putting down three rebellions at the Taos Pueblo in the last two decades of the 17th century. Through the 18th and 19th centuries Taos was an important trade center: New Mexico's annual caravan to Chihuahua, Mexico, couldn't leave until after the annual midsummer Taos Fair. French trappers began attending the fair in 1739. Plains tribes, even though they often attacked the Pueblos at other times, also attended the market festivals under a temporary annual truce. By the early 1800s Taos had become a headquarters for American "mountain men," the most famous of whom, Kit Carson, made his home in Taos from 1826 to 1868.

Taos, firmly Hispanic, stayed loyal to Mexico during the Mexican War of 1846. The city rebelled against its new U.S. landlord in 1847, killing newly appointed Gov. Charles Bent in his Taos home. Nevertheless it became a part of the Territory of New Mexico in 1850. It fell into Confederate hands for just six weeks during the Civil War, at the end of which time Carson and two other statesmen raised the Union flag over Taos Plaza and guarded it day and night. Since then Taos has had the honor of flying the flag 24 hours a day.

When the railroad bypassed Taos for Santa Fe, the population dwindled. But in 1898 two eastern artists—Ernest Blumenschein and Bert Phillips—discovered the dramatic light changes in the Taos valley and put them on canvas. By 1912 the Taos Society of Artists had placed the town on the international cultural map. Today, by some estimates more than 10% of the population are painters, sculptors, writers, musicians, or people who otherwise earn income from an artistic pursuit.

The town of Taos is merely the focal point of rugged 2,200-square-mile Taos County. Two features dominate this sparsely populated region: the high desert mesa, split in two by the 650-foot-deep chasm of the Rio Grande; and the Sangre de Cristo range, which tops out at 13,161-foot Wheeler Peak, New Mexico's highest mountain. From the forested uplands to the sage-carpeted mesa, the county is home to a great variety of wildlife. The human element includes the Native Americans, still at home in ancient pueblos, and Hispanic farmers who continue to irrigate their farmlands by centuries-old methods.

1 Orientation

Arriving

BY AIR The **Taos Municipal Airport** (☎ 758-4995) is about eight miles northwest of town on U.S. 64. **Horizon Air Services** (☎ toll free **800/547-9308**) provides local Cessna 310 services to communities and national parks of the region. **Pride of Taos** (☎ 758-8340) meets incoming flights and provides shuttlebus service to Taos and the Taos Ski Valley.

BY BUS The **Taos Bus Center,** Paseo del Pueblo Sur at the Chevron station (☎ 758-1144), is not far from the Plaza. **Greyhound/Trailways** and **TNM&O Coaches** arrive and depart from this depot several times a day. For more information on these and two local bus services to and from Albuquerque and Santa Fe, see "Getting There," in Chapter 2.

BY CAR Most visitors arrive in Taos via either N.M. 68 or U.S. 64. Northbound travelers exit I-25 at Santa Fe, follow U.S. 285 as far as San Juan Pueblo, and continue on the divided highway when it becomes N.M. 68. Taos is about 79 miles from the I-25 junction. Travelers southbound from Denver on I-25 exit about 6 miles south of Raton at U.S. 64, and follow it about 95 miles to Taos. Another major route is U.S. 64 from the west (214 miles from Farmington).

Tourist Information

The **Taos County Chamber of Commerce,** at the junction of U.S. 64 and N.M. 68 (P.O. Drawer I), Taos, NM 87571 (☎ **505/758-3873,** or toll free **800/732-TAOS**), is open year-round, daily from 8am to 5pm; closed major holidays. **Carson National Forest** also has an information center in the same building as the chamber.

City Layout

The Plaza is a short block west of Taos's major intersection—where U.S. 64 (**Kit Carson Road**) from the east joins N.M. 68, **Paseo del Pueblo Sur** (also known as South Pueblo Road or South Santa Fe Road). U.S. 64 proceeds north from the intersection as **Paseo del Pueblo Norte** (North Pueblo Road). **Camino de la Placita** (Placitas Road) circles the west side of downtown, passing within a block of the other side of the Plaza. Many of the streets that join these thoroughfares are winding lanes lined by traditional adobe homes, many of them over 100 years old.

Most of the art galleries are located on or near the Plaza, which was bricked over several years ago, and along neighboring streets.

MAPS To find your way around town, pick up a free copy of the Taos map from the chamber of commerce.

2 Getting Around

By Bus and Taxi

Two private companies serve Taos. Pride of Taos (☎ **758-8340**) operates a summer trolley that runs daily from 9am to 5pm from the Sagebrush Inn to Taos Pueblo on a 45-minute schedule, for $7 ($3 for children). In winter, Pride of Taos's shuttlebus service links town hotels and Taos Ski Valley four times a day for $7 round-trip. A night bus ($10) brings skiers staying at the ski valley into town for dinner and returns them to their lodgings.

Faust's Transportation (☎ **758-3410**) offers town taxi service daily from 7am to 10pm, with fares of $7 anywhere within the city limits for up to two people ($2 per additional person), $12 to the airport, and $25 to Taos Ski Valley.

By Car

With offices at the Taos airport, **Payless Rental Cars** (☎ **751-1110**) is reliable and efficient. **Hertz** (☎ **776-2229**) is located at Taos Mountain Lodge, 1 mile from Taos Ski Valley. **Friday Motors** at 1040 Paseo del Pueblo Norte (☎ **758-2252**) is another option.

PARKING Parking can be difficult during the summer rush, when the stream of tourists' cars moving north and south through town never ceases. Not everyone knows about all the free parking lots, however, especially about the municipal lot behind the Taos Community Auditorium, just off Paseo del Pueblo Norte a block north of the Plaza traffic signal. The town office lot, located off Caminode la Placita, is also free. Another lot just to the north of the Plaza has parking meters. Two commercial lots, one behind the Plaza and another off Kit Carson Road, charge a small fee for all-day parking.

WARNINGS FOR DRIVERS Reliable paved roads lead to take-off points for side trips up poorer forest roads to many recreation sites. Once you get off the main roads, you won't find gas stations or cafés. Four-wheel-drive vehicles are recommended on snow and much of the otherwise-unpaved terrain of the region. If you're doing some off-road adventuring, it's wise to go with a full gas tank, extra food and water, and warm clothing—just in case. At the more-than-10,000-foot elevations of northern New Mexico, sudden summer snowstorms are not unknown.

ROAD CONDITIONS Information on road conditions in the Taos area can be obtained from the **State Police** (☎ **758-8878,** or **505/983-0120,** for which there is no charge within New Mexico). Also, for highway conditions throughout the state call the **State Highway Department** (☎ toll free **800/432-4269**).

By Bicycle or on Foot

Bicycle rentals are available from the **Gearing Up Bicycle Shop,** 129 Paseo del Pueblo Sur (☎ **751-0365**); **Hot Tracks Cyclery & Ski**

Touring Service, 729 Paseo del Pueblo Sur (☎ **751-0949**); and
Native Sons Adventures, 715 Paseo del Pueblo Sur (☎ **758-9342**).

Most of Taos's attractions can easily be covered on foot as they
are within a few blocks of the Plaza.

Fast Facts: Taos

Airport See "Orientation" earlier in this chapter.

Area Code The telephone area code for all of New Mexico is **505**.

Business Hours Most **businesses** are open Monday through Friday from 10am to 5pm, though some may open an hour earlier
and close an hour later. Many tourist-oriented **shops** are also open
on Saturday mornings, and some art galleries are open all day Saturday and Sunday, especially during peak tourist seasons. **Banks**
are generally open Monday through Thursday from 9am to 3pm
and on Friday from 6am to 6pm. Call establishments for specific
hours.

Car Rentals See "Getting Around," earlier in this chapter.

Climate Only 50 feet lower than Santa Fe in elevation, Taos is
similar in climate to the state capital. Summer days are dry and
sunny, except for frequent afternoon thunderstorms; winter days
are often bracing, with snowfalls common but rarely long-lived.
Average summer temperatures range from lows of 50°F to highs
of 87°F. Winter temperatures vary between an average low of
9°F and a high of 40°F. Annual rainfall is 12 inches; annual snowfall is 35 inches in town, 300 inches at Taos Ski Valley, elevation
9,207. (A foot of snow is equal to an inch of rain.)

Currency Exchange It's difficult to exchange money in Taos (it
could take up to a week), so it's advisable to do it before you get to
Taos. However, if you have time, try these major banks: First State
Bank of Taos (☎ **758-6600**) is on the Plaza; Centinel Bank of
Taos (☎ **758-6700**) has a branch at Paseo del Pueblo Sur; and
Peoples Bank has two offices in Taos, one on Paseo del Pueblo
Sur (☎ **758-4500**) and one on Paseo del Pueblo Norte
(☎ **758-4211**).

Dentists If you need dental work, try Dr. Walter Jakiela, 536
Paseo del Pueblo Norte (☎ **758-8654**); Dr. Larry J. Cook, 1399
Weimer Rd. (☎ **758-9777**); and Dr. Tom Simms, 623-B Paseo
del Pueblo Sur (☎ **758-8303**).

Doctors Members of the Taos Medical Group, on Weimer Road
(☎ **758-2224**), are highly respected. Also well thought of are
Family Practice Associates of Taos, on Don Fernando Street
(☎ **758-3005**), a short distance west of the Plaza.

Driving Rules See "Getting Around," earlier in this chapter.

Drugstores The Taos Pharmacy, in Piñon Plaza on Paseo del
Pueblo Sur (☎ **758-3342**) next door to Holy Cross Hospital, is

open Monday through Friday from 9am to 6pm and on Saturday from 9am to 5pm.

Emergencies Dial **911** for police, fire, and ambulance.

Eyeglasses Taos Eyewear, in Cruz Alta Plaza (☎ **758-8758**), handles most needs Monday through Friday between 8:30am and 5pm. It also has emergency service.

Hairdressers and Barbers Spirits of Beauty, 223 Paseo del Pueblo Sur (☎ **758-1178**), and Kachina Beauty Salon, 413 Paseo del Pueblo Norte (☎ **758-8727**), welcome drop-ins of either sex. There are numerous other shops in town.

Hospital The Holy Cross Hospital, 630 Paseo del Pueblo Sur (☎ **758-8883**), has 24-hour emergency service. Serious cases are transferred to Santa Fe or Albuquerque. At press time, the hospital had plans to move to a new location at Weimer Road off Paseo del Cañyon, so be sure to call and verify the address at the time of your visit.

Hotlines The following hotlines are available in Taos: battered women (☎ **785-9888**), poison control (☎ toll free **800/432-6866**), and rape crisis center (☎ **758-9888**).

Information See "Information and When to Go," in Chapter 2; also "Orientation," earlier in this chapter.

Laundry and Dry Cleaning Peralta Laundry & Dry Cleaning, 1018 S. Santa Fe Rd. (☎ **758-0239**), a couple of miles south of downtown, is open daily.

Library The Harwood Library and Museum, on Ledoux Street near the Plaza (☎ **758-3063**), has a general collection for Taos residents, a children's library, and special collections on the Southwest and Taos art. (The library plans to move at the end of '95, so call then for new address.)

Liquor Laws As in Santa Fe, bars must close by 2am Monday through Saturday and can open only between noon and midnight on Sunday. The legal drinking age is 21.

Lost Property Check with the police (☎ **758-2216**).

Mail The main Taos Post Office is at 318 Paseo del Pueblo Norte, Taos, NM 87571 (☎ **758-2081**), a few blocks north of the Plaza traffic light. There are smaller offices in Ranchos de Taos (☎ **758-3944**) and at El Prado (☎ **758-4810**). The ZIP Code for Taos is 87571.

Maps A free city map can be obtained from the Taos County Chamber of Commerce, at the junction of U.S. 64 and N.M. 68 (☎ **758-3873**). Good, detailed city maps can be found at Fernandez de Taos Bookstore, 109 N. Taos Plaza (☎ **758-4391**).

Newspapers The *Taos News* (☎ **758-2241**) and the *Sangre de Cristo Chronicle* (☎ **377-2358**) appear weekly on Thursday. The *Albuquerque Journal, The New Mexican* from Santa Fe, and the

Denver Post are easily obtained at the Fernandez de Taos Bookstore on the Plaza.

Photographic Needs   Check Plaza Photo, 106B Juan Largo Lane, just off North Taos Plaza (☎ **758-3420**). Repairs must go to Santa Fe and usually require several days. For film processing you can go to Plaza Photo or Ultima Photo Images, 133A Bent St. (☎ **758-4406**). Both places have same-day service. If you need your pictures developed in a hurry, take your film to April's 1-Hour Photos, at 613E N. Pueblo Rd.   (☎ **758-0515**).

Police   In case of emergency, dial **911**. All other inquiries should be directed to Taos Police, Civic Plaza Drive (☎ **758-2216**). The Taos County Sheriff, with jurisdiction outside the city limits, is located in the county courthouse on Paseo del Pueblo Sur (☎ **758-3361**).

Radio   Local stations are KKIT-AM (1340) for news, sports, weather, and a daily event calendar at 6:30am (☎ **758-2231**); and KTAO-FM (101.7), which broadcasts an entertainment calendar daily (☎ **758-1017**).

Religious Services   The biggest Catholic church in town is Our Lady of Guadalupe Church, west of the Plaza on Camino de la Placita (☎ **758-9208**). Visitors often enjoy attending a service at the famous San Francisco de Asis Church, four miles south of the Plaza in Ranchos de Taos (☎ **758-2754**). Masses are mainly in English, but each church has a Sunday-morning Spanish-language mass.

Other denominations active in Taos include Assemblies of God, Baptist, Brethren, Church of Christ, Episcopal, Foursquare Gospel, Friends, Jehovah's Witnesses, Methodist, and Presbyterian; Mormon; Jewish; Baha'i; and Eckankar.

Shoe Repairs   Ranchero Boot and Leather Enterprise, at 323 Paseo del Pueblo Sur (☎ **758-1243**), has a convenient location.

Taxes   Gross receipts tax for Taos town is 6.8125% and for Taos county it's 6.3125%. There is an additional local bed tax of 3.5% in Taos town and 3% on hotel rooms in Taos County.

Taxis   See "Getting Around," earlier in this chapter.

Telephones   The area code for New Mexico is **505**. Local calls are usually 25¢. You must dial 505 plus the telephone number when calling any area within New Mexico outside Taos.

Television   Channel 2, the local access station, is available in most hostelries. For a few hours a day there is local programming. Cable networks carry Santa Fe and Albuquerque stations.

Time   Taos, like all of New Mexico, is in the mountain time zone. It's two hours later than New York, one hour later than Chicago, and one hour earlier than Los Angeles. Daylight saving time is in effect from April to October.

Useful Telephone Numbers For information on road conditions in the Taos area, call the state police (☎ **758-8878**), or dial toll free **800/432-4269** (within New Mexico) for the state highway department. Taos County offices are at **758-8834.** The KKIT 24-hour weather line is **758-4267.**

13

Taos Accommodations

Taos has some 1,350 rooms in 60 hotels, motels, condominiums, and bed-and-breakfasts. Most of the hotels and motels are located on Paseo del Pueblo Sur and Norte, with a few scattered just east of the town center along Kit Carson Road. The condos and B&Bs are mostly scattered throughout Taos's back streets.

During peak seasons, visitors without reservations may find a vacant room hard to come by. **Taos Central Reservations,** P.O. Box 1713, Taos, NM 87571 (☎ **505/758-9767,** or toll free **800/821-2437**), might be able to help.

There are another 400-or-so rooms in 15 condo lodges at or near the Taos Ski Valley. The **Taos Valley Resort Association,** P.O. Box 85, Taos Ski Valley, NM 87525 (☎ **505/776-2233,** or toll free **800/776-1111**), can book these as well as unadvertised condominium vacancies.

Some three dozen bed-and-breakfasts are listed with the Taos Chamber of Commerce. The **Taos Bed & Breakfast Association** (☎ **505/758-4747,** or toll free **800/876-7857**), with strict guidelines for membership, will provide information and make reservations for member homes.

And **Affordable Meetings & Accommodations,** P.O. Box 1258, Taos, NM 87571 (☎ **505/751-1292,** or toll free **800/290-5384**), will help you find accommodations from bed-and-breakfasts to home rentals, hotels, and cabins throughout Taos and northern New Mexico. They'll also help you arrange rental cars and reservations for outdoor activities like white-water rafting, horseback riding, fishing/hunting trips, and ski packages, among other things.

Unlike in Santa Fe, there are two high seasons in Taos: winter (the Christmas-to-Easter ski season) and summer. Spring and fall are shoulder seasons, often with lower rates. The period between Easter and Memorial Day is notoriously slow in the tourist industry here, and many restaurants and other businesses take their annual vacations at this time. Book well ahead during ski holiday periods (especially Christmas) and during the annual arts festivals (late May to mid-June and late September to early October).

In these listings, the following categories describe peak-season price ranges: "Expensive," over $100 per night double; "Moderate," $75 to $100; "Inexpensive," $45 to $75; "Budget," less than $45 per night double. Tax of 10.3125% in Taos town and 9.8125% in Taos County is added to every hotel bill.

1 The Taos Area

Expensive

HOTELS/MOTELS

★ **The Historic Taos Inn,** 125 Paseo del Pueblo Norte, Taos, NM 87571. ☎ **505/758-2233,** or toll free **800/TAOS-INN.** $ Fax 505/758-5776. 39 rms. TEL

Rates: $75–$160 double, depending on the type of room and season. CB, DC, MC, V.

The last century of Taos history is alive and well within the walls of this atmospheric inn. The inn is made up of several separate adobe houses dating from the mid-1800s, which surrounded a small plaza complete with communal town well. Dr. T. Paul Martin purchased the complex in 1895; he was Taos County's first physician, and for many years the only one. In 1936, a year after the doctor's death, his widow, Helen, enclosed the plaza—now the inn's magnificent two-story lobby—installed indoor plumbing (the first in Taos!), and opened the Hotel Martin. In 1981–82 the inn was restored; it's now listed on the State and National Registers of Historic Places. Today guests find an inn of hospitality and charm, combining 20th-century elegance with 19th-century ambience. The lobby is graced with interior balconies overlooking the town well, reborn as a tiered fountain. Above it rises a stained-glass cupola. Large vigas adorn the ceiling, hand-woven rugs and outstanding artwork cover the walls, and visitors relax in Taos-style bancos facing a sunken pueblo-style fireplace in one corner of the room.

No two guest rooms are alike. While all are furnished in regional style, they differ in size, shape, and craft items—and thus each has a distinct personality. All rooms contain Taos-style furniture built by local artisans, and original Native American, Hispanic, and New Mexican artwork decorates the interiors. All have custom hand-loomed bedspreads, and 31 rooms have fireplaces.

Dining/Entertainment: Doc Martin's, with outstanding southwestern cuisine, is one of Taos's leading dining establishments (see Chapter 14). The Adobe Bar, popular among Taos artists and other locals, has live entertainment on select weeknights, snacks, margaritas, and an espresso-dessert menu.

Facilities: Rooms for nonsmokers and the disabled; seasonal outdoor swimming pool, year-round Jacuzzi in greenhouse.

Quail Ridge Inn, Ski Valley Rd. (P.O. Box 707), Taos, NM 87571. ☎ **505/776-2211,** or toll free **800/624-4448.** Fax 505/776-2949. 110 rms. 60 suites. TV TEL

Rates: $75–$135 single or double; $170–$280 suite. Rates depend on season; 2% gratuity added to all rates. Additional person $10 extra; children under 18 stay free in parents' room. DC, MC, V.

This sports-oriented lodge bills itself as a family resort and conference center. Tennis and skiing are popular at this contemporary pueblo-style hotel, which spreads across several acres of open sagebrush about 4 miles north of Taos and three-quarters of a mile east of U.S. 64, en route to the ski valley approximately 14 miles away.

Four room options are available at the Quail Ridge Inn, which won an award from *Western Home* magazine for architect Antoine Predock when it opened in 1978. Smallest are "hotel rooms," which can each sleep four on a queen-size bed and queen-size sleeper sofa.

Next are studios, actually semisuites with full kitchens and patios or balconies. One-bedroom suites, the most popular accommodations, each consist of a studio with a connecting hotel room. Half a dozen separate casitas contain spacious two-bedroom suites of about 1,600 square feet each.

Every room, no matter its size, has a big fireplace, huge closets, and full shower/baths with private hot-water heaters. Kitchenettes are fully stocked and each includes a stove, refrigerator, microwave oven, and dishwasher. The decor is breezy southwestern with light woods, dried-flower arrangements in handcrafted pottery, and various pieces of local art and artifacts.

Dining/Entertainment: Carl's French Quarter (☎ 776-8319), specializing in Cajun/Créole cuisine, is one of Taos's most popular restaurants. Lunches are strictly prebooked group affairs (no individual diners); but dinner is when Carl's bounces like Basin Street. Appetizers—seafood filet gumbo, shrimp-and-artichoke bisque—run $3.50 to $7.95. Main courses—shrimp Créole, blackened chicken, and Cajun prime rib—are $12.95 to $22.95. Dessert favorites are chocolate marquise cake and key lime pie. There's also a kids' menu. The lounge serves New Orleans cocktails like hurricanes and mint juleps.

Services: Valet laundry.

Facilities: Rooms for nonsmokers; year-round heated swimming pool, hot tubs and saunas, six outdoor and two indoor tennis courts, four racquetball/squash courts, summer volleyball pit, fitness center with weights and exercise room.

BED & BREAKFASTS

⭐ **Casa de las Chimeneas**, Cordoba Lane at Los Pandos Road (P.O. Box 5303), Taos, NM 87571. ☎ 505/758-4777. Fax 505/758-3976. 4 rms, 1 suite. TV TEL

Rates (including breakfast): $112 single; $122–$130 double; $148 suite (for two). MC, V.

This qualifies as Taos's luxury B&B. Its four rooms, each of them a work of art, each with a private entrance, look out on a beautifully landscaped private garden. The two-room suite includes an old library and two fireplaces; it's furnished with marble-topped antiques, a comfortable reading couch, a bentwood rocker, and a game table complete with chess and backgammon. Lace-trimmed bed linens cover a sheepskin mattress. The Blue Room and Willow Room have similar charm. The new Garden Room has a separate entrance off the herb, vegetable, and rose garden and features a fireplace as well as a skylit bathroom with a tab/shower combination and a deep soaking tab for one. Original art and hand-quilted spreads hang throughout and are for sale. Room minirefrigerators are stocked with complimentary soft drinks, juices, and mineral water. Bathrobes are supplied in each room. A full gourmet breakfast is served daily. A large hot tub is in a courtyard. Smoking is not permitted.

Moderate

Holiday Inn Don Fernando de Taos, Paseo del Pueblo Sur
(P.O. Drawer V), Taos, NM 87571. ☎ **505/758-4444,** or
toll free **800/HOLIDAY.** Fax 505/758-0055. 124 rms, 26 suites.
A/C TV TEL

Rates: $79–$95 single; $89–$105 double; $105–$135 suite. Rates depend on season; Christmas season rates higher. Additional person $10
children 19 and under stay free in parents' room. AE, CB, DC, DISC,
JCB, MC, V.

Taos's newest major hotel, opened in 1989, is like a modern Pueblo
village spread across landscaped grounds on the south side of town.
Half a dozen adobe-style two-story building clusters, each named for
a noted New Mexico artist, surround private courtyards. Standard
rooms, appointed in a soft Southwest-motif decor with Pueblo paintings on the walls, each feature hand-carved New Mexican wood
furnishings, two double beds or a king-size bed and sleeper sofa, and
a special doorside niche for skis and boots. Suites each offer a sitting
room, fireplace, and wet bar (not stocked).

Dining/Entertainment: Don Fernando's Restaurant, open daily
from 6:30am to 2pm and 5 to 10pm, serves a variety of regional breakfasts and lunches. An all-you-can-eat soup-and-salad lunch buffet
($5.95) is served Monday through Friday from 11:30am to 2pm.
Dinner main courses ($9.95 to $18.95) include steaks, chicken, pasta,
and seafood dishes. A children's menu is available. The Fernando's
Hideaway lounge, built around a large adobe fireplace, has a happy
hour Monday through Friday from 5 to 7:30pm.

Services: Room service, valet laundry, courtesy van, 24-hour desk.

Facilities: Rooms for nonsmokers and the disabled; outdoor swimming pool, hot tub, tennis court.

Kachina Lodge de Taos, 413 Paseo del Pueblo Norte
(P.O. Box NN), Taos, NM 87571. ☎ **505/758-2275,** or
toll free **800/522-4462.** Fax 505/758-9207. 118 rms. 4 suites.
A/C TV TEL

Frommer's Cool for Kids: Hotels

El Pueblo Lodge (see p. 180) A slide, year-round swimming
pool, and hot tub set in 2¹/₂-acre grounds will please the kids; a
barbecue, some minikitchens with microwave ovens, laundry facilities, and the rates will please their parents.

Kachina Lodge de Taos (see p. 170) An outdoor swimming pool
and snack machines in the summer here make a great late-afternoon
diversion for hot, tired, and cranky kids.

Quail Ridge Inn (see p. 168) The year-round swimming pool
and tennis courts will keep active kids busy during the day when
it's time for a parent's siesta.

Taos Accommodations

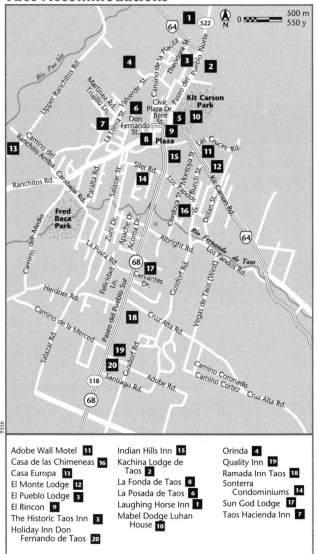

Adobe Wall Motel **11**
Casa de las Chimeneas **16**
Casa Europa **13**
El Monte Lodge **12**
El Pueblo Lodge **3**
El Rincon **9**
The Historic Taos Inn **5**
Holiday Inn Don
  Fernando de Taos **20**

Indian Hills Inn **15**
Kachina Lodge de
  Taos **2**
La Fonda de Taos **8**
La Posada de Taos **6**
Laughing Horse Inn **1**
Mabel Dodge Luhan
  House **10**

Orinda **4**
Quality Inn **19**
Ramada Inn Taos **18**
Sonterra
  Condominiums **14**
Sun God Lodge **17**
Taos Hacienda Inn **7**

Rates: $85–$145 single or double; $120–$150 suite. Additional person $8 extra; children under 12 stay free in parents' room. AE, DC, DISC, MC, V.

A Pueblo-style motel with bright-blue trim, this long-established lodge is an art lover's dream. The art gallery, which connects the lobby to the lodge's restaurants, has a changing exhibit of paintings and other works from the Taos Gallery. The Navajo Living Room, a comfortable space for indoor games or fireside reading, is full of valuable antique Navajo rugs. Rooms—there is a wide variety—are each appointed with custom-made Taoseño furniture, including armoire, headboards, table, and chairs. Many have a couch or love seat; all have huge bathrooms and a second sink at the vanity in an outer dressing area.

Dining/Entertainment: The Hopi Dining Room (open daily from 5:30 to 10pm for dinner) is an elegant restaurant with a gourmet family-style menu (steaks, chicken, seafood) priced at $10 to $14. The Kiva Coffee House, open daily from 6am to 5:30pm, serves filling breakfasts and Mexican-style lunches for under $8. The Zuni Lounge is open nightly, and the Kachina Cabaret (see Chapter 17) draws big-name acts. A Taos Pueblo dance troupe performs nightly in summer. No pets are allowed.

Services: Guest services desk (in summer).

Facilities: Rooms for nonsmokers; outdoor swimming pool, hot tub, coin-op laundry; ski shop adjacent.

La Fonda de Taos, South Plaza (P.O. Box 1447), Taos, NM 87571. ☎ **505/758-2211,** or toll free **800/833-2211.** 24 rms, 3 suites. A/C TEL

Rates: $70 single; $80 double; $120 suite. AE, MC, V.

An old-time, family-owned hotel, La Fonda hosted many of Taos's most glamorous guests in the 1940s, 1950s, and 1960s. The only lodging on the Plaza, it frankly has seen better days. Today it's most often visited by drop-ins who want a look at owner Saki Karavas's fine art collection, including Old West–style paintings on the walls of the heavy-beamed lobby. Ten original nudes by author D. H. Lawrence are sealed away in a private room for viewing by special request; Lawrence brought them to Taos when they were banned in England, along with his novel *Lady Chatterley's Lover,* in 1929.

Rooms, gaily decorated with red carpets and blue trim, have double or twin beds. Furnishings include dressers and desks; local phone calls are free. Guests can get their video-game fix in the TV room on the mezzanine.

Services: Valet laundry.

Neon Cactus Hotel, 1523 Paseo del Pueblo Sur (P.O. Box 5702), Taos, NM 87571. ☎ **505/751-1258.** 4 rms. A/C

Rates (including continental breakfast): Jan, Apr–June, and Sept–Dec 18, $65–$85 double; $105 quad. The rest of the year, $85–$125 double; $125–$145 quad. AE, MC, V.

The Neon Cactus is a delightful change of pace from some of the other hotels and bed-and-breakfasts in New Mexico. You won't find one hint of southwestern decor anywhere in this hotel, and if you're a movie buff you're not likely to miss it one bit. Each of the rooms here pays homage to a film star—for instance, the Marilyn Monroe Room is decorated with photographs that document the "many moods of Marilyn" and authentic period furnishings. The dominant color scheme in the room is black and white. There's a queen-size bed as well as a pull-out couch, so this room can sleep up to four. The bathroom in the Marilyn Monroe Room is something to behold: It features a Roman-style oversize sunken tub complete with bubble bath. The Rita Hayworth Room is done in rich reds, has two queen-size beds, and features an inviting reading nook. The Hayworth Room adjoins the Casablanca Room (the Hayworth Room may be rented on its own, but the Casablanca Room must be rented in conjunction with the Hayworth), which is my favorite room in the hotel. The small room is filled with Oriental rugs, tapestries, and pillows, but the best part is the built-in Turkish-style curtained twin bed. It sits a couple of feet above the floor and is surrounded by bookshelves. The reading lamp invites guests to climb into bed, close the curtains, and read themselves to sleep. The other two rooms, the James Dean Room and the Billie Holiday Room, are equally well thought-out. Each of the rooms is stocked with biographies of the star for which it's named, and there's a growing film library downstairs in the art deco sitting room. All rooms have private decks, and guests enjoy discount rates at the adjacent Taos Spa. An extended continental breakfast is included in the rates, and there's a Jacuzzi available for guest use.

Rancho Ramada, 615 Paseo del Pueblo Sur, Taos, NM 87571. ☎ **505/758-2900,** or toll free **800/RAMADA.** Fax 505/758-1662. 124 rms. A/C TV TEL

Rates: $98 double; $190 suite for two. Rollaway $15 extra; children under 18 stay free in parents' room. AE, CB, DC, DISC, EU, JCB, MC, V. **Parking:** Free.

Recently renovated, the Ramada is a large adobe-style building with a traditional bell tower. The newly designed lobby has a sitting area in front of a fireplace as well as some bancos on the front wall. The brightly colored and unusual murals on the lobby walls were specially done for the Ramada.

Each spacious room has a king-size bed or two queen-size beds and other standard furnishings, including a vanity table. Each suite has a living room with a pull-out couch, a gaslight kiva-style fireplace, and a full bath, as well as a full-size bedroom (two beds) with a full bath. Each room can be entered separately.

Dining/Entertainment: The Fireside Cantina Restaurant and Lounge, located just off the lobby, is open Monday through Friday from 6am to 1pm and on Saturday and Sunday from 6am to 11am. In the evenings it's open daily from 4 to 11pm for dinner. It's a pleasant, bright environment for breakfast, and in the evenings it can be sectioned off with the "adobe walls on wheels" and made more intimate for dinner or drinks by the fire.

Services: Room service, valet laundry, courtesy van.

Facilities: Rooms for nonsmokers and the disabled; indoor swimming pool, Jacuzzi, sun deck.

Sagebrush Inn, Paseo del Pueblo Sur (P.O. Box 557), Taos, NM 87571. ☎ **505/758-2254,** or toll free **800/428-3626.** Fax 505/758-5077. 81 rms, 19 suites. A/C TV TEL

Rates (including breakfast): $75 single; $90–$105 double; $120–$147 suite. Additional person $7 extra; children under 12 stay free in parents' room. AE, CB, DC, MC, V.

Originally called the Chamisa Inn, this hotel was built in Pueblo Mission style in 1929, about three miles south of the Plaza near Ranchos de Taos.

Georgia O'Keeffe, probably the most famous artist to have worked extensively in the Southwest, lived and painted for six months in the 1930s in a third-story room at this venerable hotel.

Most of the rooms face either an open grass courtyard, the outdoor swimming pool, or the stables. Traditional viga ceilings are complemented by earth-patterned decor and standard furnishings. Suites in "Sagebrush Village" have kiva fireplaces and beautiful hand-carved furniture. Each has a king-size bed in the bedroom, a Murphy bed in the main living area, two full baths, and charcoal drawings of local Native Americans on the walls. If you decide to stay at the Sagebrush you should know that you're paying for the hotel's history—not its amenities.

Dining/Entertainment: Los Vaqueros Room is open for dinner daily from 5:30 to 10pm. A complimentary full breakfast is served to guests daily from 6:30 to 11am in the Sagebrush Dining Room. The lobby bar is one of Taos's most active nightspots for live music and dancing (see Chapter 17).

Services: Courtesy van.

Facilities: Swimming pool, hot tub, tennis courts.

$ Sonterra Condominiums, 206 Siler Rd. (P.O. Box 5244), Taos, NM 87571. ☎ 758-7989. 9 suites. TV TEL
Rates: $49–$119 per day single or double, $775–$1,100 per month. Additional person $10 extra. MC, V.

This pleasant and secluded complex is four blocks from the Plaza. Surrounded by a high adobe wall and cedar or latilla fence, these one-story, Pueblo-style condos face into a central garden courtyard with a graceful Mexican fountain. Every unit has a full kitchen, stocked with all cookware and utensils, and containing a refrigerator, four-burner stove, microwave oven, and coffee maker. Each has a private outdoor patio. Three have fireplaces, for which a complimentary firelog is provided. Regional art, from paintings to Taos-style drums employed as night tables, makes each room a bit different from the next. No pets.

Facilities: Hot tub, solar-paneled guest laundry.

BED & BREAKFASTS

★ Adobe & Pines Inn, N.M. 68 (Box 837), Ranchos de Taos, NM 87557. ☎ **505/751-0947,** or toll free **800/723-8267.** Fax 505/758-8423. 5 rms. TV
Rates (including breakfast): $95–$145 single or double. MC, V.

After some traveling in Europe, the owners, Chuck and Charil, decided that they wanted to open a bed-and-breakfast inn. The only problem is that they didn't quite know where—until they ended up in Taos and fell in love with what, after six months of renovation, is now the Adobe & Pines Inn. It's located directly off N.M. 68, about 1 1/2 miles from the recreation area at Hwy. 570 (driving north from Santa Fe), or 0.3 miles from St. Francis Plaza (driving south from Taos town). If you're driving from Santa Fe, the entrance will be on your right; you can't really see the inn itself from the street, but you will see the multicolored posts that mark the driveway.

As you drive down to the house you'll see the horses out front, and you'll undoubtedly be awed by the 80-foot length of the Grand Portal. The inn is a 150-year-old adobe home that has been turned into one of the most beautiful and peaceful guesthouses I have stayed in. The inn rests amid four acres of pine and fruit trees (the land here is sacred—the Native Americans once stopped here to pray for a good hunt on their way to the hunting grounds, and again on their way back to thank the gods for their successes). Each room has a private entrance, which affords you all the privacy you could ever need. All rooms have fireplaces (two even have a fireplace in the bathroom), and each is decorated uniquely. The room called Puerta Azul is a wonderful, cozy space with an antique writing desk and royal-blue accents. Puerta Verde, done in deep greens, has a wonderful old retablo (ask Chuck and Charil about it), a sitting area, and a queen-size canopy bed. Puerta Turquese, my favorite, is a guest cottage that is separate from the rest of the house; it has a full kitchen and is done in bright pastels. The wonderful "broken tile mosaic" floors, laid about a hundred years ago by a man who did only a select few in the whole town of Taos, run throughout the whole guesthouse. The colors (turquoise, yellow, maroon, black, and peach) in the tile floor have been picked up in the rest of the decor. You can enjoy a fire under a down comforter while in bed, or you can relax in a jet whirlpool bath in front of a fire in the bathroom. Two new rooms, Puerta Violetta and Puerta Rosa, are welcome competition for Puerta Turquese. Chuck and Charil have outdone themselves with the addition of these bright, colorful rooms. Puerta Rosa, with its two-person soaking tub, cedar sauna, and fireplaced bathroom, is a mini-spa in itself. The bedroom has been furnished with a unique wrought-iron bed designed by Charil. Puerta Violetta is the only room on the second floor of the inn, and its main attraction is the spectacular view from a picture window which faces the bed. From the bed you'll have a wonderful view of the Taos night sky. In addition to a large bathroom with a two-person jet tub, Puerta Violetta has a private patio, making it a great place for a romantic evening of stargazing and sipping champagne.

In the evening, Chuck, Charil, and Rascal (their dog) serve hors d'oeuvres in front of a roaring fire in the living room, which is decorated with local art (on sale), including paintings, sculptures, and greeting cards. Some of this artwork is Charil's own—in fact, the paper sculpture hanging above the reception desk is hers. Morning brings a treat—a delicious full breakfast in front of the fire in the glassed-in breakfast room. Chuck and Charil are very gracious hosts, and they will help you plan activities to suit your interests; they'll also give you suggestions as to how you might want to spend your time in Taos. You really can't go wrong here; if I could give this place two stars I would!

Casa Europa, 840 Upper Ranchitos Rd. (HC 68, Box 3F), Taos, NM 87571. ☎ **505/758-9798,** or toll free **800/525-TAOS** for reservations. 6 rms.

Rates (including full breakfast): $70–$135 double. Additional person $20 extra. MC, V.

This cream-colored Mediterranean-style pueblo, 1³/₄ miles west of the Plaza, was built of adobe and vigas two centuries ago and fully renovated in 1983. The elegant rooms, each with full private bath, vary in furnishings: One, for example, has a marble whirlpool and enameled wood stove; another has a full-size Jacuzzi and fireplace, with glass doors opening onto a courtyard. In fact, there are eight fireplaces and 14 skylights in Casa Europa. Regional artwork in the rooms can be purchased. There's a sitting room for reading and/or conversation; coffee and pastries are offered here each day between 3 and 4pm, and during ski season hors d'oeuvres are served from 5 to 6pm. A full gourmet breakfast is served each morning. Smoking is not permitted.

El Rincon, 114 Kit Carson Rd., Taos, NM 87571. ☎ **505/758-4874.** 12 rms. TV

Rates (including continental breakfast): $49–$109 double. AE, MC, V.

Across the street from the Kit Carson Home and Museum (see Chapter 15) is the former home of 19th-century cultural leader La Dona Luz Lucero de Martinez. The inn comprises two dwellings separated by a flower-filled courtyard where breakfast is served in warm weather. Fine art and hand-carved furniture are scattered through both houses. Hostess Nina Meyers, an artist, has added trim and other decorations in her happy and colorful style. Each room is unique, but all have private baths, coffee pots, and VCRs; all but one have small refrigerators, and only two lack kiva fireplaces. Some of the rooms have been made up with Asian or Old West themes. Adjacent to the B&B is the Original Trading Post of Taos, still run by Rowena Martinez, widow of Native American trader and founder Ralph Meyers.

Hacienda del Sol, 109 Mabel Dodge Luhan Ln. (P.O. Box 177), Taos, NM 87571. ☎ **505/758-0287.** 8 rms (6 with bath). MC, V.
Rates: $55–$75 single, $65–$120 double.

Not far from the Plaza on the north side of Taos, Hacienda del Sol is a lovely, quiet bed and breakfast in a surprising location—directly behind the Lottaburger. Housed within the main building is the original 190-year-old adobe structure, easily recognized by its low ceilings and pueblo doorways. Like many of the homes in Taos, Hacienda del Sol has a wonderful history. The home was once owned by art patroness Mabel Dodge Luhan, and it was here that author Frank Waters wrote *The People of the Valley*. On the far side of the inn's well-manicured grounds is the adjoining Taos Pueblo. All the guest rooms are constructed of adobe and many of them feature kiva fireplaces built by Carmen Velarde, New Mexico's most sought after kiva fireplace artist. Each room is furnished with handcrafted Southwestern-style furnishings, antiques, and original art (for sale). Down comforters, clock radios with tape decks and a selection of cassettes, refrigerators, terrycloth robes, and private baths (each supplied with a basket of items you might have forgotten to bring with you) are added luxuries here. The spacious Sala del Don, located in the main building, was once Tony Luhan's room; it features a beautiful screen handcrafted by Lydia Garcia. The Casita is a separate building that houses two guest rooms which can be rented separately or as a unit. Both rooms have fireplaces and mountain-view bathtubs. Los Amantes ("The Lovers") is indeed for lovers—the two-person black Jacuzzi, situated on a mahogany platform directly beneath a skylight, is the perfect place to spend a romantic evening of stargazing. One room even has a private steam room. The extended continental breakfast here consists of fresh-baked goodies, fresh-squeezed juice, fruit, and the inn's special blend of coffee. Refreshments are also served every evening from 5pm. An outdoor hot tub offering spectacular views of Taos Mountain is available for guest use in half-hour blocks. Hacienda del Sol is an excellent choice for those traveling with children—it's one of only a handful of bed and breakfasts that will accept children of any age.

La Posada de Taos, 309 Juanita Lane (P.O. Box 1118), Taos, NM 87571. ☎ **505/758-8164.** 5 rms, 1 cottage.

Rates (including breakfast): $65–$105 single or double. Additional person $10 extra. No credit cards.

There's room for 12 guests here, in five rooms and a self-contained honeymoon cottage. Each of the small but charming units has a tiled private bath and is decorated with an array of international art and country pine antique furnishings. La Casa, the cottage, has its own fireplace and a double bed in a loft with a skylight. The Beutler Room has a king-size bed, wood stove, Jacuzzi, and games table. Two other units also each have a stove or fireplace. The sixth unit has a queen-size bed, a fireplace, and a large skylighted bathroom with a Jacuzzi. A full breakfast is served each morning.

★ **Little Tree Bed & Breakfast,** P.O. Box 960, El Prado, NM 87529. ☎ **505/776-8467.** 4 rms.

Rates (including breakfast): $70–$85 double. MC, V.

Little Tree is one of my favorite Taos bed-and-breakfasts, partly because it's located in a beautiful, secluded setting, and partly because it's built out of real adobe—not stucco like most of the new buildings in the area. The Giddens, who call themselves "refugee Dallasites," came to New Mexico and just fell in love with everything about the northern region of the state—especially the architecture. When they decided to move to Taos they began researching authentic adobe architecture and together came up with a floor plan for their new home. They ran the plans by an architect and, along with a couple of women who are expert adobe builders, began construction.

(It's interesting to note that throughout history women have built adobe homes because working with mud was considered too menial for men.)

The rooms are smallish, but charming and very cozy. They all have adobe floors, which are warm in the winter because the heat runs through the floors, making for a much healthier environment. All rooms have queen-size beds, private baths, and access to the portal and courtyard garden, at the center of which is the "little tree" for which the inn is named. The Piñon and Juniper Rooms have fireplaces and private entrances. The Piñon and Aspen Rooms have sunset views. The Spruce Room is western in feeling and is decorated with beautiful quilts.

In the main building, the living room has a traditional viga-and-latilla ceiling and tierra blanca adobe (adobe that's naturally white; if you look closely at it you can see little pieces of mica and straw). If you develop a real interest in adobe architecture, there are a number of books available for your reading pleasure. Three cats—Miss Kitty, Mister Mud, and Fred—entertain, and the hummingbirds that visit enchant guests as they enjoy a healthy breakfast on the portal in warmer months. On arrival, guests are treated to refreshments.

Mabel Dodge Luhan House, 240 Morada Lane (P.O. Box 3400), Taos, NM 87571. ☎ **505/758-9456,** or toll free **800/84-MABEL.** 19 rms (5 with bath).

Rates (including breakfast): $75–$150. Additional person $17.50 extra. MC, V.

This inn is also called Las Palomas de Taos because of the throngs of doves (*palomas*) that live in bird condominiums on the property. Like so many other free spirits, they were attracted by the flamboyant Mabel Dodge (1879–1962), who came to Taos in 1916. She and her fourth husband, a full-blooded Pueblo named Tony Luhan, enlarged this 200-year-old home to its present 22-room size in the 1920s. The Spanish Colonial–style portal and flagstone placita are hidden behind an adobe wall and shaded by huge hardwood trees. All main rooms have viga ceilings, arched Pueblo-style doorways, hand-carved Hispanic doors, kiva fireplaces, and dark hardwood floors. Guest rooms in the main building have antique furnishings. Six have fireplaces; baths are private or shared. Eight more guest rooms were recently added with the erection of a second building. All the new accommodations have fireplaces. During much of the year, rooms are reserved for educational workshop attendees. The Mabel Dodge Luhan House is now a National Historic Landmark.

Orinda B&B, 461 Valverde St. (P.O. Box 4451), Taos, NM 87571. ☎ **505/758-8561,** or **800/847-1837.** 3 rms, 1 suite.

Rates (including continental breakfast): $65–$85 double. Additional person $10 extra. MC, V.

This B&B has the delightful advantage of being in town but also in the country. Though only a 10-minute walk from the Plaza, it's tucked beneath huge trees with a view across pasture land to Taos Mountain. Thick adobe walls keep it warm in winter and cool in summer. Innkeepers Cary and George Pratt share their living room, including a TV, sound system, and wood-burning stove, with guests. Works by local artists adorn the walls of the dining room, where a hearty continental breakfast is served daily. Two rooms comprise the Vigil Suite, where a sitting room with a fireplace and refrigerator separates two bedrooms. The Truchas Room, with traditional southwestern decor, has a private entrance, fireplace, and bath. Pets and smoking are not permitted.

Taos Hacienda Inn, 102 LaLoma Plaza (P.O. Box 4159), Taos, NM 87571. ☎ **505/758-1717,** or toll free **800/530-3040.** 7 rms. TV TEL

Rates (including breakfast): $95–$125 standard double; $145–$185 artist's studio: $135–$300 suite. Discounts available. AE, MC, V.

As you drive into the parking area, you'll see the Taos Hacienda Inn perched atop a small hill. As you enter the reception area, you'll be immediately relaxed by the abundance of green plants and a slow, gurgling fountain. Local art (for sale) is displayed in all public spaces of this comfortable and spacious adobe home (some of which was built in the 1800s).

Each room is uniquely decorated, though all have the same amenities—such as bathrobes, fireplaces, fresh flowers, TVs, telephones, and queen- or king-size beds. Some rooms have patios, and there are a couple of suites and artists' studios with kitchenettes. Cary's Studio—named for Cary Moore, a longtime resident of the home—has a full kitchenette and sleeps up to six. The Happy Trails Room, which is distinctly different from the rest of the rooms in the house, has wonderful pine paneling, a brass bed, and chaps and spurs hanging decoratively. A couple of the rooms have incredible views of Taos Mountain. All the furniture is handcrafted.

In the morning, a breakfast of fresh fruit, different kinds of juice, fresh breads, muffins, croissants, and a daily special hot item, perhaps a breakfast burrito with Jerry's special green chiles, is served. In the early evening you'll find southwestern hors d'oeuvres or homemade cookies and coffee waiting for you to snack on while you're planning your evening.

Inexpensive

El Monte Lodge, 317 Kit Carson Rd. (P.O. Box 22), Taos, NM 87571. ☎ **505/758-3171.** 13 rms. TV TEL

Rates: $54–$59 single; $85–$95 double. Kitchenette units $10 extra. AE, DISC, MC, V.

Century-old cottonwood trees stand in a parklike picnic area, complete with barbecue grills and children's playground, outside this friendly 1930s motel. Four blocks east of the Plaza, it's old-fashioned but homey, built in traditional adobe style with protruding vigas, painted yellow, and framed by flower gardens. The rooms, many with fireplaces, occupy eight small buildings. The eclectic decor features considerable Pueblo art. Four rooms have fully stocked kitchenettes; there's a free guest laundry. Pets are permitted for an extra $5.

El Pueblo Lodge, 412 Paseo del Pueblo Norte (P.O. Box 92), Taos, NM 87571. ☎ **505/758-8700,** or toll free **800/433-9612.** Fax 505/758-7321. 42 rms, 4 suites. TV TEL

Rates (including continental breakfast): $43–$48 single; $63 double; $73–$215 suite. Additional person $7–$10 extra. AE, MC, V.

The setting here is special: nicely landscaped 3¹/₂-acre grounds, complete with cottonwood and towering fir trees, gardens, barbecue pits, and lawn furniture. Throw in a year-round outdoor swimming pool and hot tub, and it's no surprise this lodge is popular with families. All the brightly colored rooms have southwestern decor and refrigerators. Rooms with kitchenettes and fireplaces are also available. Laundry facilities are free to guests. A light complimentary breakfast is served daily.

★ **Laughing Horse Inn,** 729 Paseo del Pueblo Norte (P.O. Box $ 4889), Taos, NM 87571. ☎ **505/758-8350,** or toll free **800/776-0161.** 14 rms (3 with bath). TV

Rates (including continental breakfast): $42–$55 single; $48–$60 double; $98 suite. MC, V.

Occupying the print shop of the 1920s "Laughing Horse Press," the inn is an unmistakable stucco structure with lilac-purple trim located a mile north of the Plaza on the right. Guests can choose between sunny dorm rooms, cozy private rooms, a deluxe solar-heated penthouse, or guesthouses. The private rooms have sleeping lofts, cassette decks, TVs, and VCRs, and some have fireplaces. Bathrooms are shared. The penthouse has a private solar bedroom and enclosed sleeping loft, a private bath, a wood stove, a big-screen TV, and video and audio decks. The guesthouses have living rooms, fireplaces, private baths, and queen lofts; one has a full kitchen. The two guesthouses adjoin for large parties. The inn has a common room around a big fireplace, a games room, and a café where continental breakfasts are served and a refrigerator is stocked for use on the honor system. There's an outdoor hot tub, a masseuse (by appointment), and mountain bikes free for guests' use.

Quality Inn, 1023 Paseo del Pueblo Sur, Taos, NM 87571. ☎ **505/758-2200,** or toll free **800/845-0648.** Fax 505/758-9009. 99 rms. 2 suites. A/C TV TEL

Rates (including breakfast in low seasons): $65–$85 single or double; $135–$150 suite. Additional person $7 extra; children under 18 stay free in parents' room. AE, CB, DC, DISC, EU, JCB, MC, V.

Newly renovated, this Quality Inn is nearer the Carson National Forest (a short trek east) than the Taos Plaza (about two miles north). Rooms have nice decorative touches like mirrors framed with copperwork and R. C. Gorman prints. There are 11 units with king-size beds; two suites have kitchenettes. The inn has a restaurant (open daily from 6:30am to 2pm and 5:30 to 9pm) and lounge and a heated outdoor swimming pool and hot tub.

Sun God Lodge, 919 Paseo del Pueblo Sur (P.O. Box 1713), Taos, NM 87571. ☎ 505/758-3162. 55 units. TV TEL

Rates: $67.65 single; $74.30–$85.35 double; $100.90 suite; $105–$139 casita. AE, MC, DISC, V.

An adobe structure, this motel offers 1¹/₂ acres of landscaped grounds. After a recent renovation, the rooms are done in southwestern decor, all with ceiling fans, double or queen- or king-size beds (with Navajo-patterned spreads), prints and lithographs by Taos artists on the walls, and complimentary bedside coffee service. There are some new accommodations with kitchenette areas (fully supplied with dishes and utensils, coffee makers, and minirefrigerators) and living rooms with kiva fireplaces (wood and firestarter are supplied), remote-controlled TVs, and niches with howling coyotes or kachinas. There are outdoor grills and a hot-tub room.

Budget

$ **Abominable Snowmansion Skiers' Hostel,** Taos Ski Valley Rd., Arroyo Seco (P.O. Box 3271), Taos, NM 87571. ☎ 505/776-8298. 60 beds.

Rates (including full breakfast in winter): $11.50–$50 per bed, depending on size of accommodation and season. MC, V.

Located in the small community of Arroyo Seco, about 8 miles north of Taos and 10 miles from the Taos and 10 miles from the Taos Ski Valley, this lodging attracts many young people. It's clean and comfortable for those happy with dormitory-style accommodation. Toilets, shower rooms, and dressing rooms are segregated by sex. A two-story lodge room focuses around a circular fireplace and features a piano and games area. Lodging is also offered in traditional teepees and smaller bunkhouses in the campfire area. Tent camping is permitted outside. Guests can cook their own meals or indulge in home-cooked fare.

Adobe Wall Motel, 227 Kit Carson Rd. (P.O. Box 1081), Taos, NM 87571. ☎ 505/758-3972. 20 rms. TV

Rates: $44 single; $50 double. Additional person $6 extra; children under 12 stay free in parents' room. AE, MC, V.

Once a stagecoach stop, this motel has cozy units each with king- or queen-size beds, handmade Mexican furniture, and leather-upholstered chairs. All rooms have showers; some also have tubs. There are no private phones, but guests can use a pay phone in the lobby, where there's also complimentary coffee, tea, and cider.

Indian Hills Inn, 233 Paseo del Pueblo Sur (P.O. Box 1229), Taos, NM 87571. ☎ 505/758-4293, or toll free 800/444-2346. 50 rms, 7 suites. TV TEL

Rates (including continental breakfast): $50–$55 single; $60–$65 double; $80–$85 suite. AE, DISC, MC, V.

Just a short walk south of the Plaza, this stuccoed adobe building has undergone a major facelift. Its well-lit units have king- or queen-size beds and other standard furnishings, including cable TVs. Local phone calls are free. Rooms feature regional artwork, antique maps, and southwestern-motif bedspreads. Suites have kitchens; some have fireplaces. Behind the hotel are a swimming pool and picnic area with barbecues.

Taos Motel, 4175 Paseo del Pueblo Sur (P.O. Box 729), Ranchos de Taos, NM 87557. ☎ **505/758-2524,** or toll free **800/323-6009.** 28 rms. TV TEL

Rates: $29–$48 single or double. Children under 12 stay free in parents' room. AE, DISC, MC, V.

A Spanish Colonial–style building with spiral pillars and corbels and a red tile roof, this is Taos's southernmost motel. Rooms have double beds and built-in desk/dressers, and local phone calls are free. Free coffee is offered in the lobby daily from 7am to 11pm. The Taos RV Park is located next door and is open all year.

2 Taos Ski Valley

For information on the skiing and the facilities offered at Taos Ski Valley, see "Sports and Recreation" in Chapter 15.

Expensive

HOTELS

Hotel Edelweiss, Taos Ski Valley, NM 87525. ☎ **505/776-2301.** 20 rms. A/C TV TEL

Rates: $125–$150 single or double. MC, V.

This quiet, elegant hotel offers family-style accommodations right on the ski slopes. There's French cuisine for breakfast and lunch, with après-ski coffees and pastries.

Inn at Snakedance, P.O. Box 89, Taos Ski Valley, Taos, NM 87525. ☎ **505/776-2277,** or toll free **800/322-9815.** Fax 505/776-1410. 60 rms. TV TEL

Rates: Nov 23–Dec 16 and Mar 26–Apr 8, $115 standard or fireplace double. Dec 17–23, Feb 4–16, and Feb 20–Mar 25, $175 standard double; $195 fireplace double. Dec 24–31 and Feb 17–19, $210 standard double; $230 fireplace double. Jan 1–Feb 3, $155 standard double; $180 fireplace double. Rates are lower in the off season. MC, V.
Parking: Free at Taos Ski Valley parking lot.

Located in the heart of Taos Ski Valley, the Inn at Snakedance is the only modern hotel in the area that offers ski-in/ski-out privileges. The most attractive feature of this hotel is that it's literally only 10 yards from the ski lift, which means that you won't have to drag your skis, boots, and children onto the shuttle bus to get to the lift and you can ski right back to the hotel if you get cold or tired. The original structure that stood on this site (part of which has been restored for use as part of the hotel today) was known as the Hondo Lodge.

Before there was a Taos Ski Valley, Hondo Lodge served as a refuge for fishermen, hunters, and artists. It was built of enormous pine timbers that had been cut for a copper-mining operation in the 1890s, and was literally nothing more than a place for the men to bed down for the night. Today the Inn at Snakedance offers much more than just a place to lay one's head in the evening. The guest rooms are comfortable and many of them feature wood-burning fireplaces. All the furnishings are modern, the rooms are done in jade and maroon with floral-print draperies, and the windows (many of which offer mountain views) open to let in the fresh mountain air. All rooms have cable TV, minirefrigerators and wet bars (not stocked), and bathrooms with standard shower/tubs and a separate vanity area. Some rooms adjoin, connecting a standard hotel room with a fireplace room—perfect for families. Smoking is prohibited in the guest rooms and most public areas.

Dining/Entertainment: The Hondo Restaurant and Bar offers dining and entertainment daily in ski season (schedules vary off-season), and also sponsors wine tastings and wine dinners. Grilled items, salads, and snacks are available on an outdoor deck. The slopeside bar offers great views.

Services: Shuttle service to nearby hotels, shops, and restaurants.

Facilities: Minispa (with hot tub, sauna, exercise equipment, and massage facilities), massage therapist on site, in-house ski storage and boot dryers, convenience store (with food, sundries, video rental, and alcoholic beverages).

CONDOMINIUMS

Hacienda de Valdez, Ski Valley Rd. (P.O. Box 5651), Taos, NM 87571. ☎ **505/776-2218.** 13 units. A/C TV TEL
  Rates: Winter, $220–$300. Summer, $85–$160. AE, DISC, MC, V.

Located about eight miles from the Ski Valley, these Pueblo-style luxury condo units have fully equipped kitchens with microwave ovens, fireplaces (with firewood provided), queen-size beds, and color TVs. There are outdoor hot tubs and daily maid service.

Kandahar Condominiums, P.O. Box 72, Taos Ski Valley, NM 87525. ☎ **505/776-2226.** Fax 505/776-2481. 27 units. A/C TV TEL
  Rates: $65–$136, depending on season. AE, MC, V.

These condos have the highest location on the slopes—and with it, ski-in/ski-out access. Facilities include an exercise room, a Jacuzzi, a steam room, a professional masseur, a laundry, and a conference and party facility. American Educational Institute seminars are held weekly in season.

Sierra del Sol Condominiums, P.O. Box 84, Taos Ski Valley, NM 87525. ☎ **505/776-2981,** or toll free **800/523-3954.** 32 units. TV TEL
  Rates: $112–$165. **Closed:** Summer. MC, V.

Located just a two-minute walk from the lifts, these condo units have fully equipped kitchens, fireplaces, and balconies. There are two hot tubs and saunas on the premises. Two-bedroom units sleep up to six; one-bedrooms and studios are also available.

Twining Condominiums, P.O. Box 696, Taos Ski Valley, NM 87525. ☎ **505/776-8873,** or toll free **800/828-2472.** 19 units. TV TEL
Rates: $125–$320. AE, DISC, MC, V.

Studios and two-bedroom units with lofts have fireplaces, color TVs, and fully equipped kitchens with dishwashers. There are also a hot tub and sauna. The main lift area is just a three-minute walk away.

Moderate

LODGES & CONDOMINIUMS

Amizette Inn, Taos Ski Valley Rd. (P.O. Box 756), Taos Ski Valley, NM 87525. ☎ **505/776-2451,** or toll free **800/446-TAOS.** 12 rms. A/C TV TEL
Rates: $110–$153 single or double. AE, CB, DC, DISC, MC, V. **Closed:** Summer.

Open for ski season only, this lodge has a hot tub and redwood sauna, tanning deck, and full-service restaurant. The spacious rooms with separate sitting areas and panoramic river and mountain views are perfect for a romantic getaway.

Austing Haus, Taos Ski Valley Rd. (P.O. Box 8), Taos Ski Valley, NM 87525. ☎ **505/776-2649,** or toll free **800/748-2932.** 36 rms. TV TEL
Rates (including continental breakfast): $50–$145 single or double. DC, MC, V.

About 1¹/₂ miles from the ski resort, the Austing Haus has a restaurant and hot tub. Guests have a choice of rooms that ranges from a standard hotel unit to luxury fireplace rooms that feature four-poster beds. Incidentally, it's the largest and tallest timber frame building in the United States.

Taos Mountain Lodge, Taos Ski Valley Rd. (P.O. Box 698), Taos Ski Valley, NM 87525. ☎ **505/776-2229.** 10 suites. A/C TV TEL
Rates: $59–$165 suite. AE, MC, V.

About 1 mile west of the valley are these loft suites (that accommodate up to four) with queen-size beds, fully equipped kitchenettes with microwave ovens, living rooms, and private spa rooms.

Thunderbird Lodge, P.O. Box 87, Taos Ski Valley, NM 87525. ☎ **505/776-2280** or **505/776-2238.** 32 rms.
Rates (including three meals): $118–$180 double. AE, MC, V.

Located 150 yards from the slopes on the north ("sunny") side of the valley, the Thunderbird's extras include a superb restaurant with a large wine cellar, superb Saturday-evening buffet, and nightly entertainment in the bar. An International Jazz Festival is hosted annually for two weeks in January. Packages are available. The lodge has a sauna, Jacuzzi, and conference facilities. Twenty-four rooms in the main lodge each have a double and a single bed or a set of bunk beds. Eight rooms in the chalets are larger (including some family rooms) with queen-size beds.

3 RV Parks & Campgrounds

Carson National Forest, P.O. Box 558, Taos, NM 87571.
☎ **505/758-6200.**
There are nine national forest campsites within 20 miles of Taos, all
open from April or May until September or October, depending on
snow conditions. For information on other public sites, contact the
Bureau of Land Management, 224 Cruz Alta Rd., Taos, NM 87571
(☎ **505/758-8851**).

Questa Lodge, two blocks from N.M. 522 (P.O. Box 155), Questa,
NM 87556. ☎ **505/586-0300.** 24 units.
Rates: Full RV hookup, $15 per day, $160 per month. **Closed:** Nov–Apr.

Taos RV Park, Paseo del Pueblo Sur (P.O. Box 729), Ranchos de Taos,
NM 87557. ☎ **505/758-1667,** or toll free **800/323-6009.** 29 units.
Rates: $12 without RV hookup, $15 with RV hookup.

Taos Valley RV Park and Campground, 120 Estes Rd. off N.M.
68; 5749 NDCBU, Taos, NM 87571. ☎ **505/758-4469.** 92 units.
Rates: $14 without RV hookup, $17–$19 with RV hookup. **Closed:**
Nov 2–Feb.

14

Taos Dining

R ESTAURANTS IN TAOS ARE VERY INFORMAL. NOWHERE IS A COAT AND TIE mandatory; in the winter you'll see diners in ski sweaters and blue jeans even at the finest restaurants. The informality doesn't extend to a disregard for reservations, however; especially in peak season, make them well in advance and keep them or cancel.

In the listings below, an "Expensive" restaurant is one with most main courses $15 or higher; "Moderate" has main courses from $10 to $15; and "Inexpensive," $6 to $10; and "Budget," less than $6.

1 Expensive

Doc Martin's, in the Taos Inn, 125 Paseo del Pueblo Norte.
☎ 758-1977.

Cuisine: CONTEMPORARY SOUTHWESTERN. **Reservations:** Recommended.

Prices: Appetizers $4–$8.25; main courses $14.50–$19.50; breakfast $3.95–$7; lunch $4.50–$8.50. CB, DC, MC, V.

Open: Breakfast/lunch daily 7:30am–2:30pm; dinner daily 5:30–10pm.

This portion of the Taos Inn comprises Dr. Paul Martin's former home, office, and delivery room. In 1912, painters Bert Philips (Doc's brother-in-law) and Ernest Blumenschein hatched the concept of the Taos Society of Artists in the Martin dining room. Art still predominates here, from paintings to cuisine. The food here is widely acclaimed, and the wine list has received numerous "Awards of Excellence" from *Wine Spectator* magazine.

Breakfast may include the local favorites: huevos rancheros (fried eggs on a blue-corn tortilla smothered with chile and Jack cheese) or "The Kit Carson" (eggs Benedict with a southwestern flair). Light fare for lunch includes a Pacific ahi tuna sandwich or Caesar salad. For the heartier appetite, the northern New Mexican casserole (layers of blue-corn tortillas, pumpkin-seed mole, calabacitas, and Cheddar) or Doc's chiles rellenos (fresh roasted green chiles stuffed with caramelized onions, herbs, and Jack cheese) will do the trick. For dinner, start with the salmon gordita (salmon cake, made with fresh salmon and served with a house mustard sauce) or the goat-cheese-and-potato terrine. Follow it with the homemade onion ravioli stuffed with onion compote and served with calabacitas in a roast-garlic sauce, or the Southwest lacquered duck (poached, roasted, and grilled duck breast served over julienne duck-leg meat and red-chile broth with posole and mango relish). If you've still got room after all this, you can finish your meal with a choice of exquisite desserts.

★ **Lambert's of Taos,** 309 Paseo del Pueblo Sur. ☎ **758-1009.**
Cuisine: CONTEMPORARY AMERICAN. **Reservations:** Recommended.
Prices: Main courses $10.50–$18.50 AE, DC, MC, V.
Open: Lunch Mon–Fri 11:30am–2:30pm; dinner daily 6–9pm.

Zeke Lambert, a former San Francisco restaurateur who was head chef at Doc Martin's for four years, opened this fine dining establishment in late 1989 in the historic Randall Home near Los Pandos

Road. Now, in simple but elegant surroundings, he presents a new and different menu every night.

Diners can start with the likes of homemade duck pàté with roasted garlic, a spinach-and-basil salad with sautéed mushrooms, or grilled lamb tenderloin. Main courses always include fresh seafood, such as tuna with yams and garlic butter, or Dungeness crab cakes with dipping sauce and pickled vegetables. Other more-or-less typical main dishes could be pepper-crusted lamb with red-wine demi-glace and garlic pasta, sautéed breast of duck served with black beans, or cassoulet with duck confit and lamb sausage. To accommodate different appetites, all main courses are offered in two sizes. Desserts are outstanding, like chocolate oblivion truffle torte and sour-cream cognac cake. Espresso coffees, beers, and wines are poured.

★ **Stakeout Grill & Bar,** Stakeout Dr., just off N.M. 68.
☎ 758-2042.
Cuisine: INTERNATIONAL. **Reservations:** Recommended.
Prices: Appetizers $4.95–$10.95; main courses $13.95–$26.95. AE, CB, DC, DISC, EU, MC, V.
Open: Dinner daily 5–10pm; brunch Sun 10am–2pm.

I love this restaurant. Maybe it's because you have to drive about a mile up a dirt road toward the base of the Sangre de Cristo mountains, and once you get there (you'll think I'm insane for sending you up Stakeout Drive in the black of night, and you'll think you're never going to get there) you've got one of the greatest views of Taos. Or maybe it's because after you're inside, you're enveloped in the warmth of its rustic decor (which is a great contrast to the close-to-white exterior); there are paneled walls and creaking hardwood floors and a crackling fireplace in the winter. The food is marvelous. You can start with baked Brie with sliced almonds and apples or escargots with walnuts and garlic. Move on to a wonderful filet mignon, wrapped in bacon and cooked to your liking; or my favorite (and the chef's), the honey-almond duck, which is never fatty and always leaves you feeling a little sticky, but *very* satisfied. Finish your meal with some fresh pastry and a cappuccino. You'll really be missing something if you don't get to Stakeout while you're in Taos.

★ **Villa Fontana,** N.M. 522, five miles north of Taos.
☎ 758-5800.
Cuisine: ITALIAN. **Reservations:** Recommended.
Prices: Appetizers $4–$11.50; main courses $19–$25. AE, CB, DC, DISC, JCB, MC, V.
Open: Lunch Tues–Fri 11:30am–2pm; dinner daily 6pm–late.

Carlo and Siobhan Gislimberti like to talk about "peccato di gola"—lust of the palate. The couple brought it with them to Taos when they left their home in the Italian Dolomites, near the Austrian border. They have their own herb garden, and Carlo, a master chef, is a member of the New Mexico Mycological Society—wild mushrooms are a major element in many of his kitchen preparations. Also something of an artist, Carlos displays his own work throughout the restaurant.

Taos Dining

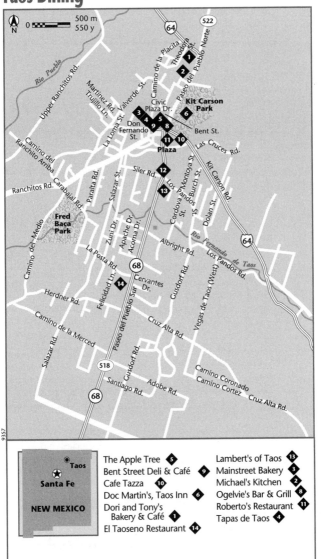

The Apple Tree	5	Lambert's of Taos	13
Bent Street Deli & Café	9	Mainstreet Bakery	3
Cafe Tazza	10	Michael's Kitchen	2
Doc Martin's, Taos Inn	6	Ogelvie's Bar & Grill	8
Dori and Tony's Bakery & Café	1	Roberto's Restaurant	11
El Taoseno Restaurant	14	Tapas de Taos	4

Meals are truly gourmet. Diners can start with scampi alla Veneziana (shrimp in a brandy Aurora sauce) or paté ricco de fegatini alla moda (homemade chicken-liver paté). Main courses include whole Dover sole with fresh herbs, pheasant breast with dried blueberries and demi-glace, and grilled beef tenderloin with brandy, balsamic vinegar, and green peppercorns. Dinners are served with salad, fresh vegetables, and potatoes or rice. Outdoor dining in the summer offers pleasant mountain and valley views.

2   Moderate

The Apple Tree, 123 Bent St. ☎ 758-1900.

Cuisine: INTERNATIONAL. **Reservations:** Recommended.
Prices: Appetizers $4.50–$8.95; main courses $10.95–$18.95. CB, DC, DISC, MC, V.
Open: Lunch Mon–Fri 11:30am–3pm; dinner daily 5:30–9pm; brunch Sat–Sun 10am–3pm.

Eclectic music pervades the four elegant adobe rooms of this fine restaurant, a block north of the Plaza. Original paintings by Taos masters overlook the candlelit service indoors; outside, diners sit at wooden tables on a graveled courtyard beneath spreading apple trees.

Daily specials supplement a standing menu with international flavor. A very popular item is velarde carnitas enchiladas (pork layered between blue-corn tortillas with apple chutney, sour cream, and white Cheddar). There's a limited children's menu, and the chef will modify dishes to suit special dietary needs whenever possible.

Casa de Valdez, Paseo del Pueblo Sur. ☎ 758-8777.

Cuisine: NEW MEXICAN. **Reservations:** Recommended.
Prices: Appetizers $5.95–$6.50; main courses $7.95–$18.95. AE, DISC, MC, V.
Open: Mon–Tues and Thurs–Sat 11:30am–9:30pm, Sun 4–9:30pm.

You can't really miss the Casa de Valdez—it's the only A-frame building in the area. It's located 2¹/₂ miles south of the Plaza. The interior looks more like a mountain home than a New Mexican restaurant because of the wood paneling, which makes it a cozy environment for a quiet dinner for two. The extremely friendly staff know many of their customers by name. The menu is predictable as far as New Mexican cuisine goes, with blue-corn enchiladas, bean burritos, and tamales. You can also get spareribs and barbecued chicken. Personally, I think the sopaipillas served at the Casa de Valdez are the best around—they practically melt in your mouth.

Frommer's Cool for Kids: Restaurants

El Taoseño Restaurant   (see p. 193) The jukebox and games room will keep everyone happy while waiting for tacos and enchiladas at low prices here.

Casa de Valdez   (see p. 190) Parents will feel comfortable dining with children here, and the menu is simple enough to please even the pickiest of palates.

Ogelvie's Bar & Grill, 1031 East Plaza. ☎ **758-8866.**

Cuisine: INTERNATIONAL. **Reservations:** Not accepted.
Prices: Appetizers $2.95–$7.50; main courses $5.50–$9.50 at lunch,
$8.50–$19.50 at dinner. AE, MC, V.
Open: Summer, breakfast/lunch daily 10am–4pm; dinner daily 5–10pm.
Winter, lunch daily 11am–4pm; dinner daily 5–10pm.

Like Ogelvie's in Albuquerque and Santa Fe, this is a casual restaurant with rich wood decor. Homemade soups, burgers and other
sandwiches, and huevos (eggs) de casa Ogelvie's are hits on the lunch
menu. Dinner might include shrimp Hawaiian, fresh trout piñon,
steaks, and regional specialties, like fajitas, burritos, and enchiladas,
as well as a few pasta dishes. A lively bar with an outdoor deck overlooks the Plaza.

---

3 **Inexpensive**

$ **Bent Street Deli & Cafe,** 120 Bent St. ☎ **758-5787.**

Cuisine: DELI. **Reservations:** Recommended.
Prices: Breakfast $2–$6.50; lunch $2.25–$7; dinner $10–$13. MC, V.
Open: Mon–Sat 8am–9pm.

This popular café is a short block north of the Plaza. Outside, a flower
box surrounds sidewalk-café-style seating beneath large
blue-and-white umbrellas. Inside, baskets and bottles of homemade
jam lend a homey country feel. The menu features breakfast burritos
and homemade granola for the morning hours; 18 deli sandwiches,
plus a "create-your-own" column, for lunch; and various quiche,
pasta, chicken, and fish dishes for dinner.

Caffè Tazza, 122 Kit Carson Rd. ☎ **758-8706.**

Cuisine: CAFE. **Reservations:** Not accepted.
Prices: All items under $10. No credit cards.
Open: Daily 8am–6pm (to 10pm on performance nights).

This cozy three-room café is a gathering spot for local community
groups, artists, performers, and poets—in fact, it's home to SOMOS,
the Society of the Muse of the Southwest. Plays, films, comedy, and
musical performances take place on weekends (and on some weeknights in summer) in the café's main room. The walls are constantly
hung with the works of local emerging artists who have not yet made
it to the Taos gallery scene. Locals and tourists alike enjoy sitting in
the café, taking in the scene while sipping a cappuccino or espresso.
Of course, the food is quite good as well. Soups, sandwiches, tamales, croissants, and pastries are all popular.

★ **Michael's Kitchen,** 305 Paseo del Pueblo Norte. ☎ **758-4178.**

Cuisine: NEW MEXICAN/AMERICAN. **Reservations:** Not accepted.
$ **Prices:** Breakfast $2.85–$8.45; lunch $2.65–$8.25; dinner $5.25–
$10.75. MC, V.
Open: Daily 7am–8:30pm.

A couple of blocks north of the Plaza is this eatery, a throwback to earlier days. Between its hardwood floor and viga ceiling are various knickknacks on posts, walls, and windows: a deer head here, a Tiffany lamp there, and several scattered antique wood stoves. Seating is at booths and tables. Meals, too, are old-fashioned, as far as quality and quantity for price. Breakfasts, including a great variety of pancakes and egg dishes, are served all day (because they're so popular), as are luncheon sandwiches. Dinners range from veal Cordon Bleu to knackwurst and sauerkraut, plantation fried chicken to enchiladas rancheros, fish and chips to New York steak. There's also a children's menu.

Roberto's Restaurant, 122 Kit Carson Rd. ☎ 758-2434.
   Cuisine: NEW MEXICAN. **Reservations:** Recommended.
   Prices: Appetizers $2.85–$5; main courses $6.50–$11.95. MC, V.
   Open: Summer, lunch Wed–Mon noon–2:30pm; dinner Wed–Mon 6–9pm. Winter, most weekends.

Hidden within a warren of art galleries opposite the Kit Carson Museum (see Chapter 15) is this local gem, which for more than 25 years has focused on authentic native dishes. Within this 160-year-old adobe are three small high-ceilinged dining rooms, each with hardwood floors and a maximum of five tables; there's a corner fireplace in one of them. Everyday dishes include tacos, enchiladas, tamales, and chiles rellenos. All meals start with sopaipillas and are accompanied by homemade refried beans with chicos (dried kernels of corn). Beer and wine only are served. Note that Roberto is an avid skier and, as a result, winter hours are unpredictable at best.

Tapas de Taos Cafe, 136 Bent St. ☎ 758-9670.
   Cuisine: NEW MEXICAN/TAPAS. **Reservations:** Not accepted.
   Prices: Tapas $3.75–$7.50; main courses $2.95–$9.95. MC, V.
   Open: Breakfast Mon–Fri 8:30–11am; lunch Mon–Fri 11:30am–3pm; dinner Mon–Sat 5:30–9:30pm, Sun 5:30–9pm; brunch Sat–Sun 10:30am–3pm.

If you're familiar with Mexican culture, you'll recognize the theme decor at Tapas de Taos Cafe. It's representational of the Mexican Day of the Dead (Dia de los Muertos). The rows of black skulls that line the walls of the dining room in this 300-year-old adobe may not be everyone's idea of a good time, but they certainly are unique. Breakfast items here include the traditional huevos rancheros and breakfast burritos, but you can also get hotcakes with maple syrup if you're in the mood for something sweet. Bolillos, pan dulce, empanadas, cookies, and pastries are baked fresh daily. The tapas menu is short but excellent, and includes items such as spicy Vietnamese fried calamari, pork-and-ginger potstickers, and a shrimp-and-vermicelli fritter. Other menu offerings include chiles rellenos, fajitas, enchiladas, tacos, and chimichangas. You can get a variety of coffees, including cafe macchiata, cappuccino, cafe latte, and espresso. Outdoor patio dining is available during the warmer months. There's a kids' menu.

Wild & Natural Cafe, 812 Paseo del Pueblo Norte. ☎ **751-0480.**

Cuisine: ORGANIC/VEGETARIAN. **Reservations:** Accepted for parties of 6 or more.
Prices: All items under $10. DISC, MC, V.
Open: Mon–Sat 11am–9pm.

When traveling it's often difficult to find a place to eat if you're a vegetarian, but in Taos the choice is easy. In fact, the Wild & Natural Cafe was voted "Natural Food Restaurant of the Year" by *New Mexico Naturally* in 1994. Lunches feature soups, salads, sandwiches, veggie burgers, steamed vegetables, southwestern dishes, and low-fat daily specials. At dinner you might try the Thai green curry, East Indian dahl, lemon-ginger squash, or a vegetable burrito. There's an espresso bar, as well as organic wine, fresh vegetable juices, local beer, fruit smoothies, and dairy-free desserts. Take-out orders are available.

4 Budget

Dori & Tony's Cafe, 402 Paseo del Pueblo Norte. ☎ **758-9222.**

Cuisine: AMERICAN/ITALIAN. **Reservations:** Not necessary.
Prices: Breakfast $3.45–$6; lunch $2.50–$6.75; dinner $4.25–$7. No credit cards.
Open: Mon–Sat 7am–10pm; dinner daily 5–9pm; brunch Sun 8am–1pm.

This delightful find, next door to the Taos Post Office, is a gathering place for the Taos literary and artistic crowd. In fact, if you read John Nicholl's *Nirvana Blues*, you'll recognize the Prince Whales Cafe as Dori & Tony's. Twenty-two years ago when Dori's opened, bagels were a mainstay on the menu, but they turned out to be a hard sell in the beginning. No one in Taos had ever heard of a bagel before. Now it's a different story. Dori's regulars come here so frequently that they keep their own personal coffee mugs hanging above the kitchen doorway. The café also hosts changing art exhibits and musical performances by local artists. Breakfast burritos are popular in the mornings, as are bagels, eggs, pancakes, and granola. In the afternoon the menu offers sandwiches, soups, salads, and pizzas. Now that Dori has taken her son Tony into partnership, the café offers quite an extensive Italian dinner menu with favorites such as bruschetta, antipasto, lasagne, fettuccine Alfredo, roasted chicken breast with fresh rosemary, and deep-dish pizza. Pastries are homemade daily, and espresso coffees are served all day. Beer and wine are available.

El Taoseño Restaurant, 819 South Santa Fe Rd. ☎ **758-4142.**

Cuisine: NEW MEXICAN/AMERICAN.
Prices: Main courses $1.25–$11.95. MC, V.
Open: Mon–Sat 6am–10pm, Sun 6:30am–3pm.

A long-established local diner, El Taoseño has a jukebox in the corner and local art (for sale) on the walls. There are daily specials like barbecued chicken and Mexican plates; standard fare includes everything from huevos rancheros to enchiladas and tacos. Locals flock here for the breakfast burrito. There's a separate low-fat menu available.

Mainstreet Bakery & Cafe, Guadalupe Plaza, Camino de la Placita. ☎ 758-9610.

Cuisine: NATURAL FOODS. **Reservations:** Not necessary.
Prices: $4.95–$12.95. No credit cards.
Open: Mon–Tues 7:45am–3pm, Wed–Sun 7:45am–10pm.

About a block and a half west of the Plaza, this has become possibly Taos's biggest counterculture hangout. The image is fostered by the health-conscious cuisine and the wide selection of newspapers, magazines, and other reading material advocating alternative lifestyles. Coffee and pastries are served all day; vegetarian breakfasts and (on weekends) lunches are very popular.

15

What to See & Do in Taos

WITH A HISTORY STEEPED IN THE INFLUENCES OF PRE-COLUMBIAN civilization, Spanish colonialism, and the Wild West; an array of outdoor activities ranging from ballooning to world-class skiing; and a healthy portion of modern culture—Taos has something to offer almost everybody. Its pueblo is the most accessible in New Mexico and its museums offer a world-class display of regional history and culture. Spectacular scenery embraces even those who prefer the comfort of a car.

Suggested Itineraries

If You Have Only One Day

Spend at least two hours of it at the Taos Pueblo. You'll also have time to see the Millicent Rogers Museum and to browse in some of the town's fine art galleries. Try, too, to make it to Ranchos de Taos to see the San Francisco de Asis Church.

If You Have Two Days

Spend the first day as outlined above. On the second day, explore the Kit Carson Historic Museums—the Martinez Hacienda, the Kit Carson Home, and the Ernest L. Blumenschein Home. And head out of town for the view from the Rio Grande Gorge Bridge.

If You Have Three Days or More

Spend the first two days as outlined above. If you have more time, drive the "Enchanted Circle" through Red River, Eagle Nest, and Angel Fire. You may want to leave a full day for shopping, or perhaps drive up to the Taos Ski Valley for a look-see. Of course, if you're here in the winter with skis, that's your first priority.

1 The Top Attractions

Taos Pueblo, P.O. Box 1846, Taos Pueblo, NM 87571. ☎ 758-9593.

No other site in Taos is as important or as famous. The community of 1,500, about $2^1/_2$ miles north of the Plaza, forms a world of its own. The northernmost of New Mexico's 19 pueblos, it has been the home of the Tiwa tribes for more than 900 years.

Two massive, multistoried adobe apartment buildings appear much the same today as when a regiment from Coronado's expedition first saw them in 1540. Houses are built one upon another to form porches, balconies, and roofs reached by ancient ladders. The distinctive flowing lines of shaped mud, with a straw-and-mud exterior plaster, are typical of pueblo architecture throughout the Southwest. The buildings blend in with the land around them, as the houses are made of the earth itself. Bright-blue doors repeat the clear blue of the sky that frames the brown buildings. Between the complexes trickles a fast-flowing creek, the Rio Pueblo de Taos. A footbridge

Taos Attractions

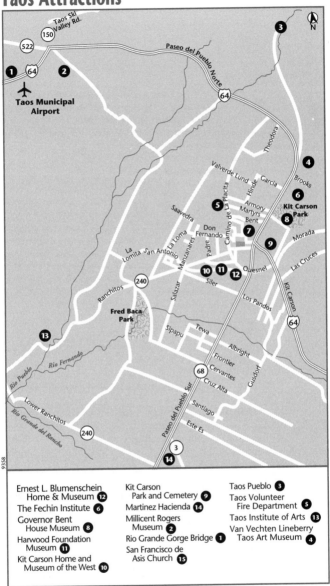

Ernest L. Blumenschein Home & Museum **12**	Kit Carson Park and Cemetery **9**	Taos Pueblo **3**
The Fechin Institute **6**	Martinez Hacienda **14**	Taos Volunteer Fire Department **5**
Governor Bent House Museum **8**	Millicent Rogers Museum **2**	Taos Institute of Arts **13**
Harwood Foundation Museum **11**	Rio Grande Gorge Bridge **1**	Van Vechten Lineberry Taos Art Museum **4**
Kit Carson Home and Museum of the West **10**	San Francisco de Asis Church **15**	

joins the two shores. To the northeast looms Taos Mountain, its long fir-covered slopes forming a timeless backdrop to the old pueblo.

Though the Tiwa were essentially a peaceful agrarian people, they are better remembered as having spearheaded the only successful revolt by Native Americans in U.S. history. Launched by Pope (Po-*pay*) in 1680, the uprising drove the Spanish from Santa Fe until 1692 and from Taos until 1698.

Native American culture and religion have persisted since. Taos is one of the most conservative of all North American tribal communities, still eschewing such modern conveniences as electricity and plumbing. Arts and crafts and other tourism-related businesses support the economy, along with government services and ranching and farming.

As you explore the pueblo and absorb insights into its people's lifestyle, you can visit those studios, munch on homemade oven bread, look into the new **San Geronimo Chapel,** and wander past the fascinating ruins of the old church and cemetery. You're expected to ask permission from individuals before taking their photos; some ask a small payment, but that's for you to negotiate. Kivas and other ceremonial underground areas are taboo.

San Geronimo is the patron saint of the Taos Pueblo and his feast day on September 30 combines Catholic and pre-Hispanic traditions. **The Old Taos Trade Fair** on that day is a joyous occasion, with footraces, pole climbs, and crafts booths. Dances are performed the evening of September 29. Other annual events include a turtle dance on **New Year's Day,** deer or buffalo dances on **Three Kings Day** on January 6, and corn dances for **Santa Cruz Day** on May 3, **San Antonio Day** on June 13, **San Juan Day** on June 24, **Santiago Day** on July 23, and **Santa Ana Day** on July 24. The **Taos Pueblo Powwow,** a dance competition and parade drawing tribes from throughout North America, is held the weekend after July 4 on reservation land off N.M. 522. **Christmas Eve** bonfires mark the start of the children's corn dance, the **Christmas Day** deer dance, or the three-day-long Matachines dance.

Admission: $6 per vehicle or $2 per person. Still camera $5, video camera $10, sketching $15, painting $35; no photography permitted on feast days.

Open: Summer, daily 8am–5pm; winter, daily 9am–4pm. **Closed:** A month every year in late winter or early spring (before making travel plans, you should call in advance to make sure it will be open when you get there).

★ **Millicent Rogers Museum,** off N.M. 522, four miles north of Taos. ☎ 758-2462.

Taos's most interesting collection is in this museum, founded in 1953 by family members after the death of Millicent Rogers. Rogers was a wealthy Taos émigré who compiled a magnificent array of aesthetically beautiful Native American arts and crafts beginning in 1947. Included are Navajo and Pueblo jewelry, Navajo textiles, Pueblo pottery, Hopi and Zuni kachina dolls, paintings from the Rio Grande Pueblo people, and basketry from a wide variety of southwestern tribes. The collection continues to grow through gifts and museum acquisitions.

Since the 1970s the scope of the museum's permanent collection has been expanded to include Hispanic religious and secular arts and crafts, from Spanish and Mexican Colonial to contemporary times. Included are santos (religious images), furniture, weavings, *colcha* embroideries, and decorative tinwork. Agricultural implements, domestic utensils, and craftspeople's tools dating from the 17th and 18th centuries are also displayed.

The museum gift shop has a fine collection of superior regional art. Temporary exhibits, classes and workshops, lectures, and field trips are scheduled throughout the year.

Admission: $4 adults, $3 seniors, $1 children 6–16; $8 families.

Open: Daily 9am–5pm. **Closed:** New Year's, Thanksgiving, and Christmas Days.

★ **Kit Carson Historic Museums,** P.O. Drawer CCC, Taos, NM 87571. ☎ 758-0505.

This foundation operates three historical homes as museums, affording glimpses of early Taos lifestyles. The Martinez Hacienda, Kit Carson Home, and Ernest Blumenschein home each has its individual-appeal.

The **Martinez Hacienda,** Lower Ranchitos Road, Hwy. 240 (☎ 758-1000), is one of the only Spanish Colonial haciendas in the United States that's open to the public year-round. This was the home of merchant and trader Don Antonio Severino Martinez, who bought it in 1804 and lived there until his death in 1827. Located on the west bank of the Rio Pueblo de Taos about two miles southwest of the Plaza, the hacienda was built like a fortress, with thick adobe walls and no exterior windows, to protect against raids by Plains tribes.

Twenty-one rooms were built around two *placitas,* or interior courtyards. Most of the rooms open today contain period furnishings: They include the bedrooms, servants' quarters, stables, a kitchen, and even a large fiesta room. Exhibits in one newly renovated room tell the story of the Martinez family and life in Spanish Taos between 1598 and 1821, when Mexico assumed control.

Don Antonio Martinez, who for a time was *alcalde* (mayor) of Taos, owned several caravans that he used in trade on the Chihuahua Trail to Mexico. This business was carried on by his youngest son, Don Juan Pascual, who later owned the hacienda. His eldest son was Padre Antonio José Martinez, northern New Mexico's controversial spiritual leader from 1826 to 1867.

Kit Carson Historic Museums has developed the hacienda into a living museum with weavers, blacksmiths, and wood carvers. Demonstrations are scheduled daily; including during the Old Taos Trade Fair the last weekend in September when they run virtually nonstop. The Trade Fair recalls days when Native Americans, Spanish settlers, and mountain men met here to trade with each other. It's open daily from 9am to 5pm.

The **Kit Carson Home and Museum of the West,** East Kit Carson Road (☎ 758-4741), located a short block east on the Plaza intersection, is the town's only general museum of Taos history. The 12-room adobe home, with walls 2¹/₂ feet thick, was built in 1825 and purchased in 1843 by Carson, the famous mountain man,

Indian agent, and scout, as a wedding gift for his young bride, Josefa Jaramillo. It remained their home for 25 years, until both died (a month to the day apart) in 1868.

A living room, bedroom, and kitchen are furnished as they might have been when occupied by the Carsons. The Indian Room contains artifacts crafted and utilized by the original inhabitants of Taos Valley; the Early American Room has an array of pioneer items, including a large number of antique firearms and trappers' implements; and the Carson Interpretive Room presents memorabilia from Carson's unusual life. In the kitchen is a Spanish plaque that reads: *Nadie sabe lo que tiene la olla mas que la cuchara que la menea* (Nobody better knows what the pot holds than the spoon that stirs it).

The museum bookshop, with perhaps the town's most comprehensive inventory of New Mexico historical books, is adjacent to the entry. It's open daily from 8am to 6pm in summer, 9am to 5pm in winter.

The **Ernest L. Blumenschein Home & Museum,** 222 Ledoux St. (☎ 758-0330), a block and a half southwest of the Plaza, recalls and re-creates the lifestyle of one of the founders (in 1915) of the Taos Society of Artists. An adobe home with garden walls and a courtyard, parts of which date to the 1790s, it was the home and studio of Blumenschein (1874–1960) and his family beginning in 1919. Period furnishings include European antiques and handmade Taos furniture in Spanish Colonial style.

Blumenschein was born and raised in Pittsburgh. His arrival in Taos in 1898 came somewhat by accident. After training in New York and Paris, he and fellow painter Bert Phillips were on assignment for *Harper's* and *McClure's* magazines of New York when a wheel of their wagon broke during a mountain traverse 30 miles north of Taos. Blumenschein drew the short straw and carried the wheel by horseback to Taos for repair. He later recounted his initial reaction to the valley he entered: "No artist had ever recorded the New Mexico I was now seeing. No writer had ever written down the smell of this air or the feel of that morning sky. I was receiving . . . the first great unforgettable inspiration of my life. My destiny was being decided."

That spark later led to the foundation of Taos as an art colony. An extensive collection of work by early 20th-century Taos masters is on display in several rooms of the home. Among the modern works are paintings by Blumenschein's daughter, Helen. The home and museum are open daily from 9am to 5pm.

Admission: Three museums, $8 adults, $6 seniors, $5 children 6–16; family rate, $15. Two museums, $6 adults, $5 seniors, $4 children; family rate, $13. One museum, $4 adults, $3 seniors, $2.50 children; family rate, $6. All museums free for children under 5.

Open: Summer, Kit Carson Home, daily 8am–6pm; Martinez Hacienda, daily 9am–5pm; Blumenschein Home, daily 9am–5pm. Winter, all museums, daily 9am–5pm.

Taos Area

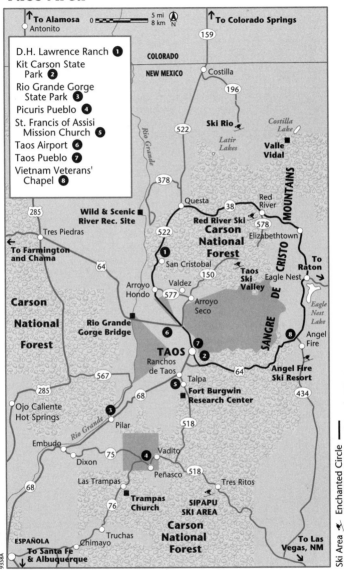

To Alamosa
Antonito
0 — 5 mi
8 km
N

To Colorado Springs
159

D.H. Lawrence Ranch ❶
Kit Carson State Park ❷
Rio Grande Gorge State Park ❸
Picuris Pueblo ❹
St. Francis of Assisi Mission Church ❺
Taos Airport ❻
Taos Pueblo ❼
Vietnam Veterans' Chapel ❽

COLORADO
NEW MEXICO
Costilla
196
Ski Rio
Costilla Lake
Latir Lakes
Valle Vidal
522
Rio Grande
378
Wild & Scenic River Rec. Site
285
Tres Piedras
Questa
38
Red River
Carson National Forest
522
Red River Ski
578
Elizabethtown
To Farmington and Chama
64
San Cristobal
❶
150
Taos Ski Valley
Eagle Nest
To Raton
Arroyo Hondo
Valdez
577
Arroyo Seco
Eagle Nest Lake
Carson National Forest
Rio Grande Gorge Bridge
❻
❼
❷
❽
Angel Fire
TAOS
Ranchos de Taos
❺ Talpa
Fort Burgwin Research Center
64
Angel Fire Ski Resort
567
285
68
Ojo Caliente Hot Springs
❸
Pilar
518
434
Embudo
75
Vadito
Dixon
❹
Peñasco
518
Tres Ritos
68
Las Trampas
Trampas Church
SIPAPU SKI AREA
76
Truchas
Carson National Forest
ESPAÑOLA
Chimayo
To Santa Fe & Albuquerque
To Las Vegas, NM

SANGRE DE CRISTO MOUNTAINS

9358A

Ski Area ⛷ Enchanted Circle —

More Attractions

D. H. Lawrence Ranch, San Cristobal. ☎ 776-2245.

The shrine of the controversial early 20th-century author is a pilgrimage site for literary devotees. A short uphill walk from the ranch home, it's littered with various mementos—photos, coins, messages from fortune cookies—placed by visitors. The guestbook is worth a long read.

Lawrence lived in Taos off and on between 1922 and 1925. The ranch was a gift to his wife, Frieda, from art patron Mabel Dodge Luhan. Lawrence repaid Luhan the favor by giving her the manuscript of *Sons and Lovers*. Lawrence died in southern France in 1930 of tuberculosis: his ashes were returned here for burial. The grave of Frieda, who died in 1956, is outside the shrine.

The shrine is the only public building at the ranch, operated today by the University of New Mexico as an educational and recreational retreat. To reach the site, head north from Taos about 15 miles on N.M. 522, then another 6 miles east into the forested Sangre de Cristo range via a well-marked dirt road.

★ **The Fechin Institute,** 227 Paseo del Pueblo Norte (P.O. Box 832), Taos, NM 87571. ☎ **758-1710.**

The home of Russian artist Nicolai Fechin (Feh-*shin*) from 1927 until his death in 1955, this historic house memorializes the career of a 20th-century Renaissance man. Born in Russia in 1881, Fechin came to the United States in 1923, already acclaimed as a master of painting, drawing, sculpture, architecture, and woodwork. In Taos, he built a huge adobe home and embellished it with hand-carved doors, windows, gates, posts, fireplaces, and other features of a Russian country home. The house and adjacent studio are now used for Fechin Institute educational activities, as well as concerts, lectures, and other programs.

Admission: $3.

Open: May–Oct, Wed–Sun 1–5pm; Nov–Apr, by appointment.

Governor Bent House Museum, 117 Bent St. ☎ **758-2376.**

Located a short block north of the Plaza, this was the residence of Charles Bent, the New Mexico Territory's first American governor. Bent, a former trader who established Fort Bent, Colorado, was murdered in the 1847 Native American and Hispanic rebellion, as his wife and children escaped by digging through an adobe wall into the house next door. The hole is still visible. Period art and artifacts are displayed.

Admission: $1 adults, 50¢ children.

Open: Summer, daily 9am–5pm; winter, daily 10am–4pm.

Harwood Foundation Museum of the University of New Mexico, 238 Ledoux St. ☎ **758-9826.**

Some of the finest works of art ever produced in or about Taos hang on the walls of this Pueblo-style library-and-museum complex, a cultural and community center since 1923.

The museum shows paintings, drawings, prints, sculpture, and photographs by the artists of the Taos area from 1800 to the present. Featured are paintings from the early days of the art colony by members of the Taos Society of Artists, including Oscar Berninghaus, Ernest Blumenschein, Herbert Dunton, Victor Higgins, Bert Phillips, and Walter Ufer. In addition, works by Emil Bisttram, Andrew

Dasburg, Leon Gaspard, Louis Ribak, Bea Mandelman, Agnes Martin, Larry Bell, and Thomas Benrimo are included.

Also on display are 19th-century retablos, religious paintings of saints that have traditionally been used for decoration and inspiration in the homes and churches of New Mexico. The permanent collection of art includes sculptures by Patrocinio Barela, one of the leading Hispanic artists of 20th-century New Mexico.

The museum also has five or six changing exhibitions each year, many of which feature the best artists currently working in Taos.

Admission: $2.

Open: Mon–Fri 10am–5pm, Sat 10am–4pm.

Kit Carson Park and Cemetery, Paseo del Pueblo Norte.

Major community events are held in the park in summer. The cemetery, established in 1847, contains the graves of Carson and his wife, Gov. Charles Bent, the Don Antonio Martinez family, Mabel Dodge Luhan, and many other noted historical figures and artists. Plaques describe their contributions.

★ **Rio Grande Gorge Bridge,** U.S. 64, 10 miles west of Taos.

This impressive bridge, west of the Taos airport, spans the Southwest's greatest river. At 650 feet above the canyon floor, it's one of America's highest bridges. If you can withstand the vertigo, it's interesting to come more than once, at different times of day, to observe how the changing light plays tricks with the colors of the cliff walls.

★ **San Francisco de Asis Church,** Ranchos de Taos.
☎ 758-2754.

From N.M. 68, about four miles south of Taos, this famous church appears as a modernesque adobe sculpture with no doors or windows. It's often photographed (by Ansel Adams, for one) and painted (by Georgia O'Keeffe, among others) from this angle. Visitors must walk through the garden on the west side of this remarkable two-story church to enter and get a full perspective on its massive walls, authentic adobe plaster, and beauty.

Displayed on the wall is an unusual painting, *The Shadow of the Cross* by Henri Ault (1896). Under ordinary light it portrays a barefoot Christ at the Sea of Galilee; in darkness, however, the portrait becomes luminescent and the perfect shadow of a cross forms over the left shoulder of Jesus' silhouette. The artist reportedly was as shocked as everyone else. The reason for the illusion remains a mystery.

The church office and gift shop are just across the driveway to the north of the church. A slide show is also presented here. Several crafts shops surround the square.

Admission: Free; donations appreciated.

Open: Daily. Visitors may attend mass Sat at 5:30pm and Sun at 7am (Spanish), 9am, and 11:30am.

Taos Volunteer Fire Department, Inc., Camino de la Placita.
☎ 758-3386.

Art lovers might find this an unlikely destination—but it's one that shouldn't be ignored. It has an irreplaceable and excellent collection of the work of early Taos artists on display. The collection was started in the 1950s when the Taos firemen, all volunteers, asked their artist friends to decorate their recreation room. Some artists loaned paintings, but many gave them to the fire station outright—and thus it has one of the finest art collections in town.

Admission: Free.

Open: Mon–Fri 8am–4:30pm.

Van Vechten Lineberry Taos Art Museum, 501 N. Pueblo Rd. ☎ 758-2690.

As this book goes to press, Taos's newest museum, the Van Vechten Lineberry Taos Art Museum, is opening its doors. The museum is the brainchild of Ed Lineberry who lives in the spectacular home adjacent to the museum, and who conceived of the museum as a memorial to his late wife, Duane Van Vechten. An artist in her own right, Duane spent a great deal of time working in her studio which now serves as the entryway to the 20,000-square-foot main gallery of the museum. The entryway features, among other things, John Dunn's roulette wheel. Lineberry traveled throughout Europe studying the preservation and storage techniques, as well as the display space, climate control, and lighting of fine museums. As a result, the Van Vechten Lineberry Taos Art Museum is state-of-the-art. The museum is slated to display the works of Van Vechten, as well as the art of the 11 original Taos artists. Each artist will be represented by at least one piece. While the initial collection will be between 130 and 150 pieces, Mr. Lineberry hopes to acquire more work in the next few years. In addition to the main gallery space, there are smaller spaces available for traveling exhibitions, and there is a wonderful library which will be open by appointment to researchers.

Admission: $5 adults, $3 children.

Open: Call ahead for days and hours.

Art and Cooking Classes

Perhaps you're visiting Taos because it's so well known as an art community but galleries and studio visits just aren't enough to satisfy your urge to create. Well, if you're interested in pursuing an artistic adventure of your own while visiting Taos, you should definitely investigate the week-long classes in sculpture, painting, jewelry making, photography, clay working, textiles, and quite a few other media available at the **Taos Institute of Arts,** P.O. Box 2429, Taos, NM 97571 (☎ 505/758-2793). Class sizes are limited, so if you're thinking about giving these workshops a try, you should call ahead for information and prices well in advance. The fees vary from class to class and usually don't include the price of materials; they remain, however, quite reasonable.

If you've fallen in love with New Mexican and southwestern cooking during your stay in New Mexico (or even before you arrived), you might like to sign up for cooking classes with Jane Butel, a leading Southwest cooking authority and author of 12 cookbooks. At **Jane Butel's Cooking School,** 800 Rio Grande NW, Suite 14 (☎ toll free **800/473-TACO;** fax 505/243-8297), you'll learn the history and techniques of southwestern cuisine and you'll develop cooking techniques through hands-on preparation. If you opt for the week-long session you'll start by learning about chiles. The second and third days you'll try your hand at native breads and dishes, the fourth focuses on more innovative dishes, and the final day centers on appetizers, beverages, and desserts. There are also weekend sessions available. Call or fax for current schedules and fees.

3 Organized Tours

Damaso and Helen Martinez's young **Pride of Taos Tours,** P.O. Box 1192, Taos, NM 87571 (☎ **758-8340**), offers several packages, including a Taos historical tour that lasts an hour and takes tourists to the Plaza, Martinez Hacienda, and Ranchos de Taos Church ($6 adults, $3 children 12 and under).

Offering step-on guide service to the historic downtown area, **Taos Historic Walking Tours** (☎ **758-4020**) is an excellent choice. Call for schedule and prices.

4 Sports & Recreation

Taos County's 2,200 square miles embrace a great diversity of scenic beauty, from New Mexico's highest mountain, 13,161-foot **Wheeler Peak,** to the 650-foot-deep chasm of the **Rio Grande Gorge. Carson National Forest,** which extends right to the eastern city limits of Taos and cloaks a large part of the county, contains several major ski facilities as well as hundreds of miles of hiking trails through the Sangre de Cristo range.

Recreation areas are mainly in the national forest, where pines and aspen provide refuge for abundant wildlife. Forty-eight areas are accessible by road, including 38 with campsites. There are also areas on the high desert mesa, carpeted by sagebrush, cactus, and frequently wildflowers. Both terrains are favored by hunters, fishermen, and horseback riders. Two beautiful areas within a short drive of Taos are the **Valle Vidal Recreation Area,** north of Red River, and the **Wild Rivers Recreation Area,** near Questa. For full information, contact **Carson National Forest,** 208 Cruz Alta Rd. (P.O. Box 558), Taos, NM 87571 (☎ **505/758-6200**), or the **Bureau of Land Management,** 224 Cruz Alta Rd. (P.O. Box 6168), Taos, NM 87571 (☎ **505/788-8851**).

Skiing

CROSS COUNTRY

There are numerous popular Nordic trails in Carson National Forest. One of the more popular is **Amole Canyon,** off N.M. 518 near the Sipapu Ski Area, where the Taos Nordic Ski Club maintains set tracks and signs along a three-mile loop. It's closed to snowmobiles, a comfort to lovers of serenity.

Just east of Red River, with 31 miles of groomed trails in 600 acres of forest land atop Bobcat Pass, is the **Enchanted Forest Cross**

Country Ski Area (☎ 754-2374). Full-day trail passes, good from 9am to 4:30pm, are $8 for adults, much less for children. Equipment rentals and lessons can be arranged at **Miller's Crossing** ski shop on Main Street in Red River (☎ 754-2374). Nordic skiers can get instruction in "skating," mountaineering, and telemarking.

Taos Mountain Outfitters, 114 South Plaza (☎ 758-8125), offers cross-country sales, rentals, and guide service.

DOWNHILL

Five alpine resorts are located within an hour's drive of Taos. All offer complete facilities, including equipment rentals. Although exact opening and closing dates may vary according to snow conditions, it's usually safe to say that skiing will begin Thanksgiving weekend and continue into early April.

Ski vacationers who can't decide which area to patronize should look into the **Ski-3 Card.** This $15 card gives skiers $5 off regular all-lift ticket prices any day of the week (including weekends) and savings on ski lessons at the Taos Ski Valley, Red River, and Angel Fire Ski Areas. You must purchase the card prior to December 24. The Ski-3 card cannot be used between January 14 and 16, February 18 and 20, March 12 to 18, and December 26 and 31. Write to Ski-3, P.O. Box 15425, Santa Fe, NM 87506, for more information.

Ski clothing can be purchased, and ski equipment rented or bought, from several Taos outlets. Among them are **Cottam's Ski Shops,** with four locations, including the Kachina Lodge (☎ 758-1697) and Taos Ski Valley (☎ 776-8450); **Terry Sports,** on Paseo del Pueblo Norte beside the post office (☎ 758-8522) and at Taos Ski Valley (☎ 776-8292); and **Olympic Ski Shops,** on Paseo del Pueblo Sur (☎ 758-1167).

★ **Taos Ski Valley,** Taos Ski Valley, NM 87525. ☎ 505/776-2291.

The preeminent ski resort in the southern Rocky Mountains was founded in 1955 by a Swiss-German immigrant, Ernie Blake. According to local legend, Blake searched for two years in a small plane for the perfect location for a ski resort equal to his native Alps. He found it at the abandoned mining site of Twining, high above Taos. Still under the command of two younger generations of Blakes, the resort has become internationally renowned for its light, dry powder (312 inches annually), its superb ski school, and its personal, friendly manner. Even the esteemed London *Times* called the valley "without any argument the best ski resort in the world. Small, intimate and endlessly challenging, Taos simply has no equal."

Of the 72 trails and bowls, more than half are designated for expert or advanced skiers. But between the 11,800-foot summit and the 9,200-foot base, there are also ample opportunities for novice and intermediate skiers. The area has an uphill capacity of 14,000 skiers per hour on its six double chairs, one triple, two quads, and one surface tow.

With its children's ski school Taos Ski Valley has always been an excellent location for skiing families, but with the 1994 addition of an 18,000-square-foot children's center (Kinderkäfig Center), skiing with your children in Taos is an even better experience. Kinderkäfig offers every service imaginable, from equipment rental for children to babysitting services. Call ahead for more information.

Taos Ski Valley has 13 lodges and condominiums with nearly 700 beds. (See "Taos Ski Valley," in Chapter 13, for details on accommodations.) All offer ski-week packages; six of them have restaurants. There are two more restaurants on the mountain in addition to the expansive facilities of Village Center at the base. For reservations, call the Taos Valley Resort Association (☎ **505/776-2233,** or toll free **800/776-1111**).

Tickets: All lifts, $37 adults full day, $24 half day; $22 children 12 or younger full day, $16 half day; $15 seniors 65–69 full day; free for seniors over 70. Novice lifts, $20 adults, $15 children. Full rental packages, $12 adults, $5 children.

Open: Thanksgiving to the first week of Apr, daily 9am–4pm.

Red River Ski Area, P.O. Box 900, Red River, NM 87558.

☎ **505/754-2747,** or toll free **800/348-6444** for reservations.

Lodgers in Red River, as at Angel Fire, can walk out their doors and be on the slopes. Two other factors make this 35-year-old, family-oriented area special: First, its 27 trails are geared to the intermediate skier, though beginners and experts have their share; and second, good snow is guaranteed early and late in the year by snowmaking equipment that can work on 75% of the runs, more than any other in New Mexico. There's a 1,500-foot vertical drop here to a base elevation of 8,750 feet. Lifts include four double chairs, a triple chair, and two surface tows, with a skier capacity of 3,000 per hour.

Tickets: All lifts, $28 adults full day, $20 half day; $17 children 12 and under and seniors (60 and over) full day, $11 half day. Full rental packages, from $12 adults, $9 children.

Open: Thanksgiving–Apr 1, daily 9am–4pm.

Angel Fire Ski Area, P.O. Drawer B, Angel Fire, NM 87710.

☎ **505/377-6401,** or toll free **800/633-7463.**

The 30 miles of ski runs here are heavily oriented to beginning and intermediate skiers. Still, with a vertical drop of 2,180 feet to a base elevation of 8,500 feet, advanced skiers are certain to find something they like. The area's lifts—four double and two triple chairs—have an hourly capacity of 1,900 skiers.

Tickets: All day, $25 adults, $17 children.

Open: In season, daily 8:30am–4:30pm.

Sipapu Ski Area, P.O. Box 29, Vadito, NM 87579.

☎ **505/587-2240.**

The oldest ski area in the Taos region, founded in 1952, Sipapu is 25 miles southeast, on N.M. 518 in Tres Ritos canyon. It prides itself on being a small local area, especially popular with schoolchildren.

There are just one triple chair and two surface lifts, with a vertical drop of 865 feet to the 8,200-foot base elevation. There are 18 trails, half classified as intermediate. There are many different types of overnight lodging, from duplexes to a bunkhouse to camping.

Tickets: $23 adults, $18 children under 12.

Open: In season, daily 8am–4pm.

Ski Rio, P.O. Box 59, Costilla, NM 87525. ☎ **505/758-7707,** or toll free **800/2-ASK-RIO.**

Just south of the Colorado border is this rapidly expanding area (which until recently has been rapidly going in and out of business—call ahead!). Half its 64 named trails are for the intermediate skier, 30% for beginners, and 20% for advanced skiers. Also within Ski Rio are Snowboard and Snow Skate parks, as well as 13 miles of cross-country trails. Annual snowfall here is about 250 inches, and there are three chair lifts (two triple, one double) and three tows. At the ski base you can rent skis, snowboards, snowshoes, and snow skates, as well as find lodgings, restaurants, and a sports shop. Sleigh rides, dog-sled tours, and snowmobile tours are also available. The ski school offers private and group clinics (for adults and children) in cross-country and downhill skiing, snow skating, and snowboarding.

Tickets: $29 adults ($24–$21 in value season), $19 juniors 7–12, free for children 6 and under with a paying adult.

Open: In season, daily 9am–4pm.

More Sports and Recreation

BALLOONING The **Taos Mountain Balloon Rally,** P.O. Box 3096, Taos, NM 87571 (☎ **758-8321**), is held each year the last full weekend of October. (See "Northern New Mexico Calendar of Events," in Chapter 2, for details.) Recreational trips are offered by **Taos Mountain Magic Balloons** (☎ 776-8746).

BICYCLING **Taos Mountain Outfitters,** South Plaza (☎ 758-9292), offers mountain bikes for rent or sale. Carson National Forest rangers recommend several biking trails in the greater Taos area, including those in Garcia Park and Rio Chiquito for beginner to intermediate mountain bikers, and a number of Gallegos and Picuris peaks for experts. Inquire at the U.S. Forest Service office next to the chamber of commerce for an excellent handout.

Annual touring events include Red River's **Enchanted Circle Century Bike Tour** (☎ 754-2366) in mid-September.

FISHING Fishing season in the high lakes and streams opens April 1 and continues through December, though spring and fall are known as the best times for success. Rainbow, cutthroat, and brown trout and kokanee, a freshwater salmon, are commonly stocked and caught. The Rio Grande also has pike and catfish. Jiggs, spinners, or woolly worms are recommended as lure, or worms, corn, or salmon eggs as bait, but many experienced anglers prefer fly fishing.

Licenses are required, of course; they are sold, along with tackle, at several Taos sporting-goods shops. For backcountry guides, try

Deep Creek Wilderness Outfitters & Guides, P.O. Box 721, El Prado, NM 87529 (☎ **505/776-8423**) or **Los Rios Anglers** (☎ **758-2798**) in Taos.

GOLF   The par-72, 18-hole course in **Angel Fire** has been endorsed by the Professional Golfers Association. Surrounded by stands of ponderosa pine, spruce, and aspen, at 8,600 feet it's one of the highest regulation golf courses in the world. It also has a driving range and putting green. Carts and clubs can be rented at the course, and the club pro provides instruction.

Since the summer of 1993 the 18-hole golf course at the **Taos Country Club,** Ranchos de Taos (☎ 758-7300), has been open to the public. It's located just four miles south of the Plaza and is a first-rate championship golf course designed for all levels of play. In addition, there's a driving range and 9-hole course and instruction by PGA professionals.

HIKING/BACKPACKING   There are many hundreds of miles of hiking trails in Taos County's mountain and high-mesa country. They're especially well used in summer and fall, although nights turn chilly and mountain weather fickle by September.

Maps (at $2 each) and free handouts and advice on all **Carson National Forest** trails and recreation areas can be obtained from the Forest Service Building, 208 Cruz Alta Rd. (☎ **758-6200**), and from the office adjacent to the chamber of commerce on Paseo del Pueblo Sur. Both are open Monday through Saturday from 8am to 4:30pm. Detailed USGS topographical maps of backcountry areas can be purchased from **Taos Mountain Outfitters** on the Plaza (☎ **758-9292**). This is also the place to rent camping gear, if you came without your own. Tent rentals are $8 a day or $17.50 a weekend; sleeping bags, $7.50 a day or $16 a weekend.

Two wilderness areas are close to Taos and offer outstanding hiking possibilities. The 19,663-acre **Wheeler Peak Wilderness** is a wonderland of alpine tundra encompassing New Mexico's highest peak (13,161 feet). The 20,000-acre **Latir Peak Wilderness,** north of Red River, is noted for its high lake country. Both are under the jurisdiction of the Questa Ranger District, P.O. Box 110, Questa, NM 87556 (☎ **505/586-0520**).

HORSE/PACK TRIPS   The **Taos Indian Horse Ranch,** on Pueblo land off Ski Valley Road just before Arroyo Seco (☎ 758-3212, or toll free **800/659-3210**), offers a variety of guided rides. Open from 10am to 4pm daily and by appointment, the ranch provides horses for all types of riders (English, western, bareback) and ability levels. Call ahead to reserve. Rates start at $55 to $125 for a two-hour trail ride. Horse-drawn trolley rides are also offered in summer. From late November to March, the ranch offers evening sleigh rides to a bonfire and marshmallow roast at $40 a head.

Horseback riding is also offered by the **Shadow Mountain Guest Ranch,** six miles east of Taos on U.S. 64 (☎ **758-7732**). Rates at the latter are $17 to $20 per hour for trail rides.

Adventures in the Great Outdoors, P.O. Box 1618, Ranchos de Taos, NM 87557 (☎ 505/758-7332), will arrange half-day rides to a view point and back, half-day rides with a campfire lunch at a view point, or an overnight ride that includes a campfire dinner, continental breakfast, and a tent (bring your own sleeping bags, or rent them). Call or write for information and rates.

HUNTING Hunters in Carson National Forest bag deer, turkey, grouse, and band-tailed pigeons, and elk by special permit. On private land, where hunters must be accompanied by qualified guides, there are also black bear and mountain lion. Hunting seasons vary year to year, so it's important to inquire ahead with the **New Mexico Game and Fish Department** in Santa Fe (☎ 505/827-7882).

Several Taos sporting-goods shops sell hunting licenses. Backcountry guides include **Agua Fria Guide Service** (☎ 377-3512) in Angel Fire, **United States Outfitters Inc.** (☎ 758-9774) in Taos, and **Rio Costilla Park** (☎ 586-0542) in Costilla.

LLAMA TREKKING El Paseo Llama Expeditions (☎ 758-3111, or toll free 800/455-2627) utilizes U.S. Forest Service–maintained trails that wind through canyons and over mountain ridges. The llamas will carry your gear and food, allowing you to walk and explore, free of any heavy burdens. They're friendly, gentle animals that have a keen sense of sight and smell. Often, other animals, like elk, deer, and mountain sheep, are attracted to the scent of the llamas and will venture closer to hikers if the llamas are present. Llama expeditions are scheduled from June to early October. Day hikes cost $75 per person. Three- to five-day hikes cost $125 per person per day.

RIVER RAFTING Half- or full-day white-water rafting trips down the Rio Grande and Rio Chama originate in Taos and Red River. The wild **Taos Box,** a steep-sided canyon south of the Wild Rivers Recreation Area, is especially popular. Early May, when the water is rising, is a good time to go. Experience is not required, but you should wear a life jacket (provided) and be willing to get wet.

One convenient rafting service is **Rio Grande Rapid Transit,** P.O. Box A, Pilar, NM 87571 (☎ 505/758-9700, or toll free 800/222-RAFT). Rio Grande also runs the Pilar Racecourse on a daily basis. Its headquarters are at the entrance to the BLM-administered **Orilla Verde Recreation Area,** 16 miles south of Taos, where most excursions through the Taos Box end. Several other serene but thrilling floats through the Pilar Racecourse start at this point.

Other rafting outfitters in the Taos area include **Native Sons Adventures** 715 Paseo del Pueblo Sur (☎ 758-9342, or toll free 800/753-7559), **Los Rios River Runners** (☎ 758-1550, or toll free 800/338-6877), and **Rio Grande Rapid Transit** (☎ 758-9700, or toll free 800/222-RAFT).

Safety Warning: Taos is not the place in which to experiment if you aren't an experienced rafter. Do yourself a favor and check with the Bureau of Land Management (☎ **758-8851**) to make sure that you're fully equipped to go white-water rafting without a guide. Have them check your gear to make sure that it's sturdy enough—this is serious rafting!

RODEO   The **Rodeo de Taos,** held the fourth weekend of June each year, draws many of the West's leading cowboys to compete for prize money. Bronco riding, calf roping, bull riding, barrel racing, and other standard events take place at Sheriff's Posse Rodeo Arena in the county fairgrounds, off Paseo del Pueblo Sur behind the Cruz Alta Shopping Center.

SPAS   **Ojo Caliente Mineral Springs,** Ojo Caliente, NM 87549 (☎ **505/583-2233**), is on U.S. 285, 50 miles (a one-hour drive) southwest of Taos. This National Historic Site was considered sacred by prehistoric tribes. When Spanish explorer Cabeza de Vaca discovered and named the springs in the 16th century, he called them "the greatest treasure that I found these strange people to possess." No other hot spring in the world has Ojo Caliente's combination of iron, soda, lithium, sodium, and arsenic. The resort offers herbal wraps and massages, lodging, and meals. It's open in summer daily from 10am to 8pm; in winter the springs don't open until 1pm on weekdays.

The **Taos Spa & Court Club,** 111 Dona Ana Dr. (☎ **758-1980**), is a fully equipped fitness center that rivals any you'd find in a big city. There are treadmills, step machines, climbing machines, rowing machines, exercise bikes, NordicTrack, weight-training machines, saunas, indoor and outdoor hot tubs, a steam room, and indoor and outdoor pools. Thirty-five step aerobic classes a week, as well as stretch aerobics, aqua aerobics, and classes specifically designed for senior citizens are also offered. In addition, there are five tennis and two racquetball courts. Therapeutic massage is available daily by appointment. Children's programs include tennis and swimming camp, and babysitting programs are available in the morning and evening. The spa is open Monday through Friday from 6:30am to 9pm, on Saturday from 8:30am to 8pm, and on Sunday from 10:30am to 8pm. Monthly, weekly, and daily memberships are available for individuals and families. For visitors there's a daily rate of $10.

The **Northside Health and Fitness Center,** at 1307 Paseo del Pueblo Norte, in El Prado (☎ **751-1242**), is also a full-service facility, featuring top-of-the-line Cybex equipment, free weights, and cardiovascular equipment. Aerobics classes are scheduled daily, and there are indoor/outdoor pools and four tennis courts, as well as children's and senior citizens' programs.

SWIMMING   The **Don Fernando Pool,** on Civic Plaza Drive at Camino de la Placita, opposite the new convention center, admits swimmers over age 6 without adult supervision.

TENNIS There are free public courts in Taos at **Kit Carson Memorial State Park,** on Paseo del Pueblo Norte, and **Fred Baca Memorial Park,** on Camino del Medio south of Ranchitos Road, and indoor courts at the **Quail Ridge Inn** (see Chapter 13).

5 An Easy Excursion Around the Enchanted Circle

The one "don't-miss" trip from Taos is an excursion around the Enchanted Circle. This 90-mile loop, a National Forest Scenic Byway, runs through the towns of Questa, Red River, Eagle Nest, and Angel Fire, incorporating portions of N.M. 522, N.M. 38, and U.S. 64. It can be driven in two hours round-trip from Taos—but most folks take a full day, and many use several days, to accomplish it.

QUESTA Traveling north from Taos via N.M. 522, it's a 24-mile drive to Questa, most of whose residents are employed at a molybdenum mine about 5 miles east of town. En route north, the highway passes near **San Cristobal,** where a side road turns off to the D. H. Lawrence Shrine, and **Lama,** site of an isolated spiritual retreat.

If you turn west off N.M. 522 onto N.M. 378 about 3 miles north of Questa, you'll descend 11 miles on a gravel road into the gorge of the Rio Grande at the Bureau of Land Management–administered **Wild Rivers Recreation Area** (☎ **758-8851**). Here, where the Red River enters the gorge, is the most accessible starting point for river-rafting trips through the infamous Taos Box. Some 48 miles of the Rio Grande, south from the Colorado border, are protected under the national Wild and Scenic River Act of 1968. Information on geology and wildlife, as well as hikers' trail maps, can be obtained at the visitors center here. Ask for directions to the impressive petroglyphs in the gorge. River-rafting trips can be booked in Taos, Santa Fe, Red River, and other communities. (See the "Sports and Recreation" sections in Chapters 7 and 15 for booking agents in Santa Fe and Taos, respectively.)

The village of **Costilla,** near the Colorado border, is 20 miles north of Questa. This is the turnoff point for four-wheel-drive jaunts into **Valle Vidal,** a huge U.S. Forest Service–administered reserve with 42 miles of roads.

RED RIVER Turn east at Questa onto N.M. 38 for a 12-mile climb to Red River, a rough-and-ready 1890s gold-mining town that has parlayed its Wild West ambience into a pleasant resort village that's especially popular with families from Texas and Oklahoma.

This community at 8,750 feet is a center for skiing and snowmobiling, fishing and hiking, off-road driving and horseback riding, mountain biking, river rafting, and other outdoor pursuits. Frontier-style celebrations, honky-tonk entertainment, and even staged shoot-outs on Main Street are held throughout the year.

The **Red River Chamber of Commerce,** P.O. Box 870, Red River, NM 87558 (☎ **505/754-2366,** or toll free **800/348-6444**), lists more than 40 accommodations, including lodges and condominiums. Some are open winters or summers only.

EAGLE NEST   About 16 miles east of Red River, on the other side of 9,850-foot Bobcat Pass, is the village of Eagle Nest, resting on the shore of Eagle Nest Lake in the Moreno Valley. There was gold mining in this area as early as 1866, starting in what is now the ghost town of Elizabethtown about five miles north; but Eagle Nest itself (pop. 200) wasn't incorporated until 1976. The four-square-mile lake is considered one of the top trout producers in the United States and attracts ice fishermen in winter as well as summer anglers. Sailboats and windsurfers also use the lake, although swimming, waterskiing, and camping are not permitted.

If you're heading to Cimarron or Denver, proceed east on U.S. 64 from Eagle Nest. But if you're circling back to Taos, continue southwest on U.S. 38 and U.S. 64 to Agua Fria and Angel Fire.

Shortly before the Agua Fria junction, you'll see the **DAV Vietnam Veterans Memorial.** It's a stunning structure, its curved white walls soaring high against the backdrop of the Sangre de Cristo range. Consisting of a chapel and underground visitor center, it was built by Dr. Victor Westphall in memory of his son, David, a Marine lieutenant killed in Vietnam in 1968. The chapel has a changing gallery of photographs of Vietnam veterans who gave their lives in the Southeast Asian war, but no photo is as poignant as this inscription written by young Westphall, a promising poet:

> *Greed plowed cities desolate.*
> *Lusts ran snorting through the streets.*
> *Pride reared up to desecrate*
> *Shrines, and there were no retreats.*
> *So man learned to shed the tears*
> *With which he measures out his years.*

ANGEL FIRE   The full-service resort community of **Angel Fire,** approximately 12 miles south of Eagle Nest, 21 miles east of Taos, and 2 miles south of the Agua Fria junction on N.M. 38, dates only from the late 1960s but already has some 30 lodges and condominiums. Winter skiing and summer golf are the most popular activities, but there's also ample opportunity for sailing and fishing on Angel Fire Lake, tennis, racquetball, and horseback riding.

The unofficial community center is The **Legends Hotel & Conference Center,** North Angel Fire Road (P.O. Drawer B), Angel Fire, NM 87710 (☎ **505/377-6401),** a 157-room inn and restaurant with rates starting at $60.

For more information on, and full accommodations listings in, the Moreno Valley, contact the **Angel Fire/Eagle Nest Chamber of Commerce,** P.O. Box 547, Angel Fire, NM 87710 (☎ **505/377-6353,** or toll free **800/446-8117**). Or call **Angel Fire Central Reservations** (☎ toll free **800/635-9633**).

It's about 21 miles back to Taos, over 9,100-foot Palo Flechado Pass, down the valley of the Rio Fernando de Taos, and through the small community of Shady Brook.

16

Taos Shopping A to Z

Visitors come to Taos to buy fine art. Some 50-odd galleries are located within easy walking distance of the Plaza, and a couple of dozen more are a short drive from downtown. Most artists display in one or more of the galleries, which are generally open seven days a week, especially in high season. Some artists show their work by appointment only.

The best-known artist in modern Taos is R. C. Gorman, a Navajo from Arizona who has made his home in Taos for over two decades. Now in his 50s, Gorman is internationally acclaimed for his bright, somewhat surrealistic depictions of Navajo women. His **Navajo Gallery,** next door to the Blumenschein House at 5 Ledoux St. (☎ **758-3250**), is a showcase for his widely varied work: acrylics, lithographs, silk screens, bronzes, tapestries, hand-cast ceramic vases, etched glass, and more.

A good place to start an exploration of galleries is the **Stables Art Center,** operated by the Taos Art Association at 133 Paseo del Pueblo Norte (☎ **758-2036**). A changing series of fine and performing-arts exhibits introduce many of Taos's emerging artists on a rotating basis. All types of work are exhibited, including painting (from expressionism to nonrepresentationalism), sculpture, printmaking, photography, and ceramics. Admission is free; it's open Monday through Saturday from 10am to 5pm and on Sunday from 1 to 5pm, year-round.

A selection of other places to shop, listed according to their specialties, follows.

Art

Act I Gallery, 226D Paseo del Pueblo Norte. ☎ **758-7831.**

Watercolors, retablos, furniture, paintings, wood turnings, pottery, jewelry, and sculpture.

⭐ **Philip Bareiss Contemporary Exhibitions,** 15 Ski Valley Rd. ☎ **776-2284.**

The works of some 30 leading Taos artists, including sculptor Gray Mercer and watercolorist Patricia Sanford. Philip Bareiss also has a three-acre sculpture park.

Desurmont-Ellis Gallery, 121 North Plaza. ☎ **758-3299.**

Abstract and impressionist oils and watercolors, sculpture, ceramics, and jewelry, including Angie Coleman woodcuts.

⭐ **El Taller Gallery,** 119A Kit Carson Rd. ☎ **758-4887.**

Exclusive representation of Amado Peña as well as fine art by an excellent group of southwestern artists.

Fenix Gallery, 228B N. Pueblo Rd. ☎ **758-9120.**

Fine contemporary paintings, prints, and sculpture. Represents such artists as Cynthia Barber, Jane Ellen Burke, Sas Colby, Brenda Euwer, Gretchen Ewert, Alyce Frank, Jan Janerio, Sandra Lerner, Ginger Mongiello, Lee Mullican, Marcia Olever, Marsha Skinner, Pat Smith, Earl Stroh, Gregory Vose, and Ben Wade.

Gallery A, 105-107 Kit Carson Rd. ☎ **758-2343.**

The oldest gallery in town, Gallery A has contemporary and traditional paintings, sculpture, and graphics, including Gene Kloss oils, watercolors, and etchings.

Magic Mountain Gallery, 107A North Plaza. ☎ **758-9604.**

Impressionistic paintings, sculpture, ceramics, jewelry, and turned wood bowls.

★ **New Directions Gallery,** 107B North Plaza. ☎ **758-2771.**

Features Larry Bell's unique "Mirage paintings" and mixed-media paper sculptures, and work by acclaimed sculptor Ted Egri.

Quast Galleries, 229 and 133 Kit Carson Rd. ☎ **758-7160.**

Representational landscapes and figurative paintings and distinguished sculpture. Rotating national and international exhibits are shown here.

Second Phase Gallery, 110 Guadalupe Plaza. ☎ **751-0159.**

Fine antique Native American art, including Navajo rugs and blankets, Pueblo pottery, and Plains beadwork.

Shriver Gallery, 401 Paseo del Pueblo Norte. ☎ **758-4994.**

Traditional paintings, drawings, etchings, and bronze sculpture.

The Taos Gallery, 403 Paseo del Pueblo Sur. ☎ **758-2475.**

Southwestern impressionism, contemporary fine art, and bronze sculpture.

Taos Traditions Gallery, 221 Paseo del Pueblo Norte.
☎ **758-0016.**

Impressionist still lifes, figures (including nudes), and landscapes by internationally acclaimed and exceptional emerging artists.

Books

The Brodsky Bookshop, 218 Paseo del Pueblo Norte.
☎ **758-9468.**

Exceptional inventory of fiction, nonfiction, southwestern and Native American studies, children's books, topographical and travel maps, cards, tapes, and CDs.

Fernandez de Taos Bookstore, 109 North Plaza. ☎ **758-4391.**

A substantial offering of books on southwestern subjects, along with local and regional newspapers and a large array of magazines.

Kit Carson Home, E. Kit Carson Rd. ☎ **758-4741.**

Fine collection of books about regional history.

Moby Dickens Bookshop, 124A Bent St. ☎ **758-3050.**

Children's and adults' collections of Southwest, Native American, and out-of-print books.

Taos Book Shop, 122D Kit Carson Rd. ☎ **758-3733.**

Founded in 1947, this is the oldest general bookstore in New Mexico.

Crafts

Brooks Indian Shop, 108G Cabot Plaza Mall, 108 Kit Carson Rd. ☎ **758-9073.**
Jewelry, pottery, artifacts, and accessories.

Clay & Fiber Gallery, 126 W. Plaza Dr. ☎ **758-8093.**
Ceramics, fiber arts, jewelry, and wearables.

Open Space Gallery, 103B East Plaza, Taos Plaza. ☎ **758-1217.**
A cooperative gallery of contemporary arts and crafts.

Southwestern Arts, in the Dunn House, Bent St. ☎ **758-8418.**
Historic and contemporary Navajo weavings, Pueblo pottery, and jewelry. Also photography by Dick Spas.

★ **Taos Artisans Coop,** Bent Street. ☎ **758-1558.**
Local handmade jewelry, wearables, claywork, glass, drums, and baskets.

Weaving Southwest, 216 Paseo del Pueblo Norte. ☎ **758-0433.**
Contemporary tapestries by New Mexico artists, as well as one-of-a-kind rugs, blankets, and pillows.

Fashions

Bluefish, 140 E. Kit Carson Rd. ☎ **758-3520.**
If you love unique articles of clothing, you'll love Bluefish, where you'll find hand-blocked pieces of art clothing.

Twining Weavers and Contemporary Crafts, 135 Paseo del Pueblo Norte. ☎ **758-9000.**
Designer clothing by Sally Bachman. Also hand-woven rugs, blankets, and other fabrics.

Food

Casa Fresen Bakery (☎ **776-2969**), which is on the road to the Taos Ski Valley in Arroyo Seco, is a wonderful place to pick up fresh pastries, cakes, cheeses, pâtés, specialty meats, pastas, sauces, preserves, and oils. You can enjoy a sandwich right there or pick up a box lunch to take with you if you're going on a picnic. It's open daily from 7:30am to 6pm.

Furniture

Country Furnishings of Taos, 534 N. Pueblo Rd. ☎ **758-4633.**
Here you'll find unique hand-painted folk-art furniture that has become popular all over the country. The pieces are as unique and individual as the styles of the local folk artists who work on them. There are also home accessories, unique gifts, clothing, and jewelry.

Lo Fino, 201 Paseo del Pueblo Sur. ☎ **758-0298.**
Handcrafted traditional and contemporary Southwest furniture and lighting by over 30 unique and creative artists.

Taos Blue, 101A Bent St. ☎ **758-3561.**

Fine Native American and contemporary handcraft gallery.

The Taos Company, 124K John Dunn Plaza, Bent St. ☎ **758-1141.**

Interior design showroom, specializing in southwestern antique furniture and decorative accessories.

Gifts and Souvenirs

Broken Arrow Ltd., 222 North Plaza. ☎ **758-4304.**

Ceramics, weaving, jewelry, baskets, paintings, and sculpture.

Jewelry

Art Wares Art Center, North Plaza. ☎ **758-8850.**

Innovative contemporary works, featuring Phil Poirier's one-of-a-kind and limited-edition silverwork.

Taos Gems & Minerals, 637 Paseo del Pueblo Sur. ☎ **758-3910.**

Now in its 26th year of business, Taos Gems & Minerals is a fine lapidary showroom. Here you can get jewelry, specimens, and antiquities at reasonable prices.

Musical Instruments

Southwest Moccasin & Drum, 803 Paseo del Pueblo Norte.
☎ **758-9332,** or toll free **800/447-3630.**

Fine instruments handmade by master Native American drummakers from Taos Pueblo and hand-printed with designs by artists B. J. Quintana and Carl Winters. The world's second-largest selection of moccasins, plus world instruments and tapes, pottery, jewelry, weavings, rattles, fans, pipes, fetishes, and kachinas. Some of the profits go to support Native American causes.

Taos Drums, five miles south of Taos Plaza off N.M. 68.
☎ **758-9844,** or toll free **800/424-DRUM.**

Drum making is an age-old tradition that local artisans are continuing in Taos. The drums are made of hollowed-out logs stretched with rawhide and come in all different shapes, sizes, and styles. Taos Drums has the largest selection of Native American log and hand drums in the world. In addition to drums, the showroom displays southwestern and wrought-iron furniture, cowboy art, and lamps, as well as a constantly changing display of primitive folk art, ethnic crafts, Native American music tapes, books, and other information on drumming. To find Taos drums, look for the teepees and drums off N.M. 68.

17

Taos Nights

FOR A SMALL TOWN, TAOS GETS ITS SHARE OF TOP ENTERTAINMENT, attracted by the resort atmosphere and the arts community. Annual programs in music and literary arts are an integral part of Taos life, and state troupes, including the New Mexico Repertory Theater and New Mexico Symphony Orchestra, make regular visits to the town.

Many occasional events are scheduled by the **Taos Art Association,** 133 Paseo del Pueblo Norte (P.O. Box 198), Taos, NM 87571 (☎ **505/758-2052**), at the Taos Community Auditorium. The TAA imports local, regional, and national performers in theater, dance, and concerts—Dave Brubeck, the late Dizzy Gillespie, the American String Quartet, and the American Festival Ballet have performed here—and offers two weekly film series, including one for children.

You can get details on current events in the weekly *Taos News,* published Thursday. The Taos Country Chamber of Commerce (☎ **505/758-3873,** or toll free **800/732-TAOS**) publishes semiannual listings of "Taos County Events."

1   The Performing Arts

Major Annual Programs ───────────

Fort Burgwin Research Center, on N.M. 518 south of Taos.
   ☎ **758-8322.**

This historic site (of the 1,000-year-old Pot Creek Pueblo) located about 10 miles south of Taos, is a summer campus of Southern Methodist University. From mid-May through mid-August, the SMU-IN-TAOS curriculum (among other studio arts, humanities, and sciences) includes courses in music and theater. There are regularly scheduled orchestral concerts, guitar and harpsichord recitals, and theater performances that are available to the community, without charge, throughout the summer.

Music from Angel Fire, P.O. Box 502, Angel Fire, NM 87710.
   ☎ **377-3233.**

This acclaimed program of chamber, folk, and jazz music begins in mid-August with weekend concerts and continues up to Labor Day. Based in the small resort community of Angel Fire (located about 21 miles east of U.S. 64), it also presents numerous concerts in Taos and Raton.

The Major Concert and Performance Halls

Taos Civic Plaza and Convention Center, 121 Civic Plaza Dr. (☎ **758-4160**).

Taos Community Auditorium, Kit Carson Memorial State Park (☎ **758-2052**).

SOMOS Taos Poetry Circus, ☎ 758-0081.

Aficionados of the literary arts appreciate this annual event, held over four days in mid-June. Billed by SOMOS (Society of the Muse of the Southwest) as "a literary gathering and poetry showdown between nationally known writers," it includes readings, workshops, lectures, children's theater, and a banquet. The main event, held at 8pm on Saturday, is the World Heavyweight Championship Poetry Bout, 10 rounds of hard-hitting readings—with the last round extemporaneous.

SOMOS also sponsors a **Summer Writers' Series** at the Stables Art Center, with 8pm readings by noted writers, beginning the Thursday after July 4 and continuing to about Labor Day. Featured writers have included New Mexicans Tony Hillerman and John Nichols.

Taos School of Music, 360 State Rd., Arroyo Seco, Taos, NM 87514. ☎ 776-2388.

One of the oldest chamber-music programs of its kind in the United States offers from mid-June to mid-August an intensive eight-week study and performance program to advanced students of violin, viola, cello, and piano. There is daily coaching by the American String Quartet and pianist Robert McDonald. Sponsored by the Taos Art Association, the school was founded in 1963 and is located at the Hotel St. Bernard in Taos Ski Valley in Northern New Mexico.

The eight-week Chamber Music Festival is an important adjunct to the school, offering 16 concerts and seminars to the public by the American String Quartet, pianist Robert McDonald, and guest violist Michael Tree of the Guarneri Quartet, as well as concerts by the international young artists in attendance. Concerts are given at the Taos Community Auditorium and the Hotel St. Bernard.

Major Concert Halls and All-Purpose Auditoriums ——

Taos Civic Plaza and Convention Center, 121 Civic Plaza Dr. ☎ 758-5792.

Taos's pride and joy is this center, located just three short blocks north of the Plaza. Opened in 1990, it accommodates audiences of 610 in Rio Grande Hall and another 500 in adjacent Bataan Auditorium. Major concerts and other entertainment events are scheduled here.

Taos Community Auditorium, 145 Paseo del Pueblo Norte. ☎ 758-4677.

The town's primary arts facility before the construction of the civic plaza, this auditorium—located behind the Stables Art Center—seats 235 for theater. A film series is offered at 8pm every Wednesday (admission is $4).

2   The Club & Music Scene

Adobe Bar, in the Historic Taos Inn, 125 Paseo del Pueblo Norte. ☎ 758-2233.

A favorite gathering place for locals as well as visitors, the Adobe Bar is known for its live-music series (Wednesday and Sunday from 6 to 9pm) devoted to the eclectic talents of Taos musicians. The schedule offers a little of everything—classical, jazz, folk, Hispanic, and acoustic. The Adobe Bar features a wide selection of international beers, wines by the glass, light New Mexican dining, desserts, and an espresso menu.

Admission: Free.

Kachina Cabaret, at the Kachina Lodge, 413 Paseo del Pueblo Norte. ☎ 758-2275.

Top-name country and Hispanic acts—including the Desert Rose Band, the Nitty Gritty Dirt Band, and Eddie Rabbit—have performed in the cabaret. Saturday night is the big event night, starting at 9pm. The adjacent Zuni Lounge has rock bands nightly.

Admission: Varies according to performer, but usually $5 Fri–Sat.

Sagebrush Inn, Paseo del Pueblo Sur. ☎ 758-2254.

Taos's highest-energy dancing spot has country or rock performers nightly, year-round, from 9pm.

Admission: Free.

Thunderbird Lodge, Taos Ski Valley. ☎ 776-2280.

Throughout January, the Thunderbird Jazz Festival brings leading contemporary jazz musicians to perform week-long gigs at the foot of the ski slopes. Shows start at 8:30pm; dinner-and-show packages are available. The rest of the ski season, the Twining Tavern has country music on Wednesday, rock on Thursday, jazz on Friday, Warren Miller ski movies on Saturday. Two-step dance lessons.

Admission: Jazz Festival $10 and up.

18

Albuquerque

Albuquerque is the gateway to fascinating northern New Mexico, the portal through which most domestic and international visitors pass before moving on to Santa Fe and Taos.

From the rocky crest of Sandia Peak, the lights of this city of almost half a million people spread out like needlepoint on an enormous quilt at sunset. As the sun drops beyond the western horizon, it glints off the Rio Grande, flowing through Albuquerque more than a mile beneath the observation post at the top of the Sandia Peak aerial tramway.

The tram, said to be the world's longest at 2.7 miles, climbs from the northeastern outskirts of the city to the top of 10,378-foot Sandia Peak, passing high above cathedrallike crags and sparse ponderosa and aspen forest. From the summit, with keen eyes and a little imagination, you can see the site where Spanish colonists established a villa on the Old Chihuahua Trail in 1706 and named it after regional governor Don Francisco Cuervo y Valdez, the 13th Duke of Alburquerque (the first "r" was later deleted from the city's name).

Reminders of the colonial past of the "Duke City" still abound, though Albuquerque has become a major metropolis that now sprawls 16 miles from the lava-crested mesas on the west side of the Rio Grande to the steep alluvial slopes of the Sandia Mountains on the east and another 14 miles north-south through the Rio Grande valley. It boomed as a transportation center with the arrival of the railroad in 1880, but that economic explosion was nothing compared to what happened during World War II, when Albuquerque was designated as a major national center for military research and production. Its population has grown by more than 10 times in four decades.

1 Orientation

Arriving

As the transportation hub for the state of New Mexico, getting in and out of town is easy. For more detailed information about doing that, see "Getting There," in Chapter 2.

BY AIR The **Albuquerque International Airport** is in the south-central part of the city, between I-25 on the west and Kirtland Air Force Base on the east, just south of Gibson Boulevard. Sleek and efficient, the airport is served by eight national airlines and two local ones.

Most hotels have courtesy vans to take new arrivals to their accommodations. **Shuttlejack** (☎ **243-3244,** or toll free **800/452-2665** outside New Mexico) also runs a service to city hotels and on to Santa Fe. **Sun Tran** (☎ **843-9200**), Albuquerque's public bus system, also makes airport stops. There is efficient taxi service to and from the airport, plus numerous car-rental agencies.

BY TRAIN Amtrak's *Southwest Chief* arrives and departs daily from and to Los Angeles and Chicago. The station is at 314 First St. SW,

Greater Albuquerque

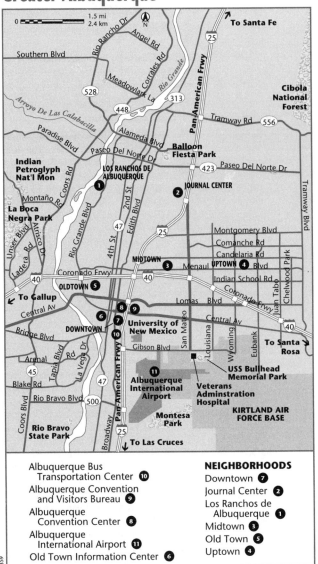

Albuquerque Bus Transportation Center **10**	**NEIGHBORHOODS**
Albuquerque Convention and Visitors Bureau **9**	Downtown **7**
Albuquerque Convention Center **8**	Journal Center **2**
	Los Ranchos de Albuquerque **1**
Albuquerque International Airport **11**	Midtown **3**
Old Town Information Center **6**	Old Town **5**
	Uptown **4**

two blocks south of Central Avenue (☎ **842-9650,** or toll free **800/USA-RAIL**).

BY BUS Greyhound/Trailways (☎ **505/243-4435** for schedules, fares, and information) and **TNM&O Coaches**

(☎ **505/242-4998**) arrive and depart from the Albuquerque Bus Transportation Center (☎ **842-9188**), adjacent to the train station at 300 Second St. SW.

BY CAR   If you're driving yourself, you'll probably arrive in the city via either the east-west Interstate 40 or the north-south Interstate 25. Exits are well marked. For information and advice on driving in New Mexico, see "Getting Around," in Chapter 2.

Tourist Information

The head office of the **Albuquerque Convention and Visitors Bureau** is at 121 Tijeras Ave. NE, first floor (☎ **505/243-3696,** or toll free **800/284-2282**). It's open Monday through Friday from 8am to 5pm. There are information centers at the airport, bottom of the escalator in the lower level, open daily from 9:30am to 8pm; and in Old Town at 303 Romero St. NW (Suite 107), open Monday through Saturday from 9am to 7pm and on Sunday from 10am to 5pm. Tape-recorded information on current local events is available from the bureau after 5pm weekdays and all day Saturday and Sunday. Call **243-3696.**

City Layout

The sprawl of the city takes a bit of getting used to. A visitor's first impression is of a grid of arterials lined with shopping malls and fast-food eateries, with residences tucked behind on side streets.

If you lay a map of Albuquerque before you, the first thing you'll notice is that it lies at the crossroads of **Interstate 25** north-south and **Interstate 40** east-west. Refocus your attention to the south-west quadrant of the X: Here you'll find both **downtown** Albuquerque and **Old Town,** center of many tourist attractions. **Lomas Boulevard** and **Central Avenue,** the old "Route 66" (U.S. 66), flank downtown on the south and north. They come together two miles west of downtown near the **Old Town Plaza,** the historical and spiritual heart of the city. Lomas and Central continue east across I-25, staying about half a mile apart as they pass by the University of New Mexico and the New Mexico State Fairgrounds. The airport is due south of the UNM campus, about three miles via Yale Boulevard. Kirtland Air Force Base—site of Sandia National Laboratories and the National Atomic Museum—is an equal distance south of the fairgrounds on Louisiana Boulevard.

Roughly paralleling I-40 to the north is Menaul Boulevard, focus of the **Midtown** and **Uptown** shopping and hotel districts. As Albuquerque expands northward, the **Journal Center** business park area, about $4^1/_2$ miles north of the freeway interchange, is getting more attention. East of Eubank Boulevard are the **Sandia Foothills,** where the alluvial plain slants a bit more steeply toward the mountain.

It's helpful when **finding an address** to know that Central Avenue divides the city into north and south, and the railroad tracks—which run just east of First Street, downtown—split it into east and west. Street names are followed by a directional: NE, NW, SE, or SW.

MAPS   The most comprehensive Albuquerque street map is the one published by First Security Bank and distributed by the convention and visitors bureau.

2 | Getting Around

A city of half a million people might seem intimidating to get around, but actually Albuquerque is easy to conquer. The wide thoroughfares and grid layout of the city, combined with efficient transportation systems, make it so.

BY PUBLIC TRANSPORTATION   Sun Tran of Albuquerque (☎ 505/843-9200) cloaks the arterials with its city bus network. Call for information on routes and fares.

BY TAXI   Albuquerque Cab (☎ 883-4888) and **Checker Cab** and **Yellow Cab** (☎ 247-8888 or 243-7777, for either) serve the city and surrounding area 24 hours a day.

BY CAR   The *Yellow Pages* list more than 30 car-rental agencies in Albuquerque. Among them are these well-known national firms: **Alamo,** at the airport (☎ 505/842-4057); **Avis,** at the airport (☎ 505/842-4080); **Budget,** at the airport (☎ 505/768-5900); **Dollar,** at the airport (☎ 505/842-4224); **Hertz,** at the airport (☎ 505/842-4235); **Rent-a-Wreck,** 500 Yale Blvd. SE (☎ 505/242-9556); and **Thrifty,** 2039 Yale Blvd. SE (☎ 505/842-8733). Those not in the airport itself are nearby and provide rapid airport pickup and delivery service.

Parking is generally not difficult in Albuquerque—nor, for that matter, is rush hour a serious problem (yet). Meters operate weekdays from 8am to 6pm and are not monitored at other times. Most hotels do not charge for parking, with the exception of the large downtown hostelries.

Fast Facts: Albuquerque

Airport   See "Orientation," earlier in this chapter.

American Express   The AmEx representative here is Atlas Travel, 5301 Central Ave. NE (☎ 505/262-2255). To report lost credit cards, call toll free **800/528-4800.**

Area Code   The telephone area code for all of New Mexico is **505.**

Climate   See "When to Go," in Chapter 2.

Emergencies   For police, fire, or ambulance, dial **911.** For non-emergencies, call **242-2677.**

Hospitals   The major facilities are **Presbyterian Hospital,** 1100 Central Ave. SE (☎ 841-1234, 841-1111 for emergency services); and **University of New Mexico Hospital,** 2211 Lomas Blvd. NE (☎ 843-2411 for emergency services).

Liquor Laws   See "Fast Facts: Santa Fe," in Chapter 4.

Mail   The Main Post Office, 1135 Broadway NE, Albuquerque, NM 87102 (☎ 848-3872), is open daily from 8am to 4pm. There are 14 branch offices, with another 13 in surrounding communities.

Newspapers and Magazines   The two daily newspapers are the *Albuquerque Tribune,* published mornings, and the *Albuquerque Journal,* published evenings. *Albuquerque Monthly* magazine covers many aspects of city life and is widely available.

Police   For emergencies, call **911.** For other business, contact the Albuquerque City Police (☎ **768-1986**) or the New Mexico State Police (☎ **841-9256**).

Radio/TV   Albuquerque has some 30 local radio stations catering to all musical tastes. Albuquerque television stations include KOB, Channel 4 (NBC affiliate); KOAT, Channel 7 (ABC affiliate); KGGM, Channel 13 (CBS affiliate); KNME, Channel 5 (PBS affiliate); and KGSW, Channel 14 (Fox and independent). There are, of course, numerous local cable channels as well.

3   Accommodations

Albuquerque's hotel glut is good news to travelers looking for quality rooms at reasonable cost. Except during peak periods—specifically, the New Mexico Arts & Crafts Fair in late June, the New Mexico State Fair in September, and the Kodak Albuquerque International Balloon Fiesta in early October—most of the city's hotels have vacant rooms, so guests can frequently request and get a lower room rate than the one posted.

In the following listing, hotels are categorized by price range: "Expensive," over $110 per night double; "Moderate," $75 to $110; "Inexpensive," $45 to $75; and "Budget," under $45.

A tax of 10.8125% is added to every hotel bill.

Expensive

Albuquerque Doubletree Hotel, 201 Marquette St. NW, Albuquerque, NM 87102. ☎ **505/247-3344,** or toll free **800/555-0444.** Fax 505/247-7025. 294 rms, 13 suites. A/C TV TEL **Rates** (including breakfast): $74–$124 single; $84–$134 double. AE, CB, DC, DISC, MC, V. **Parking:** Free.

A two-story waterfall cascades down a marble backdrop adjacent to the registration area, setting the mood in this recently vastly renovated hotel (formerly the Regent). Marble is the trademark of the pillared lobby; the elegance extends to the guest rooms, which feature custom-made southwestern furnishings and other regional touches. Guests are treated to chocolate-chip cookies on arrival.

Dining/Entertainment: La Cascada Restaurant, at the foot of the waterfall, is an airy, sidewalk café-style coffee shop serving three meals daily. Adjacent is the Bistro Bar. Upstairs, the Lobby Lounge has live music daily during happy hour.

Albuquerque Accommodations

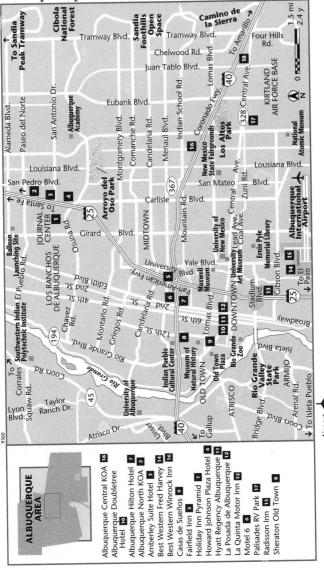

Services: Room service (6am–midnight), courtesy van to airport and Old Town, valet laundry.

Facilities: Rooms for nonsmokers and the disabled; swimming pool, weight and exercise room, gift shop, airline desks; underground passages to convention center and Galeria shopping center.

Casas de Sueños, 310 Rio Grande Blvd. SW, Albuquerque, NM 87104. ☎ **505/247-4560,** or toll free **800/CHAT-W/US.** 15 rms. TV TEL

Rates (including breakfast): $85–$250 single or double. AE, CB, DC, DISC, MC, V.

You'll know Casas de Sueños by the bright sign and the snail-shaped front of the main building (you'll know exactly what I mean when you see it, and you can't miss it). The buildings that comprise Casas de Sueños were once private homes—apparently somewhat of an artists' colony. Most of them face a courtyard that was cooperatively maintained for many years by the residents. In the spring and summer the gardens, filled with roses, are maintained by today's owners of Casas de Sueños, making this place an oasis in the middle of Albuquerque.

Each of the rooms follows an individual theme; for instance, Cupid is done in black, white, and pink and has a clawfoot tub—a nice romantic getaway. La Cascada, so named because of the fountain outside its door, has a Monet theme with its pastel colors, Monet posters, and Monet print comforter. The Kachina room has many little *kachinas* (the storytellers) scattered about. Some of the rooms have kitchens, and La Miradora has two bedrooms (with king- and queen-size beds), a living room with a fireplace, a full bath (with a two-person Jacuzzi), and a back porch with a swing overlooking a golf course. All the rooms have their own entrances.

Gordon and Maggie Johnston, the managers, serve a delicious full breakfast in the main building every morning. Works by local artists are displayed in the breakfast room. Guests have sports club privileges, and there's a massage therapist on premises. No smoking is permitted indoors. Pets are not accepted, but children 12 and older are welcome.

★ **Hyatt Regency Albuquerque,** 330 Tijeras Ave. NW, Albuquerque, NM 87102. ☎ **505/842-1234,** or toll free **800/233-1234.** Fax 505/842-1184. 395 rms, 14 suites. A/C TV TEL **Rates:** $115–$155 single or double weekdays, $85 weekends; $310–$725 suite. AE, CB, DC, DISC, MC, V. **Parking:** $7 self-parking, $11 valet.

This $60-million hotel opened in 1990 with a great deal of hoopla. Already a city landmark, the 20-story structure—which incorporates the offices of Albuquerque Plaza—makes a bold architectural statement uncharacteristic of New Mexico. The lobby features a palm-shaded fountain beneath a pyramidal skylight, and throughout the public areas of the hotel is an extensive art collection, including original Frederic Remington sculptures. The spacious guest rooms perpetuate the feeling of richness with mahogany furnishings, full-length mirrors, even data-port phone jacks for busy businesspeople.

Dining/Entertainment: McGrath's serves three meals daily in a luxurious setting of forest-green upholstery and black-cherry furniture. The Lobby Bar, noted for its whimsical oils of "where the deer and the antelope play" (at the bar), has live jazz Tuesday through Saturday nights.

Services: Room service, concierge, valet laundry.

Facilities: Rooms for nonsmokers and the disabled; outdoor swimming pool, health club (with weight/exercise equipment and masseur); shopping block (including art galleries, hair salon, florist, optician, and travel agency).

NEARBY

Salsa del Salto, P.O. Box 453, El Prado, NM 87529.
☎ **505/776-2422.** 8 rms (all with bath).
Rates: $85–$160 double. Extra person $10. MC, V.

Situated between Taos town and the Taos Ski Valley, Salsa del Salto is the perfect place for those seeking a secluded retreat within a short drive of Taos's major tourist attractions. Guest rooms in this New Mexican country lodge are tastefully decorated with pastel shades in a Southwestern motif and beds are covered with cozy down comforters. Each room offers views of the mountains or mesas of Taos, and the private bathrooms are modern and spacious. The Master's Room features a beautiful fireplace with copper detailing as well as a private door to a covered portal, and the Lobo Room faces lobo peak, one of the largest aspen stands in the Taos area. La Familia, composed of two connecting rooms, is ideal for families.

The focus here is on relaxation and outdoor activities. Innkeeper Mary Hockett is a native New Mexican who is extremely knowledgeable about the surrounding area and who enjoys horseback riding, skiing, biking, and tennis. She's happy to share information about her favorite activities with her guests. Mary's partner, Dadou Mayer, was born and raised in Nice, France, and is an accomplished chef. Dadou was also a member of the French National Ski Team, and he was recently named "The Fastest Chef in the United States" when he won the Grand Marnier Ski Race. Mayer has authored a cookbook, *Cuisine à Taos,* and has been a supervisor of the Ski School of Taos for over twenty years. Salsa del Salto is the only bed and breakfast in Taos that has a pool and hot tub as well as private tennis courts, and it's the only place in Taos where you'll be treated to a full gourmet breakfast whipped up by a true French chef. Mary bakes the muffins and breads, while Dadou serves up specialties like green chile and brie omelettes—all of which you can savor each morning in front of the massive fireplace. If you're at Salsa del Salto during the winter you'll get the added bonus of an early morning briefing about ski conditions. In short, you'll want for nothing here.

Moderate

IN ALBUQUERQUE

Albuquerque Hilton Hotel, 1901 University Blvd. NE, Albuquerque, NM 87102. ☎ **505/884-2500,** or toll free **800/27-HOTEL.** Fax 505/889-9118. 250 rms, 2 suites. A/C TV TEL

Rates: $91–$105 single; $95–$105 double; $375–$400 suite. AE, CB, DC, DISC, MC, V. **Parking:** Free.

White stuccoed corridors with petroglyph-style paintings are a trademark of this hotel. Many of the rooms are in a high-rise tower that underwent a multimillion-dollar renovation in 1988. Two floors of rooms comprise a VIP level for business travelers; cabaña rooms with 15-foot cathedral ceilings surround the outdoor pool. No pets.

Dining/Entertainment: The Ranchers Club, built like a British hunting lodge transported to the high plains, is considered by many as Albuquerque's number-one restaurant. Fine continental cuisine is complemented by more than 20 gourmet sauces. It's open Monday through Friday for lunch and Monday through Saturday for dinner. Casa Chaco is open daily for three meals, including highly regarded contemporary southwestern dinners. The Cantina, with its fajitas grill and piano bar, serves as the hotel lounge.

Services: Room service (during restaurant hours), valet laundry, courtesy van.

Facilities: Rooms for nonsmokers and the disabled; indoor and outdoor swimming pools, whirlpool, saunas, tennis courts, gift shop.

Best Western Fred Harvey, 2910 Yale Blvd. SE, Albuquerque, NM 87106. ☎ **505/843-7000,** or toll free **800/227-1117.** Fax 505/843-6307. 266 rms. A/C TV TEL

Rates: $81–$93 single; $91–$103 double. AE, CB, DC, DISC, MC, V. **Parking:** Free.

No accommodation is closer to the airport than the Best Western Fred Harvey, which is literally a stone's throw north of the main terminal. It caters to air travelers with a 24-hour desk and shuttle service, and overnight valet laundry. Rooms are appointed in pastel decor with a southwestern flair and are furnished with king-size or double beds, four-drawer dressers, leather easy chairs with ottomans, cable TV/radios, and phones. There's a restaurant on the premises that serves meals at reasonable prices. Room service, courtesy van, valet laundry, complimentary shoeshine, and rooms for nonsmokers and the handicapped are available. Pets are not permitted. Facilities include an outdoor swimming pool, coed sauna, two all-weather tennis courts, and a gift shop.

★ **Casa del Granjero,** 414 C de Baca Lane NW, Albuquerque, NM 87114. ☎ **505/897-4144.** 3 rms. MC, V.

Rates (including breakfast): $87–$107 double. Additional person $20 extra.

From the potbelly pig to the old restored wagon out front, Casa del Granjero ("The Farmer's House") is true to its name. It might come as more of a surprise, however, that the innkeepers actually are the Farmers—Butch and Victoria Farmer—and they have transformed their home into an exquisite bed-and-breakfast. The great room has an enormous sculptured adobe fireplace, comfortable bancos for lounging, a library, and scores of Old West and Native American artifacts. As a guest at Casa del Granjero you might like to curl up in front of the fire and read a book or listen to Butch's stories about an Indian fighter relative who was a scout for George Washington. If you'd rather spend a couple of hours watching a movie, but are too tired to head back into downtown Albuquerque, the 52-inch television in the den fits the bill. The three guest rooms all have kiva fireplaces and are beautifully furnished. Cuarto del Rey, with queen-size and day beds, features Mexican furnishings and handmade quilts and comforters. Cuarto de Flores has French doors that open onto a portal, and Cuarto Allegre (the largest of the rooms) has a king-size canopy bed done up in lace and satin. All the bathrooms are unique and quite beautiful. The one in Cuarto Allegre has wooden beams, corbels, and handmade Mexican tiles. In the morning, breakfast is served at the spectacular dining room table or on the portal. It includes fresh fruit, homemade pastries and breads, and a hot dish. There's an outdoor hot tub available for guest use. Smoking is permitted outdoors only, and pets are not permitted.

Hacienda Antigua, 6708 Tierra Dr., NW, Albuquerque, NM 87107. ☎ 505/345-5399. 3 rms (all with bath).

Rates (including breakfast): $85–$110 double. Extra person $15.

Located on the north side of Albuquerque, just off Osuna Road, you'll find Hacienda Antigua, a 200-year-old adobe home that was once the first stagecoach stop out of Old Town in Albuquerque. Owned for two centuries by the Yrissaris family, the hacienda retained its old world charm, and when Ann Dunlap and Melinda Moffit bought it they were careful to preserve the building's history while at the same time transforming it into a beautiful bed and breakfast. The exterior walls of the inn are remarkable in their simplicity—only the heavy carved gates bespeak the treasures that lie within. The beautifully landscaped courtyard, with its large cottonwood tree and abundance of greenery, offers a welcome respite for today's tired travelers just as it did during the days when the hacienda served as a mercantile and cantina.

The three guest rooms are furnished with antiques, and each room has a private bath. The Don Pablo Suite features a king-size bed (covered with a stunning blue quilt), a sitting room with a kiva fireplace, and a bathroom with a wonderful old pedestal bathtub/shower. A traditional "ducking door" allows guests staying in this room access to the courtyard. La Capilla is the home's former chapel, and it is furnished with lovely dark oak, a queen-size bed, a fireplace, and a beautiful carving of San Ysidro (the patron saint of farmers). Dona Manuelita features antique iron beds (full-size and twin), and traditional *bancos* by the window. The bathroom is separated from the rest of the room by a curving adobe wall which offers bathers who sink into the claw-foot tub a view of the fireplace. A gourmet breakfast is served in the garden during warm weather, and by the fire in winter. Guests also have use of the pool and hot tub. Just a 20-minute drive from the airport, Hacienda Antigua is a welcome change from the anonymity of the downtown Albuquerque high-rise hotels.

★ **Holiday Inn Pyramid,** 5151 San Francisco Rd., NE, Albuquerque, NM 87109. ☎ **505/821-3333,** or toll free **800/544-0623** or **800/HOLIDAY.** Fax 505/828-0230. 311 rms, 60 suites. A/C TV TEL

Rates: $100–$130 single; $110–$140 double; $115–$300 suite. AE, CB, DC, MC, V. **Parking:** Free.

As you drive north from Albuquerque toward Santa Fe, a spectacular stepped Aztec pyramid seems to rise from nowhere on the west side of the I-25 freeway. This major hotel and convention complex, reached via the Paseo del Norte exit (Exit 232) from I-25, is a monument to what modern hotel architecture can be like. The 10 guest floors focus around a "hollow" skylit core. Vines drape from planter boxes on the balconies, and a fountain falls five stories to a pool between the two glass elevators. Pets are accepted.

An associated hostelry is the 363-room Holiday Inn Midtown, 2020 Menaul Blvd. NE, Albuquerque, NM 87102 (☎ **505/884-2511**), where rates run slightly less than those at the Pyramid.

Dining/Entertainment: The Gallery restaurant serves fine continental cuisine nightly except Sunday; main courses run $12.50 to $24.25. The Terrace, an atrium café, is open for three meals daily; dinner prices top out at $23. The Palm Court, with its baby grand piano bar, is open daily until 10pm. The Pyramid Club attracts the younger set with video music for dancing Monday through Saturday night until 2am.

Services: Room service, concierge, 24-hour courtesy car, valet laundry.

Facilities: Rooms for nonsmokers and the disabled; indoor/outdoor swimming pool, sauna, two whirlpools, health club (with weights and exercise room), jogging trails.

★ **La Posada de Albuquerque,** 125 Second St. NW
$ (at Copper St., Albuquerque, NM 87102. ☎ **505/242-9090,** or toll free **800/777-5732.** 114 rms. 4 suites. A/C TV TEL

Rates: $82–$92 single; $92–$102 double; $175–$225 suite. AE, CB, DC, DISC, MC, V. **Parking:** Free.

Built in 1939 by Conrad Hilton as the famed hotelier's first inn in his home state of New Mexico, this twice-sold hostelry on the National Register of Historic Places feels more like Old Mexico. An elaborate Moorish brass-and-mosaic fountain stands in the center of the tiled lobby floor; old-fashioned tin chandeliers hang from the two-story ceiling. Surrounded on all sides by high archways, the total effect is of a 19th-century hacienda courtyard.

As in the lobby, all guest-room furniture is handcrafted, but here it's covered with cushions of southwestern design. There are limited-edition lithographs by R. C. Gorman and Amado Peña on the white walls, adobe-toned ceramic lamps on the tables flanking the couch, and an ample desk opposite the wood-shuttered windows.

Dining/Entertainment: Conrad's Downtown, La Posada's elegantly redesigned restaurant, features Spanish/Yucatán cuisine.

Menu offerings might include ensalata Mazatlán, paella, chicken dishes, or pesto poblano. Conrad's is open for breakfast and lunch Monday through Friday, and for dinner daily. The Lobby Bar is a favorite gathering place for evening cocktails.

Services: Room service, courtesy car, valet laundry.

Facilities: Rooms for nonsmokers and the disabled; art gallery, hair salon, gift shop; health club membership available to guests.

$ Radisson Inn, 1901 University Blvd. SE, Albuquerque, NM 87106. ☎ **505/247-0512,** or toll free **800/333-3333.** Fax 505/843-7148. 148 rms. A/C MINIBAR TV TEL

Rates: $80–$90 single; $90–$100 double. AE, CB, DC, DISC, MC, V. **Parking:** Free.

The Spanish Colonial–style Radisson (entirely renovated in 1993) is a mile from the airport. It's nice to be away from the hubbub, especially when you can lounge on the spacious deck of the swimming pool, in the center of the landscaped grounds. The rooms are decorated in emerald green and navy blue, and are furnished with king- or queen-size beds, two-drawer credenzas, tables and chairs, and cable TV/radios. Small pets are accepted.

Dining/Entertainment: Diamondback's Restaurant, open daily from 6am to 2pm and 5 to 10pm, specializes in steaks and regional dishes like pollo a la parrilla and trout Rio de Pecos. Breakfasts run $4.75 to $7.50; lunches, $6.75 to $10.95; dinners, $9.95 to $15.95. Coyote's Cantina is a popular watering hole.

Services: Room service (6am–10pm); valet laundry, 24-hour courtesy van.

Facilities: Rooms for nonsmokers; year-round outdoor swimming pool, whirlpool, lobby art gallery, free guest use of a nearby health club.

Sheraton Old Town, 800 Rio Grande Blvd. NW, Albuquerque, NM 87104. ☎ **505/843-6300,** or toll free **800/237-2133.** Fax 505/842-9863. 190 rms, 20 suites. A/C TV TEL

Rates: $100–$110 single; $110–$120 double; $140 suite. Children stay free in parents' room. AE, CB, DC, MC, V. **Parking:** Free.

No Albuquerque hotel is closer to top tourist attractions than the Sheraton. Five minutes' walk from the Old Town Plaza and overlooking two important museums, it's an ideal spot for visitors without their own vehicles who don't want to be at the mercy of taxis or rental cars. Mezzanine-level windows light the adobe-toned lobby, which is separated from the Fireside Lounge by a double-sided fireplace. Each of the guest rooms is characterized by a Pueblo craft on the wall over the beds. The southside rooms, facing Old Town, have private balconies.

Dining/Entertainment: The Customs House Restaurant, specializing in seafood and regional cuisine, serves weekday lunches and nightly dinners, with main courses ranging from $8.95 to $19.25. The Café del Sol is the Sheraton's coffeehouse; main courses run $6 to $12. Taverna Don Alberto, serving drinks off the main lobby, features dance bands on weekend nights.

Services: Room service, concierge, courtesy van, valet laundry, secretarial and babysitting services.

Facilities: Rooms for nonsmokers and the disabled; outdoor swimming pool, Jacuzzi, exercise room; Old Town Place, an attached shopping center, includes arts-and-crafts dealers, a bookstore, beauty salon, and manicurist.

NEARBY

Hacienda Vargas, El Camino Real (P.O. Box 307), Algodones, NM 87001. ☎ **505/867-9115.** 4 rms.
Rates (including breakfast): $69–$129 double. Additional person $15 extra. MC, V.

Unassuming in its elegance, Hacienda Vargas is located right on old Route 66. Owned and operated by the DeVargas family, the inn is situated in the small town of Algodones about 20 miles from Albuquerque and is a good place to stay if you're planning on spending time in both Santa Fe and Albuquerque but don't want to stay in one of the downtown hotels in either city. The walls in the entry hallway are hung with the works of local artists (for sale), and each of the guest rooms has a private entrance. All rooms are furnished with New Mexico antiques, each is individually decorated, and all have handmade kiva fireplaces. The Wagner Room, the largest of the four, looks out onto the courtyard and features a Jacuzzi tub with a skylight view. The Piñon Room has direct access to the outdoor hot tub and has a beautiful antique clawfoot bathtub. The main attraction in the Peña Room is the unique bed and headboard, and the Pueblo Room has authentic adobe walls. Hosts Jule and Paul DeVargas are extremely gracious and helpful—they'll make you feel right at home. A full breakfast is served every morning in the dining room. The only drawback here is that train tracks run directly parallel to the back of the house and during my stay the last train went by at around midnight. At all other times the inn is very quiet and restful.

La Hacienda Grande, 21 Baros Lane, Bernalillo, NM 87004. ☎ **505/867-1887.** 6 rms.
Rates (including breakfast): $79–$110 double. Additional person $15 extra. MC, V. **Parking:** Free.

La Hacienda Grande, run by brother-and-sister team Daniel Buop and Shoshana Zimmerman, opened in 1993 and has a wonderful history. The completely restored adobe home is over 250 years old and has two-foot-thick walls. It was one of two original stagecoach stops and is said to have had the very first adobe stables and an adobe corral, built to prevent horse thievery. It sits on four acres of land that was once part of the original 100-square-mile Spanish land grant, and today's kitchen was once used as the area chapel before churches were built. The courtyard, surrounded by high adobe walls, has a vortex, which once had special significance to the local native tribespeople who came here often to pray and hold ceremonies. The owners also recently learned that during the Civil War gold and silver was often stored here. The walled courtyard, the roofline of which was easily patrolled, was a perfect fortress.

Guest rooms, all featuring custom-crafted furniture, are comfortable and inviting. Much of the furniture is made of bent willow, which lends a rustic air to the hacienda. One room has a queen-size wrought-iron canopy bed, all rooms have small sitting areas and southwestern-style armoires, and four have wood-burning kiva fireplaces. Brick or tile floors are covered with throw rugs. Every morning at 7:30am thermoses of coffee are left outside guest-room doors and breakfast is served in the dining room between 8 and 8:45am. It usually consists of homemade breads, specialty honeys, fresh-ground coffees, egg dishes, fruit, and granola. You won't get anything sickly sweet for breakfast here because the emphasis is on healthy eating. Guests may make use of the living room, which has a TV and VCR available for guest use, and tea and snacks are served in the afternoon. Children under 11 are not accepted, and smoking is prohibited except on the patio.

Inexpensive

$ Amberley Suite Hotel, 7620 Pan American Fwy. NE, Albuquerque, NM 87109. ☎ **505/823-1300,** or toll free **800/333-9806.** Fax 505/823-2896. 170 suites. A/C TV TEL

Rates: $94–$104 suite for one or two; $20 higher during balloon fiesta. Discounts for longer stays, weekend arrivals, or corporate or government travelers. Additional 1 person $10 extra; children under 16 stay free in parents' room. AE, CB, DC, DISC, MC, V. **Parking:** Free.

Every room in the recently renovated Amberley Suite Hotel is a one- or two-room suite, most with a living room/kitchenette and separate bedroom; the deluxe king is an efficiency studio with a kitchen area. Kitchen facilities include a refrigerator (with complimentary beverages), a microwave oven, a coffee maker, and pots, pans, and utensils. Each living room has a swivel rocker with ottoman and a cable TV. Every bathroom is provided with a built-in hairdryer.

Dining/Entertainment: Watson's Café and Deli, open daily from 6am to 10pm, serves an all-you-can-eat breakfast buffet ($4.95) until 10am, and a summer patio barbecue Tuesday through Thursday from 5 to 9pm. The hotel manager hosts a happy-hour reception on Wednesday at 5:30pm, with cocktails, hors d'oeuvres, live music, and trivia games.

Services: 24-hour courtesy car (within a two-mile radius), free airport shuttle, valet laundry.

Facilities: Rooms for nonsmokers and the disabled; outdoor swimming pool, sauna, hot tub, weight/exercise room, guest laundry.

Best Western Airport Inn, 2400 Yale Blvd. SE, Albuquerque, NM 87106. ☎ **505/242-7022,** or toll free **800/528-1234.** Fax 505/243-0620. 120 rms. A/C TV TEL

Rates (including breakfast): $52–$59 single; $62–$67 double. AE, CB, DC, DISC, MC, V.

A landscaped garden courtyard behind the hotel is a lovely place to relax on cloudless days. The rooms, with dark-brown carpets and beige-checkered bedspreads, contain standard furnishings plus cable TV and free local phone calls. Deluxe units have refrigerators and other special touches. Breakfast is served free in the rooms, or guests can get a coupon good for $3 off their morning meal at the adjacent Village Inn.

Services: Courtesy van on call from 6am to midnight, valet laundry.

Facilities: Rooms for nonsmokers and the disabled; outdoor swimming pool, Jacuzzi; use of nearby health club.

Best Western Winrock Inn, 18 Winrock Center NE, Albuquerque, NM 87110. ☎ **505/883-5252,** or toll free **800/528-1234.** Fax 505/889-3206. 173 rms, 2 suites. A/C TV TEL

Rates (including breakfast buffet): $55–$78 single or double; $85–$110 suite. AE, CB, DC, DISC, MC, V. **Parking:** Free.

Located just off I-40 at the Louisiana Boulevard interchange, the Winrock is attached to Albuquerque's second-largest shopping center: Winrock Center. A hotel with prime appeal to international visitors, its two separate buildings are wrapped around a private lagoon and garden featuring Mandarin ducks, giant *koi* (carp), and an impressive waterfall. The comfortable rooms, many of which have private patios overlooking the lagoon, feature a pastel southwestern-motif decor.

Dining/Entertainment: The Club Room offers a breakfast buffet each morning and complimentary happy-hour drinks each evening.

Services: Valet laundry, 24-hour courtesy van.

Facilities: Rooms for nonsmokers and the disabled; heated outdoor swimming pool, guest laundry.

Fairfield Inn, 1760 Menaul Rd. NE, Albuquerque, NM 87102. ☎ 505/889-4000, or toll free **800/228-2800.** 188 rms. A/C TV TEL

Rates: $49.95 single; $59.95 double. Additional person $6 extra; children 18 and under stay free in parents' room. AE, CB, DC, DISC, MC, V.

The Fairfield Inn, owned by Marriott, is one of Albuquerque's newest hostelries. Each of the extremely clean rooms has cable TV with pay movies, one king-size bed or two double beds, and free local phone calls. There are complimentary coffee and tea in the morning (in the lobby), valet service, vending machines on every floor, and an indoor swimming pool with saunas and a Jacuzzi. You probably couldn't get more for your money anywhere else. There are rooms for both nonsmokers and the disabled available.

$ Howard Johnson Plaza Hotel, 6000 Pan American Fwy. NE (at San Mateo Blvd.), Albuquerque, NM 87109. ☎ **505/821-9451,** or toll free **800/446-4656.** Fax 505/858-0239. 138 rms, 12 suites. A/C TV TEL

Rates: $43–$71 single; $45–$81 double; $70–$110 suite. Various discount packages available. AE, CB, DC, DISC, MC, V.

Howard Johnson doesn't try to be as grand as the Pyramid (see above), but it does have a five-story lobby atrium with fountains of its own. A three-story-high tapestry reminds viewers of Albuquerque's obsession with hot-air ballooning, and there are old-fashioned flower-topped lampposts on the mezzanine deck. Private balconies are an outstanding feature of all rooms. They've got all standard furnishings, including remote-control cable TVs and phones. Pets are permitted with the manager's prior approval.

Dining/Entertainment: Earl's Café, open Monday through Friday from 6am to 10pm and on Saturday and Sunday from 7am to 10pm, offers southwestern fare for $5 to $14. The Atrium Lounge has a big-screen TV for watching sports events and a Top-40 DJ for dancing.

Services: Room service (during restaurant hours), 24-hour courtesy van, valet laundry.

Facilities: Rooms for nonsmokers and the disabled; indoor/outdoor swimming pool, sauna, Jacuzzi, weight/exercise room, guest laundry, gift shop.

La Quinta Motor Inn, 2116 Yale Blvd. SE, Albuquerque, NM 87106. ☎ **505/243-5500,** or toll free **800/531-5900.** Fax 505/247-8288. 105 rms. A/C TV TEL

Rates: $58 single; $66 double. AE, CB, DC, DISC, ER, JCB, MC, V.

Quinta (pronounced "*keen*-ta") is Spanish for villa and, like vacation homes, La Quinta motels—a 240-strong Texas-based chain—are friendly and gracious toward visitors. The rooms are appointed in pleasant modern tones. Each has a king-size or two extra-long double beds. Coffee is on 24 hours in the lobby. Small pets are accepted.

Other La Quinta Motor Inns in Albuquerque are located at 5241 San Antonio Dr. NE, off I-25 at Journal Center (☎ **505/821-9000;** fax 505/821-2399), with 130 rooms; and at I-40 and San Mateo Boulevard (☎ **505/884-3591**) with 106 rooms. All have the same rates and facilities, including adjacent restaurants.

Dining/Entertainment: Goody's restaurant is adjacent.

Facilities: Rooms for nonsmokers and the disabled; outdoor swimming pool.

Budget

Motel 6, 1701 University Blvd. NE at I-40, Albuquerque, NM 87102. ☎ **505/843-9228** or **505/891-6161.** 118 rms. A/C TV TEL

Rates: May–Oct, $27.95 single, $39.95 double; Nov–Apr, $23.95 single, $29.95 double. AE, CB, DC, DISC, MC, V.

Typical of the 16 other members of this chain scattered around New Mexico, the midtown Motel 6 is a no-frills accommodation with the essentials for a comfortable stay. Rooms are just big enough, they're clean, each has a phone and television, and there's even a swimming pool for afternoon dips.

RV Parks

Albuquerque Central Koa, 12400 Skyline Rd. NE, Albuquerque, NM 87123. ☎ **505/296-2729.** 200 sites.

Bathhouse, guest laundry, outdoor swimming pool (open summers only), convenience store. Cabins available.

Albuquerque North Koa, 555 Hill Rd., Bernalillo, NM 87004. ☎ **505/867-5227.** 101 sites.

Laundry, outdoor swimming pool (open May to October) playground, convenience store, cafe, free outdoor movies. Free pancake breakfast daily. Reservations recommended.

Palisades RV Park, 9201 Central Ave. NW, Albuquerque, NM 87121. ☎ **505/831-5000.** 110 sites.

Bathhouse, guest laundry, reception room, small convenience store, propane available, Near Old Town.

4 Dining

In these listings, the following categories define price ranges: "Expensive," most dinner main courses are priced over $15; "Moderate," most dinner main courses $10 to $15; "Inexpensive," $6 to $10; "Budget," under $6. Keep in mind that many of Albuquerque's finest restaurants are in major hotels (listed above).

Expensive

High Finance Restaurant & Tavern, 40 Tramway Rd. NE, atop Sandia Peak. ☎ **243-9742.**

Cuisine: CONTINENTAL. **Reservations:** Recommended.
Prices: Appetizers $3–$7; main courses $13.95–$35. Tramway, $9.50 with dinner reservations, $13.50 without. CB, DC, DISC, MC, V.
Open: Lunch daily 11am–4pm; dinner daily 5–9:30pm.

Since it's perched atop Sandia Peak, two miles above Albuquerque and the Rio Grande valley, diners at High Finance have a breathtaking panorama of New Mexico's largest city. The atmosphere inside is elegant yet casual.

The menu focuses on prime rib, steaks (including a wonderful steak Diane), and fresh seafood, from fresh fish to crab and lobster. Diners can also choose pasta or Mexican main dishes. Many tram riders just drop in for the view and a drink at the casual full-service bar. Smoking is permitted only in the bar.

⭐ **Le Marmiton,** 5415 Academy Blvd. NE. ☎ **821-6279.**
Cuisine: FRENCH. **Reservations:** Recommended.
Prices: Dinner $13.95–$19.95. AE, DC, MC, V.
Open: Dinner only, daily 5–9:30pm.

The name means "the apprentice," but there's nothing novice about the food or presentation. The 15 tables seat 45 people in a romantic French provincial atmosphere, with lace curtains and antique plates on shelves.

Recommended main courses include fantaisie aux fruits de mer, a mixture of shrimp, scallops, and crab in a mushroom-cream sauce

Albuquerque Dining

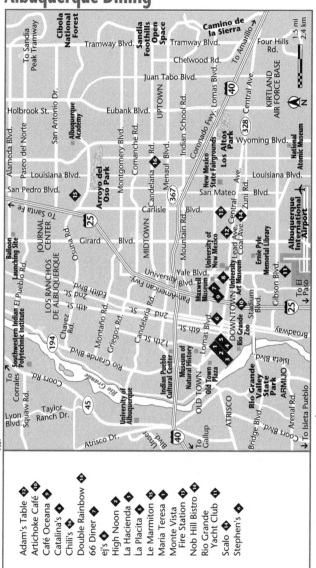

Adam's Table 🔷 2
Artichoke Café 🔷 10
Café Oceana 🔷 9
Catalina's 🔷 4
Chili's 🔷 3
Double Rainbow 🔷 7
66 Diner 🔷 8
ej's 🔷 6
High Noon 🔷 2
La Hacienda 🔷 1
La Placita 🔷 4
Le Marmiton 🔷 15
Maria Teresa 🔷 5
Monte Vista Fire Station 🔷 12
Nob Hill Bistro 🔷 14
Rio Grande Yacht Club 🔷 11
Scalo 🔷 13
Stephen's 🔷 6

on pastry; and cailles, two whole quail with a shallot-sherry-cream
sauce. If you arrive early for dinner (between 5 and 6pm) Monday
through Thursday, you can take advantage of the fixed-price light
dinners which include soup or salad, a choice of main course,
and coffee or tea for $7.95. There's a long wine list, and the
cinnamon-apple crêpes make a great dessert.

Nob Hill Bistro, 3118 Central Ave. SE. ☎ 255-5832.

> **Cuisine:** CONTINENTAL. **Reservations:** Recommended.
>
> **Prices:** Appetizers $5.95–$6.50; main courses $14.50–$19.50. DISC, MC, V.
>
> **Open:** Lunch Mon–Fri 11:30am–2pm; dinner Mon–Thurs 5:30–9pm, Fri–Sat 5:30–10pm.

For fine dining in an intimate bistro setting, Nob Hill Bistro, located in historic Nob Hill, is a perfect choice. The small dining room is bright and comfortable, with no more than a dozen white-clothed tables, and the service is extremely attentive. I recommend that you start with the classic French onion soup; with a puff-pastry topping, it's like no other you've ever had. The peppered beef carpaccio or creamed leek and crab baked in filo and served with a lemon-chervil hollandaise are also excellent ways to start your meal. For a main course I had the sautéed sterling salmon with a lemon-dill butter, which was excellent. Other offerings include chicken breast stuffed with goat cheese, basil, and a Mediterranean sauce; sautéed pork chop with herb jus lié; and sautéed duck-breast and duck-leg confit with marjoram glace de canard. Dessert selections vary daily, but I had a delightfully light (albeit very rich) flourless chocolate torte with a raspberry coulis. The wine list is excellent.

★ **Prairie Star,** 1000 Jemez Canyon Dam Rd., Bernalillo.
☎ 867-3327.

> **Cuisine:** CONTEMPORARY REGIONAL. **Reservations:** Required.
>
> **Prices:** Appetizers $5–$7; main courses $15–$24. AE, DISC, MC, V.
>
> **Open:** Dinner daily 5–10pm (lounge opens at 4pm); brunch Sun 11am–2:30pm.

A sprawling adobe home, with a marvelous view across the high plains and an adjacent golf course to Sandia Peak, is host to this intimate dining experience. The 6,000-square-foot house, on a rural site leased from Santa Ana Pueblo, was built in the 1940s in mission architectural style. Exposed vigas and full latilla ceilings, as well as hand-carved fireplaces and bancos, complement the thick adobe walls in the dining room. All art displayed on the walls is for sale.

Diners can start with smoked quail or baked cheese in puff pastry (a blend of mascarpone and Gruyere cheese scented with toasted hazelnuts and fresh tarragon). Main courses include shrimp margarita (shrimp sautéed and flambéed with tequila, fresh tomatoes, and roasted poblano chiles, and finished with lime juice and butter), veal sweetbreads (served in puff pastry with a tarragon and wild-mushroom cream sauce), lamb loin (stuffed with roast garlic, pine nuts, basil, and goat cheese), and pan-fried Truchas trout with piñon nuts. There are daily specials and a lounge at the top of a circular stairway. Private parties often reserve the patio and tiled swimming pool.

Moderate

Artichoke Cafe, 424 Central Ave. SE. ☎ 243-0200.

> **Cuisine:** CONTINENTAL. **Reservations:** Recommended.

Prices: Appetizers $4.50–$5.95; main courses $8.95–$19.95. AE, CB, DC, MC, V.
Open: Lunch Mon–Fri 11am–2:30pm; dinner Mon–Sat 5:30–10pm.

The no-frills decor is clean and tasteful, with modern art prints on azure walls, white linens on tables shaded by standing plants, and classical music playing in the background. Start your meal with an artichoke appetizer, then go on to a main dish like baked chicken stuffed with goat cheese, spinach, and roasted red pepper or New Zealand mussels with sweet Italian sausage in white wine. Crêpes, pastas, salads, sandwiches, and the like are popular at lunch. The café has an excellent list of Californian and French wines.

Cafe Oceana, 1414 Central Ave. SE. ☎ 247-2233.

Cuisine: SEAFOOD. **Reservations:** Recommended.
Prices: Appetizers $3.95–$6.95; main courses $11.95–$13.95; oysters $4.75 per half dozen, $8.95 per dozen. AE, DC, DISC, MC, V.
Open: Lunch Mon–Fri 11am–3pm; oyster hour Mon–Thurs 3–6:30pm and 10–11pm, Fri 3–6:30pm and 10:30–11:30pm, Sat 5–7pm and 10:30–11:30pm; dinner Mon–Thurs 5–11pm, Fri–Sat 5–11:30pm.

The Café Oceana is and has been Albuquerque's favorite oyster bar and fresh seafood café for years. In a New Orleans–style dining room with high ceilings and hardwood floors you can enjoy fresh oysters, fresh fish daily, scallops, crab rellenos (for the New Mexican touch), and the house special, beer-batter-fried shrimp Oceana. If you're really in the mood for New Orleans cuisine, you can also get some red beans and rice here.

The County Line Barbecue, 9600 Tramway Blvd. NE. ☎ 296-8822.

Cuisine: BARBECUE. **Reservations:** Not accepted.
Prices: Main courses $8.95–$13.95 AE, CB, DC, DISC, MC, V.
Open: Mon–Thurs 5–9pm, Fri–Sat 5–10pm, Sun 4–9pm.

This extremely popular spot doesn't take reservations, but if you call before you leave the hotel, they'll put your name on the waiting list, and by the time you get there you'll probably be next in line. If not, you can always wait at the ever-crowded bar. The restaurant is loud and always busy, but it has a spectacular view of the city lights and great food.

When you finally get a table, you'll be given a Big Chief Writing Tablet menu offering great southwestern barbecue at very reasonable prices. You might opt for barbecued chicken or a steak grilled to perfection, along with a baked potato (with your choice of toppings), beans, and coleslaw. If you're not very hungry you should probably consider going somewhere else.

The Firehouse Restaurant at the Tram, 38 Tramway Rd. ☎ 856-3473.

Cuisine: STEAKS/SEAFOOD. **Reservations:** Recommended.
Prices: Main courses $12–$18. AE, DISC, MC, V.
Open: Daily 11am–10pm. (Bar, daily noon–10pm.)

Located at the bottom of the Sandia Peak Tramway, the Firehouse has an old steam-powered fire engine serving as its bar and windows on all sides: The views of the city and the Rio Grande valley are great. Seafood, steaks, chicken, and baby pork ribs get special treatment on the mesquite grill. Of particular note are lime chicken, scallops with toasted piñon and white wine, and peppered steak. There's nightly music; guests with reservations get a discount on tram tickets.

High Noon, 425 San Felipe St. NW. ☎ **765-1455.**

Cuisine: STEAKS/SEAFOOD/NEW MEXICAN. **Reservations:** Recommended.

Prices: Appetizers $3–$7.95; main courses $8.50–$18.50. AE, CB, DC, DISC, MC, V.

Open: Lunch Mon–Sat 11am–3pm; dinner Mon–Sat 5–10pm, Sun noon–9pm.

One of Albuquerque's oldest buildings, this restaurant boasts a 19th-century saloon atmosphere with stuccoed walls, high and low ceiling beams, and historical photos on the walls. One photo depicts the original 1785 structure, which now comprises the building's foyer and santo room. The dinner menu offers a choice of beef dishes, like the house-specialty pepper steak sautéed with brandy; fish dishes, including red trout amandine; game dishes, including buffalo, venison, and caribou; and regional favorites, among them burritos, enchiladas, and fajitas.

La Hacienda Restaurant, 302 San Felipe St. NW, at North Plaza. ☎ **242-3131.**

Cuisine: NEW MEXICAN/AMERICAN. **Reservations:** Recommended for large parties.

Prices: Appetizers $3.50–$6.25; main courses $8.95–$16.95. AE, DC, MC, V.

Open: Lunch daily 11am–4pm; dinner daily 4–9pm.

A mural girding La Hacienda's outer wall tells the story of the establishment of the city of Albuquerque and the construction of this Villa de Albuquerque at the turn of the 18th century. Approached through a large and interesting gift shop, this cozy restaurant is adorned by hanging plants and chile ristras and has an intimate, laid-back atmosphere. The menu is predominantly regional, with house specialties including beef or chicken fajitas, carne adovada, tostadas compuestas, and tortilla-chile soup. Steaks, shrimp, and other American meals also are offered.

★ **Maria Teresa,** 618 Rio Grande Blvd. NW. ☎ **242-3900.**

Cuisine: CONTEMPORARY AMERICAN. **Reservations:** Recommended.

Prices: Appetizers $3.95–$7.25; main courses $10–$21. AE, CB, DC, DISC, MC, V.

Open: Daily 11am–9pm.

The city's most beautiful and classically elegant restaurant, Maria Teresa is located in the 1840s Salvador Armijo House, a national historic property furnished with Victorian antiques and paintings.

Built with 32-inch adobe bricks, the house exemplifies 19th-century New Mexican architecture, when building materials were few and defense a prime consideration. The house had 12 rooms, 7 of which (along with a large patio) are now reserved for diners. Another room is home to the 1840 Bar and lounge.

The menu features salads, pastas, and sandwiches for lunch; and a wide choice of gourmet dinners, from raspberry chicken to fresh salmon with tequila-lime butter, and from baby back ribs to regional dishes like carne y pollo asada burrito.

Monte Vista Fire Station, 3201 Central Ave. NE, Nob Hill.
☎ **255-2424.**

Cuisine: CONTEMPORARY AMERICAN. **Reservations:** Recommended.
Prices: Appetizers $4.95–$6.95; main courses $8.95–$19.95. AE, MC, V.
Open: Lunch Mon–Fri 11am–2:30pm; dinner Sun–Thurs 5–10:30pm, Fri–Sat 5–11pm. (Bar, Mon–Fri 11am–2am, Sat noon–2am, Sun noon–midnight.)

The Fire Station has been a city landmark since it was built in pure Pueblo Revival style in 1936. Its occupants no longer make fire calls, however, concentrating instead on creative cookery within an art deco interior. Appetizers include crabcakes with goat cheese on assorted baby greens with roasted garlic vinaigrette; and zucchini squash blossoms filled with ricotta and sun-dried tomatoes, served with baby greens, pancetta, and balsamic vinaigrette. Main courses include grilled marinated lamb chops with a cucumber-yogurt sauce and quail with wild mushrooms in a tawny port sauce. Try the tiramisù for dessert. There's a popular singles bar on the fourth-story landing.

★ **Rio Grande Yacht Club,** 2500 Yale Blvd. SE. ☎ **243-6111.**
$ **Cuisine:** SEAFOOD. **Reservations:** Recommended at dinner.
Prices: Appetizers $1.95–$8.95; main courses $3.50–$7.95 at lunch, $9.95–$16.95 at dinner. AE, CB, DC, DISC, MC, V.
Open: Lunch Mon–Fri 11am–2pm; dinner daily 5:30–10:30pm.

Red-white-and-blue sails are draped beneath the skylight of a large room dominated by a tropical garden. The walls are of wood strips like those of a ship's deck, and yachting prints and photos hang on the walls. Fresh fish—catfish, whitefish, bluefish, sole, salmon, grouper, mahimahi, and other denizens of the deep—are prepared broiled, poached, blackened, teriyaki, Veracruz, au gratin, mornay, amandine, and more. Diners can also opt for shrimp, steaks, ribs, chicken, and seafood-and-steak or prime rib combinations.

★ **Scalo,** 3500 Central Ave. SE, Nob Hill. ☎ **255-8782.**
$ **Cuisine:** NORTHERN ITALIAN. **Reservations:** Recommended.
Prices: Appetizers $2.50–$7.50; main courses $5.50–$8.95 at lunch, $6.95–$15.95 at dinner. AE, MC, V.
Open: Lunch Mon–Fri 11:30am–2:30pm, dinner Mon–Sat 5–11pm. (Bar, Mon–Sat 11am–1am.)

Scalo has a simple bistro-style elegance, with white linen indoor seating and outdoor tables in a covered, temperature-controlled patio.

The kitchen, which makes its own pasta and breads, specializes in contemporary adaptations of classical northern Italian cuisine.

Seasonal menus focus on New Mexico–grown produce. Featured appetizers are calamaretti fritti (fried baby squid) and caprini con pumante (goat cheese with toast, capers, roasted garlic, and sun-dried tomatoes). There's a selection of pastas for lunch and dinner, as well as meat, chicken, and fish dishes—among them pollo casino (grilled chicken with prosciutto, provolone, tomato, and arugula served on focaccia) and filetto con salsa balsamica (grilled filet of beef with rosemary, green peppercorns, garlic, and a balsamic demi-glace sauce). Dessert selections change daily.

Stephens, 1311 Tijeras Ave. NW, at 14th St. and Central Ave.
☎ **842-1773.**
Cuisine: CONTEMPORARY AMERICAN. **Reservations:** Recommended.
Prices: Appetizers $4.95–$8.95; main courses $15.95–$24.95. AE, DC, MC, V.
Open: Lunch Mon–Fri 11am–2pm; dinner Sun–Thurs 5:30–9:30pm, Fri–Sat 5:30–10:30pm.

Big bay windows face on Central Avenue, and foliage shades an enclosed patio. This modern, open, and airy restaurant was inspired by Mexico City's Hacienda Angel and features interior decor by the noted designer Richard Worthen. The eclectic menu is described as "fresh American and southwestern ingredients prepared with continental inspiration." Dishes include everything from shrimp capellini to braised lamb shank, veal schnitzel to black-bear ravioli, poached trout to New York strip steak.

Inexpensive

Adam's Table, 3619 Copper NE. ☎ **266-4214.**
Cuisine: VEGETARIAN. **Reservations:** Not required.
Prices: Main courses $5.50–$7.50. DISC, MC, V.
Open: Sun–Thurs 7am–9pm, Fri 7am–3pm.

Located in the historic Nob Hill district, just off Central Avenue, Adam's Table bills itself as "a true vegetarian restaurant" whose aim is "to educate [diners] on the wonderful principles of health: proper diet, rest, exercise, pure water, sunshine, temperance, and trust in divine power." After a meal here, I can honestly say that they absolutely succeed in the area of "proper diet." Mexican specialties include whole-wheat quesadillas smothered with sour cream, guacamole, cheese, and tomato; chiles rellenos (not fried) with cashew cheese; Adam's burrito (fried potato, tomato, green pepper, and onion, served with avocado or guacamole). All Mexican specialties are served with beans and rice and red or green chile. Other menu items include spinach or sesame noodles with pesto; pizza with bell peppers, onions, soy sauce, and olives; and an oat burger (a blend of brown rice, rolled oats, and sunflower seeds). There's an "all-you-should-eat" breakfast, lunch, and dinner buffet as well as a salad bar. Adam's offers a nice selection of natural juices, sodas, and teas, as well as tofu milk and fruit smoothies.

$ Catalina's, 400 San Felipe St. NW. ☎ 842-6907.

Cuisine: NEW MEXICAN. **Reservations:** Accepted but not necessary.
Prices: $3.50–$7.95. AE, MC, V.
Open: Breakfast Mon–Sat 8–11am; lunch Mon 11am–2pm, Tues–Sun 11am–4pm; dinner daily (summer only) 4–9pm. **Closed:** Usually mid-Jan to Mar.

Right in the heart of Old Town, set back in the rear of the Patio San Felipe del Norte courtyard, is this oft-overlooked gem in an old adobe home. The white stuccoed interior, covered with Mexican handcrafts, still has its original log beams. All meals are homemade by Catalina; the chiles rellenos are superb, as are the tacos, tostadas, enchiladas, and so forth.

Chili's Grill & Bar, 6909 Menaul Blvd. NE. ☎ 883-4321.

Cuisine: TEXAS-MEXICAN. **Reservations:** Not accepted.
Prices: Appetizers $2.25–$5.25; main courses $4.95–$9.95. AE, CB, DC, DISC, MC, V.
Open: Mon–Thurs 11am–10:30pm, Fri–Sat 11am–11:30pm, Sun 11:30am–10pm.

A casual bar and grill adjacent to the Ramada Classic Hotel, Chili's is like a small greenhouse. There are plants in baskets and pots, standing and hanging, dispersed among the antique bric-a-brac suspended from the ceilings or on shelves high above the red-tile floors. The menu focuses on hamburgers (like the verde burger, with guacamole) and southwestern grill—fajitas, chicken, ribs, steaks, and the like. There are also salads, sandwiches, and chili. The bar, which has happy hour weekdays from 3 to 6pm, is noted for its margaritas.

$ La Placita, 208 San Felipe St. NW, at South Plaza. ☎ 247-2204.

Cuisine: NEW MEXICAN/AMERICAN. **Reservations:** Recommended for large parties.
Prices: Lunch $4.25–$6.95; dinner $6.25–$13.95. AE, DISC, MC, V.
Open: Daily 11am–9pm.

Native American artisans spread their wares on the sidewalk outside the old Casa de Armijo, built by a wealthy Hispanic family in the early 18th century. The adobe hacienda, which faces the Old Town Plaza, features hand-carved wooden doorways, deep-sunk windows, and an ancient patio. Fine regional art and furnishings decorate the five dining rooms and an upstairs gallery. The house favorite is a full Mexican dinner that includes an enchilada colorado de queso, chiles rellenos, taco de carne, frijoles con queso, arroz español, ensalada, and two sopaipillas. There is also a variety of beef, chicken, and fish selections.

Budget

Double Rainbow, 3416 Central Ave. SE. ☎ 255-6633.

Cuisine: CAFE/BAKERY. **Reservations:** Not accepted.
Prices: All items under $10. No credit cards.
Open: Mon–Sat 6:30am–midnight, Sun 6:30am–11pm.

If you're a people-watcher worth your salt, you shouldn't miss a visit to the Double Rainbow, located in Albuquerque's historic Nob Hill district. Of course, people-watching isn't the only reason to stop in—Double Rainbow has great sandwiches, ice cream, and coffee too. And one of the best things about this place is its enormous selection of magazines. In fact, there are more than 700 titles, ranging from comic books to film and fashion magazines to a travel magazine for gays and lesbians. Not only will you find architectural magazines, but you'll also find *Tricycle* (a Buddhist review), and *Blues Review Quarterly*. A selection of newspapers spans the globe as well. No one will feel out of place here!

$ ej's, 2201 Silver Ave. SE. ☎ 268-2233.

Cuisine: NATURAL FOODS. **Reservations:** Not necessary.
Prices: Breakfast $2.50–$5.95; lunch $3.95–$7.50; dinner $5.25–$8.75. MC, V.
Open: Mon–Thurs 7am–11pm, Fri 7am–midnight, Sat 8am–midnight, Sun 8am–9:30pm.

A popular coffeehouse just a couple of blocks from the UNM campus, ej's roasts its own specialty coffees—and also caters to natural-foods lovers. Breakfasts include granola and croissants from ej's own bakery. Lunch features homemade vegetarian soups, tempeh burgers, organic turkey sandwiches, and cheese enchiladas. The gourmet dinner menu lists shrimp linguine, spinach fettuccine Alfredo, Monterey chicken, and a vegetarian stir-fry.

66 Diner, 1405 Central Ave. NE. ☎ 247-1421.

Cuisine: AMERICAN.
Prices: $3–$6.25. AE, DISC, MC, V.
Open: Mon–Thurs 9am–11pm. Fri 9am–midnight, Sat 8am–midnight, Sun 8am–10pm.

Like a trip back in time to the days when Martin Milner and George Maharis got "their kicks on Route 66," this thoroughly 1950s-style diner comes complete with Seeburg jukebox and full-service soda fountain. The white caps make great green-chile cheeseburgers, along with meatloaf sandwiches, grilled liver and onions, and chicken-fried steaks. Ham-and-egg and pancake breakfasts are served every morning. Beer and wine are available.

5 Attractions

Albuquerque's original town site, today known as Old Town, is the central point of interest for visitors to the city today. Here, centered around the Plaza, are the venerable Church of San Felipe de Neri and numerous restaurants, art galleries, and crafts shops. Several important museums stand nearby.

But don't get stuck in Old Town. Elsewhere in the city are the Sandia Peak Tramway, Kirtland Air Force Base and the National Atomic Museum, the University of New Mexico with its museums, and a number of natural attractions. Within day-trip range are several pueblos and a trio of national monuments (see "Excursions from Albuquerque," later in this chapter).

Albuquerque Attractions

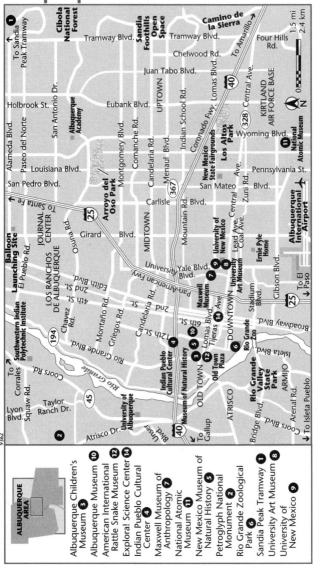

Albuquerque Children's Museum 3
Albuquerque Museum 10
American International Rattle Snake Museum 12
Explora! Science Center 14
Indian Pueblo Cultural Center 4
Maxwell Museum of Anthropology 7
National Atomic Museum 11
New Mexico Museum of Natural History 5
Petroglyph National Monument 2
Rio Grande Zoological Park 6
Sandia Peak Tramway 1
University Art Museum 8
University of New Mexico 9

The Top Attractions

⭐ **Old Town,** northeast of Central Ave. and Rio Grande Blvd. NW.
A maze of cobbled courtyard walkways lead to hidden patios and
gardens where many of Old Town's 150 galleries and shops are located. Adobe buildings, many refurbished in Pueblo Revival style in

the 1950s, focus around the tree-shaded **Plaza**, created in 1780. Pueblo and Navajo artisans often display their pottery, blankets, and silver jewelry on the sidewalks lining the Plaza.

The buildings of Old Town once served as mercantile shops, grocery stores, and government offices; but the importance of Old Town as Albuquerque's commercial center declined after 1880, when the railroad came through $1^1/4$ miles east of the Plaza and businesses relocated nearer the tracks. Old Town clung to its historical and sentimental roots, but the quarter was disintegrating until it was rediscovered in the 1930s and 1940s by artisans and other shop owners, and tourism burgeoned as an industry.

The first structure built when colonists established Albuquerque in 1706 was the **Church of San Felipe de Neri,** facing the Plaza on its north side. The house of worship has been in almost continuous use for 285 years.

The Albuquerque Museum conducts guided **walking tours** of Old Town's historic buildings during the summer, Wednesday through Friday at 11am and on Saturday and Sunday at 1pm. For visitors who don't find those times convenient, the museum publishes a brochure for a self-guided walking tour of Old Town.

★ **Sandia Peak Tramway,** 10 Tramway Loop NE. ☎ 856-7325. The world's longest tramway extends $2^3/4$ miles from Albuquerque's northeastern city limits to the summit of 10,360-foot Sandia Peak. A 15-minute ride up on the tram is a memorable experience, rising from urban desert at its base to lush mountain foliage in the Cibola National Forest at its peak . . . and dropping about 20°F in temperature in the process. Animals viewed on the wild slopes from the tram occasionally include bears, bighorn sheep, deer, eagles, hawks, and a rare mountain lion. The view from the observation deck encompasses more than 11,000 square miles, well beyond Santa Fe and Los Alamos to the north.

The Sandia Peak tram is a "jigback"; in other words, as one car approaches the top, the other nears the bottom. The two pass halfway through the trip, in the midst of a $1^1/2$-mile "clear span" of unsupported cable between the second tower and the upper terminal.

There are popular and high-priced restaurants at the tramway's summit, **High Finance,** and at the base, **The Firehouse** (see "Albuquerque Dining," earlier in this chapter). Special tram rates apply with dinner reservations.

Admission: $12.50 adults, $9.50 seniors and children 5–12, free for children under 5.

Open: Memorial Day–Labor Day, daily 9am–10pm; spring and fall, Thurs–Tues 9am–9pm, Wed 5–9pm; ski season, Mon–Tues and Thurs–Fri 9am–9pm, Wed noon–9pm, Sat–Sun 8am–9pm. **Directions:** To reach the base of the tram, take I-25 north to the Tramway Road/Alameda exit, then proceed east about 5 miles on Tramway Road (N.M. 556); or take Tramway Boulevard (N.M. 541) north of I-40 approximately $8^1/2$ miles. Turn east the last half mile on Tramway Road.

⭐ **Indian Pueblo Cultural Center,** 2401 12th St. NW.
☎ **843-7270,** or toll free **800/766-4405.**

Owned and operated as a nonprofit organization by the 19 pueblos of New Mexico, this is a fine place to begin an exploration of the local Native American culture. Located about a mile northeast of Old Town, this museum—modeled after Pueblo Bonito, a spectacular 9th-century ruin in Chaco Culture National Historic Park—consists of several parts.

In the basement, a permanent exhibit depicts the evolution from prehistory to present of the various pueblos, including displays of the distinctive handcrafts of each community. Note, especially, how pottery differs in concept and design from pueblo to pueblo. The displays include a series of remarkable photographs of Pueblo tribe members taken between 1880 and 1910, a gift of the Smithsonian Institution. The Pueblo House Children's Museum, also located on the premises, is a hands-on museum that gives children the opportunity to learn about and understand the evolution of Pueblo culture.

Upstairs is an enormous gift shop—a fine place to price the Pueblo peoples' colorful ceramics, weavings, and paintings before bartering with private artisans. The code of ethics of the Indian Arts and Crafts Association guarantees work here to be stylistically authentic, the creations of pueblo members only. A gallery displays a variety of ancient and modern works from different pueblos, with exhibits changing monthly.

Local Native American dancers perform and artisans demonstrate their crafts expertise in an outdoor arena surrounded by original murals. An **annual craft fair** is held on July 4th weekend, the first weekend in October, and Thanksgiving weekend.

A **restaurant,** open for breakfast and lunch daily from 7:30am to 4pm, emphasizes the cornmeal-based foods of the Pueblo people. Daily specials are priced at $4, although an ample meal is posole, treated dried corn with beef, chili, and oven-fried bread.

Admission: $3 adults, $2 seniors, $1 students, free for children 4 and under.

Open: Daily 9am–5:30pm; restaurant, daily 7:30am–4pm. **Closed:** New Year's, Thanksgiving, and Christmas Days. **Directions:** From Lomas Boulevard, turn north on 12th Street. The Cultural Center is on the left, just beyond the I-40 underpass. From midtown, head west on Menaul Boulevard and turn left onto 12th Street; the center will be on the right.

⭐ **Albuquerque Museum,** 2000 Mountain Rd. NW.
☎ **243-7255** or **242-4600.**

The largest collection of Spanish Colonial artifacts in the United States is featured here. Among the objects held in the museum's collection are arms and armor used during the Hispanic conquest, medieval religious artifacts and weavings, maps from the 16th to 18th centuries, and coins and domestic goods traded during that same period. A multimedia audiovisual presentation, *Four Centuries:*

A History of Albuquerque, depicts the history of the mid–Rio Grand region from the Spanish conquest to the present. "History Hopscotch" is a hands-on history exhibition designed specifically for children. There's also a gallery of early and modern New Mexico art, with permanent and changing exhibits; and a major photo archive. A gift shop offers a variety of souvenirs and other wares.

Admission: Free; donations appreciated.

Open: Tues–Sun 9am–5pm. **Closed:** Major holidays.

More Attractions

Los Colores Museum, 4499 Corrales Rd., Corrales. ☎ 898-5077.

If you're staying in a bed-and-breakfast on the outskirts of Albuquerque, take some time to stop by Los Colores Museum. Housed in the historic Alejandro Gonzales House, the museum is dedicated to the weaving traditions of New Mexico. The focal point of the museum is a collection of about 200 antique Mexican serapes that represent over 200 years of weaving tradition. You'll also see exhibits of traditional and contemporary New Mexican folk art.

Admission: Free.

Open: Sat–Sun 1–4pm, other days by appointment.

★ **National Atomic Museum,** Wyoming Blvd. and K St., Kirtland Air Force Base. ☎ 845-6670.

This museum is the next-best introduction to the nuclear age after the Bradbury Science Museum in Los Alamos. It traces the history of nuclear weapons development beginning with the top-secret Manhattan Project of the 1940s, including a copy of the letter Albert Einstein wrote to Pres. Franklin D. Roosevelt suggesting the possible development of an atomic bomb. A 51-minute film, *Ten Seconds That Shook the World,* is shown four times daily, at 10:30am, 11:30am, 2pm, and 3:30pm.

There are full-scale models of the "Fat Man" and "Little Boy" bombs, displays and films on peaceful applications of nuclear technology and other alternative energy sources. Fusion is explained in a manner that a layperson can begin to understand; other exhibits deal with the problem of nuclear waste. Outdoor exhibits include a B-52 "Stratofortress," an F-1015D "Thunderchief," and a 280mm atomic cannon. A tour that lasts about an hour takes visitors through the development of the first nuclear weapons to today's technology. You'll also see a solar-powered TV and be able to test your budgeting skills as you use the Energy-Environment Simulator to manipulate energy allocations to make the planet's supplies last longer. The museum is directly across the street from the International Nuclear Weapons School, adjacent to Sandia National Laboratory.

Admission: Free. Visitors must obtain passes at the Wyoming or Gibson Gate of the base. Children under 12 not admitted without parent or adult guardian.

Open: Daily 9am–5pm. **Closed:** New Year's, Easter, Thanksgiving, and Christmas Days.

Petroglyph National Monument, 6900 Unser Blvd. NW, west of Coors Rd. ☎ **823-4016** or **897-8814.**

Albuquerque's western city limits are marked by five extinct volcanoes. Adjacent lava flows were a hunting and gathering area for prehistoric Native Americans, who lived in the area and left a chronicle of their beliefs etched and chipped in the dark basalt boulders. Some 15,000 of these petroglyphs have been found in several concentrated groups at this archeological preserve. Plaques interpret the rock drawings—animal, human, and ceremonial forms—to visitors, who may take four hiking trails, ranging from easy to moderately difficult, winding through the lava. The 45-minute Mesa Point trail is the most strenuous but also the most rewarding.

Camping is not permitted in the park; it's strictly for day use, with picnic areas, drinking water, and restrooms.

Admission: $1 per vehicle.

Open: Summer, daily 9am–6pm; winter, daily 8am–5pm. **Closed:** State holidays.

Rio Grande Nature Center State Park, 2901 Candelaria Rd. NW. ☎ **344-7240.**

Located on the Rio Grande Flyway, an important migratory route for many birds, this wildlife refuge extends for nearly a mile along the east bank of the Rio Grande. Numerous nature trails wind through the cottonwood bosque, where a great variety of native and migratory species can be seen at any time of year. The center publishes a checklist to help visitors identify them, as well as several self-guiding trail brochures.

Housed in a unique building constructed half aboveground and half below, the visitor center contains classrooms, laboratory space, a library, a gift shop, and exhibits describing the history, geology, and ecology of the Rio Grande valley. Interpreted hikes are scheduled every weekend.

Admission: $1 adults, 50¢ children 6 and older, free for children under 6.

Open: Daily 10am–5pm. **Closed:** New Year's, Thanksgiving, and Christmas Days.

University of New Mexico, Yale Blvd. NE, north of Central Ave. ☎ **277-0111.**

The state's largest institution of higher learning stretches across an attractive 70-acre campus about two miles east of downtown Albuquerque, north of Central Avenue and east of University Boulevard. The five campus museums, none of which charges admission, are constructed (like other UNM buildings) in a modified pueblo style. Popejoy Hall, in the south-central part of campus, hosts many performing-arts presentations, including those of the New Mexico Symphony Orchestra; other public events are held in nearby Keller Hall and Woodward Hall.

The **Maxwell Museum of Anthropology,** situated on the west side of campus on Redondo Drive at Ash Street NE (☎ **277-4404**), is an internationally acclaimed repository of southwestern anthropological finds. It's open Monday through Friday from 9am to 4pm, on Saturday from 10am to 4pm, and on Sunday from noon to 4pm; closed holidays.

The **University Art Museum** (☎ 277-4001), in the UNM College of Fine Arts adjoining Popejoy Hall on Cornell Street, just north of Central Avenue, is a multilevel museum focusing on 19th- and 20th-century American and European artists. It's open Monday and Wednesday through Friday from 9am to 4pm, on Sunday from 1 to 4pm, on Tuesday from 9am to 5pm; closed holidays. A gift shop offers reproductions of many of the works displayed.

The intimate **Johnson Gallery** at 1909 Las Lomas Blvd. NE (☎ 277-4967), on the north side of the central campus, features more than 2,000 works by the late Raymond Jonson, a leading modernist painter in early 20th-century New Mexico, as well as works by contemporary artists. The gallery is open on Tuesday from 9am to 4pm and 5 to 8pm, and Wednesday through Friday from 9am to 4pm.

In Northrop Hall (☎ 277-4204), about halfway between the Maxwell Museum and Popejoy Hall in the southern part of the campus, the adjacent **Geology Museum** and **Meteoritic Museum** (☎ 277-1644) cover the gamut of recorded time from dinosaur bones to moon rocks. The 3,000 meteorite specimens held here comprise the sixth-largest collection in the United States. The Geology Museum is open Monday through Friday from 8am to 5pm; the Meteoritic Museum, Monday through Friday from 9am to noon and 1 to 4pm.

Finally, the **Museum of Southwest Biology,** in the Biology Annex adjacent to Northrop Hall (☎ 277-5340), has few displays but has extensive research holdings of global flora and fauna, especially representative of southwestern North America, Central America, South America, and parts of Asia. Call for times and other information.

6 Cool for Kids

Albuquerque Children's Museum, 800 Rio Grande Blvd. NW. ☎ 842-5525.

At the Albuquerque Children's Museum there's something for everyone: bubbles, whisper disks, a puppet theater, a giant loom, a dress-up area, zoetropes, a capture-your-shadow wall, art activities, science demonstrations, and a giant pin-hole camera. The museum also sponsors wonderful educational workshops. "The Me I Don't Always See" was a health exhibit designed to teach children about the mysteries of the human body, and recently, the museum sponsored a Great Artists Series that featured live performances about artists' lives and work followed by an art activity.

Admission: $3 children 2–12, $1 ages 13 and up, free for kids under 2.

Open: Tues–Sat 10am–5pm, Sun noon–5pm.

American International Rattlesnake Museum, 202 San Felipe St. NW ☎ 242-6569.

This unique museum, located just off Old Town Plaza, has living specimens of common, uncommon, and very rare rattlesnakes of North, Central, and South America in naturally landscaped habitats. Oddities such as albinos and patternless rattlesnakes are included, with a popular display for youngsters—baby rattlesnakes. Over 30 species can be seen, followed by a seven-minute film on this essential contributor to the ecological balance of our hemisphere. Throughout the museum are rattlesnake artifacts of early American history, Native American culture, medicine, the arts, and advertising.

You'll also find a gift shop that specializes in Native American jewelry, T-shirts, and other memorabilia with ties to the natural world and the Southwest, all with an emphasis on rattlesnakes.

Admission: $2 adults, $1 children.

Open: Daily 10am–6:30pm.

Explora Science Center, 401 1st Plaza, Suite 68. ☎ 842-6188.

Children and adults alike will enjoy a trip to the Explora Science Center, a hands-on science and technology museum. The flight demonstrator captures the imaginations of all museum-goers, while the gravity well both entertains and fascinates. Kids won't soon forget time spent in the echo tube either.

Admission: $2 adults, $1 children 5–17 and seniors 62 and older, free for children 4 and under.

Open: Wed–Sat 10am–5pm, Sun noon–5pm.

★ **New Mexico Museum of Natural History & Science,** 1801 Mountain Rd. NW. ☎ 841-8837.

Two life-size bronze dinosaurs stand outside the entrance to this modern museum, opposite the Albuquerque Museum. Inside, innovative video displays, polarizing lenses, and black lighting enable visitors to stroll through geologic time. You can walk a rocky path through the Hall of Giants, as dinosaurs fight and winged reptiles swoop overhead; step into a seemingly live volcano, complete with simulated magma flow; or share an Ice Age cave, festooned with stalagmites, with saber-toothed tigers and woolly mammoths. Hands-on exhibits in the Naturalist Center permit use of a video microscope, viewing of an active beehive, and participation in a variety of other activities. For an additional charge the giant-screen Dynamax Theater puts you into the on-screen action.

There's a gift shop on the ground floor, and the highly regarded Museum Café (see "Dining," earlier in this chapter) on the mezzanine.

Admission: $4 adults, $3 seniors, $2 children 3–11. Museum and Dynamax, $7 adults, $5 seniors, $3 children 3–11. Children under 12 must be accompanied by an adult.

Open: Daily 9am–5pm. **Closed:** Christmas and Mon in Jan and Sept.

Rio Grande Zoological Park, 903 10th St. SW. ☎ 843-7413.

Open-moated exhibits with animals in naturalized habitats are a treat for zoo-goers. Highlight exhibits include the giraffes, sea lions (with underwater viewing), the cat walk, the bird show, and ape country with its gorilla and orangutans. More than 1,200 animals of 300 species live on 60 acres of riverside bosque among ancient cottonwoods. The zoo has an especially fine collection of elephants, reptiles, and native southwestern species. A children's petting zoo is open during the summer. There are numerous snack bars on the zoo grounds, and La Ventana Gift Shop carries film and souvenirs.

Admission: $4.25 adults, $2.25 children and seniors. Children under 12 must be accompanied by an adult.

Open: Daily 9am–5pm, with extended hours in summer. **Closed:** New Year's, Thanksgiving, and Christmas Days.

7 Sports & Recreation

Spectator Sports

BASEBALL　The Albuquerque Dukes, 1990 champions of the Class AAA Pacific Coast League, are the number-one farm team of the Los Angeles Dodgers. They play 72 home games from mid-April to early September in the city-owned 30,000-seat Albuquerque Sports Stadium, 1601 Stadium Blvd. SE, at University Boulevard (☎ 243-1791).

BASKETBALL　The University of New Mexico team, nicknamed the Lobos, plays an average of 16 home games from late November to early March. Capacity crowds cheer the team at the 17,121-seat University Arena (fondly called "The Pit") at University and Stadium Boulevards. The arena was the site in 1983 of the annual National Collegiate Athletic Association championship tournament.

BOXING　Albuquerque has several professional boxing gyms. Local bouts, whose sites have varied, have featured top contenders in various weight divisions. Several nationally ranked boxers live and train in the Albuquerque area.

FOOTBALL　The UNM Lobos football team plays a September to November season, usually with five home games, at the 30,000-seat University of New Mexico Stadium, opposite both Albuquerque Sports Stadium and University Arena at University and Stadium Boulevards.

HORSE RACING　**The Downs at Albuquerque,** 201 California St. (☎ 262-1188 for post times), is in the state fairgrounds near Lomas and Louisiana Boulevards NE. Racing and betting—on thoroughbreds and quarter horses—take place on Wednesday, Friday, and Saturday from late January to June and during the state fair in September. The Downs has a glass-enclosed grandstand, exclusive club seating, valet parking, and complimentary racing programs and tip sheets.

RODEO   The All-American Pro Rodeo, a key event on the national professional rodeo circuit, takes place the second through third weekends of September each year as a part of the New Mexico State Fair. Tickets—at $5 general, $9 reserved—must be ordered from fair officials (☎ toll free **800/235-FAIR**).

Recreational Sports

BALLOONING   Visitors not content to watch the colorful craft rise into the clear-blue skies have a choice of several hot-air balloon operators from whom to get a ride, at rates starting about $100 per person:

Braden's Balloons Aloft, 9935-B Trumbull Ave. SE (☎ **281-2714**).

Cameron Balloons, 2950 San Joaquin Ave. SE (☎ **265-4007**).

Rainbow Ryders, 430 Montclaire SE (☎ **268-3401**).

World Balloon Corporation, 4800 Eubank Blvd. NE (☎ **293-6800**).

The annual **Albuquerque International Balloon Fiesta** is held the first through second weekends of October. See "Northern New Mexico Calendar of Events," in Chapter 2, for details.

BICYCLING   Albuquerque is a major bicycling hub in the summer, both for road racers and mountain bikers. Full information on competition and touring, as well as rentals, can be obtained from **Gardenswartz Sportz**, 2720 San Mateo Blvd. NE (☎ **884-6787**).

HIKING/BACKPACKING   The 1.6-million-acre **Cibola National Forest** offers ample opportunities. In the Sandia Mountain section alone are 18 recreation sites, though only one—Cedro Peak, about four miles southeast of Tijeras—allows overnight camping. For details, contact the Sandia Ranger Station, N.M. 337 south toward Tijeras (☎ **381-3304**).

Elena Gallegos/Albert G. Simms Park, near the base of the Sandia Peak Tramway at 1700 Tramway Blvd. NE (☎ **291-6224** or **768-3550**), is a 640-acre mountain picnic area with hiking-trail access to the Sandia Mountain Wilderness.

RIVER RAFTING   This mainly takes place farther north, in the Santa Fe and especially the Taos areas. Check with **Wolf Whitewater Kayak Canoe School & River Tours,** P.O. Box 666, Sandia Park, NM 87047 (☎ **505/281-5042**).

In mid-May each year, **The Great Race** takes place on a 14-mile stretch of the Rio Grande through Albuquerque. Eleven categories of craft, including rafts, kayaks, and canoes, race down the river. Call **505/768-3490** for details.

SKIING   The **Sandia Peak Ski Area** has twin base-to-summit chair lifts to its upper slopes at 10,360 feet, and a 1,700-foot vertical drop. There are 25 trails, 14 of them geared to intermediates, with several beginners' runs above the day lodge and ski-rental shop. Three chairs and two pomas accommodate 3,400 skiers an hour. All-day lift tickets are $25 for adults, $18 for children; rental packages are $11 for adults, $9 for kids. The season runs from the Christmas holidays through March. Contact 10 Tramway Loop NE (☎ 505/296-9585) for more information, or call the hotline for ski conditions (☎ 505/242-9052).

Cross-country skiers can enjoy the trails of the **Sandia Wilderness** from the ski area, or can go an hour north to the remote **Jemez Wilderness** and its hot springs.

8 Savvy Shopping

Visitors interested in regional specialties will find many artists and galleries, although not so concentrated as in Santa Fe and Taos. The galleries and regional fashion designers around the Plaza in Old Town make a sort of shopping center of their own for tourists, with more than 40 merchants represented. The Sandia Pueblo people run their own crafts market on their reservation land off I-25 at Tramway Road, just beyond Albuquerque's northern city limits.

Albuquerque has the two largest shopping malls in New Mexico within two blocks of one another, both on Louisiana Boulevard just north of I-40—Coronado Center and Winrock Center.

Business hours vary from store to store and from shopping center to shopping center. In general, it's safe to say that shops will be open Monday through Saturday from 10am to 6pm, but many have extended hours; some have reduced hours; and a few, especially in shopping malls or during the high tourist season, are open Sunday.

Albuquerque sales tax is 5.8125%.

Best Buys

Southwestern regional items are the things to look for in Albuquerque. That includes **arts and crafts** of all kinds, from traditional Native American and Hispanic to contemporary works. In local Native American art, look for silver and turquoise jewelry, pottery, weavings, baskets, sand paintings, and Hopi kachina dolls. Hispanic folk art, including handcrafted furniture, tinwork and retablos, and religious paintings, are worth seeking out. Contemporary art focuses primarily on paintings, sculpture, jewelry, ceramics, and fiber art, including weaving.

The Major Concert and Performance Halls

Keller Hall, University of New Mexico, Cornell Street at Redondo Drive South (☎ 277-4402).

KiMo Theatre, 419 Central Ave. (☎ 848-1374).

Popejoy Hall, University of New Mexico, Cornell Street at Redondo Drive South (☎ 277-3121).

South Broadway Cultural Center, 1025 Broadway Blvd. (☎ 848-1320).

By far the greatest concentration of **galleries** is in Old Town; others are spread around the city, with smaller groupings in the university district and the northeast heights. Consult the brochure published by the Albuquerque Gallery Association, "A Select Guide to Albuquerque Galleries," or Wingspread Communications' annual *The Collector's Guide to Albuquerque,* widely distributed at shops. Once a month, usually from 5 to 9:30pm on the third Friday, the Albuquerque Art Business Association (☎ 292-7537) sponsors an ArtsCrawl to dozens of galleries and studios. If you're in town, it's a great way to get to know the artists.

Other things to keep your eyes open for are **fashions** in southwestern print designs; **gourmet items,** including blue-corn flour and chile ristras; and **souvenirs** unique to the region, especially local Native American and Hispanic creations.

9 Albuquerque Nights

Albuquerque has an active performing-arts and nightlife scene, as befits a city of half a million people. The performing arts are naturally multicultural, with Hispanic and (to a lesser extent) Native American productions sharing time with Anglo works—they include theater, opera, symphony, and dance. In addition, many national touring companies appear in the city. Country music predominates in nightclubs, though aficionados of rock, jazz, and other forms of music can find them here as well.

Full information on all major cultural events can be obtained from the **Albuquerque Convention and Visitors Bureau** (☎ 505/243-3696, with a taped recording of local events after business hours). Current listings can be found in the two daily newspapers; detailed weekend arts calendars can be found in the Thursday-evening *Tribune* and the Friday-morning *Journal.* The monthly *On the Scene* also carries entertainment listings.

Tickets for nearly all major entertainment and sporting events can be obtained from TicketMaster, 4004 Carlisle Blvd. NE (☎ 884-0999 for information, or 842-5387 to place credit- or charge-card orders on American Express, MasterCard, or Visa). Discount tickets are often available for midweek and matinee performances. Check with specific theaters or concert halls.

The Performing Arts

CLASSICAL MUSIC

Chamber Orchestra of Albuquerque, 2730 San Pedro Dr. NE, Suite H-23. ☎ 881-2078.

This 31-member professional orchestra, conducted by music director David Oberg, performs an October to June season, primarily at St. John's United Methodist Church, 2626 Arizona St. NE. The concerts include a subscription series of six classical concerts (in October, November, January, March, May, and June), an all-baroque concert in February, concerts for children in February and April, and a joint concert with the University of New Mexico Chorus. The orchestra regularly features guest artists of national and international renown.

Admission: Tickets, $12–$21, depending on seating and performance.

New Mexico Symphony Orchestra, 3301 Menaul Blvd. NE, Suite 4, Albuquerque, NM 87107. ☎ **881-9590,** or toll free **800/251-6676** for tickets.

NMSO musicians may be the busiest performing artists in New Mexico. During its 1994–95 season, the orchestra will perform about 60 classical, pops, and chamber concerts in a September to May season, not including at least two dozen ensemble programs.

Nine pairs of classical and pops concerts are presented at Popejoy Hall on the University of New Mexico campus. A chamber series, "Symphony in the Sunshine," is heard on six Sunday afternoons at the Sunshine Music Hall, 120 Central Ave. SW (☎ **764-8825**).

Admission: Tickets, Popejoy Hall concerts, $15–$26 adults, $12–$21 students, $5 Hot Tix (available 15 minutes prior to performances); Symphony in the Sunshine, $13 adults, $6 students and seniors.

DANCE

New Mexico Ballet Company, 3620 Wyoming Blvd. NE (P.O. Box 21518), Albuquerque, NM 87154. ☎ **984-2501.**

Founded in 1972, the state's oldest ballet company performs an October to April season at Popejoy Hall. It typically includes a fall production like *The Legend of Sleepy Hollow,* a December performance of *The Nutcracker* or *A Christmas Carol,* and a contemporary spring production.

Admission: Tickets, $10–$16 adults, $5–$8 students.

THEATER

Albuquerque Civic Light Opera Association, 4201 Ellison Rd. NE. ☎ **345-6577.**

Five major Broadway musicals are presented each year at Popejoy Hall during a March to December season. Each production is staged for three consecutive weekends, including two Sunday matinees.

In 1994, its 27th season, ACLOA presented *South Pacific, The Fantasticks, Chicago, Big River,* and *The Music Man.*

Admission: Ticket prices vary. $9–$17.50 adults, $7–$15.50 students and seniors.

Albuquerque Little Theatre, 224 San Pasquale Ave. SW. ☎ 242-4750.

This 65-year-old amateur theater presents six plays annually during a September to May season. Productions cover the gamut from classical to contemporary, comedy to mystery, drama to musical. The 1994–95 calendar included *A Chorus Line, Count Dracula, The Best Christmas Pageant Ever, You Can't Take It with You, Steel Magnolias,* and *Lend Me a Tenor.*

La Compañía de Teatro de Albuquerque, 518 First St. NW.
☎ 242-7929.

One of only 10 major professional Hispanic companies in the United
States and Puerto Rico, La Compañía stages four productions at the
KiMo Theatre between October and June. Comedies, dramas, and
musicals are offered, along with one Spanish-language play a year.

Admission: Tickets, $8 adults Thurs and Sun, $9 Fri–Sat; $7 stu-
dents, seniors, and children Thurs and Sun, $8 Fri–Sat.

Vortex Theatre, Buena Vista, just South of Central Ave.
☎ 247-8600.

An 18-year-old community theater known for its innovative productions, the Vortex is Albuquerque's "Off Broadway" theater, present-
ing plays ranging from classic to original. The company mounts 10
shows a year, including (in 1994) the Tony Award–winning *Dancing at Lughnasa,* the bawdy Greek comedy *Lysistrata,* and
Shakespeare's *Macbeth.* Performances take place on Friday and
Saturday at 8pm and on Sunday at 6pm. The black-box theater
seats 90.

Admission: Tickets, $7 adults, $6 students and seniors, $5 chil-
dren 13 and under; $5 for everyone Sun.

MULTIPURPOSE PERFORMANCE HALLS

Keller Hall, Cornell St. at Redondo Dr., University of New Mexico.
☎ 277-4402.

The Fine Arts Department's main auditorium, with seating for 336,
hosts numerous musical concerts throughout the year, including
student recitals and concerts. It's best known for its two annual
distinguished faculty and guest artist series, with seven chamber music
and solo concerts each from August to December and from January
to June.

Admission: Tickets, $6 general admission, $3 students, $2.50
seniors.

★ **KiMo Theatre,** 419 Central Ave. NW, at Fifth St. ☎ 848-1370
for information, **764-1700** for tickets (Mon–Fri 11am–5pm).

Albuquerque's historic showcase of the performing arts is a tribute
to the region's Native American cultures. Opened in 1927, the
KiMo's architecture is a colorful adaptation of the adobe pueblo and
its interior decor emphasizes Native American motifs. Handmade tiles
adorn the lobby; wall paintings simulate Navajo sand paintings;
murals of the legendary Seven Cities of Cibola stand outside the
balcony seating area; even the design of the box office is based on a
kiva. And then there's the remarkable lighting: White plaster buffalo skulls with lights in their eye sockets adorn the mezzanine col-
umns and outline the ceiling of the theater itself.

The 750-seat theater, owned by the City of Albuquerque, is the
home of La Compañía de Teatro de Albuquerque. In addition, it
hosts numerous theater, dance, and music groups. The KiMo and
the city also sponsor a series of touring shows of national and international importance.

Admission: Tickets, $5–$25, depending on seating and performance. Series tickets are available at a discount, and there are discounts for children.

Popejoy Hall, Cornell St. at Redondo Dr., University of New Mexico. ☎ 277-3121.

A multipurpose performing-arts facility, Popejoy Hall is Albuquerque's leading venue for major musical entertainment. Seating 2,094, it's the home of the New Mexico Symphony Orchestra, the Albuquerque Civic Light Opera Association, the New Mexico Ballet Company, and UNM's highly popular September to April "Broadway" series featuring major New York productions. (For information on each of the local companies, see the descriptions above.)

Adjacent Woodward Hall is the site of Albuquerque's June Music Festive (☎ 888-1842), a series of five concerts featuring nationally and internationally known string quartets with guest artists from leading symphony orchestras, during the first two weeks following Memorial Day. Season subscription tickets are $65 to $85; single tickets, $16 to $25 for adults, $10 for students.

Admission: Tickets, Broadway series, $20–$38 (discounts for students, faculty, staff, and seniors). For prices of other events, see the descriptions of specific companies, above.

South Broadway Cultural Center, 1025 Broadway Blvd. SE. ☎ 848-1320.

Funded by the city of Albuquerque, the SBCC presents a diversity of multicultural programming in the performing arts—from blues singers to avant-garde comedy, Mexican dance theater to medieval troubador melodies. The center, which seats 315, includes a 3,000-square-foot gallery space and a 2,000-square-foot multipurpose room. There's also a large library. Open Monday through Saturday from 9am to 5:30pm, it's located on the northwest corner of Broadway Boulevard and Garfield SE, three blocks north of Stadium Boulevard.

Admission: Tickets for touring shows, $5 adults, $2 children 12 and under.

The Club and Music Scene

COMEDY CLUBS/DINNER THEATER

Downtown Funnies, 407 Central Ave. NW. ☎ 247-8727.

A "cappuccino comedy club," Downtown Funnies is a popular place for live entertainment Wednesday through Saturday nights.

Admission: Cover varies.

Laffs Comedy Caffè, 3100 Juan Tabo Blvd., at Candelaria Rd. NE. ☎ 296-JOKE.

Top acts from each coast, including comedians who have appeared on the "Late Show with David Letterman" and HBO, also appear at Albuquerque's top comedy club. Show times are Tuesday through Sunday at 8pm, with second shows on Friday and Saturday at

10:30pm. Tuesday is "Best of Albuquerque Night." Wednesday is smoke-free night; Thursday and Sunday are Laff's T-shirt nights. The caffè serves dinner nightly from 6pm.

Admission: Cover varies.

Mystery Cafe, in La Posada de Albuquerque, 125 Second St. NW. ☎ **237-1385.**

If you're in the mood for a little dinner theater, the Mystery Cafe might be just the ticket. You'll help the characters in this ever-popular, delightfully funny show solve the mystery as they serve you a four-course meal. Reservations are a must. Call for show times and prices.

COUNTRY MUSIC

Caravan East, 7605 Central Ave. NE. ☎ **265-7877.**

"Always a dance partner" boasts this large country-and-western club east of the State Fairgrounds. Two bands share stage time Monday through Saturday from 5pm to 2am and on Sunday from 4:30pm to midnight; there are occasional national acts. Tuesday is ladies' night. Happy hour is 4:30 to 7pm, and there's a free dinner buffet from 5 to 7pm.

Admission: Free Sun–Thurs, $3 Fri–Sat.

Midnight Rodeo, 4901 McLeod Rd. NE, near San Mateo Blvd. ☎ **888-0100.**

The Southwest's largest nightclub of any kind, Midnight Rodeo not only has bars in all corners of its enormous domicile, it even has its own shopping arcade, including a boutique and gift shop. A DJ spins records daily until closing; the hardwood dance floor is so big (5,000 square feet) that it resembles an indoor horse track. Free dance lessons are offered on Sunday from 5:30 to 7pm and on Tuesday from 7 to 8pm. A busy kitchen serves simple but hearty meals to dancers who work up appetites, and there's a $3 buffet Monday through Friday from 5 to 7pm.

Admission: Free Sun–Thurs, $3 Fri–Sat.

ROCK/JAZZ

Beyond Ordinary, 211 Gold SW. ☎ **764-8858.**

Albuquerque's alternative-rock hangout has live music, including reggae, and a DJ spinning progressive disks on Friday and Saturday from 7pm to 1:30am and on Sunday from 7pm to midnight. An art gallery exhibits equally alternative paintings. Happy hour is Wednesday through Friday from 4 to 8pm.

Admission: $4.

Brewsters Pub, 312 Central Ave. SW. ☎ **247-2533.**

Wednesday through Saturday nights, Brewsters Pub offers live entertainment in a "sports bar"–type setting. There are 24 beers on tap, as well as a wide variety of bottled beer. Sports fans can enjoy the game on a big-screen TV. Barbecue is served at lunch and dinner.

Admission: Cover varies.

The Cooperage, 7220 Lomas Blvd. NE. ☎ 255-1657.

Jazz, rhythm-and-blues, rock, and salsa keep dancers hopping on Friday and Saturday nights inside this gigantic wooden barrel.

Admission: $3–$5.

Dingo Bar, 313 Gold SW. ☎ 243-0663.

The Dingo Bar is one of Albuquerque's premier rock clubs. There's live entertainment nightly that runs from punk rock to classic rock 'n' roll and jazz.

Admission: Cover varies, depending on the performer.

More Entertainment

Albuquerque's best nighttime attraction is the **Sandia Peak Tramway** (see "Attractions," earlier in this chapter) and its two restaurants, High Finance at the summit and the Firehouse at the base (see "Dining," earlier in this chapter). Both offer a view nonpareil of the Rio Grande valley and the city lights.

The best place to catch foreign films, art films, and limited-release productions is the **Guild Cinema,** 3405 Central Ave. NE (☎ 255-1848). For film classics, check out the **UNM SUB Theater,** on the UNM campus (☎ 277-5608), with double features Wednesday through Sunday, changing nightly.

Major Albuquerque **first-run theaters** include the Coronado Six Theater, 6401 Uptown Blvd. NE (☎ 881-5266); Del Norte Cinema Four, 7120 Wyoming Blvd. NE (☎ 823-6666); United Artists Four Hills 12 Theater, 13160 Central Ave. SE, at Tramway Boulevard (☎ 275-2114); Ladera Six Cinema, 3301 Coors Blvd. NW (☎ 836-5606); Montgomery Plaza-5, 165 Montgomery Plaza NE, at San Mateo Boulevard (☎ 881-1080); San Mateo Cinema 8, 631 San Mateo Blvd. NE (☎ 889-3051); United Artists 8 at High Ridge, Tramway Boulevard at Indian School Road (☎ 275-0038); and Winrock 6 UA Cinema, 201 Winrock Center NE (☎ 883-6022). The **Albuquerque Drive-In Theatre,** Montgomery Boulevard NE and I-25 (☎ 345-8641), has six theaters, all showing double features beginning at 8pm.

The **Isleta Gaming Palace,** 11000 Broadway Blvd. SE (☎ 869-2614), is a luxurious, air-conditioned bingo parlor with a full-service restaurant, no-smoking section, and free bus transportation on request. Doors open daily at 9pm for the video casino, and bingo begins at noon and 6:30pm on Saturday and Sunday; weekdays gaming begins at 6:30pm.

10 Excursions from Albuquerque

Pueblos and Monuments

Ten Native American **pueblos** are located within an hour's drive of central Albuquerque. One national and two state monuments preserve another five ancient pueblo ruins.

The active pueblos nearby include Acoma, Cochiti, Isleta, Jemez, Laguna, Sandia, San Felipe, Santa Ana, Santo Domingo, and Zia. Of them, Acoma is the most prominent.

In visiting pueblos, certain **rules of etiquette** apply: Remember to respect them as people's homes; don't peek into doors and windows or climb on top of buildings; stay out of cemeteries and ceremonial rooms, such as kivas, as these are sacred grounds; don't speak during dances or ceremonies, or applaud after their conclusion; silence is mandatory. Most pueblos require a permit to carry a camera or to sketch or paint on location. Several pueblos prohibit picture taking at any time.

★ **Acoma Pueblo,** P.O. Box 309, Acoma, NM 87034.
☎ **252-1139** or **552-6604.**

The spectacular "Sky City," a walled adobe village perched high atop a sheer rock mesa 365 feet above the 6,600-foot valley floor, is said to have been lived in at least since the 11th century—the longest continuously occupied community in the United States. Native legend says it has been inhabited since before the time of Christ. Both the pueblo and its mission church of **San Estevan del Rey** are National Historic Landmarks.

The Keresan-speaking Acoma (*Ack*-uh-mah) pueblo boasts about 4,400 inhabitants, but only about 50 reside year-round on the 70-acre mesa top. They make their livings from tourists who come to see the large church, built in 1639 and containing some examples of Spanish Colonial art, and to purchase the pueblo's thin-walled white **pottery,** with brown-and-black designs.

Start your tour at the **visitor center** at the base of the mesa. There is a **museum** and **café** here. A 16-seat **tour bus** climbs through a rock garden of 50-foot sandstone monoliths and past precipitously dangling outhouses to the mesa's summit. There's no running water or electricity in this medieval-looking village; a small reservoir collects rainwater for most uses, and drinking water is transported up from below. Wood-hole ladders and mica windows are prevalent among the 300-odd adobe structures.

Admission: $6 adults, $5 seniors, $4 children 6–18, free for children under 6. Still photography $5, sketching or painting $40; video cameras are prohibited.

Open: Summer, daily 8am–7pm; spring, daily 8am–6pm; fall and winter, daily 8am–5pm. One-hour tours begin every 20 minutes. **Closed:** July 10–13. **Directions:** To reach Acoma from Albuquerque, drive west approximately 52 miles to the Acoma–Sky City exit, then about 12 miles southwest.

Salinas Pueblo Missions National Monument, P.O. Box 496, Mountainair, NM 87036. ☎ **847-2585.**

The Spanish conquistador's Salinas Jurisdiction, on the east side of the Manzano Mountains (southeast of Albuquerque), was an important 17th-century trade center because of the salt extracted by the Native Americans from the salt lakes. Franciscan priests, utilizing native labor, constructed missions of adobe, sandstone, and limestone for the native converts. The ruins of some of the most durable—along with evidence of preexisting Anasazi and Mogollon cultures—are highlights of a visit to Salinas Pueblo Missions National Monument. The monument consists of three separate units: the ruins of Abo, Quarai, and Gran Quivira. They are centered around the quiet town of Mountainair, 75 miles southeast of Albuquerque at the junction of U.S. 60 and N.M. 55.

Abo (☎ **847-2400**) boasts the 40-foot-high ruins of the Mission of San Gregorio de Abo, a rare example of medieval architecture in the United States. **Quarai** (☎ **847-2290**) preserves the largely intact remains of the Mission of La Purisima Concepción de Cuarac (1630). Its vast size, 100 feet long and 40 feet high, contrasts with the modest size of the pueblo mounds. A small museum in the visitor center has a scale model of the original church, with a selection of artifacts found at the site. **Gran Quivira** (☎ **847-2770**) once had a population of 1,500. Las Humanes has 300 rooms and seven kivas. Rooms dating to 1300 can be seen. There are indications that an older village, dating to 800, may have previously stood here. Ruins of two churches (one almost 140 feet long) and a convento have been preserved. A museum with many artifacts from the site, a 40-minute movie showing the excavation of some 200 rooms, plus a short history video of Las Humanes are in the visitor center.

All three pueblos and the churches that rose above them are believed to have been abandoned in the 1670s. Self-guided tour pamphlets can be obtained at the units' respective visitor centers and at the Salinas Pueblo Missions National Monument Visitor Center in Mountainair, on U.S. 60 one block west of the intersection of U.S. 60 and N.M. 55. The visitor center offers an audiovisual presentation on the region's history, a bookstore, and an art exhibit.

Admission: Free.

Open: Sites, daily 9am–5pm. Visitor center in Mountainair, daily 8am–5pm. **Closed:** New Year's and Christmas Days. **Directions:** Abo is 9 miles west of Mountainair on U.S. 60. Quarai is 9 miles north of Mountainair on N.M. 55. Gran Quivira is 25 miles south of Mountainair on N.M. 55. All roads are paved.

Coronado State Monument, N.M. 44 (P.O. Box 95), Bernalillo, NM 87004. ☎ **867-5351.**

When the Spanish explorer Coronado traveled through this region in 1540–41 while searching for the Seven Cities of Cíbola, he wintered at a village on the west bank of the Rio Grande—probably one located on the ruins of the ancient Anasazi pueblo known as Kuaua. Those excavated ruins have been preserved in this state monument.

Hundreds of rooms can be seen, and a kiva has been restored so that visitors can descend a ladder into the enclosed space, once the site of sacred rites. Unique multicolored murals, depicting human and animal forms, were found on successive layers of wall plaster in this and other kivas here; some examples are displayed in the monument's small archeological museum.

Admission: $2 adults, free for children 15 and under.

Open: Summer, daily 9am–6pm; winter, daily 8am–5pm. **Closed:** Major holidays. **Directions:** To get to the site, 20 miles north of Albuquerque, take I-25 to Bernalillo and N.M. 44 west.

Jemez State Monument, N.M. 4, Jemez Springs. ☎ 829-3530.

All that's left of the Mission of San José de los Jemez, founded by Franciscan missionaries in 1621, is preserved at this site. Visitors find massive walls standing alone, its sparse, small door and window openings underscoring the need for security and permanence in those times. The mission was excavated between 1921 and 1937, along with portions of a prehistoric Jemez pueblo. The pueblo, near the Jemez Hot Springs, was called Giusewa—"place of the boiling waters."

A small **museum** at the site exhibits artifacts found during the excavation, describes traditional crafts and foods, and weaves a thread of history of the Jemez peoples to the 21st century in a series of displays. An interpretive trail winds through the ruins.

Admission: $2 adults, free for children 15 and under.

Open: May–Sept 15, daily 9:30am–5:30pm; Sept 16–Apr, daily 8:30am–4:30pm. **Closed:** New Year's, Thanksgiving, and Christmas Days. **Directions:** The state monument is located about 14 miles north of the state monument. From Albuquerque, take N.M. 44; to N.M. 4 (it will be on your right) and follow the signs.

The Turquoise Trail

New Mexico 14 begins about 16 miles east of downtown Albuquerque, at I-40's Cedar Crest exit, and winds some 46 miles to Santa Fe along the east side of the Sandia Mountains. Best known as "The Turquoise Trail," this state-designated scenic and historic route traverses the revived "ghost towns" of Golden, Madrid, and Cerrillos, where gold, silver, coal, and turquoise were once mined in great quantities. Modern-day settlers, mostly artists and craftspeople, have brought a renewed frontier spirit to the old mining towns.

GOLDEN Golden is approximately 10 miles north of the Sandia Park junction on N.M. 14. Its sagging houses, with their missing boards and the wind whistling through the broken eaves, make it a purist's ghost town. There's a general store widely known for its large selection of well-priced jewelry, as well as a bottle seller's "glass garden." Nearby are the ruins of a pueblo called **Paako,** abandoned around 1670. Such communities of mud huts were all the Spaniards ever found on their avid quests for the gold of Cíbola.

MADRID Madrid is about 12 miles north of Golden. Madrid and neighboring Cerrillos were in a fabled turquoise-mining area dating back into prehistory. Gold and silver mines followed, and when they faltered, there was still coal. The Turquoise Trail towns supplied fuel to locomotives of the Santa Fe Railroad until the 1950s, when the railroad converted to diesel fuel. Madrid (pronounced with the accent on the first syllable) used to produce 100,000 tons of coal a year. But the mine closed in 1956. Today this is a village of artists and craftspeople seemingly stuck in the 1960s: Its funky, ramshackle houses have many counterculture residents, the "hippies" of yore, who operate several crafts stores and import shops.

The **Old Coal Mine Museum** (☎ 473-0743) invites visitors to go down into a real mine, saved from the abandoning of the town. The old mine offices, steam engines, machines, and tools are shown. It's called a "living" museum because blacksmiths, metalworkers, and leatherworkers ply their trades here in restoring parts and tools found in the mine. It's open daily; admission is $1.

Next door, the **Mine Shaft Tavern** continues its lively career with buffalo steaks on the menu and live music daily, attracting folks from Santa Fe and Albuquerque. It's adjoined by the **Madrid Opera House,** claimed to be the only such establishment on earth with a built-in steam locomotive on its stage. (The structure was an engine repair shed; the balcony is made of railroad track.)

CERRILLOS   Cerrillos about three miles north of Madrid, is a village of dirt roads that sprawls along Galisteo Creek. It appears to have changed very little since it was founded during a lead strike in 1879; the old hotel, the saloon, even the sheriff's office have a flavor very much like an Old West movie set. It's another 15 miles to Santa Fe and I-25.

Index

Now Save Money On All Your Travels By Joining FROMMER'S™ TRAVEL BOOK CLUB The World's Best Travel Guides At Membership Prices!

Frommer's Travel Book Club is your ticket to successful travel! Open up a world of travel information and simplify your travel planning when you join ranks with thousands of value-conscious travelers who are members of the *Frommer's Travel Book Club.* Join today and you'll be entitled to all the privileges that come from belonging to the club that offers you travel guides for less to more than 100 destinations worldwide. **Annual membership is only $25.00 (U.S.) or $35.00 (Canada/Foreign).**

The Advantages of Membership:

1. Your choice of **three free** books (any **two** *Frommer's Comprehensive Guides, Frommer's $-A-Day Guides, Frommer's Walking Tours* or *Frommer's Family Guides*—plus **one** *Frommer's City Guide, Frommer's City $-A-Day Guide* or *Frommer's Touring Guide*).
2. Your own subscription to the **TRIPS & TRAVEL** quarterly newsletter.
3. You're entitled to a **30% discount** on your order of any additional books offered by the club.
4. You're offered (at a small additional fee) our **Domestic Trip-Routing Kits.**

Our **Trips & Travel** quarterly newsletter offers practical information on the best buys in travel, the "hottest" vacation spots, the latest travel trends, world-class events and much, much more.

Our **Domestic Trip-Routing Kits** are available for any North American destination. We'll send you a detailed map highlighting the best route to take to your destination—you can request direct or scenic routes.

Here's all you have to do to join:

Send in your membership fee of $25.00 ($35.00 Canada/Foreign) with your name and address on the form below along with your selections as part of your membership package to the address listed below. Remember to check off your three free books.

If you would like to order additional books, please select the books you would like and send a check for the total amount (please add sales tax in the states noted below), plus $2.00 per book for shipping and handling ($3.00 Canada/Foreign) to the address listed below.

FROMMER'S TRAVEL BOOK CLUB
P.O. Box 473
Mt. Morris, IL 61054-0473.
(815) 734-1104

[ ] **YES!** I want to take advantage of this opportunity to join Frommer's Travel Book Club.

[ ] My check is enclosed. Dollar amount enclosed   *

(all payments in U.S. funds only)

Name _____

Address _____

City _____ State _____ Zip _____

All orders must be prepaid.

To ensure that all orders are processed efficiently, please apply sales tax in the following areas: CA, CT, FL, IL, IN, NJ, NY, PA, TN, WA and CANADA.

*With membership, shipping & handling will be paid by Frommer's Travel Book Club for the three free books you select as part of your membership. Please add $2.00 per book for shipping & handling for any additional books purchased ($3.00 Canada/Foreign).

Allow 4-6 weeks for delivery. Prices of books, membership fee, and publication dates are subject to change without notice. Orders are subject to acceptance and availability.

Please send me the books checked below:

FROMMER'S COMPREHENSIVE GUIDES

(Guides listing facilities from budget to deluxe,
with emphasis on the medium-priced)

	Retail Price	Code		Retail Price	Code
☐ Acapulco/Ixtapa/Taxco, 2nd Edition	$13.95	C157	☐ Jamaica/Barbados, 2nd Edition	$15.00	C149
☐ Alaska '94-'95	$17.00	C131	☐ Japan '94-'95	$19.00	C144
☐ Arizona '95 (Avail. 3/95)	$14.95	C166	☐ Maui, 1st Edition	$13.95	C153
☐ Australia '94-'95	$18.00	C147	☐ Nepal, 2nd Edition	$18.00	C126
☐ Austria, 6th Edition	$16.95	C162	☐ New England '95	$16.95	C165
☐ Bahamas '94-'95	$17.00	C121	☐ New Mexico, 3rd Edition (Avail. 3/95)	$14.95	C167
☐ Belgium/Holland/ Luxembourg '93-'94	$18.00	C106	☐ New York State, 4th Edition	$19.00	C133
☐ Bermuda '94-'95	$15.00	C122	☐ Northwest, 5th Edition	$17.00	C140
☐ Brazil, 3rd Edition	$20.00	C111	☐ Portugal '94-'95	$17.00	C141
☐ California '95	$16.95	C164	☐ Puerto Rico '95-'96	$14.00	C151
☐ Canada '94-'95	$19.00	C145	☐ Puerto Vallarta/ Manzanillo/ Guadalajara '94-'95	$14.00	C028
☐ Caribbean '95	$18.00	C148			
☐ Carolinas/Georgia, 2nd Edition	$17.00	C128	☐ Scandinavia, 16th Edition (Avail. 3/95)	$19.95	C169
☐ Colorado, 2nd Edition	$16.00	C143	☐ Scotland '94-'95	$17.00	C146
☐ Costa Rica '95	$13.95	C161	☐ South Pacific '94-'95	$20.00	C138
☐ Cruises '95-'96	$19.00	C150	☐ Spain, 16th Edition	$16.95	C163
☐ Delaware/Maryland '94-'95	$15.00	C136	☐ Switzerland/ Liechtenstein '94-'95	$19.00	C139
☐ England '95	$17.95	C159	☐ Thailand, 2nd Edition	$17.95	C154
☐ Florida '95	$18.00	C152	☐ U.S.A., 4th Edition	$18.95	C156
☐ France '94-'95	$20.00	C132	☐ Virgin Islands '94-'95	$13.00	C127
☐ Germany '95	$18.95	C158	☐ Virginia '94-'95	$14.00	C142
☐ Ireland, 1st Edition (Avail. 3/95)	$16.95	C168	☐ Yucatan, 2nd Edition	$13.95	C155
☐ Italy '95	$18.95	C160			

FROMMER'S $-A-DAY GUIDES

(Guides to low-cost tourist accommodations and facilities)

	Retail Price	Code		Retail Price	Code
☐ Australia on $45 '95-'96	$18.00	D122	☐ Israel on $45, 15th Edition	$16.95	D130
☐ Costa Rica/Guatemala/ Belize on $35, 3rd Edition	$15.95	D126	☐ Mexico on $45 '95	$16.95	D125
☐ Eastern Europe on $30, 5th Edition	$16.95	D129	☐ New York on $70 '94-'95	$16.00	D121
☐ England on $60 '95	$17.95	D128	☐ New Zealand on $45 '93-'94	$18.00	D103
☐ Europe on $50 '95	$17.95	D127	☐ South America on $40, 16th Edition	$18.95	D123
☐ Greece on $45 '93-'94	$19.00	D100	☐ Washington, D.C. on $50 '94-'95	$17.00	D120
☐ Hawaii on $75 '95	$16.95	D124			
☐ Ireland on $45 '94-'95	$17.00	D118			

FROMMER'S CITY $-A-DAY GUIDES

	Retail Price	Code		Retail Price	Code
☐ Berlin on $40 '94-'95	$12.00	D111	☐ Madrid on $50 '94-'95	$13.00	D119
☐ London on $45 '94-'95	$12.00	D114	☐ Paris on $45 '94-'95	$12.00	D117

FROMMER'S FAMILY GUIDES

	Retail Price	Code		Retail Price	Code
☐ California with Kids	$18.00	F100	☐ San Francisco with Kids	$17.00	F104
☐ Los Angeles with Kids	$17.00	F103	☐ Washington, D.C. with Kids	$17.00	F102
☐ New York City with Kids	$18.00	F101			

FROMMER'S CITY GUIDES

(Pocket-size guides to sightseeing and tourist
accommodations and facilities in all price ranges)

	Retail Price	Code		Retail Price	Code
☐ Amsterdam '93-'94	$13.00	S110	☐ Nashville/Memphis, 1st Edition	$13.00	S141
☐ Athens, 10th Edition (Avail. 3/95)	$12.95	S174	☐ New Orleans '95	$12.95	S148
☐ Atlanta '95	$12.95	S161	☐ New York '95	$12.95	S152
☐ Atlantic City/Cape May, 5th Edition	$13.00	S130	☐ Orlando '95	$13.00	S145
☐ Bangkok, 2nd Edition	$12.95	S147	☐ Paris '95	$12.95	S150
☐ Barcelona '93-'94	$13.00	S115	☐ Philadelphia, 8th Edition	$12.95	S167
☐ Berlin, 3rd Edition	$12.95	S162	☐ Prague '94-'95	$13.00	S143
☐ Boston '95	$12.95	S160	☐ Rome, 10th Edition	$12.95	S168
☐ Budapest, 1st Edition	$13.00	S139	☐ San Diego '95	$12.95	S158
☐ Chicago '95	$12.95	S169	☐ San Francisco '95	$12.95	S155
☐ Denver/Boulder/Colorado Springs, 3rd Edition	$12.95	S154	☐ Santa Fe/Taos/ Albuquerque '95	$12.95	S172
☐ Dublin, 2nd Edition	$12.95	S157	☐ Seattle/Portland '94-'95	$13.00	S137
☐ Hong Kong '94-'95	$13.00	S140	☐ St. Louis/Kansas City, 2nd Edition	$13.00	S127
☐ Honolulu/Oahu '95	$12.95	S151	☐ Sydney, 4th Edition	$12.95	S171
☐ Las Vegas '95	$12.95	S163	☐ Tampa/St. Petersburg, 3rd Edition	$13.00	S146
☐ London '95	$12.95	S156	☐ Tokyo '94-'95	$13.00	S144
☐ Los Angeles '95	$12.95	S164	☐ Toronto '95 (Avail. 3/95)	$12.95	S173
☐ Madrid/Costa del Sol, 2nd Edition	$12.95	S165	☐ Vancouver/Victoria '94-'95	$13.00	S142
☐ Mexico City, 1st Edition	$12.95	S170	☐ Washington, D.C. '95	$12.95	S153
☐ Miami '95-'96	$12.95	S149			
☐ Minneapolis/St. Paul, 4th Edition	$12.95	S159			
☐ Montreal/ Quebec City '95	$11.95	S166			

SPECIAL EDITIONS

	Retail Price	Code		Retail Price	Code
☐ Bed & Breakfast Southwest	$16.00	P100	☐ National Park Guide, 29th Edition	$17.00	P106
☐ Bed & Breakfast Great American Cities	$16.00	P104	☐ Where to Stay U.S.A., 11th Edition	$15.00	P102
☐ Caribbean Hideaways	$16.00	P103			

FROMMER'S WALKING TOURS

(With routes and detailed maps, these companion guides
point out the places and pleasures that make a city unique)

	Retail Price	Code		Retail Price	Code
☐ Berlin	$12.00	W100	☐ New York	$12.00	W102
☐ Chicago	$12.00	W107	☐ Paris	$12.00	W103
☐ England's Favorite Cities	$12.00	W108	☐ San Francisco	$12.00	W104
☐ London	$12.00	W101	☐ Washington, D.C.	$12.00	W105
☐ Montreal/Quebec City	$12.00	W106			

FROMMER'S TOURING GUIDES

(Color-illustrated guides that include walking tours,
cultural and historic sites, and practical information)

	Retail Price	Code		Retail Price	Code
☐ Amsterdam	$11.00	T001	☐ New York	$11.00	T008
☐ Barcelona	$14.00	T015	☐ Rome	$11.00	T010
☐ Brazil	$11.00	T003	☐ Scotland	$10.00	T011
☐ Hong Kong/Singapore/ Macau	$11.00	T006	☐ Sicily	$15.00	T017
			☐ Tokyo	$15.00	T016
☐ Kenya	$14.00	T018	☐ Turkey	$11.00	T013
☐ London	$13.00	T007	☐ Venice	$9.00	T014

Please note: If the availability of a book is several months away, we may have back issues of guides to that particular destination. Call customer service at (815) 734-1104.